NORWEGIAN
FJORD HORSE.

ON YOUR OWN TIME

The FORTUNE Guide
to Executive Leisure

MARILYN WELLEMEYER

ON YOUR OWN TIME

The FORTUNE Guide to Executive Leisure

LITTLE, BROWN AND COMPANY
BOSTON   TORONTO

COPYRIGHT © 1987 BY MARILYN WELLEMEYER

ALL RIGHTS RESERVED. NO PART OF THIS BOOK MAY BE REPRODUCED
IN ANY FORM OR BY ANY ELECTRONIC OR MECHANICAL MEANS,
INCLUDING INFORMATION STORAGE AND RETRIEVAL SYSTEMS,
WITHOUT PERMISSION IN WRITING FROM THE PUBLISHER, EXCEPT
BY A REVIEWER WHO MAY QUOTE BRIEF PASSAGES IN A REVIEW.

FIRST EDITION

This book is published by arrangement with *Fortune* magazine;
it is based on articles that were originally published in "On Your
Own Time," *Fortune* magazine, and copyrighted by Time Incorporated.

Library of Congress Cataloging-in-Publication Data

Wellemeyer, Marilyn.
    On your own time.

    Articles originally published in Fortune magazine.
    Includes index.
    1. Recreation.   2. Executives — Recreation.
2. Professional employees — Recreation.   I. Title.
II. Title: Fortune guide to executive leisure.
GV181.2.W44   1987   790   87-14348
ISBN 0-316-92949-2

Designed by Robert G. Lowe

RRD OH

Published simultaneously in Canada
by Little, Brown & Company (Canada) Limited

PRINTED IN THE UNITED STATES OF AMERICA

No man is really happy or safe without a hobby, and it makes precious little difference what the outside interest may be — botany, beetles or butterflies, roses, tulips or irises; fishing, mountaineering or antiquities — anything will do so long as he straddles a hobby and rides it hard.
— Sir William Osler, M.D., 1909

CONTENTS

ACKNOWLEDGMENTS ix

INTRODUCTION xi

Part One VACATIONS AND WEEKENDS

SPORTING HOLIDAYS 1
Learning to Sail 1
Scuba Diving 2
European Tennis Camps 4
Golfers' Grand Tour of Scotland 6
Heli-Skiing in Canada 7
Ski Touring 9
Deep-Sea Game Fishing 11
Salmon Fishing in Iceland 13
Pheasant Shooting in Denmark 14
Schools for Wing-Shooters 15

EXPEDITIONS AND EXPLORATIONS 18
Bicycling Through Europe 18
Walking Through Europe 19
Trekking in Nepal 21
Mountaineering Alpine Style 23
Mountaineering Expeditions:
Seven Summits 24
On Camera Safari in Africa 26
Touring by Kayak 27

FAMILY ADVENTURES 30
Reunions with Hubie Clark's Clan 30
A Wonderful Year in the Wilderness 31
Horsepacking in the Western Wilds 33
Rafting with Outward Bound 35
Canoeing in the Arctic 36
Vacationing with Little Kids 38

PURPOSEFUL VACATIONS 41
Earthwatch Volunteers 41
Friends of French Art 42
Fighting Fat 44

Part Two SPORTS AND GAMES

FOR FITNESS AND FUN 47
In the Competitive Swim 47
Business Cyclists 48
Running: Marathons and Less 49
Triathlons for Ultimate Athletes 52
Soccer: The World's Most Popular Sport 54
Fitness for Your Kids 55

WITH RACKET, CLUB, AND MALLET 58
High-Tech Golf and Tennis Schools 58
Low-Handicap Golfers 60
Championship Tennis for Amateurs 62
Squashing the Competition 63
Croquet's New Version 64
Polo's Perilous Pleasures 66

ON THE WATER 69
Board Sailing for Stand-Up Thrills 69
Rowing: For Getting an Oar In 71
White Water's Seductive Challenge 73
Water-Skiing, from Slalom to Jumping 75

ON WHEELS AND WINGS 77
Auto Racing: Vroom at the Top 77
Motorcycling: Free and Close to Nature 79
Ballooning, with the Wind 80
Learning to Fly 82
Civil Air Patrol: Knights of the Sky 84

IN WINTER 86
Ski Racing Alpine Style 86
Ski Racing: Cross-Country 88
Ski Patrol: Samaritans of the Slopes 90
Senior Hockey: More Brains, Less Brawn 91
Curling, with Broomsticks and Stones 93

CONTENTS

TO CHALLENGE THE MIND   95
  Bridge in the Big Leagues   95
  Chess vs. the Computer   97

Part Three HOBBIES

PERFORMING   99
  Jamming in a Jazz Band   99
  In Tune with the Classical Beat   101
  A Place in the Chorus   102
  Barbershop Harmony   104
  The Rewarding Applause of Theater   105
  Ballroom Dancing   107

CREATING   109
  Working Your Way with Wood   109
  Painting and Sculpting   110
  Through the Camera's Eye   112
  Photographers' Workshops   113

FOR COLLECTORS AND
CONNOISSEURS   116
  Art: How Not to Get Stung   116
  Classic Cars   117
  Appreciating Wine   119

THE NATURAL WORLD   123
  Astronomy: In Touch with the Universe 123
  At Home with Orchids   125
  Gardening for Gourmets   126
  Watching the Mystery of the Birds   128
  Campaigning for Top Show Dog   129
  Putting Hunting Dogs on Trial   131
  Improving Wildlife Habitats   132

COMMUNITY SERVICE   135
  Volunteer Firemen   135
  Running for Office in Suburbia   137
  The Joys of Hands-On Philanthropy   138

INDEX   141

vii

ACKNOWLEDGMENTS

Originally published in *Fortune* magazine under the heading "On Your Own Time," the articles in this guide have been updated and expanded to include additional sources of information. The articles feature on-the-scene reporting and personal interviews by members of *Fortune*'s editorial staff, as well as photographs taken expressly for *Fortune*.

For giving me the enviable assignment of regularly writing these articles I thank *Fortune*'s former Managing Editor Robert Lubar. For authorizing this book my thanks go to former Managing Editor William S. Rukeyser, and for encouraging the book's completion, to Managing Editor Marshall Loeb.

Credit for deft editing of the original magazine articles, before revisions for the book, goes to Richard Armstrong, Charles G. Burck, Geoffrey Colvin, Allan T. Demaree, Donald D. Holt, the late Emmet John Hughes, Carol Junge Loomis, Harold B. Meyers, and Wyndham Robertson.

While I wrote most of the original articles, and have revised virtually all of them, I wish to recognize the following present and former members of the staff of *Fortune*, each of whom wrote one or two of the magazine articles: Charles G. Burck, Eleanore Carruth, Stuart Gannes, Judson Gooding, Lee Griggs (of *Time*), Patricia Langan, Jeremy Main, Walter McQuade, Thomas Moore, and Faye Rice. Many of *Fortune*'s researchers and reporters worked with dedication on the original articles. Those most frequently assigned include Rosalind Klein Berlin, Anne B. Fisher, Faye Rice, Suzy Spencer, Caroline Parker Young, and Jay Zebrowski.

The updating and revision of 25 articles benefited immeasurably from the reporting skills of Dorothy Ferenbaugh. Contributions came also from Elizabeth Baker, Frances Fiorino, Barbara Loos, Eleanor Nadler Schwartz, and Renata von Stephasius.

For providing computer disks with the original *Fortune* articles I am grateful to Donald G. Biglands, Manager of Editorial Operations.

For picture editing I thank Maureen Duffy Benziger of *Fortune,* and for copyediting the final manuscript, Emily Mikszto Salzberg.

At Little, Brown & Co., I am indebted to former editor Ann Sleeper, who asked me to undertake this book. For seeing it to completion I thank editors Fredrica S. Friedman, Christina Ward, and Betsy Pitha, and designer Robert Lowe.

Finally I wish to thank all of the executives, many interviewed expressly for this guide, who enthusiastically consented to share their experiences.

INTRODUCTION

He hath no leisure who useth it not.
— George Herbert, 1640

This book celebrates leisure, not mere free time but activity freely chosen for joy and fulfillment. Today most of us belong to the "leisure class" in a universe of unprecedented opportunity. No barriers deny our desires: neither time, nor distance, nor age, nor lack of skill, not even money. Scientists invite us on expeditions to Borneo or Swaziland; we jet there and back on a fortnight's leave, tax-deductible. Lifelong sports programs keep amateur athletes competing forever, smacking the hockey puck at 60. Schools teach any skills we fancy — undersea photography or how to fly.

Increasingly leisure competes with work as central to satisfaction in life. Unlike their workaholic fathers, many of today's managers are not willing to give up personal interests for more work. They want to spend their own time in stimulating outside pursuits that let them discover and extend themselves.

We Americans invest close to $350 billion a year in leisure, much of it as passive consumers of entertainment and tourist fare. Are we satisfied with our returns? The challenge is in the choosing.

On these pages some 300 men and women, from their 20s to their 60s, achievers in business and in 77 leisure activities, offer the testimony of their experience. They pour quantities of energy and creativity into their performance as travelers, sportsmen, hobbyists, and volunteers in community service. They return to business refreshed for the challenges ahead. Besides fitness and self-discovery, many look to shared recreation to cultivate family and social relationships.

Courage and competition often mark their commitments. Michael Levin, 35, president and chief executive of Titan Industrial, a 400-employee steel import-export firm in New York City, is an ocean racer who recently took up polo. "Active sports, with a chance of injury, a physical penalty for making a mistake, force you to focus on something other than business," Levin says, "and they help you to come back to problems you've left behind with your mind clearer."

While work can be more satisfying to managers than it is to some others, business professionals look more and more to outside avocations for personal rewards. Garry Stout, 43, an advisory financial analyst for IBM's information network division in Tampa, Florida, has applied his talent as a water-skier to putting on shows. "I've spent 20 years at IBM and hope to spend 20 more," he says, "but at no time do I expect I'll ever get a standing ovation from 10,000 people for it."

The selection of activities offered here is eclectic rather than all-inclusive. Some articles describe once-in-a-lifetime experiences. Others profile pursuits that call for long-term commitment of time and personal resources.

Requirements in talent, time, equipment, and money, as well as the risks and rewards, are presented, and sources of further information are suggested.

A few caveats can avoid misunderstandings. Some nonprofit sports and hobby organizations operate with rotating volunteer officers and headquarters, so more than one inquiry may be required. And inevitably travel organizers will change rates and programs.

Let this guide get you off the mark and on the track of active leisure for fun and fulfillment, or at least a few dreams.

PART ONE
VACATIONS AND WEEKENDS

SPORTING HOLIDAYS
Learning to Sail

■ Savoring newfound command as he prepares to turn the 24-foot sloop upwind, David Preefer shouts, "Ready about!" His mates respond, "Ready!" Pushing the tiller hard to leeward, Preefer sings out, "Hard alee!" Jib and mainsail swing from port to starboard, and the boat comes about in a 12-knot breeze, carving a 90-degree arc through the turquoise sea. "That was much better," calls instructor Jennifer Adam, 22, from her perch on the aft deck. "It was perfect," rejoins Preefer, 41, an executive with First Montgomery Properties of Cherry Hill, New Jersey.

One of the mates was Preefer's — his wife, Karen Zimmerman, 31, senior study director with the marketing analysis division of Booz Allen & Hamilton, a management consulting firm. Seeking an active vacation in a warm climate, they enrolled in February in a five-day vacation course for new sailors at the Annapolis Sailing School's branch on St. Croix in the U.S. Virgin Islands. It is one of hundreds of commercial sailing schools from the Virgin Islands to Hawaii that attempt to turn new sailors into old salts.

What school should an able body choose? That depends on what kind of boat you want to sail, where you want to learn — at a resort or close to home — and how much time and money you want to spend. It also depends on how good the school is, something not always easy to find out. The American Sailing Association, founded in 1980 to set standards for sailing instruction offered commercially, publishes a list of 200 schools that it certifies.

The list is useful, but not all-inclusive. The Annapolis Sailing School, founded on Chesapeake Bay in 1959, is the oldest and largest school in the U.S., with eight locations, including Texas and Arkansas. But, with a reputation long preceding ASA, it is not a member. Nor is its closest competitor, Steve Colgate's Offshore Sailing School, founded in 1964. It operates on New York's City Island, 30 minutes from Manhattan, and at five resorts, from the British Virgins to Newport, Rhode Island.

To learn basic sailing takes a minimum of 12 hours of intensive instruction, at least two-thirds of it aboard a boat. It can take 30 or so hours to develop confidence and proficiency. In their five-day Annapolis course on St. Croix, Preefer and Zimmerman were assigned to a boat with a physician and an AT&T communications technician.

At 9 A.M. daily the four met their instructor to review nautical lingo (shrouds and stays, not wires) and knots (square and figure eight), and to preview tasks aboard — rigging sails, casting off, docking. They saw how to find wind direction (look at the strands of yarn called telltales tied high on the shrouds) and how to steer (push the tiller away from the direction you want to go). On the last two days the novices sailed to other islands for lunch and snorkeling, with their instructor aboard only to answer questions.

A five-day (six-night) beginners' vacation package for two costs $990 at the Annapolis school on St. Croix, in the Danish colonial town of Christiansted, with rooms at Best Western's Holger Danske Hotel across the street. Preefer and Zimmerman chose other quarters. Without hotel, the

At the Annapolis Sailing School's Virgin Islands branch, instructor Jennifer Adam (left, rear) keeps an eye on her students: at the tiller, David Preefer; watching the sails, Karen Zimmerman (dark glasses) and Dr. Patricia Mikes.

1

VACATIONS AND WEEKENDS

course is $690 for two, $361 for one. Summer package rates are lower.

At Steve Colgate's Offshore Sailing School on Captiva Island, off Fort Myers on Florida's Gulf Coast, the learn-to-sail winter vacation package lasts eight days and seven nights, with 26 hours of instruction, and typically costs $1,006 per person. That's with two sharing a one-bedroom condominium at the South Seas Plantation resort, which also offers tennis and golf. Without hotel, the beginners' course at all Offshore locations is $395 per person; other courses are more.

Live-aboard cruising is the dream of many a nautical neophyte. This requires special instruction on sizable boats. Rüdiger Koch, 41, president of Intra Corp., a maker of carpet-printing machinery in Spartanburg, South Carolina, and his wife, Ehrengard, started with Offshore's learn-to-sail package on Captiva over the Christmas holidays. The next summer at the Annapolis Sailing School's branch in St. Petersburg, Florida, the couple took their children, ages 5 and 10, on a five-day, live-aboard vacation cruise. A flotilla of six or so boats, from 26 to 37 feet, cruise along a fixed route, with a daytime instructor aboard and a chief instructor accompanying the fleet in a motorboat. But most learning is by doing. The cost of $1,265 for the 37-footer, which sleeps six, does not include provisions. The Kochs have since bought a 31-foot racer-cruiser for weekend sailing on a lake near home.

To charter a boat for ocean cruising, they needed more instruction. Charter agencies often require certification of skills from sailors who wish to cruise bareboat without a professional crew. Both the Annapolis and Offshore schools offer certification. Students learn to plan a cruise, operate the auxiliary engine, navigate, anchor, use the marine radio telephone, and keep a log.

Aspiring racers may end up at Offshore's Captiva Island School. Seasoned racers can also sharpen skills in an intensive course at the ASA-certified schools operated by J World of Newport, Rhode Island, which use boats in the J/24 class. Though best known for its racing program, J World offers all kinds of sailing instruction in three ports that vary with the seasons. At Newport, San Francisco, and Key West a five-day course costs $535 without bed and board.

You don't have to take a vacation to learn sailing. Weekenders can often find courses to fit their schedules. When he was Secretary of Transportation, Drew Lewis, 53, slated to become chairman of Union Pacific in October 1987, slipped out of Washington incognito with his wife, Marilyn, to take the Annapolis Sailing School's 12-hour, $180 weekend course. The New York Sailing School, winner of ASA's "School of the Year" award in 1984, 1985, and 1986, is located on City Island and offers a 26-hour "master's course" for novices at $345.

Evening courses taught by the California Sailing Academy of Marina del Rey, an ASA school, are available at UCLA's extension school in Los Angeles. Each course costs $225 and consists of four weekly three-hour lectures on campus and seven three-hour sails at Marina del Rey. Alice Leahey, 39, a bank vice president, took Sailing I and II and then raced in the academy's Tuesday evening Sunset Series. She turned into such a good hand that when the starting gun went off July 4 for the 1985 Transpacific Race from Los Angeles to Waikiki, she had one of nine coveted berths crewing aboard the 48-foot *Azahara*. On the 13th day at sea it finished 13th overall in a fleet of 66.

FOR FURTHER INFORMATION

American Sailing Association, 13922 Marquesas Way, Marina del Ray, CA 90292; (213)-822-7171.

Annapolis Sailing School, Box 3334, Annapolis, MD 21403; (800)-638-9192 or (301)-267-7205.

Steve Colgate's Offshore Sailing School, 190 E. Schofield St., City Island, Bronx, NY 10464; (800)-221-4326 or (212)-885-3200.

Instructional videotapes may be purchased from ASA or Offshore; rented from Annapolis.

PUBLICATIONS

Cruising World, monthly, $19.95; 524 Thames St., Newport, RI 02840; (401)-847-1588.

Fundamentals of Sailing, Cruising & Racing by Stephen Colgate (New York: Norton, 1978), $24.95.

Sail magazine, monthly, $21.75; 100 First Ave., Charlestown, MA 02129-2097; (800)-247-2504 or (617)-241-9500.

The Sailor's Handbook edited by Halsey C. Herreshoff (Boston: Little, Brown, 1983), $14.95.

Soundings (marine newspaper), monthly, $16; Essex, CT 06426; (203)-767-3200. ∎

Scuba Diving

∎ When John and Janet Frishman were courting in Florida, he agreed to take dancing lessons if she would learn scuba diving, his passion. The cardinal rule of diving is never do it alone, and relying on someone else is a big part of its appeal. In just one November week Janet got her C card, a diver's basic certificate, at a dive shop in Pompano Beach. Without a C card, dive centers will not rent or sell the equipment that is the diver's life-support system. By year-end the couple had married and moved to the Boston area, where Janet, 34, runs a marketing promotion company, and John, 36, is national sales manager for Servolift/Eastern, a maker of food service equipment. They combine business and diving on Florida trips, vacation in prime Caribbean dive spots, and have turned into avid undersea photographers.

More than 2.7 million Americans are active divers and another 350,000 are certified each year, most of them by three national organizations: the Professional Association of Diving Instructors (PADI); the National Associa-

SPORTING HOLIDAYS

tion of Underwater Instructors (NAUI); and the YMCA. Fatalities annually number about 2.5 per 100,000 divers. Many fail to obey the rules in an environment not their own.

To escape from the human habitat into the exotic marine environment of contoured corals, sea fans, shoals of parrot fish, multicolored grouper, even moray eels and barracuda, the key is the self-contained underwater breathing apparatus, or scuba, invented by Jacques-Yves Cousteau. You breathe through your mouth via a regulator with a valve that draws compressed air through a hose from a tank strapped to your back. Your air supply, or pressure in the tank, registered by a gauge, should never go below 500 pounds per square inch under water.

To descend several fathoms, explore the aquatic panorama, and then resurface, you don't need the swimming prowess of a Johnny Weissmuller. You wear a weighted belt and a buoyancy compensator. This inflatable vest, with carbon dioxide cartridges for reflation, enables you to maintain "neutral buoyancy," moving neither up nor down while you glide with the fish. A depth gauge and a timepiece help you figure how long and how deep you can stay. As water pressure on your body increases at lower depths, safe time limits decrease: 60 minutes at 60 feet, 50 at 70 feet, and 20 at 100 feet. There pressure equals four atmospheres, the limit for most recreational divers. Below 100 feet, special "decompression diving" equipment is needed to avoid "the bends" on ascent.

A scuba diving course for entry-level certification requires about 31 hours: classroom instruction, exercises in a pool, an exam, and demonstration of scuba skills plus four supervised dives to depths from 30 to 60 feet in open water. All equipment is provided to start, but you will soon need your own fins, mask, and snorkel. Athletic clubs and dive shops nationwide offer evening and weekend courses.

In the Caribbean off Bonaire, Charles I. Robins (left) and Ralph G. Doerfling of Detroit snap yellowtail snappers.

If you are unsure you will like diving, most dive shops offer an introduction at little or no cost. An entry-level course costs an average $150, plus fees for the required dives, travel to a lakeside or seaside resort not included. A year after getting her C card, Janet Frishman took an advanced open-water course ($75) to enhance her skills.

First immersion at a resort spawns many a diver. Robert Thompson Jr., 32, president of Redshaw in Pittsburgh, a producer of computer software for the insurance industry, tried an introductory dive on St. Thomas during a cruise in the Virgin Islands. He fell in love with the sport, took his class work near home and the dives for his C card back on St. Thomas.

Many diving resorts give the full course for certification. On Bonaire, 1,200 miles southeast of Miami, one of the world's best diving sites, where reef walls hang with corals and pulsate with vivid fish, four hotels offer instruction, plus one-week vacation packages, varying seasonally from $600 to $1,200 per person in a double room.

To preserve their underwater holidays, lots of divers catch those fleeting fish on film or videotape. On Bonaire for a week's diving, Charles I. Robins, 55, president of Met-Chem Testing Laboratories in Dearborn, Michigan, which serves the aircraft and automotive industries, enrolled in a two-day underwater photography course with Photo Bonaire at the Flamingo Beach Hotel. The first morning, the instructor explains how to operate the Nikon-made Nikonos cameras, which, linked to a strobe light, can automatically find the correct exposure. Students and instructor then dive for "macro" shots, or closeups of tiny "critters," from one to a few inches long, using a 35-mm lens. The instructor positions the students' cameras and signals when to shoot. Photo Bonaire processes the film (Ektachrome or Fujichrome), and in late afternoon the instructor projects and critiques the slides. "I took those? Unbelievable," said Robins as he viewed the first day's pictures. "Just look at how good they are!"

Next day the divers try wide-angle photography of larger subjects — fish and each other — with a 28-mm lens. The camera is held two to four feet from the subject, tilted up toward the surface to brighten the background. The cost: $154 for the two-day course; $220 for a one-day videotaping course. Prices include use of equipment.

Janet and John Frishman bought a Nikonos camera and shot by trial and error with mixed results before turning to Photo Bonaire for coaching on wide-angle techniques. Shooting through water was a lot different from shooting through air. Water magnifies, making fish and people appear much closer than they are. That makes it hard to get the focus and lighting right. Since improving their skill, the Frishmans bought the 1985 Nikonos-V, which costs around $450.

The most in-depth instruction in underwater photography at a resort is given from May through September by Jim and Cathy Church, authors of three books on this

VACATIONS AND WEEKENDS

specialty. Their series of ten week-long courses, formerly given on St. Thomas, where Rob Thompson of Pittsburgh studied with them, has moved to Grand Cayman, 450 miles south of Miami. Tuition of $495 includes six and a half days of instruction, textbooks, film processing, and critiques. Rental of a Nikonos camera is $80, or students may bring cameras of any make. The cost of accommodations at Sunset House, with double room, most meals, and six full days of diving, is $791 per person.

Live-aboard cruises to remote destinations fulfill the dreams of seasoned underwater adventurers. Several aquariums — Boston's New England, Chicago's Shedd, and Honolulu's Waikiki — conduct natural history study tours that include diving. Commercially, La Mer in New York offers cruises to 12 destinations, ranging from the Caribbean ($895 a week) to the Maldives in the Indian Ocean ($2,900 for 12 days). See & Sea of San Francisco features 18 sites from Baja California ($995 a week) to Australia's Great Barrier Reef ($2,450 a week). Some See & Sea cruises feature photo seminars with well-known underwater photographers. For $7,000 or $8,000 both agencies invite you on a cruise to South Australia to descend in cages and face the Great White Shark.

FOR FURTHER INFORMATION

Underwater Society of America; membership, $15 a year, includes bimonthly newsletter *Visibility;* P.O. Box 628, Daly City, CA 94017; (415)-595-8492.

SCUBA DIVING INSTRUCTION

National Association of Underwater Instructors (NAUI), P.O. Box 14650, Montclair, CA 91763; (714)-621-5801.
National YMCA Scuba Program, Oakbrook Square, 6083-A Oakbrook Parkway, Norcross, GA 30093; (404)-662-5172.
Professional Association of Diving Instructors (PADI), 1243 E. Warner Ave., Santa Ana, CA 92705; (714)-540-7234.

UNDERWATER PHOTOGRAPHY INSTRUCTION

Jim and Cathy Church, P.O. Box 80, Gilroy, CA 95021-0080; (408)-842-9682.
Photo Bonaire, c/o Divi Hotels, 520 W. State St., Ithaca, NY 14850; (800)-FOR-DIVI or (607)-277-3484.

TRAVEL FOR DIVERS

La Mer, Suite 817, 823 United Nations Plaza, New York, NY 10017; (800)-DIVE-NOW or (212)-599-0886.
See & Sea, Suite 250, 50 Francisco St., San Francisco, CA 94133; (800)-DIV-XPRT or (415)-434-3400.

PUBLICATIONS

Hidden Seascapes by Feodor Pitcairn and Kirstin Pitcairn (Boston: Little, Brown / New York Graphic Society, 1984), $70.
Howard Hall's Guide to Successful Underwater Photography (Port Hueneme, CA: Marcor Publishing, 1982), $14.95.
Mastering Underwater Photography by Carl Roessler (New York: Morrow, 1985), $12.95.

The New Science of Skin and Scuba Diving by The Council for National Cooperation in Aquatics, (Piscataway, NJ: New Century, 6th ed., 1986), $10.95.
Skin Diver magazine, monthly, $19.94; P.O. Box 3295, 6725 Sunset Blvd., Los Angeles, CA 90028; (213)-854-2470.
Sport Diver Manual by Jeppesen Sanderson (Englewood, CO: Jeppesen Sanderson, 11th printing, 1986), $9.78.
The Sport Diving Catalog: A Comprehensive Guide & Access Book by Herb Taylor (New York: Harper & Row, 1986), $10.95.
Undercurrent (reviews of resorts and equipment), monthly; $28 a year; Atcom Building, 2315 Broadway, New York, NY 10024; (212)-873-5900.
Underwater USA newspaper, monthly, $9.95; P.O. Box 705, Bloomsburg, PA 17815; (800)-228-DIVE or (717)-784-6081. ∎

European Tennis Camps

■ In settings that combine tennis with tourism, you can add top spin to your game at camps where European operators serve up multilingual instructors. Training can be intense — or an invigorating adjunct to good living. Some camps are summer flowers, others bloom year-round.

Tennis is only one attraction of Windmill Hill Place, a 20-acre estate near Hailsham in East Sussex, 66 miles south of London and ten minutes from the sea. In a well-appointed Georgian mansion, guests enjoy the atmosphere of an English country house party. A week's holiday package includes seven nights, with three meals served each day, and five days of instruction on eight grass

At the Palace Hotel in the Swiss resort of Gstaad, players from California warm up for coaching.

SPORTING HOLIDAYS

or six hard-surface outdoor courts (plus four indoor courts for all-weather play). Andy Briant, 40, the English-born general manager of tennis at California's Lodge at Pebble Beach, sends players over every year, often combining a week at Windmill Hill with a week in London during the Wimbledon tennis championships.

At Windmill Hill, coaching consists of two hours on the courts each morning, with the pupil-instructor ratio averaging six to one. Every student is videotaped daily during the first hour and a half of instruction. After a coffee break, the tapes are played back for analysis and discussion before students return to the courts for another hour's coaching. "It's a great advantage to actually see your faults rather than just talk about them," said George Edwards Jr., 58, chairman and president of A. W. Stern, a paper-box manufacturer in San Francisco, and a member of one of Briant's groups. Edwards, who plays at San Francisco's Olympic Club, found that the week at Windmill Hill improved his game.

In the afternoon, players may join "stroke of the day" clinics, enter round-robin tournaments, swim in the heated outdoor pool, or arrange for golf or horseback riding nearby. They might even take in one of the major pro tennis tournaments at nearby Eastbourne. Edwards especially enjoyed excursions through the historic countryside. Hastings, where the Normans triumphed in 1066, is only minutes away. The week climaxes on Saturday with a doubles tournament and the awarding of prizes.

The cost per person in a double room ranges from around 216 pounds (about $345) in late March to 280 pounds (about $448) in July, taxes and tips not included. Weekend and midweek packages are also available most of the year, except in the high summer season. Rooms with private baths cost more. Should players choose to stay elsewhere, the tennis coaching program, space permitting, may be taken without room and meals at about half the full cost. These package rates are contingent upon participation of at least 25 players. Though the players need not all belong to the same party, this arrangement suits clubs and other groups traveling together.

For first-rank coaching amid luxury, the turreted Palace Hotel in the Swiss ski resort of Gstaad is a smash. Here Roy Emerson, 48, the Australian who won the U.S. Open in 1961 and 1964, and Wimbledon in 1964 and 1965, holds four tennis weeks each June and July. In August and September, Nikki Pilić, 45, Yugoslav coach of the German Davis Cup team, offers two tennis weeks, plus a ski-tennis combination in March on nearby indoor courts. During the occasional summer mountain squall, the hotel chauffeurs players to those indoor courts in a white Rolls-Royce.

Emerson, who spends most of the year as resident pro at the John Wayne Tennis Club in Newport Beach, California, limits the number of players to 36 for each week in Gstaad, with an instructor for every four. Instructors group players by ability. "I don't mind working with be-ginners. At least they don't have any faults to unlearn," says Emerson. Focusing on a different stroke each day, he first diagrams movements on a board for players lounging about him on a patio. Since social tennis is the objective of most of his students, Emerson ends each day's instruction with tips on doubles strategy.

"The week certainly helped me," said Gerard Burns, 50, president of National Communications Corp., a San Francisco company that sells long-distance telephone services. His wife, Helen, was not a tennis player, Burns added, but "now that we've seen what Roy does for beginners, we plan to come back, and she will take lessons." Burns and his wife turned into Emerson regulars in Gstaad. Robert Doner, 59, a Southern California real estate developer and a follower of Emerson from the years when he was resident tennis pro at the John Wayne Tennis Club in Newport Beach, has attended nine Emerson weeks at Gstaad.

An Emerson tennis week at the Palace includes six nights and five days, five hours of instruction per day with videotaping, room with bath, all meals, unlimited use of indoor and outdoor heated pools, the sauna, and even a massage. Rates, which the Palace quotes only in Swiss francs, include tips and taxes, but not air fare. In 1987 it cost 2,120 Swiss francs (about $1,400) for the June weeks; 2,270 francs (about $1,500) in July. Spouses or other companions not enrolled for tennis pay, depending on the week, from 50% to 60% of the full program. By comparison a five-night stay at John Gardiner's luxurious Tennis Ranch in Carmel Valley, California, costs a minimum of $1,400 per person.

How to get a grip on the training racket? One source is the U.S. Tennis Association's *World Tennis* magazine, which frequently carries articles on foreign camps and resorts, and publishes a directory of tennis camps worldwide each January. Check the ratio of instructors to students, total hours of instruction, the use of videotaping and playback, and the after-hours availability of courts. You're just as well off to miss the school-holiday months at large European camps — unless you have youngsters with you. Spring and early fall are winners for adults in most places.

FOR FURTHER INFORMATION

John Gardiner's Tennis Ranch, P.O. Box JGTR, Carmel Valley, CA 93924; (408)-659-2207.

Palace Hotel, CH-3780 Gstaad, Switzerland; (41)-030 83131; telex 922-222; or Leading Hotels of the World, (800)-223-6800.

Windmill Hill Tennis Centre, P.O. Box 505, Pebble Beach, CA 93953; (408)-625-1939; or Windmill Hill Place, Hailsham, East Sussex BN27 4RZ England; (44)-0323-832552.

PUBLICATIONS

Tennis magazine, monthly, $17.94 a year; 5520 Park Ave., Trumbull, CT 06611-0395; (203)-373-7000.

VACATIONS AND WEEKENDS

Wimbledon: Centre Court of the Game by Max Robertson (Sausalito, CA: Parkwest Publications, 1984), $16.95.

World Tennis magazine, monthly, $15.94; P.O. Box 6042, Palm Coast, FL 32037; (800)-423-1780. ∎

Golfers' Grand Tour of Scotland

■ The devoted golfer's dream of playing those historic Scottish links, where the game began five centuries ago, came true for a group of low-handicap amateurs from California's Monterey Peninsula Country Club. Grandly calling themselves the British Open Links Challenge Team, they set out one spring day to tour those courses where the British Open Gold Championship challenges the world's best players and several more of Scotland's finest links.

These men from Monterey were among some 44,000 foreigners, 25,000 of them Americans, who make the annual pilgrimage to Scotland's golfing shrines. The country is small, so it is simple to tee off on different courses on successive mornings. Scottish clubs and resorts are eager to attract foreigners, so play can usually be arranged.

Golf in Scotland fittingly conforms to an image of Scottish ruggedness and hardiness. The courses feature gale-force winds, sand traps a person can get lost in, and hard, fast, tricky greens that demand that most testing of golf strokes, the comeback putt. The links—literally, the word means sandy hills along the sea—have been contoured not by bulldozers but by seas receding after the Ice Age. Many of those traps began when burrowing sheep sought protection against the wind. The rough is tough native gorse, a couple of feet high. And the wild winds must be fought on foot: golf carts are almost never found on Scottish courses.

The idea of accepting the challenges and enjoying the bold beauty of golf's birthplace came up when the players from Monterey Peninsula were trapped in their clubhouse one Sunday morning by California rain—weather far milder than they would cheerfully play in once they got to Scotland. Andy Nottenkamper, 42, a manufacturer's representative in the San Francisco area with Office Products Sales, remarked how he would like to play the championship courses they had been seeing on TV. His friends immediately gave Nottenkamper the job of arranging a trip. He turned to Michael Roseto's Wide World of Golf in Carmel, one of several U.S. travel agencies that specialize in golf tours. Roseto decided to go along.

The playing tour was arranged for 16 golfers, lasted 11 days, and provided 14 rounds of golf. In different summers one of five Scottish courses has been the scene of the British Open: Troon and Turnberry on the west coast, St. Andrews, Carnoustie, and Muirfield on the east. The touring golfers played all of them, plus six other striking courses: historic Prestwick on the west coast, near the airport; the inland resort of Gleneagles; Edinburgh's Royal Burgess; and courses at Gullane and North Berwick.

The tour started at Turnberry, where the Ailsa links resemble the famed course at Pebble Beach, familiar to these Monterey players. Several holes at Turnberry run along a high bluff above the sea; the ninth tee has a guard rail. The sun was shining at Turnberry when Tom Watson beat Jack Nicklaus by a stroke to win the British Open in 1977, in July.

But at Turnberry in May, the touring Californians were pummeled by near-freezing temperatures and 60-mile-an-hour winds that dashed rain and sleet in their faces. Dale Eberly, the owner of Salinas Valley Ford, a large automobile dealership, and at nearly 70 the oldest man on the tour, bought a tam-o'-shanter and a down vest, and woolen mittens he pulled on between strokes. He and a few others also played the British ball, which is smaller than the American one (1.62 inches in diameter instead of 1.68) and plays better against the wind. All the Californians were good golfers: Nottenkamper had a 2 handicap, and none had a handicap over 11. But only four broke 100 in that first round at Turnberry.

Two days later, the group played at Troon, where 69 U.S. professionals would enter that year's British Open. The first nine holes at Troon run out along the water; the home nine holes are inland. One of the most famous is the

At Troon in Scotland, Californians from the Monterey Peninsula Country Club sight down the fifth fairway. From left: Andy Nottenkamper (between the caddies), Douglas Scott, Charles Pius, Leo Futch.

SPORTING HOLIDAYS

"postage stamp" eighth, at 126 yards the shortest hole on any British Open course, with traps surrounding the green. The hole recalls the 120-yard seventh at Pebble Beach, with the green perched over water. In 1973, 41 years after he won his first British Open, 71-year-old Gene Sarazen shot a hole in one on the postage stamp in his last Open. Harrison Robinson, 43, an Oakland attorney with the Monterey group, thought for a moment that he had a hole in one. But he was left with a three-foot putt, missed it, and ended up at par.

Roseto's itinerary called for two days at St. Andrews, the grandest of grand old courses. In that cathedral and university town, the license issued to the proprietor of the Old Course in 1552 obliged him "not to plough up any part of said golf links in all time coming." Since then, the hand of nature has done far more to the Old Course than the hand of man. A public course, St. Andrews is the home of the Royal and Ancient Golf Club, the British equivalent of the United States Golf Association.

By the time the touring golfers got to St. Andrews, they were used to keeping their drives low against the wind, and were trading their pitching wedges for clubs with low lofts on approach shots to defeat the hard, slippery greens. "Hit a high shot in California, where our greens are watered, and the ball stops where it hits," remarked Douglas Dusenbury, 39, an attorney who is a partner in HD&A Real Estate in Carmel. "In Scotland the ball keeps rolling."

In the unexpected sunshine at St. Andrews Leo Futch, co-owner of the Fairway Stores supermarket chain, and four-time club champion at Monterey Peninsula, with a 4-handicap, shot a 76. Lesser golfers can be paralyzed at the top of their backswings by the sudden thought of the hazards waiting to swallow their shots. These carry such terrifying names as Coffin, Grave, Cat's Trap, Lion's Mouth, Hell, and the Valley of Sin.

With obstacles like those, not even the most colorful caddies can help much. At Carnoustie, perhaps the most difficult course, some caddies dress formally in collar, tie, and overcoat. One occasionally brings his black collie. Puzzling over a downhill putt at Gleneagles, one player asks his caddie how hard to hit it. Came the reply: "No' too much, sir, but remember it'll no' get there by itself."

The pleasures of play mingled with the pleasures of food and drink. The group's final banquet, at the Johnstounburn House in Humbie, East Lothian, included *cullen skink,* a finnan haddie soup unmatchable outside Scotland, noisettes of lamb with lemon sauce, and soufflé Grand Marnier. Back in California, with a golfer's certainty, Dale Eberly remarked: "In Scotland they play this game as God *intended* it."

At the group's request, Michael Roseto began planning a two-week return tour, with an extended itinerary. Ireland's west coast drew them first. Proceeding to Dublin's Portmarnock course, they then played the very fine Royal County Down Golf Club at Newcastle. Back in Scotland, at Troon, they joined foursomes with local club members. Bad weather again dogged the Californians, presenting them with even more severe golfing tests. As spectators, they took in the British Open, played that year at England's Royal St. George's, before they flew home from London.

In 1987 a Wide World of Golf 16-day package tour of play on Irish and Scottish courses cost $2,475 per person, plus coach-class round-trip air fare, about $980 from San Francisco. Arrangements included a chartered bus, de luxe hotels, most meals, and green fees. Caddies' fees, about $20 per round, and other incidentals were extra.

FOR FURTHER INFORMATION

Wide World of Golf, P.O. Box 5217, Dolores near 6th, Carmel, CA 93921; (408)-624-6667.
The British Tourist Authority provides names of other travel companies that arrange golfing tours; 40 W. 57th St., New York, NY 10019; (212)-581-4700.

PUBLICATIONS
AA Guide to Golf Courses in Britain by the Automobile Association (Basingstoke, Hampshire, England: Fanum House, 1984), $11.95.
Golf: A Royal and Ancient Game by R. Clark (Cambridge, MA: Charles River Publishing, 1976), $25.
Golf Digest, monthly, $19.94; 5520 Park Ave., Trumbull, CT 06611-0395; (800)-PAR-GOLF or (203)-373-7000.
Golf Magazine, monthly, $15.95; P.O. Box 2786, Boulder, CO 80322-3733.
Good Golf Guide to Scotland by David Hamilton (New York: Penguin Books, 1982), $11.95.
The Royal & Ancient by F. Ward-Thomas (New York: Columbia University Press, 1980), $14.95.
The World of Golf edited by Gordon Menzies (Sausalito, CA: Parkwest Publications, 1984), $19.95. ∎

Heli-Skiing in Canada

∎ Long considered a macho preserve for superskiers, the world's largest helicopter-skiing operation, Canadian Mountain Holidays, has been changing its image. For Gene Tremblay, 45, senior vice president at Wellington Management Co. in Boston, the difference is startling: "When I first skied in the wilds of British Columbia in 1976, I was basically scared to death. The pressure to keep up was enormous." In 1985 Tremblay returned to try CMH's new approach for the uninitiated—the intro-week. "After the chopper landed the first day, instead of tearing straight down, we took the easy way around a precipice, with an instructor along as well as a guide."

VACATIONS AND WEEKENDS

The rewards of helicopter-skiing are tantalizing. Rather than coping with crowds and lift lines, skiers hop into a waiting helicopter that carries them to the longest runs to be found in untracked deep powder. Unlike those at conventional ski resorts, the runs are not groomed and patrolled. Heli-skiing is a fast, physically demanding sport. And there are risks: bad weather, rapidly changing conditions, avalanches.

Hard-core "repeaters," as CMH tags its loyal followers, feel the ultimate experience in skiing hasn't been compromised, even with the coming of less skilled skiers. After eight trips, Nicholas Connor, 37, an American businessman based in Japan, wouldn't miss a season. Mitchell Field, 38, a contractor from Southern California who came in 1978, still finds the skiing among trees that he loves. Heli-skiing is the only skiing these people do. As Field's wife, Holly Manion, 35, a realtor, says, "It's like swimming in a pool for years and then discovering the ocean."

And for them there's only one ocean — 3,700 square miles of wilderness in eastern British Columbia. Heli-skiing there is dominated by Hans Gmoser, 54, an Austrian mountaineer who started CMH in the Purcell Mountains in 1965. Today his network of seven areas handles 2,500 international heli-skiers each season.

Though several U.S. and European ski resorts offer day trips by helicopter, and smaller Canadian operators offer packages with accommodations, what makes CMH unique are its three remote, self-sufficient lodges designed specifically for heli-skiing: the Bugaboos, the Cariboos, and Bobbie Burns. At each, 44 skiers escape from the outside world to live and ski in splendid isolation for an entire week. No newspapers, TV, or telephones intrude. "My office can't call me. I'm literally forced to relax," says Nick Connor. His family business in Tokyo acts as liaison between Asian and Western retailers. "All you have to do here is ski. No hassling crowds, rent-a-cars, or dinner reservations. That stuff leaves me mentally and physically exhausted."

Connor and his wife, Kathy, 32, pile into a CMH bus in Calgary for a four- to six-hour drive to a staging area where skiers and luggage are moved to Bell jet helicopters for the flight into one of the three lodges. Built of stucco and cedar, these seem more like a friend's place in the mountains than a hotel. Rooms with twin beds come with or without private baths. Dining is family style, so you get to know the other skiers at meals. Dress is informal. Night life revolves around a small bar that closes at 10 P.M.

The camaraderie that develops is part of the experience. "It's not a social thing, requiring 100 outfits," notes Holly Manion. "At dinner you might find King Juan Carlos of Spain on one side of you and a taxi driver from Calgary on the other. You're all there for one thing — the skiing."

The day begins with a 7:30 breakfast call. After they are instructed on the use of Skadis, small radio transmitter-receivers for use in case of an avalanche, the skiers form four groups of ten, based on ability. Each group is led by a professional mountain guide. His job is to find the safest runs with the best conditions. In the Bugaboos alone there are 140 possibilities, but most groups average about eight runs a day. The pickups and landings of one helicopter are scheduled in a way that leaves little time for falls en route or resting.

While one group is unloading skis at the top, another is at the midpoint of a run descending 3,000 vertical feet, knee-deep in powder. If visibility goes, the helicopter is grounded at the lodge. Skiers can retreat to cross-country runs with equipment provided, to toboggan races, or a quiet sauna.

Holly Manion feels lucky that she's never lost heli-ski time owing to bad weather, but after her first week at Bobbie Burns in 1982 she swore she would never come back. An advanced intermediate skier, she found she wasn't up to breakable crust and a fast pace. "I kept falling. On my first run I met Mitch Field. He dug me out, and said, 'What are you doing up here? You can't handle this.' "

After the trip, the two Californians dated and Holly was persuaded to give heli-skiing another chance at Christmas. "That time I was mentally prepared and in the right condition. Now I'm the first one out at the helicopter pad." With two trips a year, at the end of 1985 Holly joined an elite group of 350 — the million-footers. Mitch had already logged two million feet.

In March of 1985 Mitch and Holly had decided to get married where they met — on a run at Bobbie Burns. A CMH staff member quietly arranged for a justice of the

After landing at the summit in the Canadian Bugaboos, skiers huddle against a blast of noise and snow from the departing helicopter.

SPORTING HOLIDAYS

peace to helicopter in when their group stopped for a midday break. "We stepped over to the edge of a clearing with two friends as attendants," Holly recalls. "After the ceremony, we all just skied down and no one else knew what was going on—until talk on the interlodge radio revealed CMH's first wedding."

Despite its prestige with dedicated experts, CMH business fell off during the 1981–82 recession. Hans Gmoser decided to cultivate a new market—the intermediate skiers who had been warned for years that they couldn't handle the runs. Intro-weeks are designed for new skiers as well as for those who want a more leisurely pace and to improve technique. A special heli-ski designed by Rossignol for CMH conditions is included in the package. Gene Tremblay noticed a big difference: "My eastern iceboards didn't work so well."

Tremblay convinced six neighbors from Wayland, Massachusetts, ages 35 to 55 with no experience in powder, to try an intro-week at Bobbie Burns in February of 1985. "The first day looked beautiful, but the snow was crusty, so we'd sink through. There was always someone to help you recover after a header and give you pointers. You get as much instruction as you want. It's not a class, but you learn about edge setting, controlling speed, and proper stance."

There was none of the Marine Corps mentality that marked his first trip. Tremblay found that the new skiers were encouraged to take their time. "There was no feeling that we were the bunnies. We landed at the same place as everyone else. But they then created a safe spot for our group to crash and burn, to experiment a little." Tremblay made reservations to return—this time with a group from his office.

In 1985–86, 170 skiers tried intro-weeks. Hans Gmoser thinks it's clear that "one need not be a superjock to enjoy heli-skiing." Intro-weeks rotate among the seven CMH areas, so skiers should specify the area they prefer. Two are based at small-town motels in case you like TV, newspapers, and different faces.

Intro-weeks cost the same as regular seven-day packages, which vary by date and location. The season runs from mid-December to mid-April. With a private bath, prices range from $2,280 to $3,395 Canadian for 1987–88. (CMH quotes all prices in Canadian dollars.) A standard twin with shared bath: $2,095 to $3,310. This includes room, meals, guides, the use of skis and poles, transfers from Calgary, and local taxes. After you complete 100,000 feet of skiing, you are charged $31.50 per 3,280 feet.

Though an expensive sport, heli-skiing can be a bargain for Americans with the advantage of a favorable exchange rate ($1.00 U.S. to $1.30 Canadian in early 1987). "It's the only thing in my life that costs about the same as in 1976," says Gene Tremblay. Perhaps that's one reason his April intro-week was fully booked the previous Oc-

tober. Try to plan about six months ahead for holiday or spring weeks.

FOR FURTHER INFORMATION

CMH Heli-Skiing, P.O. Box 1660, Banff, Alberta, Canada T0L 0C0; (403)-762-4531, telex 03-826509. ∎

Ski Touring

∎ Cross-country skiers are gliding from lodge to lodge, inn to inn, or hut to hut, in ski areas from the Sierras to the Alps. In North America ski touring is moving deeper into the wilderness, but with more creature comforts. Ski area operators, resort owners, and innkeepers have added many services for cross-country skiers. They maintain trails, rent equipment, and provide instruction, guides, maps, and itineraries tailored to a person's ability and desires.

With the temperature at 22 degrees, Dawn Flakne, 27, a computer engineer, set out one sunny December morning from the Gunflint Lodge, near the Minnesota-Ontario border, to explore Minnesota's Superior National Forest. For a week she skied alone along the well-marked Banadad Trail and its tributaries, covering up to 12 miles a day and staying each night at a lodge or hut. The snow was three feet deep, but the trail had been groomed. She skirted lakes that were not yet solidly frozen and skied along a 1,967-foot ridge. On that first day, near sparkling Gunflint Lake, she glimpsed a mother moose with calf. As the days passed she saw a lot more moose and got within 20 yards of a bull. "I was snapping pictures like crazy," she recalls.

Some skiers prefer to stay in one hostelry and tour the surrounding trails. Others, like Dawn Flakne, want to move on day by day. Flakne, who works for UOP, an Allied-Signal company in Des Plaines, Illinois, arranged her tour with Minnesota's Gunflint Trail Lodge to Lodge Ski Association, an organization of lodge operators. She paid $70 a night, all meals and services included.

One night she stayed in a midtrail hut just outside the Boundary Waters Canoe Area, where structures of any kind are forbidden. The hut is a circular tent with a wood floor, modeled on a Mongolian yurt. There is an outhouse, and two of the hut operators, Barbara and Ted Young, who live nearby on Young's Island, cut a hole in the ice on a lake for fresh water. They prepare and serve a steaming Mongolian firepot dinner of assorted meats and vegetables, and provide cots with sleeping bags. Since Flakne was traveling alone, Barbara Young stayed with her overnight.

The four rustic lodges, each operated by a different owner, offer private rooms or cabins, hot showers, stick-to-the-ribs breakfasts and dinners taken family style with the owners, and a pack lunch for the trail. Each lodge lays out an itinerary for the day and shuttles guests' cars with

9

VACATIONS AND WEEKENDS

baggage by road to the next overnight stop. If skiers are late in reaching the next lodge, the operators will start a search — an important service in the wilderness, especially for a skier alone.

While Flakne has made similar cross-country trips in the Midwest and felt comfortable going it alone, not all skiing experts approve. By the time her trip ended, she was skiing in sub-zero temperatures. Cross-country skiers suffer fewer injuries than downhillers — one injury per day per thousand vs. two to three injuries for downhill skiers. But cross-country enthusiasts can be at greater risk of hypothermia, a dangerous drop in body temperature. A sprained ankle in the wilderness could result in death before help arrives.

"The fun of cross-country skiing is the rhythm of its motion and the phenomenally beautiful places it gets you to in winter," says Thomas A. Barron, 34, president of the Prospect Group Inc., a venture capital company in New York City, who has skied cross-country in many places, including Maine and Yosemite. An expert who learned the sport as a youngster in Colorado and has taught many friends, Barron finds four out of five adults can master the technique. Some skiers compare it to sliding across a floor in bedroom slippers.

Beginners can practice the rhythmic shoulder, arm, and leg motions on a tracked trail with instruction at a ski center before attempting long-distance inn-to-inn or backwoods touring. Directories of major cross-country areas in the U.S. appear in *Cross Country Skier* magazine and in *Ski X-C,* an annual issued by *Backpacker* magazine.

In New England, dozens of centers give instruction and rent equipment. For an easy start, the Woodstock Ski Touring Center in the foothills of Vermont's Green Mountains offers lessons and half-day tours, from golf course terrain to gentle forested slopes. At its center in Pinkham Notch, New Hampshire, the Appalachian Mountain Club offers several workshops in ski touring. These are given on weekends in January, February, and March for $50, plus $32.50 a day for lodging and meals at the center.

Inn-to-inn skiing, long a fixture in rural New England, is enhanced by the marking of the first 50 miles of Vermont's Catamount Trail, a 280-mile passage planned to run through the Green Mountains from Massachusetts to Quebec. For intermediate cross-country skiers, the Churchill House Inn in Brandon, Vermont, organizes the Catamount Excursion, a weekly self-guided tour with north-to-south skiing over parts of the trail. The five-night tour, with stops at four traditional New England inns for dinner, bed, and breakfast, costs $398 per person, double occupancy. That includes a trail lunch, ski-area fees, and shuttle service.

Groups can organize their own inn-to-inn tours in New Hampshire with the help of the Jackson Ski Touring Foundation, a nonprofit organization in the village of Jackson, New Hampshire. The foundation maintains the largest cross-country trail system in the Northeast, 91 miles. It provides maps and a list of lodgings, and advises on itineraries.

In Aspen, Colorado, the Tenth Mountain Trail Association, named for the Tenth Mountain Division's ski troops who trained in the area during World War II, has opened its fourth hut, on a 40-mile trail heading north toward Beaver Creek. Not for beginners, skiing in this back country requires heavy packs while breaking trail in deep snow at elevations of 8,000 to 11,000 feet. But one of the stops, the Diamond J Guest Ranch, boasts a sauna and a Jacuzzi. William F. Russell, 60, chairman of Russell Aives Mills Ltd., sweater manufacturers in Deer Park, New York, led an Appalachian Mountain Club group on a five-day tour, using professional guides. Guides are available through the trail association.

Europe's ski touring adventures vary from rugged to refined. In Norway, lodge-to-lodge wilderness touring for experienced intermediate or advanced skiers is available in the Hardangervidda region through Worldwide Nordic USA of Wisconsin. The price for an 11-day tour with six days of skiing: $1,425, including air fare from New York.

Village-to-village skiing features gentler pleasures. Mountain Travel of Albany, California, offers three nine-day trips in the Jura mountains of Switzerland, along the French border. Skiers spend five hours a day on prepared trails of moderate challenge, covering about 12 miles. They stop at inns for lunch, while their baggage is transported to simple hotels featuring hot baths and five-course dinners. Cost, excluding air fare: $950 per person in double rooms.

In Austria's Steiermark region, Butterfield & Robinson of Toronto offers nine-day trips with seven days of skiing accompanied by an instructor and one or two guides. Instead of taking prepared trails, participants ski along rivers and over meadows. Skiers stay at small guest houses, some centuries old. Cost, excluding air fare: $1,295 per person in double rooms. Trips end with a celebration. That has the sound of *Gemütlichkeit.*

FOR FURTHER INFORMATION

Appalachian Mountain Club, Pinkham Notch Camp, P.O. Box 298, Gorham, NH 03581; (603)-466-2727.

Butterfield & Robinson, 70 Bond St., Toronto, Ontario, Canada M5B 1X3; (800)-387-1147 or (416)-864-1354.

Catamount Trail Association; membership, $20, includes newsletter and map; P.O. Box 897, Burlington, VT 05402-0897.

Churchill House Inn, Catamount Excursion, Rt. 73, Brandon, VT 05733; (802)-247-3300.

Gunflint Trail Lodge to Lodge Ski Association, Box 100, Grand Marais, MN 55604; (800)-328-3325 or (218)-388-2294.

Jackson Ski Touring Foundation, P.O. Box 216, Jackson, NH 03846; (603)-383-9355.

Mountain Travel, 1398 Solano Ave., Albany, CA 94706; (800)-227-2384 or (415)-527-8100.

SPORTING HOLIDAYS

Tenth Mountain Trail Association, 1280 Ute Ave., Aspen, CO 81611; (303)-925-5775.
Woodstock Ski Touring Center, Woodstock Inn, Woodstock, VT 05091; (802)-457-2114.
Worldwide Nordic USA Travel Service, P.O. Box 185, Hartland, WI 53029; (414)-367-7227.

PUBLICATIONS

Backcountry Skiing: The Sierra Club Guide to Skiing off the Beaten Track by Lito Tejada-Flores (San Francisco: Sierra Club Books, 1981), $8.95.
Backpacker magazine, bimonthly, $18; CBS Magazines, 1515 Broadway, New York, NY 10036; (800)-525-0643 or (303)-447-9330. Publishes *Ski X-C* annually, $3.95.
Cross Country Skier magazine, five issues a year, $9.97; Rodale Press, 33 E. Minor St., Emmaus, PA 18090; (215)-967-5171.
Ski Country: Nordic Skiers' Guide to the Minnesota Arrowhead by Robert Beymer (Virginia, MN: W. A. Fisher Co., 1986), $8.95. ■

Deep-Sea Game Fishing

■ Now that mounting a tiger's head on the library wall is widely considered an act of environmental vandalism, what can the heavyweight sportsman do to flaunt his prowess? What avoids endangered species, yet maintains the proper mixture of huge expense, exotic location, and a titanic struggle concluding in the capture of imposing prey? The answer is deep-sea game fishing, which usually means going after tuna, sailfish, or marlin.

The pursuit of big fish in deep water can become a grand, expensive passion. It possessed Zane Grey and Ernest Hemingway, who were among its pioneers. Today the sport has a large following among top U.S. businessmen. They support most of the game fish centers of the world, which are in the Caribbean, up and down the Pacific and Atlantic coasts, and off Hawaii, Panama, and Australia.

Stephen Sloan, a New York real estate developer who holds 19 world records for game fish, has no trouble explaining his enthusiasm. He says, "There's a pantheism involved. To see one of these animals come out of the sea and try to shake the hook is fabulous." While many fishermen still mount their trophies, Sloan notes: "Unlike a big-game hunter, you don't have to kill. You can let the fish go and let it live."

That pantheistic feeling can come dear. A day's charter in Mexico, currently about the cheapest place to fish, runs to at least $225 for a 30-foot boat, about the smallest most fishermen would find comfortable, and a more luxurious 38-footer rents for $450. Prices can go a lot higher. In the Azores, Sloan and two partners rent out the 43-footer they own jointly for $10,000 a week, including air fare and hotel for two. Less-than-wealthy fishermen can spread the costs because most boats can accommodate up to four people. Once a fisherman is hopelessly hooked, he will probably have to own a boat. A fully rigged 38-foot model made by Topaz costs about $300,000, and a 60-footer fit for heavy seas made by Egg Harbor will cost around $850,000.

Trolling slowly in a 38-footer through the deep blue water a few miles off the southern tip of Baja California, with sere hills jutting up behind the town of Cabo San Lucas, it is easy to see why people like Sloan spend fortunes fishing around the world. In the distance a whale slaps the sea with its tail. Giant rays fling themselves out of the ocean. A huge sea turtle drifts by. Then the skipper high on the bridge sees the scimitar dorsal of a marlin slitting the sea off the starboard beam. He accelerates and swings around to pass in front of the fish. The deckhand yanks a live mackerel out of the bait box, hooks it just above the mouth, and lets it out on about 40 feet of line. The maneuver draws the live bait slowly in front of the lazing marlin. The big fish moves tantalizingly toward the bait, but decides it isn't hungry. A couple of hundred yards off, another boat is luckier. A marlin weighing perhaps 150 pounds is dancing on its tail in its own spray as it tries to shake the hook.

The deep sea off Cabo San Lucas, where the Pacific meets the Sea of Cortez, churns with fish. William Doner, a vice president of Caesars Palace in Las Vegas, says, "You

A four-rod fisherman, Irwin Pines, whose company manages buildings in Florida and New Jersey, trolls off Bimini in his boat, *Send Money.*

VACATIONS AND WEEKENDS

can get bigger fish in other places, but this is the finest all-round fishing in the world." He was so taken by the fishing at Baja that he bought a house there and runs a fleet of seven charter boats out of Cabo San Lucas. "We get an average of one marlin a day on our boats," he says, "and you can't do that anywhere else." Boats in Doner's Tortuga Fleet rent for $275 a day, less in summer.

When W. Matt Parr, an Irish-born American expatriate, began attracting corporate executives to Baja to fish at his resorts after World War II, they could come only by yacht or private plane. Now jets from Los Angeles and other cities serve nearby San José del Cabo, opening the resort to the merely affluent, who stay at one of Parr's three stunning resorts, each with its own fishing fleet. Rooms on the American plan at the Cabo San Lucas, the oldest of his hotels, start at $65 a day per person, and boats with captain and crew rent for an average $325 a day. The hotel takes cash and traveler's checks but requires advance arrangements for payments by credit card. It has no telephone, so make reservations through its U.S. office.

Fishing has been good for decades in the Caribbean and along the East Coast of North America. Sportsmen move north from Venezuela as the big fish follow the warming waters. Tournaments are popular all along the route of the fish, with prizes ranging from a trophy to $25,000 or more in cash. An old favorite of tournament anglers is the Bimini Big Game Fishing Club, which is open to the public and offers boat slips. Rooms start at $96. Fishermen can charter 31-foot boats made by Bertram for $450 a day. Serious fishermen also look to other islands in the Bahamas, such as Treasure Cay, Chub Cay, and Walker's Cay.

Montauk, at the tip of Long Island, is one of the best sport-fishing bases along the East Coast. Beginning in July, the big boats speed out to the great underwater canyon 60 miles offshore where fishing for marlin and tuna is hottest. Montauk Marine Basin, operated by Carl Darenberg Jr. and Sr., charters boats of up to 54 feet for the two-day trip to the canyon and back at costs from $1,800 to $2,000. Smaller boats for fishing closer to shore cost $595 a day.

Coastal waters off Chile and Peru and around Hawaii and New Zealand all offer good game fishing. Tropic Star Lodge at Piñas Bay, on the Pacific coast of Panama 150 miles from Panama City, is exclusively a fishing resort. The lodge houses up to 28 people in weekly shifts and sends them out Sunday through Friday in a fleet of 31-foot Bertrams to seek marlin, sailfish, and less renowned game. The comfortable lodge costs $2,650 for a week's room and board; that includes the fishing and transportation by small plane from Panama City. The owner, Conway Kittredge, suggests reservations as much as a year in advance.

Those who want to land a "grander" — a fish of 1,000 pounds or more — inevitably turn to Australia's Great Barrier Reef. Bill Doner, whose hallway in Cabo San Lucas is dominated by the massive head and bill of a 1,234-pound black marlin he caught off Australia, figures he spent about $15,000 for one week's fishing off the reef. Qantas flies twice a week from San Francisco to Cairns in Queensland, one base for fishing the reef. Fishing International arranges trips to Australia.

While no major game fish are endangered, some are getting scarce in places. Partly as a result, fishing customs are changing. Some anglers will no longer kill fish they do not plan to eat. Light tackle, which requires more skill in landing a big fish, is increasingly popular. Matt Parr of Baja California is especially proud of his world record for catching a 205-pound striped marlin on line rated to stand only an 8-pound pull. That may seem something like leading an angry elephant through Times Square on a string, but even a little drag tires a big fish eventually, and the clever angler can bring him alongside.

Competitions in which the angler kills his fish are giving way to tag-and-release competitions. When the fish is brought alongside, the deckhand implants a numbered plastic dart in its shoulder and releases the fish to live and hit the hook another day. But for anglers whose lives cannot be complete without a giant trophy above the mantelpiece, game fishing still provides a chance to win one without worry of imperiling a species.

FOR FURTHER INFORMATION

International Game Fish Association; membership, $20 a year, includes *International Angler,* a bimonthly newsletter, plus the annual *World Record Game Fishes;* 3000 E. Las Olas Blvd., Fort Lauderdale, FL 33316; (305)-467-0161.

Fishing International, P.O. Box 2132, 4000 Montgomery Dr., Santa Rosa, CA 95405; (707)-542-4242.

Australian Tourist Commission, 489 Fifth Ave., New York, NY 10017; (800)-445-4000.

Bahamas Tourist Office, Suite 415, 255 Alhambra Circle, Coral Gables, FL 33134; (305)-442-4860.

Bimini Big Game Fishing Club and Hotel, P.O. Box 523238, Miami, FL 33152; (800)-327-4149 or (809)-347-2391.

Cabo San Lucas Hotel (Baja California), P.O. Box 48088, Los Angeles, CA 90048; (800)-421-0777 or (213)-205-0055.

Chub Cay Club, P.O. Box 661067, Miami Springs, FL 33266; (305)-445-7830.

Finisterra Tortuga Sportfishing Fleet (Baja California), 18700 MacArthur Blvd., Irvine, CA 92715; (714)-752-9010.

Mexican Government Tourism Office, Suite 1002, 405 Park Ave., New York, NY 10022; (212)-838-2949.

Montauk Marine Basin, West Lake Dr., Montauk, NY 11954; (516)-668-5900.

Tropic Star Lodge (Piñas Bay, Panama), Suite 200, 693 N. Orange Ave., Orlando, FL 32801; (305)-843-0124.

Walker's Cay Hotel & Marina (Abaco, Bahama Islands), 700 S.W. 34th St., Fort Lauderdale, FL 33315; (800)-327-3714 or (305)-522-1469.

PUBLICATIONS
Angler's Guide to Baja California by Tom Miller (Huntington Beach, CA: Baja Trail, 1984), $6.95.

SPORTING HOLIDAYS

Marlin, The Magazine of Big Game Fishing, $22 for six issues; P.O. Box 12902, Pensacola, FL 32576; (904)-434-5571.

Motor Boating & Sailing, monthly, $15.95 a year; P.O. Box 10075, Des Moines, IA 50350; (800)-247-5470 or in Iowa (800)-532-1272.

The Old Man and the Sea by Ernest Hemingway (New York: Scribner, 1983), $9.95.

Salt Water Sportsman, monthly, $19.95 a year; 186 Lincoln St., Boston, MA 02111; (617)-426-4074.

The Undiscovered Zane Grey Fishing Stories edited by George Reiger (Piscataway, NJ: New Century, Winchester Press, 1983), $29.95. ∎

Salmon Fishing in Iceland

■ Just 35 miles below the Arctic Circle, at Husavik on the northeast coast of Iceland, a Fokker Friendship turboprop bounced to a landing. It brought a party of Americans and Canadians in search of what many deem the freshwater fisherman's supreme prize, the Atlantic salmon. Scanning clouds scudding over snowcapped mountains that Sunday afternoon, these anglers fervently hoped for a week of foul weather. Even in July that could mean near-freezing temperatures and rain. At 65 degrees, when summer sun warms northern waters, the salmon lie low.

"Salmon fishing has a mystique about it," says Randolph A. Marks, 52, chairman and co-owner of American Brass Co. in Buffalo, New York. He has pursued the elusive catch on Quebec's northern rivers and Anticosti Island, in New Brunswick, and on Scotland's River Tay. This was his sixth trip to Iceland.

The Atlantic salmon, called by the Romans *salmo,* or leaper, presents a unique challenge. Pacific salmon are generally fished by trolling with bait and lures as they feed near a river's mouth before going upstream to spawn. But the Atlantic species is caught upriver, with a casting rod and fly. A trout will take a fly that matches whatever insects it may be nibbling. But a salmon does not feed once it starts upriver. Salmon take flies only out of irritation, perhaps, say Iceland's guides, to defend their territory from an invader.

In the U.S. in recent years the Atlantic salmon, confronted with intruders, has all but vanished. Dams and logging make many rivers impassable for the leaper from the sea, and pollution makes them uninhabitable. In Canada and Europe poaching on rivers and commercial netting at sea have diminished the salmon population. But Scotland, Norway, and especially Iceland still offer good midsummer angling.

Iceland reserves most of its 60 unblemished salmon rivers for the sportsman. Though its economy is based on fish, the government has long prohibited the netting of salmon within 200 miles offshore. Tourists wielding fly rods in rivers provide more revenue per salmon than do commercial fishermen casting nets at sea. The government strictly limits the number of rods allowed on a salmon river. All tackle brought in must be accompanied by a certificate of disinfection to prevent spreading disease to Iceland's rivers.

Even Iceland's catch varies in cycles. Lodges keep logs of the daily catch, and each season rivers are stocked with smolts, the young salmon. In the early 1980s sporting anglers brought in fewer salmon than the more than 20 per rod per week in the 1970s. But 1985 marked a turnaround.

Frontiers International Travel, specialists in fishing and wing-shooting trips, offer rods and accommodations from late June until early August on three of Iceland's rivers: the Grimsa, the Midfjardara, and the Laxa i Adaldal. That's Icelandic for "salmon river in the Adal valley." Randy Marks likes the Laxa, noted for the size of its salmon and of its catch.

A few hayfields back from the Laxa, at the lodge on the Arnes farm, guests pay $4,900 per rod per week at the peak of the season, in late July. That includes 12 hours of fishing per rod per day for six days, plus two half-days, with guide, bed and board, and a third of the rod's catch. This lodge can put seven rods on the eight beats, or fishing stations, that it owns or leases along a five-mile stretch of the Laxa. Since the lodge sleeps ten, for $3,000 each, two persons can share time on a rod. In August a combination trout and salmon week on the upper Laxa costs $3,790 per rod. Air fare, transfers, and hotel in Reykjavik, the capital, are not included.

Hoping for one more hit before a summer day in Iceland ends at 10 P.M., Montreal stockbroker C. Athol Gordon casts for salmon on the Laxa i Adaldal.

VACATIONS AND WEEKENDS

After a smorgasbord breakfast, served around 7 A.M., the fishermen went to the river, two in the car of each gillie, or guide. Some of the first-timers had pictured the Laxa as a forbidding torrent. Instead they found a pastoral stream, full of deep quiet holes, merely punctuated by rapids.

Marks brought three of his 40 rods to Iceland: the customary 10½- and 9½-foot graphites, with 9-pound test line; and a traditional but unusual two-handed 14½-foot salmon rod that takes 11-pound line. With the latter he can alternate hands, to keep from tiring in the wind.

Instead of the dry flies that anglers use for trout at the height of the season, wet flies on double hooks are customary for salmon. And the gillies get anglers to cast out far more line than for trout. For salmon the caster directs the line downstream, diagonally across the current. Then he allows it to drift slowly across a pool, back toward the bank, and plays the line gently, if at all. It's a subtle game that ideally ends with a good fight.

At beat No. 1, Marks's gillie, Jafet Olafsson, rowed him out to a deep mid-river pool, while his partner cast from shore. Both anglers got a hit at once. The shore caster's fish headed upstream and broke free. When Marks felt his fish turn downstream, he pulled his rod up sharply, striking the fish. It ran a couple of hundred yards, drawing the line all the way through its backing. After a 35-minute fight, Marks pulled in a 28-pounder, twice the usual size.

On balmy days the anglers caught more of the Laxa's filmy underwater plant life than fish. With the sun shining through clear water, the salmon didn't rise much and the pesky weeds had proliferated, fouling flies and lines.

But on the best days, standing in the flowing water as late as 10 P.M. during the long northern evenings, the fishermen lost all sense of time. Families of ducks paddled by. Arctic terns glided over the treeless landscape. On the grassy banks strewn with tiny flowers sheep grazed. Except for the whip of lines and whir of reels, the fishermen heard only hay rakes and lowing cattle in the fields, and once in a while the great splash of a salmon leaping upstream.

At 11 P.M. the anglers sat down to a dinner of exquisitely poached salmon, or some other local delicacy. On the final evening, they dined on baked whole salmon garnished with tomatoes in their mouths. Next day each picked up his share of the catch, and some bought more — fresh, smoked, or pickled — packed to travel.

FOR FURTHER INFORMATION

Frontiers International Travel, P.O. Box 161, Wexford, PA 15090; (800)-245-1950 or (412)-935-1577.

The Atlantic Salmon Federation; membership, $40 per year, includes the quarterly *Atlantic Salmon Journal* ($11 per year to non-members); P.O. Box 429, St. Andrews, New Brunswick, Canada E0G 2X0; (506)-529-8889.

PUBLICATIONS

The Atlantic Salmon by Lee Wulff (Piscataway, NJ: New Century, Winchester Press, 1983), $27.95.

Daughter of Fire: A Portrait of Iceland by Katharine Scherman (Boston: Little, Brown, 1976), $16.95.

Iceland Tourist Board, Scandinavian National Tourist Offices, 655 Third Ave., New York, NY 10017; (212)-949-2333.

Iceland: The Visitor's Guide by David Williams (Cambridge, MA: Bradt Enterprises, 1985), $19.95. ■

Pheasant Shooting in Denmark

■ The common ring-necked pheasant, with its green head, scarlet-circled eyes, and golden breast, is an exotic Oriental import, introduced into the U.S. and Europe in the 19th century. South Dakota once harbored more of these coveted game birds than any other place on earth. But after World War II, intensive agriculture cleared hedgerows and destroyed nesting places, and harvesters left little food in the fields. The pheasant population, and the bag for upland bird shooters, nose-dived. The number may vary from year to year, but many states limit the hunter's quarry of wild birds to two or three cocks a day.

So Raymond Plank, 65, and his wife, Lollie, have taken to traveling each November thousands of miles from Minneapolis to Denmark, where in one exceptional day he has shot up to 125 pheasants, twice the normal bag, and his wife, some 90. "The shooting is unbelievable," exclaims Plank, chairman of Apache Corp., an oil and gas exploration company. "The birds are strong, fast, high-flying, and challenging." And, he adds, "it's an opportunity to see what Denmark might have been like for the landed gentry 100 years ago at the lovely historic places where we shoot." A week's escorted holiday with four days of shooting costs a bundle in a package offered by Frontiers International Travel: from $6,890 to $8,990 in 1987. Non-shooters can come along for $2,290.

Special European practices of game management and gunning make possible these bountiful shoots. Pheasants yield a cash crop twice over for Danish landowners. Their gamekeepers breed and release the young into their woodlands at six weeks or so, months before the shooting season. From late October through November, shooting parties pay for the privilege of harvesting this crop, usually about half the number of birds released. And the estates sell each day's quarry, at $4 to $5 per bird, undressed, to restaurants or for export.

Europe's style of "driven shoot," which goes back to feudal times, gives the gunner scores of well-placed tar-

SPORTING HOLIDAYS

gets. Instead of walking fields with dogs to flush out their own birds, as American shotgunners do, Europeans wait with the dogs in a clearing facing the woods. Beaters walk through the woods beating the bushes to roust birds from their cover. Hence gunners get shots at birds coming toward them, as well as passing shots.

Americans have been joining driven shoots in Britain since the 1960s, when many stately homes opened their grouse moors and pheasant fields to paying guns. They discovered Denmark's more plentiful birds in the late 1970s. Frontiers accommodates 12 shooters per week. While they are in the field, non-shooting wives and companions can spend their days sight-seeing.

Before the start of a day's shooting, the gamekeeper or master of the hunt at an estate informs his guests of the safety rules. Automatic guns are illegal in Denmark. Only double-barreled, side-by-side or over-and-under shotguns are allowed, preferably 12 gauge. When loaded, barrels should point up at least 45 degrees, to avoid an accidental shot that could hit the beaters. Anything that flies is fair game, but not animals. At the end of this lecture, little glasses of *krabask,* the traditional schnapps with bitters served before a shoot, are often passed around.

Stationed about 50 yards apart in the field, the shooters become part of a small army deployed by the gamekeeper. Behind them stand the dog handlers, with black Labradors to retrieve the fallen game; beside each shooter, a loader keeps a second gun ready so the guest can shoot continually. Once all shooters are ready, the gamekeeper gives a blast on his hunting horn to signal the beaters to advance.

As some 20 beaters approach through the woods, shooters hear the muffled, "yep, yep, yep" of their call and a crescendo of rhythmic tapping as their sticks hit tree trunks. Suddenly a beater alerts the shooters to ready their guns. They hear the screechy cackles of a cock, then sight birds coming over the treetops one by one. The birds can fly 120 feet high and 45 miles an hour — a challenge to any shotgun, especially in the wind. As they heave into view, shots ring out down the line. A panting dog yelps as he sees a bird hit, leaps in the direction of its downward somersault, and is on the spot before it reaches the ground. Soon the air is adrift with feathers and the smell of powder. When the beaters reach the edge of the woods, facing the shooters, the gamekeeper sounds the signal to unload. Four or five such drives each morning and two or three more in the afternoon, all in different locations on one estate, make a day's shooting.

Following Continental tradition, the ladies join the shooters at the manor house for cocktails and game parade. In this ceremony the estate owner, gamekeeper, and shooters gather in the courtyard to honor the fallen birds, laid out in rows on the cobblestones, and to thank all who contributed to the drives' success. The gamekeeper announces the number of birds shot, typically from 600 to 1,200, raises his horn, and sounds taps. "It's quite a thing," notes Plank. "They show great respect for the birds and the beaters."

Frontiers President Michael Fitzgerald says that during a standard four-day shoot, for 12 guns on four estates, each shooter will have a chance at from 2,200 to 2,400 birds. A party typically shoots two days on the Jutland peninsula, and two on the island of Fyn. There parties on the highest-priced trips take over one of the world's finest small hotels, the Falsled Kro, a 19th-century inn with 13 rooms and an outstanding restaurant.

"It's a week that you talk about a long time before and a long time afterward," says Forrest Braden, a rancher from Yuma, Arizona, and a dealer for John Deere farm machinery in Mexico. He has shot all over the world, and hasn't missed a season in Denmark since Frontiers started offering trips in 1976.

"One of the neat things about it is the camaraderie," says Plank, who looks forward to going with the same people time and again. A four-year relationship on these trips with one businessman led to his joining the board of Plank's Apache Corp.

FOR FURTHER INFORMATION

Frontiers International Travel, P.O. Box 161, Wexford, PA 15090; (800)-245-1950 or (412)-935-1577.

PUBLICATIONS
The Hunt by John G. Mitchell (New York: Penguin, 1981), $4.95.
Seasons of the Hunter edited by Robert Elman (New York: Knopf, 1985), $17.95. ■

Schools for Wing-Shooters

■ Ever since their father took them on elephant safaris in Kenya as children, the Havens brothers have been shooting. Timothy M. Havens, 41, president of Newbold's Asset Management in Philadelphia, hunts whenever he can; John P. Havens, 30, a securities trader and principal at the investment banking firm of Morgan Stanley in New York, is a regular skeet-shooter on Long Island. But along with some American friends who joined them for a pheasant shoot in Yorkshire in November, they spent an afternoon at a school outside London run by Holland & Holland Ltd., which makes some of the world's most expensive guns. This was their first formal instruction in the art of shotgunning. "You get to think you know everything," says Tim. "But people who shoot a lot get sloppy. You can always learn."

The very idea of going to school to learn to shoot birds is new to most Americans. Until a generation or so ago, boys

15

VACATIONS AND WEEKENDS

got guns for Christmas, and, by trial and error, learned from their elders to track plentiful wild game. But the ways of hunting in America are changing. Suburban sprawl has banished the sport from ever-increasing areas of the country. More and more Americans follow the European practice of paying to shoot game raised expressly for release on preserves, with seasons often lasting from October until March. (A directory of 128 preserves is available from the National Shooting Sports Foundation.)

Such sport can be expensive. Though costs vary with the quality of the birds, amenities, and service, a shooter can spend $400 a day (meals and lodging extra) to bag a dozen quail on a plantation in Georgia. Memberships in hunting clubs that lease land can cost thousands of dollars. Sharpened skills help wing-shooting enthusiasts make the most of their investments. And, with instruction increasingly available, the sport is broadening: More women are taking up arms. The Greater Houston Gun Club offers a popular Saturday clinic for women novices, at $30.

Until recently most instructors of sport shooting in the U.S. taught only skeet and trap, where clay targets are launched at predictable speeds, distances, and angles. The requisite skill is calculating how far ahead of the target to fire, a method called the sustained lead. But real birds do not fly as predictably as clay ones do: Sustaining a lead is a formidable challenge for the sometime bird-shooter. Even such exponents of the technique as Fred Missildine, 69, former world champion skeet- and trapshooter, allow that wing-shooters rarely get enough practice to succeed with the technique. At the Cloister Hotel on Sea Island, Georgia, where he says he has instructed such luminaries as former Exxon Chairman Clifton C. Garvin Jr., Missildine teaches both the sustained lead and a variant of the English method.

The shooter using the English method (sometimes called the Churchill method after the gunsmith and coach who devised it) does not calculate a lead. He mounts the gun to his shoulder as he sights the bird and shoots, turning his body in one swing-through motion, as in golf. In theory if the gun is properly mounted and the rhythm and timing of the swing are correct, the shot and the bird will intersect without conscious planning.

Instruction in the English method is becoming more popular in the U.S. Holland & Holland instructors visit regularly, with itineraries arranged by Griffin & Howe, a New York gunsmith. Orvis, a fishing and hunting outfitter, offers sessions from July until October near its Manchester, Vermont, headquarters, then sets up shop until January near Tallahassee, Florida. *The Orvis Wing-Shooting Handbook* by Bruce Bowlen (Nick Lyons Books, $8.95) explains the company's interpretation of the English method. Near Houston the Highland Bend Shooting School in Fulshear gives instruction year-round except for the hunting season, when shooters take to the fields. Pachmayr, a Los Angeles hunting supplier, gives summer sessions in the "instinctive" method, an American technique, taught by the military, among others, and much like the English method but simpler.

To find out how the English method works, two stockbrokers from Kidder Peabody's Philadelphia office took a lesson at the Fairfield Shooting School near Chestertown, Maryland. (The cost: $200 for the pair for a two-hour session.) A. John Gregg, 39, a vice president and sales manager, and Charles Boinske, 24, an account executive, began with the introductory part of a videotape, "Gameshooting," produced by Holland & Holland. It demonstrates the importance of stance, placement of hands, eye-hand coordination, mount, and swing-through.

In the field, instructor Charles "Chick" Darrell, 39, had the men go through the motions they had seen in the video. Boinske faced a 15-foot target-launcher tower, left foot slightly forward with heels six inches apart, and readied his gun with the stock under his right arm and the barrel resting in his left hand; his extended left arm would help him move the gun in the swing-through. Gregg, a left-hander, was his mirror image.

As soon as Darrell released the clay pigeons by remote control, his pupils mounted stocks and fired, swinging and pivoting in the direction of the targets. Boinske, who had previously shot only with rifles at stationary targets, found that a lot to remember. Gregg had to overcome a habit of hesitating in midswing. But soon both were breaking pi-

John P. Havens (right) of Morgan Stanley in New York sharpens his shotgunning at the school run by Holland & Holland Ltd. near London.

SPORTING HOLIDAYS

geons. Later they shot at clays coming from a 50-foot tower that simulated passing geese or doves.

English-style training is even providing an alternative to traditional skeet- and trapshooting. Those targets are so predictable that the goal is to break 100% of them—a tension-filled quest for perfection that turns off many recreational shooters. Sporting Clays, as the new game is called, sets launchers for unpredictable trajectories; breaking 80% of the targets is a high score, and the exercise is more relaxed. In 1984 the Highland Bend School introduced the sport to the U.S. By 1986 regional tournaments were held in New Hampshire and Maryland. "This is a substitute for hunting that the whole family can enjoy," says Bob L. Davis, 40, president of Dove Oil & Gas Co. in Houston and head of the new United States Sporting Clays Association.

On the last day of their pheasant shoot in Yorkshire, where beaters tapped the bushes to flush game released months before, the Havens brothers and their six friends downed 297 birds. They left most with caretakers on the property. But those they brought back to the chef at Brown's Hotel in London made a delectable farewell dinner. Meanwhile, in Maryland, Jack Gregg sat in a blind all day, but nary a fowl winged over. Whatever its merits, the English method is no better than the American at making birds appear in the sky.

FOR FURTHER INFORMATION

National Shooting Sports Foundation, Box 1075, Riverside, CT 06878; (203)-637-3618.

United States Sporting Clays Association, Suite 490 East, 50 Briar Hollow, Houston, TX 77027; (713)-622-8043.

Fairfield Shooting School, Pheasantfield Shooting Preserve, Rt. 3, Box 245A, Chestertown, MD 21620; (301)-758-1824.

Highland Bend School, P.O. Box 580, Fulshear, TX 77441; (713)-341-0032.

Holland & Holland Ltd., 35 Bruton St., London, England WIX 8JS; (44)-1-499-4411; or c/o Griffin & Howe, Suite 1011, 36 W. 44th St., New York, NY 10036; (212)-921-0980.

Holland & Holland's instructional videotape, "Game Shooting," $49.95; Blacksmith Corp., P.O. Box 424, Southport, CT 06490; (800)-531-2665.

Orvis Shooting Schools, 10 River Rd., Manchester, VT 05254; (802)-362-3900.

Pachmayr Shotgun Hunting School, 1875 S. Mountain Ave., Monrovia, CA 91016; (800)-423-9704 or (818)-357-7771.

EXPEDITIONS AND EXPLORATIONS

Bicycling Through Europe

■ Halfway through a nine-day bicycle tour of the Chianti region of Tuscany in Italy, Arthur S. Labatt, 53, president of Trimark Investment Management, a Toronto mutual fund company, was fully adjusted to pedaling by day and feasting by night. In late May 1985, at a veal and pasta dinner in a 17th-century villa 27 miles south of Florence, Labatt, a member of the Canadian brewing family, summed up his day's cycling: "On the downhills I thought about the business meetings I just came from in Japan. On the uphills I thought about what I was going to eat."

European bike touring, once for the young and frugal, attracts executives of all ages. Some do it on their own. Barton M. Biggs, 54, chairman of the asset management division of the New York investment banking firm of Morgan Stanley, took his family — his wife, Judy, 49, and their three children ranging in age from 17 to 24 — on a 1984 biking trip through Normandy and Brittany. Says Biggs, "Two weeks of this kind of thing sure puts into perspective a stock market that took a dive in the first week and made most of the loss back in the second week."

But even seasoned travelers like Labatt and his wife, Sonia, 48, often prefer to bike in groups. In the summer of 1985 more than a dozen tour operators sent some 3,000 vacationers on plush pedaling excursions. In groups of 15 to 25, fitness-minded adults took two-wheeled trips through the scenic areas of Europe, from the dunes of Ireland to the outskirts of Venice.

The trips vary in difficulty according to the daily distance covered and the hilliness of the terrain. But most prearranged tours offer trips that average 20 to 30 miles per day and pose little trouble for anyone who feels comfortable on a bicycle and exercises regularly. Prices range from $500 a week to $1,500, depending on the service and luxury provided, as well as the country chosen and its exchange rates.

Choosing a tour is usually a matter of deciding on a location and date. But availability is also a factor: popular trips sponsored by well-established operators sell out months in advance. Three magazines help bring cyclists and tour organizers together: *Bicycling, Bicycle Guide,* and *Bicycle USA.* The latter publishes *The Bicyclists' Almanac* every January, giving state-by-state information. The March "TourFinder" issue lists tour organizers along with departure dates, prices, and a brief description of routes. The League of American Wheelmen, the cyclists' organization that publishes *Bicycle USA,* sells reprints of the list for $3.

One advantage of a tour is that the cyclists carry no baggage, which travels on a support van, or "sag wagon," along with spare bicycle tires and parts for mechanical repairs. The sag wagon gets its name because tired travelers can call it a day and hop aboard with their bikes whenever they like. If a tour member is injured — a cyclist fell and broke his arm on the Chianti tour — the van is available for emergency hospital runs.

While seasoned cyclists may prefer to take their own bicycles along, shipping them can be a nuisance. Most airlines require that bikes be boxed, and each airline has its own rules on how that is to be done — wheels on or off, for example. Many trip organizers provide comfortable touring bikes to participants at low cost. The bikes often come with seats that are easy to adjust and dual brake handles. These are important comfort and safety features for over-the-road travel. Tour operators recommend that riders bring their own handlebar bags and rain gear. Helmets aren't widely used in Europe, but wearing them makes sense as a safety measure. Special bike clothing — padded gloves, tight-fitting shirts and shorts, and hard-sole biking shoes — is popular but not essential.

"For most people, biking is only half the attraction. It's picnic, pâté, and Pommard all the way," promises Butterfield & Robinson, the Toronto-based organizer of the Chianti tour that Arthur and Sonia Labatt took. The agency signed up 2,600 Americans and Canadians to bike through Europe on 19 routes in 1987 and stay at first-class hotels. Rates average $200 per day. On these deluxe tours Butterfield & Robinson takes care of all the logistics. Guides accompanying each group plan the day's route, usually choosing lightly traveled back roads.

Although guides will plot longer, more strenuous routes

EXPEDITIONS AND EXPLORATIONS

for serious cyclists, an average day's run is four hours or so. Even slowpokes have plenty of time along the way to picnic outdoors, eat at Michelin-starred restaurants, and visit châteaux. At day's end everyone gathers for an aperitif and dinner at the night's lodgings, which range from centuries-old country villas, such as a former home of the Medici family, to spectacular resort hotels with marble baths and gold-plated faucets.

Sightseeing and the chance to get close to people along the way are important parts of the bicycle tour. Guides organize visits to attractions that most tourists never see. On the Labatts' Chianti tour, the group pedaled up a twisting Tuscan road to the hilltop wine estate of Badia a Coltibuono, on the grounds of an 11th-century monastery. After meeting the owner for a wine tasting, the cyclists inspected wine cellars and the monastery's early-Renaissance frescoes. Said Judith Bernstein, 36, an independent management consultant to the New York City Health and Hospitals Corporation, a municipal agency, "This is about as far as I can get from a hospital in Queens."

The previous day, Bernstein and W. Gary Atkinson, 31, a project manager for Beacon Corp., a Boston real estate development firm, had pulled their bikes under the eaves of a house for shelter from a brief rain shower. Says Atkinson, "The owner came out and invited us inside. He served us wine from his own vineyard." Before they left, their host suggested that the two get married. Says Bernstein, "We don't speak Italian, but we communicated very well."

Elizabeth Marcus Russell, 38, an associate merchandise manager at the Brown Group, a St. Louis-based shoe manufacturer, used to go on cross-country mountain treks. She was drawn to the Chianti trip by the promise of nights in beautiful villas and outstanding meals. Says Russell: "With trekking, you carry your own food, and there's just so much cabbage and beans that you can stand." The chance to sweat is a powerful attraction for other bikers. "I like exercise. Lying on a beach would bore me to death," says Alan Sayers, 53, vice president of Cadillac Fairview, a Toronto-based real estate development company.

Henry O. Timnick, 54, an executive with Clayton & Dubilier, a private investment company in New York, toured Bavaria in 1984 on a trip organized by Gerhard's Bicycle Odysseys of Portland, Oregon. "When we were going through the Black Forest in Germany, it was like being in a cathedral," he recalls. That kind of memory brings you back. In 1985 Timnick took a 15-day Gerhard trip through Switzerland, France, and Italy.

FOR FURTHER INFORMATION

The League of American Wheelmen; membership, $22 a year, includes *Bicycle USA* magazine, nine issues a year, the annual *Bicycle USA Almanac;* Suite 209, 6707 Whitestone Rd., Baltimore, MD 21207; (301)-944-3399.

Butterfield & Robinson, 70 Bond St., Toronto, Ontario, Canada M5B 1X3; (800)-387-1147 or (416)-864-1354.

Gerhard's Bicycle Odysseys, 4949 S.W. Macadam, Portland, OR 97201; (503)-223-2402.

PUBLICATIONS

Bicycle Guide, nine issues a year including annual *Buyers Guide,* $11.95; Raben Publishing, 711 Boylston St., Boston, MA 02116; (800)-358-8888 or (617)-236-1885.

Bicycling, ten issues a year, $15.97; Rodale Press, 33 E. Minor St., Emmaus, PA 18090; (800)-441-7761 or (215)-967-5171.

Cycling in Europe by Nicholas Crane (Newbury Park, CA: Haynes Publications, 1977), $12.95.

Cyclist's Britain (New York: Hunter Publishing, 1986), $12.95.

Europe by Bike by Karen & Terry Whitehill (Seattle: The Mountaineers, 1987), $10.95.

Walking Through Europe

■ They met at Ireland's Shannon Airport shortly after 7 A.M. one Monday in July, 12 sleepy Americans from Hawaii, California, Illinois, and Maryland. By midafternoon they had turned into resolute walkers, clambering over a rough stone wall in County Clare to tramp up the roll of a meadow mantled in velvety green. Suddenly the land ran out and they stood atop the sheer Cliffs of Moher, which from their highest point drop 668 feet straight to the Atlantic. Stunned out of jet lag, the walkers gazed on a vista of promontories jutting for five miles down the coast.

This was the first of 15 hikes on a three-week walking tour over byways and trails in Ireland, Wales, England, and Scotland, organized by Mountain Travel of Albany, California. The 12 walkers included an industrialist from Palo Alto, a computer engineer from Rockwell International, a

In Ireland's County Clare, walkers on tour met two new entrepreneurs. Their charge for a donkey photo: 10 pence; for a ride: 50 pence. No one rode.

VACATIONS AND WEEKENDS

bank vice president, a retired builder, a retired food industry executive, and a psychiatrist, most with spouses.

Immersed in landscape, the walker gets to know a place better than the sedentary tourist shut inside a car or bus. Walkers like the exercise, but more than that, they like going where wheelmen can't, where sheep graze and Stone Age tombs and Iron Age fortresses rest in rocky fields. In Ireland one bird watcher on the Mountain Travel tour added at least ten species to his life list of birds. The walker's leisurely pace encourages encounters with local people and free-flowing conversation among companions.

The way certain travel companies arrange things, walkers can enjoy these experiences without the chores of camping or the burden of backpacking. A van carries bags, and at night hikers enjoy the comforts of country inns. On some tours, travelers ride partway to cover the maximum terrain; other tours are built around guided hikes in one or two areas that return to the same base each night. The group meeting at Shannon had chosen a motor-and-foot combination from among the 150 itineraries offered by Mountain Travel worldwide. Their trips are ranked by difficulty; this tour was one of the easiest on the feet.

At Shannon the 12 travelers packed themselves cozily into a blue Datsun van with their tour leader, Paddy O'Leary, 49, at the wheel. O'Leary's year-round job is director of Ireland's Association for Adventure Sports, which trains teachers of climbing and kayaking. The group covered some 550 miles in seven days, around Ireland and into Northern Ireland. Every day O'Leary led a scenic hike off the beaten track: up Croghaun Mountain on Achill Island; through Tollymore Forest Park in Northern Ireland; to the legendary hilltop grave of Queen Maeve, a favored spot of poet William Butler Yeats. In Dublin the group took a walking tour guided by university students.

From Rosslare, on Ireland's southeast tip, the Americans crossed by ferry to Fishguard, Wales. Here Mike Banks, a British explorer, and his wife, Patricia, both 61, took the travelers in two minibuses, and on foot, for 12 days — across southern Wales, northward through the western shires of England, and along the southwest coast of Scotland.

At their first small country hotel, a young Irish lawyer played the pipes to entertain the walkers, and some Irish guests danced an impromptu jig. Dinner sometimes included fresh salmon or lobster, and breakfasts were hearty: gooseberries on occasion, but regularly porridge, bacon, sausage, eggs, grilled tomatoes, and scones with jam. Unusually dry weather in Ireland allowed the group to picnic at midday in open fields or shady glens on bread, cheese, fruit, and juice bought in village stores. In Britain a pub lunch was usual.

Mountain Travel has replaced this ambitious itinerary with two trips: a fortnight in Ireland ($1,990), and 17 days in the English and Scottish highlands ($1,950). The cost includes everything except air fare, lunches, and dinners.

Britain is walker's heaven, with 96,000 miles of public footpaths mapped in detail and maintained by the Ramblers' Association and various public authorities. The views are marvelous and the only equipment needed is a good pair of walking shoes. Travelers can book tours in particular areas with prearranged itineraries, van and guide services, plus hotels. The Wayfarers, a British firm with a representative in New York, conducts one-week walking tours from May until October in several parts of England, through Thomas Hardy country in the south or James Herriot's Yorkshire, for example. The cost: 485 pounds (about $780).

Walkers seeking to conquer Europe on foot without paying anyone for the privilege can arrange their own tours and set their own pace. James Donley, 51, head of Donley Communications in New York City, hoofed it alone 220 miles coast to coast from the North Sea to the Irish Sea. He backpacked provisions and often slept out. The next year Donley, his wife, Mary Todd, and her 9-year-old son, each carrying packs, took a week's 100-mile amble along the Cotswold Way, from near Stratford-on-Avon south to Bath. They easily found bed and breakfast at farmhouses.

Up-to-date information on footing it in the British Isles, as well as in France, Germany, Switzerland, and Austria, all laced with clearly marked and well-maintained footpaths, is usually available in the U.S. from the government tourist offices of those countries. On the Continent, Mountain Travel offers easy to moderately challenging trips in Czechoslovakia, France, Italy, and Spain. Nine-day walking tours guided by specialists around the Swiss and Italian lake districts or through Tuscan vineyards are given by Butterfield & Robinson of Toronto for $1,500, all-inclusive except for air fare. Serenissima, a London-based firm with a New York City branch, presents a series of eight- to ten-day bus-and-walking tours in France, Spain, and Italy, priced from $1,224 to $2,936, including air fare from London.

Some hikers seek more strenuous outings. Fred Jacobson Alpine Trails Ltd. of New York attracts many physically fit hikers from the caverns of Wall Street. From June through September, Fred Jacobson, 48, a marketing man with the investment firm of William D. Witter, leads six 17-day holidays in different Swiss locales for $1,845 each, including breakfasts and dinners. Air fare, midweek advance purchase excursion from New York, is $776. Hikers, limited to 25 per group, spend eight nights in one mountain center and seven in another, savoring Swiss hospitality and good cuisine in small hotels. Jacobson's groups hike six to 15 miles along different trails each day, climbing 3,000 to 4,500 feet in six to eight hours. Warns Katherine Lorenz, 40, a vice president at Continental Illinois in Chicago, "If you hike with Jacobson, you have to keep up." Fear not: anyone desiring a change of pace can take one of the slower walks offered daily.

FOR FURTHER INFORMATION

Butterfield & Robinson, 70 Bond St., Toronto, Ontario, Canada M5B 1X3; (800)-387-1147 or (416)-864-1354.

Fred Jacobson Alpine Trails Ltd., c/o Chappaqua Travel, 24 S. Greeley Ave., Chappaqua, NY 10514; (914)-238-5151.

Mountain Travel, 1398 Solano Ave., Albany, CA 94706; (800)-227-2384 or (415)-527-8100.

Serenissima Travel, Suite 2312, 41 E. 42nd St., New York, NY 10017; (800)-358-3330 or (212)-953-7720.

Sierra Club, membership, $33 a year, includes *Sierra* magazine, bimonthly ($12 for nonmembers); January issue contains a calendar of trips; Outing Department, 730 Polk St., San Francisco, CA 94109; (415)-776-2211.

The Wayfarers, c/o Mary McCarty, Apt. 4R, 307 E. 91st St., New York, NY 10128; (212)-369-4322.

PUBLICATIONS

Backpacker magazine, bimonthly, $18; CBS Magazines, 1515 Broadway, New York, NY 10036; (800)-525-0643 or (303)-447-9330.

A Coast to Coast Walk by A. Wainwright (Kendal, Westmorland, England: Westmorland Gazette, 1973), £3.73.

The National Trust Book of Long Walks in England, Scotland and Wales by Adam Nicolson (London: Pan Books, 1984), $15.95.

The New Complete Walker by Colin Fletcher (New York: Knopf, 1982), $14.95

One-Hundred Hikes in the Alps by Ira Spring and Harvey Edwards (Seattle; The Mountaineers, 1984), $9.95.

Tramping in Europe by J. Sydney Jones (Englewood Cliffs, NJ: Prentice-Hall, 1984), $7.95.

Turn Right at the Fountain by George W. Oakes and Alexandra Chapman (New York: Henry Holt, 1981), $9.95.

Walking magazine, bimonthly, $9.95; Raben Publishing, 711 Boylston St., Boston, MA 02116; (800)-358-8888 or (617)-236-1885.

Walking Europe Top to Bottom by Susanna Margolis and Ginger Harmon (San Francisco: Sierra Club Books, 1986), $10.95.

Walking in France by Rob Hunter (Newbury Park, CA: Haynes, 1986), $9.95. ∎

Trekking in Nepal

∎ From the terraced village of Namche Bazar, Bowen H. McCoy and his friend, Samuel F. Pryor III, hiked toward the roof of the world. The steep trail hugged the side of a gorge dropping thousands of feet to a river below. Directly ahead of them loomed Mount Everest. In his diary Pryor called it "easily the most spectacular sight I have ever seen in my life. One either had to stop and look at the view or walk, watching the trail. It was impossible to do both." That was in 1975. "Buzz" McCoy, who heads the Los Angeles office of the investment banking firm of Morgan Stanley, has returned three times since then to explore on foot the unique landscape and culture of the kingdom of Nepal. And Sam Pryor, a partner in the Wall Street law

EXPEDITIONS AND EXPLORATIONS

firm of Davis Polk & Wardwell, was drawn back in the fall of 1985.

Thousands of hikers trek the remote foothills of the Himalayas each spring and autumn for an intimate look at the world's highest mountains. Monsoon rains bar summer treks and cold weather precludes all but a few short midwinter excursions at rather low altitudes. Treks do not require technical mountaineering with ropes and pitons. But hikers should start in good physical shape, with an adventurous spirit adaptable to the unexpected, outdoor clothing for weather that can range from tropical to arctic, and they should stop for rest as they ascend, to acclimatize to high altitude.

On that first trip McCoy and Pryor joined a party of eight hikers to follow the classic route toward Everest. Their goal was the 18,192-foot summit of Kala Pattar. Less than ten air-miles from Everest's summit, it offers a clear view across the ice fall to the base camps from which Sir Edmund Hillary and other climbers mounted their heroic expeditions. Could these hurried executives reach their goal in only three weeks away from jobs and families?

Instead of following the traditional 25-day walk-in route, their timetable required flying from Katmandu, Nepal's capital, at 4,500 feet, to Lukla's tiny airstrip, a cliffside yak pasture at 9,200 feet, thus compressing a ten-day climb into 30 minutes. Carrying only light day packs, they set out with their Sherpa *sirdar* (leader) and his retinue of three guides, four cooks, who would feed them a basic diet of potatoes, rice, cabbage, and tea, 25 porters, and seven yaks.

No one appeared in better condition than Buzz McCoy, then 38. He regularly ran 20 miles a week, took climbing holidays, and had scaled peaks as high as Kilimanjaro, 19,350 feet. No one appeared in worse shape than Sam Pryor, then 47, who had been laid up with a leg infection that began as a jogging blister. Loaded with antibiotics, he headed for Everest hobbling with a walking stick.

A test of endurance came the fourth day on the trail, along with the spectacular view of Everest that Pryor recorded. Climbing out of the Sherpa capital of Namche Bazar at 11,300 feet, the trekkers hiked almost straight up to 12,000 feet before dipping to 10,665 feet for lunch by the river. Pryor and McCoy then led the way up the switchbacks to their campsite at 12,670 feet, near the Buddhist monastery of Thyangboche. By the time they arrived, Pryor had fully recovered, but McCoy was feeling the first signs of mountain sickness — headache and nausea.

This malaise, apparently caused by lack of oxygen, is common above 10,000 feet, can become serious over 11,500, and, if ignored, can be fatal. The only cure is a rapid descent. Pryor's lame start had evidently worked in his favor. While he rested in camp a couple of afternoons, McCoy had eagerly climbed ahead to reconnoiter the trail and may have overexerted. He grew worse and three days

VACATIONS AND WEEKENDS

later, near 16,000 feet, he heard the telltale rattle of edema in his lungs. Reluctantly McCoy heeded the ruling of the group's leader and started down, with an orthopedic surgeon who was a fellow trekker, plus a guide, porter, cook, and two yaks.

Adversity turned to advantage when they went down to the villages and got acquainted with a culture and people McCoy had feared they might miss. Of their caravan's ascent, he had noted: "Our small tent city and incredible logistics kept us from being anything but distant observers." Below 13,000 feet, McCoy quickly recovered. He and the doctor came to be celebrated guests in the homes of their retainers, people with no wheeled vehicles, no glass, no radios. The Americans got to see the spirit rooms in these homes, with their Tibetan scrolls and carved stone figures. They visited one of Hillary's schools for the Sherpas and a Buddhist monastery, where they were shown a purported yeti scalp.

Meanwhile Pryor, along with a 44-year-old Colorado woman and a 71-year-old veteran trekker, had gained the top of Kala Pattar, negotiating the last thousand feet in a halting sequence of ten small steps, a pause, five deep breaths, and so on. It was, Pryor recalled, a perfectly cloudless afternoon, and he could make out the routes various expeditions had taken up Everest's face. But on the way down he had time for only one brief visit in the *sirdar's* home. Three weeks had not been enough.

On return treks McCoy explored different parts of Nepal, with no ill effects. Without Pryor, but with a close-knit half dozen other business friends, he hiked ten days below 11,000 feet in the Annapurna region along ancient trade routes, still plied by ponies with bells. Easter sunrise illuminating the peaks of the Annapurna massif proved a mystical experience. Most of the arrangements for this trip, including Sherpa guide Per Temba, who has twice climbed Everest, were made through mountaineer Al Read, now with InnerAsia, an adventure touring company in San Francisco.

In 1980 McCoy led 17 Stanford alumni on a natural history trek through the 12,500-foot-high Langtang Valley, between Everest and Annapurna, amid forests festooned with rhododendron and orchid blossoms. And on sabbatical leave in 1981 he walked with an anthropologist 600 miles in two months, climbing above 15,000 feet several times. They spent 30 days hiking in a 200-degree arc around the Annapurna massif, one of the most beautiful and popular walks in Nepal. Each day they walked seven hours, ate four meals their cook devised, and read, wrote, or meditated for six hours. "I did everything right. It's clear that in 1975 I did everything wrong," says McCoy.

Pryor, in the fall of 1985, retraced the same route toward the Everest base camp that he and McCoy had climbed in 1975, but under different conditions: an added week, colder weather with rougher terrain, a smaller party. Pryor's sons, Daniel, 24, and Joseph, 21, and a friend, Todd Clark, 21, made a foursome. Torrential floods from melting October snows had devastated the trail between Lukla and Namche Bazar, so the trekkers had to slog through rocks, fallen trees, and mud. They adjusted their pace to acclimatize to the altitude, trekking six hours a day and stopping to rest a full day at 10,000 feet, at 12,000, and at 14,000. Above that they were unprepared for the extra snow and ice they found on the Khumbu Glacier, and could have used more warm clothing including leggings. They picked up ice axes en route, but lacked crampons. It took two days to cross a stretch that had taken four hours in 1975, so they had to spend longer hours on the trail. But the Sherpa *sirdar* and cook, both English-speaking, extended the warmth of their hospitality to the small group, inviting them to their homes back in Namche Bazar.

When they were ready to depart, Pryor's party experienced one of the inconveniences of modern travel to the Nepalese highlands. At Lukla they found hundreds of people waiting for the Royal Nepalese Air Force's Twin Otter planes, which can ferry only 75 passengers per day back to Katmandu. Bad weather had backed up flights, as it often does. After two days, Pryor negotiated a ride for his party on an army helicopter — for a consideration of $1,500 in traveler's checks. He was fully reimbursed by Mountain Travel, the outfitters who had arranged the trip.

Headquartered in Albany, California, near Berkeley, the company specializes in adventure travel and can tailor private independent treks for small parties in several remote areas of the world. It also offers scheduled walking trips in 50 countries for individuals who wish to join a Mountain Travel group. On both kinds of trips the company provides all transportation, equipment, food, and personnel from the staging area. The cost of a 31-day group trip similar to Pryor's is $2,290. That includes a few days in a Katmandu hotel in double rooms. Air fare to Katmandu is not included, but that flight to Lukla and back surely is.

FOR FURTHER INFORMATION

InnerAsia Expeditions, 2627 Lombard St., San Francisco, CA 94123; (800)-551-1769 or (415)-922-0448.
Mountain Travel, 1398 Solano Ave., Albany, CA 94706; (800)-227-2384 or (415)-527-8100.

PUBLICATIONS

Classic Walks of the World edited by Walt Unsworth (Newbury Park, CA: Haynes, 1985), $14.95.
A Guide to Trekking in Nepal by Stephan Bezruchka (Seattle: Mountaineers, 1985), $10.95.
Rhythms of a Himalayan Village by Hugh R. Downs (New York: Harper & Row, 1980), $9.95.
Trekking in the Nepal Himalaya by Stan Armington (Emeryville, CA: Lonely Planet, 1985), $7.95. ■

EXPEDITIONS AND EXPLORATIONS

Mountaineering Alpine Style

■ Mountaineering seems to rope in adventurous executives as they rise in their careers. Edward E. Matthews, 55, executive vice president for finance at American International Group (AIG), a worldwide insurance company based in New York, decided at age 41 to step up from trail hiking to technical climbing, with ropes and protective equipment. His frequent climbing partner in recent years, Philip Erard, 54, senior vice president for corporate finance at the investment banking firm of Wertheim & Co. in New York, started at 34.

Getting to the mountaintop, Erard discovered, brings mental, physical, even metaphysical, renewal and camaraderie. "In the city we think we are masters of our environment. In the mountains you realize that nature is a far more imposing force than you are," notes Erard. "You feel insignificant." In the intense physical effort and mental concentration of getting the best footholds, the climber escapes totally from the world beneath him. A well-conditioned, agile body is a must for getting up a pitch, and it's easy to lose eight or so pounds during a two-week mountain holiday. Climbing is a team sport requiring at least two for safety. The rope that ties climbers to the mountain, and to each other, is the lifeline of the team; handling it makes each climber responsible for every other one, creating personal bonds.

Mountaineers must master many skills on rock, snow, and ice. Schools and groups of private guides in the U.S. and Europe teach how to use the ropes, carabiners (metal rings for threading rope), pitons or chocks, nuts, and hammers that prevent falls and protect the climber. On ice they show how to climb with crampons on boots and use axes for self-arrest. They also teach the mechanics of belaying, or securing the lead climber at the end of the rope in case of a fall, and rappelling, or descent on a rope.

Erard first learned those skills during two weeks at a Swiss mountain climbing institute, Rosenlaui, at Meiringen in the Bernese Oberland region, one of some 20 mountaineering schools in Switzerland. Matthews attended three schools in the U.S. At Rainier Mountaineering in Mount Rainier National Park he took a five-day seminar in snow and ice climbing, which finished with an ascent to the 14,410-foot summit of Rainier's glaciated peak. At the Exum school of mountaineering near Jackson Hole, Wyoming, in Grand Teton National Park, Matthews learned more about climbing rock faces. And at the Yosemite Mountaineering School in California's Yosemite National Park, he learned crack-climbing techniques. All of these schools teach beginners as well as advanced climbers. Different specialties come from differences in their local terrain.

Matthews and Erard are both active in the American Alpine Club, a group of distinguished climbers and a leading source of information on mountaineering. To belong, a climber must be proposed by two members, one of whom has to certify his climbing ability. Once he is accepted, a climber's name is published in the club's newsletter and any member has a chance to object.

Most of the world's great mountains and the best routes for climbing them are described in guidebooks and rated by degree of difficulty, generally from 5.0 to 5.13 in the U.S., and from I to VI in Europe. Erard says his level of skill, 5.8 to 5.9, is sufficient for most of the classic climbs in North America and Europe. "Classic climbs" in mountaineering parlance are especially beautiful ones along routes following natural lines that local mountaineers consider the way to go.

Matthews and Erard spend two weeks each summer traversing the classic routes of the Alps, where the sport of mountaineering began when the English started bagging peaks in the 1850s. "The Alps are a particularly good place to climb because of the enormous variety and accessibility of the routes, and the extensive system of huts along these routes," Erard points out. This combination of accessibility and huts means small parties carrying only rucksacks can make rapid ascents of easy-to-reach mountains, a style of climbing known as "alpine." It differs from "expeditionary climbing" on, say, Alaska's Mount McKinley, which requires a lengthy approach where climbers carry supplies and set up camps for days or weeks at a time.

From July to September the 14,690-foot Matterhorn draws as many as 60 climbers on a fine day to its unique pyramidal peak. They usually start from Zermatt, where English-speaking guides are available for 520 Swiss francs (about $340). On the first afternoon, climber and guide ascend 5,000 feet (partway by cable car if desired) to the Hornli Hut. Here for $45 they can have dinner, a blanket, a few hours' sleep, dormitory style, and breakfast. At 3 A.M. climbers rope up and head for the summit, straight up 4,500 feet of gneiss. Though not technically difficult, the ascent is physically grueling. But, Erard recalls, "one of the most beautiful sights I have seen in my life is the rising sun striking the top, bathing it in a golden luminescence." The goal is to reach the top by about 8 A.M. and get back to Zermatt by midday, before afternoon clouds shroud the mountain.

Italy's Dolomites with their steep brown, gold, and white limestone spires have more recently challenged the skills of Matthews and Erard. And they persuaded two climbing friends to join them: Bob Allen Street, 48, a Houston oil producer, and William Phillips, 57, chairman of the Ogilvy Group, the New York–based advertising company. The Dolomites are technically harder to climb than many of the popular Swiss routes, but the huts are more comfortable and more reasonably priced. And in Italy the

23

VACATIONS AND WEEKENDS

weather is more predictable than in the western Swiss Alps, an important factor for a business person with limited time. To save time the foursome hired two Austrian guides familiar with the area. A guide's fee is $150 a day. In the Italian hut at Madonna di Campiglio, 40 miles southwest of Bolzano, the Americans paid around $30 per day for semiprivate rooms—instead of a communal dormitory—with cots, sheets, hot water, even a shower, and two meals. Now that's life at the top.

FOR FURTHER INFORMATION

American Alpine Club, 113 E. 90th St., New York, NY 10128; (212)-722-1628.

Appalachian Mountain Club; membership, $40 a year, includes monthly *Appalachia;* 5 Joy St., Boston, MA 02108; (617)-523-0636.

Austrian National Tourist Office, 500 Fifth Ave. (20th fl.), New York, NY 10110; (212)-944-6880.

Colorado Mountain School, Box 2062, Estes Park, CO 80517; (305)-586-5758.

The EMS Climbing School, Main St., North Conway, NH 03860; (603)-356-5433; or 1428 15th St., Denver, CO 80202; (305)-571-1160.

Exum Mountain Guides, Grand Teton National Park, Box 56, Moose, WY 83012; (307)-733-2297 or, in winter, (415)-922-0448.

International Mountain Climbing School, P.O. Box 239, Conway, NH 03818; (603)-447-6700 or 356-5287.

Mountain Guides Alliance, Box 266, North Conway, NH 03860; (603)-356-5310.

Outward Bound USA, 384 Field Point Rd., Greenwich, CT 06830; (800)-243-8520 or (203)-661-0797.

Rainier Mountaineering, 201 St. Helens Ave., Tacoma, WA 98402; (206)-627-6242; or, in summer, (206)-569-2227.

Swiss National Tourist Office, 608 Fifth Ave., New York, NY 10020; (212)-757-5944.

Yosemite Mountaineering School and Guide Service, Yosemite National Park, CA 95389; spring and fall (209)-372-1233 or, in summer, 372-1355.

PUBLICATIONS

Climbing magazine, bimonthly, $15; Box E, Aspen, CO 81612; (303)-925-3414.

Mountain Magazine, bimonthly, $17.50; Box 184, Sheffield S11 9DL, England.

Mountaineering: The Freedom of the Hills edited by Ed Peters (Seattle: Mountaineers, 4th ed., 1982), $17.

Outside magazine, monthly, $18; P.O. Box 54715, Boulder, CO 80322-4715. ■

Mountaineering Expeditions: Seven Summits

■ Could a Hollywood mogul and a Dallas financier, both over 50, retrace the heroic steps of a 33-year-old New Zealand beekeeper and a 39-year-old Nepalese tribesman to make history of their own? Thirty years after Sir Edmund Hillary and Tenzing Norgay scaled Everest, Frank Wells, then vice chairman of Warner Bros., and Richard Bass, owner-developer of Utah's Snowbird ski resort, set out for the 29,028-foot summit. At 51 and 53 they were older than any of the 127 climbers who had already scaled it. "The odds of our making it at our ages are one in a hundred," Wells told a press conference in Katmandu just before setting out in March of 1983 for the six-week climb. Said Bass to correspondent Elizabeth Hawley: "It'll be a miracle if we make it, but we gotta try."

Everest was only one of seven summits, the highest peak on each continent, that the pair had set their hearts on conquering in just one year. Each had climbed a bit as students, but had only recently tried mountaineering again and was instantly rehooked. Independently Bass and Wells had each conceived the idea of taking the seven summits. Introduced by friends, they met in August of 1981 over a brief lunch at the Warner Bros. studio. With a handshake, Bass, a former Texas geologist, and Wells, a former Rhodes scholar and *Stanford Law School Review* editor, formed a partnership to climb those seven peaks together in a single year—1983. Wells would take leave from his job, and Bass would play hooky from the pressures of financing his ski resort.

Expeditionary climbing to the world's highest peaks, remote and glacier-mantled, is an adventure that requires a superbly conditioned body capable of carrying a heavy pack of supplies and gear in thin air at high altitude, proficiency in a variety of mountaineering techniques, tolerance for camping out in very low temperatures and high winds, teamwork with experienced guides, daunting logis-

Ski resort developer Richard Bass fastens his gaiter en route to the first of his seven summits: snow-topped Aconcagua in Argentina.

EXPEDITIONS AND EXPLORATIONS

tics, and deep pockets. Those prerequisites did not deter Bass and Wells, both relative novices.

Earlier that year Bass had tried his first expeditionary climb, on a dare. A 29-year-old female employee, Marty Hoey, ski patroller at Snowbird and professional guide on Alaska's Mount McKinley, had coldly told him that he lacked the physical conditioning and mountaineering training to reach the top of McKinley. Six months later, with Hoey as guide, Bass, his four children, and a small party set out. "I remember feeling scared and inadequate as I started up the Kahiltna Glacier on skis, bent over with 70 pounds on my back, and pulling a 35-pound sled," he later confessed. "It now fully struck me that this was a major climb, a giant leap into the unknown." Thirteen days later, with the temperature 37 degrees below zero, he stood at 20,320 feet on the highest summit in North America. En route he had learned some basic climbing and mountaineering skills: how to use an ice ax, crampons, ropes with carabiners. But above all he learned the importance of mental attitude in overcoming physical discomfort. He did it by reciting poetry. And he was elated to find his compact physique well suited to high altitude. Coming down, he hit on his notion of the seven summits. No more experienced than Bass, Wells had decided to go for the peaks after climbing 15,771-foot Mont Blanc, the highest Alp.

Four of their seven summits required expeditionary climbs in certain seasons: in January, South America's 22,834-foot Aconcagua in Argentina; before the summer monsoon, Asia's supreme Everest; in July, North America's McKinley; in November, Antarctica's 16,864-foot Vinson Massif. Three alpine-style climbs required only day packs: Africa's 19,340-foot Kilimanjaro in August; Europe's 18,510-foot Mount Elbrus in the U.S.S.R. in September; Australia's 7,310-foot Mount Kosciusko in December. To help organize the expeditions, and accompany them, they recruited leading professional mountaineers.

To test themselves, they made three practice climbs, starting immediately in September of 1981 with Mount Elbrus, and Aconcagua in January of 1982. Bass got to the top of both; Wells reached neither. In the spring of 1982, Bass's goad, Marty Hoey, arranged for them to join, and help underwrite, a climb up Everest's north face via Tibet, led by Louis Whittaker, who had been on the first American team to conquer Everest in 1961. Bass reached 25,000 feet, carrying a 40-pound load, and Wells 23,700, both without oxygen flasks. Bad weather forced the expedition to turn back, soon after Marty Hoey died in a fall.

Their 1983 seven-summits odyssey got off to a good start when both men scaled Aconcagua. The budget for the year approached $650,000, according to Bass. Antarctica took $200,000 of that and Everest about $250,000. An extra $150,000 would go to filming the seven climbs. To supply the Everest expedition in March, seven Twin

Otter flights ferried more than six tons of gear and provisions from Nepal's Katmandu airport to Lukla at 9,000 feet. From there 175 porters and 25 yaks moved the loads to 17,800 feet, where 35 Sherpas ran the base camp and carried provisions to higher camps.

Bass and Wells trudged 40 miles from Lukla to the base camp, following their team of nine Americans, a Nepalese official, and the expedition's leader, Gerhard Lenser, 54, manager of a German travel agency. Nepal allows only a few groups to climb Everest each year, scheduled far in advance. So Wells and Bass teamed up with Lenser, who had obtained his permit years earlier but needed financing. Though their expedition put seven climbers on the summit, Bass and Wells were not among them. With supreme effort, making up in will power what they lacked in physical power, Wells got to 26,000 feet and Bass to a tantalizing 28,000. Thwarted by 100-mile-an-hour winds for four days, they had to come down.

The five remaining summits they did conquer. Wells carefully organized the logistics for Antarctica's Vinson Massif, previously scaled by only two parties. A chartered DC-3, fitted with skis for Arctic oil-field work, flew climbers and supplies from California to the Nimitz Glacier at the foot of the mountain. The Chilean air force made a fuel drop. The weather, with temperatures at −40 degrees, prolonged their stay from six to 16 days.

The adventure didn't end with the seven-summits year. Persevering, Bass returned to Everest in the fall of 1984, without Wells, whose wife, Luanne, had told him that if he risked Everest a third time, she would not be home if and when he returned. Staying home, as it turned out, opened up a new business challenge. In September 1984 Wells was tapped to be president of the Walt Disney Company. Bass went with two American mountaineers and promises of climbing permits from a Nepalese expedition that was cleaning up the trails. The permits never materialized. But in the spring of 1985, Bass and one of his mountaineer companions were back for yet another try, this time with a large Norwegian expedition.

Frank Wells wasn't sure just how he would feel if his buddy made it without him. In New York on business, he answered the phone at 3 A.M. to hear that on April 30, Dick Bass had reached the summit of Everest and returned safely to camp. At 55, Bass had set a record as the oldest man, by five years, to reach the top of the world, and to have conquered all seven summits. "I cried. I was hugely thrilled. I called everybody I knew," says Wells. "This was a final chapter we could both share, a more complete adventure than if neither of us had made it."

The adventure of expeditionary climbing is available to seasoned mountaineers, willing to take their peaks at a less concentrated rate than Bass and Wells. Several mountaineering schools and guide services organize trips. The American Alpine Institute of Bellingham, Washington, offers three- to four-week expeditions to several Western

VACATIONS AND WEEKENDS

Hemisphere peaks. And for 1988 Mountain Travel scheduled six of the seven summits, skipping only Everest. Prices rise from $1,690 for Aconcagua to a steep $19,000 for Antarctica's Vinson Massif.

FOR FURTHER INFORMATION

American Alpine Institute, 1212 24th St., Bellingham, WA 98225; (206)-671-1505.

InnerAsia Expeditions, 2627 Lombard St., San Francisco, CA 94123; (800)-551-1769 or (415)-922-0448.

Mountain Travel, 1398 Solano Ave., Albany, CA 94706; (800)-227-2384 or (415)-527-8100.

PUBLICATIONS

The American Alpine Journal, an annual (New York: American Alpine Club), $15.95.

Ascent: The Autobiography of Peter & Sir Edmund Hillary (New York: Doubleday, 1986), $17.95.

Everest: A Mountaineering History by Walt Unsworth (Boston: Houghton Mifflin, 1981), out of print.

Peaks, Passes and Glaciers by Walt Unsworth (Seattle: Mountaineers, 1981), $20.

The Seven Summits Odyssey by Richard Bass and Frank Wells, with Rick Ridgeway (New York: Warner Books, 1986), $18.95.

The Six Mountain Travel Books by Eric Shipton (Seattle: Mountaineers, 1986), $30. ∎

On Camera Safari in Africa

■ In Swahili, the lingua franca of East Africa, "safari" simply means "journey" and can even apply to a trip to the local market. But elsewhere "safari" is synonymous with high adventure, and perhaps a little danger. It conjures up visions of hunters in pith helmets stalking bravely through the bush after wild animals, trailed by a long line of black gun-bearers and half-naked porters carrying bundles on their heads. Old-time guides recall that on foot, in areas rampant with malaria and sleeping sickness, it often took four months to cover the 120 miles from Nairobi to the areas of most plentiful game in western Kenya.

Today the trip takes less than three hours on a tarmac road. Game safaris are still exciting adventures, now within reach of those of moderate means. They are safe and comfortable enough to be enjoyed by anyone aged 9 to 90. Once you lay out the $1,400-or-so round-trip fare between the U.S. and Nairobi, for $1,500 you can take a ten-day group tour of game reserves via minibus with comfortable lodgings in the bush. If that's too tame, you can invest about from $1,500 to $2,500 a day in a shooting safari for the once legendary "big five"—lion, leopard, elephant, rhino, buffalo—nowadays the big four, with rhino practically unavailable. A shooting safari comes complete with professional hunters, trackers, skinners, and bearers. In Ernest Hemingway's heyday, four out of five safaris were bang-bang. Today, owing partly to worldwide concern for wildlife, all but one in 20 are click-click.

While most old safari hands approve of photographic safaris, they resent the rise of motel-like concrete lodges and bridges and well-worn tracks with so many signposts that it's impossible to get lost. But there are still places where one can get away from gaggles of tourist groups. A tented safari in the Hemingway tradition takes small parties to unspoiled stretches of the great game plains of western Kenya and sometimes Tanzania.

As soon as he wound up investor Kirk Kerkorian's deal to sell MGM to Turner Broadcasting, Los Angeles lawyer Stephen Silbert took off in the summer of 1985 to join friends already on a photographic tented safari he had planned in Kenya. Silbert, 44, president of MGM/UA Communications Co., had dreamed of this romantic adventure for years. He engaged Abercrombie & Kent International, specialists in luxurious tented safaris in Kenya, Tanzania, and selected African hinterlands, to custom-tailor a trip in Kenya. His party of six included his daughter, Tracy, then 13, and a couple with a daughter, 14.

"Tented safaris come with four-wheel-drive vehicles that take you places minibuses can't go, right to the game, close-up," explains Geoffrey Kent, 45, A&K's managing director. "Of course, they cost more, but a real safari is one of the world's last remaining adventures, basically a once-in-a-lifetime thing. It's worth doing right." Kent was born on safari and grew up in Kenya. He took over and expanded his father's safari business into a worldwide travel enterprise. A&K lists its traditional Hemingway tented safari, with 13 days in Kenya and visits to two parks

The lions are rather blasé about posing for pictures in the Ngorongoro Crater in northern Tanzania.

EXPEDITIONS AND EXPLORATIONS

and one reserve, at $4,995 per person without air fare in the high seasons, July to October and December to March, when migrating game is most visible. The Silbert party's 18-day safari, with an added reserve, cost proportionately more.

Outside Nairobi the Silbert party visited the Amboseli and Aberdare national parks, the Samburu and Masai Mara game reserves. Their guide, John Cook, a safari escort for ten years, traveled with the Americans over every mile, by chartered twin-engine plane, minibus with pop-up top, land cruiser, and balloon. They spent ten nights in three tent camps set up exclusively for them. And they had three nights in two special lodges, and two at the Mount Kenya Safari Club, an elegant resort where one dresses for dinner. "One of our party wasn't sure she would like tenting, so we decided we would try a little of everything," explains Silbert. "She instantly realized tenting was best. It gives you a much greater feeling of being in Africa."

A staff of ten—cooks, tent stewards, and helpers—trucked supplies and baggage, preceding the Silbert party to each campsite. At every one the travelers got hot showers, and in the cool high country hot-water bottles at night to warm their feet. "I have never slept as well," says Silbert. Days started with tea or coffee, brought to the tents. And at sundown as the party sat around the campfire, stewards presented trays of drinks and warm cashews. "The food was unbelievable—beef Wellington, chocolate or orange soufflés," Silbert reports.

The two lodges where they stayed feature special facilities for game viewing. In the Aberdare National Park, north of Nairobi, the Ark lodge is built over a watering hole. Through windows of a dungeon at animal level, the Silbert party watched elephant, rhino, and buffalo come to drink. Floodlights make all-night viewing possible, and a buzzer alerts guests to unusual sightings. Farther north in the Samburu Game Reserve, the Samburu River Lodge on the Uaso Nyiro River also keeps lights on, and rigs meat to attract game.

"Every day was an adventure. You never knew what you would see, from lions feeding on a Cape buffalo to crocodiles in the river where we fished," Silbert recalls. From the Samburu the party flew to their final stop, due west of Nairobi in the Masai Mara Reserve. It is home to the highest concentration of game in all of Kenya, and the Americans camped there for five nights. "We saw animals everywhere, 100 to 1,000 at once," exclaims Silbert. "In the water there were always eight to ten hippos."

Inevitably the Americans witnessed both the savage and the peaceable sides of the animal kingdom. Silbert had anticipated that he would not want to see a kill. But when he saw a cheetah take a Thompson's gazelle to feed her weeks-old baby, he realized this is the way animals survive. And when he ascended on his first balloon ride, out of a permanent camp 30 minutes from his party's campsite,

he found it "one of the most peaceful moments of my life, gazing down on lions, gazelle, zebra."

Silbert brought back his African game trophies in some 800 pictures. A few animals even cooperated—one leopard, usually a very elusive animal, stayed up a tree for an hour on the river in the Samburu. And the sounds of his videotape recreate different times of day: baboons fighting in the trees in the mornings, and zebra braying in the evening. "I could have stayed another month," he says. "There are so many parts we didn't see."

FOR FURTHER INFORMATION

Abercrombie & Kent International, 1420 Kensington Rd., Oak Brook, IL 60521-2106; (800)-323-7308 or (312)-954-2944.
Kenya Tourist Office, 424 Madison Ave., New York, NY 10017; (212)-486-1300.

PUBLICATIONS

Field Guide to the National Parks of East Africa by John G. Williams (New York: Viking Penguin), $24.95.
The Flame Trees of Thika by Elspeth Huxley (New York: Penguin, 1982), $4.95.
The Green Hills of Africa by Ernest Hemingway (New York: Scribner, 1985), $4.95.
The Kenya Pioneers by Errol Trzebinski (New York: Norton, 1986), $19.95.
Out of Africa and Shadows on the Grass by Isak Dinesen (New York: Random House, 1985), $4.95.
Portraits in the Wild: Animal Behavior in East Africa by Cynthia Moss (Chicago: University of Chicago Press, 1982), $11.95.
Safari: The African Diaries of a Wildlife Photographer by Gunter Ziesler and Angelika Hoifer (New York: Facts on File, 1984), $24.95.
Silence Will Speak: A Study of the Life of Denys Finch Hatton and His Relationship with Karen Blixen by Errol Trzebinski (Chicago: University of Chicago Press, 1986), $8.95. ■

Touring by Kayak

■ Kayak touring takes paddlers to shallow coves and rocky coastlines they could never reach by deeper-drawing motorboats or sailboats. In the 1980s kayaking has flourished on the island-studded Northwest Coast and Down East among Maine's coastal islands.

On a sparkling Saturday morning ten novice kayakers and three guides hurried to start their weekend tour among the San Juan Islands, some 60 miles north of Seattle. To paddle the three miles from Guemes Island to Cypress Island, they had to cross the Bellingham Channel between high and low tides. Otherwise they risked getting caught in a riptide, which would make for tough going, possibly danger.

John Besteman, 51, an executive at Boeing Computer Services, slipped into the aft of a 20-foot kayak and

VACATIONS AND WEEKENDS

snapped the sprayskirt around the cockpit's edge to keep the inside dry. In the forward cockpit his wife, Kay, set the rhythm of their strokes with her twin-bladed paddle; Besteman synchronized his paddle with hers and controlled the rudder with foot pedals. As if wishing them smooth passage, an eagle glided between treetops. A pair of playful seals popped out of the kelp.

Besteman turned instant enthusiast: "We became part of nature, only inches above the water in our kayaks, using our muscle power, seeing everything, and feeling the salt spray," he recalls. Says Robert Miles, 56, president of ROI Computer Co. in Seattle: "We were enthralled in a different world."

Though best known as sea kayaking, the sport offers pleasure on almost any open water without dangerous rapids and has recently taken hold in the Midwest. Shaun Devlin, 50, a Ford manager, and his wife, Sheila, took to kayaking on the Great Lakes, where cruising is often best along the Canadian shores.

Today's version of the ancient Eskimo sealskin craft, touring kayaks are more seaworthy than canoes and their nimble white-water brethren. They are less tippy than canoes because the paddler sits on the floor instead of a raised seat, lowering the center of gravity, and the bottom is relatively flat. Speed comes with a narrow tapered hull, longer than a white-water kayak's, that with normally vigorous paddling slices through water at three knots.

A Chinook touring kayak for one from Aquaterra costs about $650; a double costs $1,850 for Eddyline's San Juan, the kind the Bestemans paddled, or $1,890 for a folding Klepper. Invented in Germany in 1907, today's improved Klepper knocks down to 37 wooden pieces, a rubber hull, and a canvas deck that fit in two bags for checking on a plane.

Kayak cruising differs from white-water kayaking as much as cross-country skiing does from downhill. River runners, in their highly maneuverable craft, need a half dozen strokes; cruising kayakers require basically one forward stroke, plus a brace maneuver to keep the boat from capsizing. That makes sea kayaking look deceptively simple. But it requires a knowledge of navigation and seamanship — familiarity with tides, winds, and waves. On an Easter weekend a kayaker suffered hypothermia and drowned in New York's Jamaica Bay after capsizing.

Only intrepid voyagers once attempted sea kayaking expeditions. Today guided paddling tours put sea kayaking within reach of most fit adults. Expedition packages range from a 15-day July odyssey in a Greenland fjord near the Arctic Circle ($2,200) to a winter fortnight's 100-mile paddle among the dolphins, porpoises, and whales in Baja California's Sea of Cortez ($830), both offered by Ecosummer Canada Expeditions of Vancouver.

Several North American outfitters and schools for paddlers — listed often in *Canoe* magazine — offer short sea kayaking trips with instruction. Off Camden, Maine, one-day guided trips are $50 from Sea Touring Kayak Center; its weekend camping trips cost $180 and its three-day instructional clinic $210.

The San Juan Islands trip was organized by Northwest Outdoor Center of Seattle. For $98 per person the new paddlers got kayaks, equipment for two days of guided paddling, and an evening's briefing on what to expect and what to do. After their successful crossing, they were served Saturday night dinner of fresh salmon grilled on the beach. They brought their own breakfast, lunch, and overnight camping gear.

Next day extraordinarily high winds delayed their departure until midafternoon, emphasizing the need for guidance and instruction. As they paddled back, a powerboat circled with passengers taking pictures of the nine kayaks as though they were a pod of whales. Says John Besteman: "I felt a certain distance from those people, sort of 'you guys don't understand.'"

For more rugged schooling in the watery wilderness, Michael Jacoby, 30, a vice president in the Chicago office of Bankers Trust, chose a week at Outward Bound's Hurricane Island school in Maine. The focus was preparing for and surviving a kayak expedition at sea, and learning to recover from a capsize. Nine students planned and executed the trip, with two guides trailing as observers. They paddled eight hours, with three short breaks, to reach their camping ground, a beach where mussel-studded shoals provided part of their supper. Jacoby says, "I would love to do more kayaking." Tuition: one week, $700; 11 days, $1,100.

At weekend symposiums experts speak and manufacturers offer kayaks for test-paddling. In Michigan, the

Within sight of Mount Baker in Washington State, Susan Dearborn and Robert Miles embark on a weekend of kayak touring in the San Juan Islands.

EXPEDITIONS AND EXPLORATIONS

Great Lakes Kayak Touring Symposium takes place in June; admission $50. In Castine, Maine, L.L. Bean holds a symposium in August; registration, which does not include bed and board, $50. And in September the West Coast Sea Kayaking Symposium takes place at Port Townsend, Washington.

While you're getting inspired, start working those shoulders and arms; although kayaking does not require great strength, it demands a lot of stamina.

FOR FURTHER INFORMATION

Association of North Atlantic Kayakers; membership, $12 a year, includes *ANorAK,* bimonthly newsletter; 14 Heather Dr., Suffern, NY 10901; (914)-357-3448.

INSTRUCTION AND TOURS

L.L. Bean Atlantic Coast Sea Kayaking Symposium, Freeport, ME 04033; (207)-865-4761.

Ecosummer Canada Expeditions, 1516 Duranleau St., Vancouver, British Columbia, Canada V6H 3S4; (604)-669-7741.

Great Lakes Touring, 3721 Shallow Brook, Bloomfield Hills, MI 48013; (313)-644-6909.

Hurricane Island Outward Bound School, P.O. Box 429, Mechanic St., Rockland, ME 04841; (800)-341-1744 or (207)-594-5548.

Northwest Outdoor Center, 200 West Lake Ave. North, Seattle, WA 98109; (206)-281-9694.

Sea Touring Kayak Center, 123A Elm St., Camden, ME 04843; (207)-236-9569.

SUPPLIERS

Aquaterra, P.O. Box 1357, Easley, SC 29641; (803)-855-1987.

Eddyline Kayak Works, P.O. Box 281, Mukilteo, WA 98275; (206)-743-9252.

Klepper America, 35 Union Square W., New York, NY 10003; (212)-243-3428.

PUBLICATIONS

Canoe magazine, six issues a year, $12; includes *Canoe/Kayak Buyer's Guide;* P.O. Box 3146, Kirkland, WA 98083; (800)-MY-CANOE or (206)-827-6363. Publishes *Starting Out,* annually, $3.95.

Derek C. Hutchinson's Guide to Sea Kayaking (Seattle: Pacific Search Press, 1985), $12.95.

Sea Kayaker, quarterly, $10 a year; 6327 Seaview Ave. N.W., Seattle, WA 98107; (206)-789-6413.

Sea Kayaking: A Manual for Long-Distance Touring by John Dowd (Seattle: University of Washington Press, 1986), $8.95. ∎

FAMILY ADVENTURES
Reunions with Hubie Clark's Clan

■ After lunch at quayside that began with lobsters and ended with a riotous Greek dance, Hubie Clark and his spirited clan of 13 linked arms and high-stepped to the music right onto their chartered yacht. This was the second day of a two-week cruise in June aboard the 100-foot motor yacht *Arvi,* which carried the Clark family from Piraeus through the Gulf of Corinth and around the Ionian Islands. As they headed for a late afternoon swim in a quiet cove, the mood of the Californians and their Greek crew sparkled like sun on a rippling sea.

Of all the family vacations E. H. "Hubie" Clark Jr., chairman of Baker Hughes in Orange, California, and his wife, Patty, had taken, this one was especially joyous. The week before, the youngest of their six children, Rebecca, 20, had married Stephen Kane, son of another Baker executive, and the newlyweds had joined the family for their honeymoon. Three married sons were aboard with their wives, another with his fiancée, and their youngest son had flown in from his job in Singapore. They embarked on the senior Clarks' 33rd wedding anniversary. "I'd had this desire for gosh knows how many years," said Clark, then 53, "to take everybody who's dear to me and just get on a boat and sort of own the world."

The Clark clan's holidays, now biennial affairs, succeed not only because they feature fancy trips. Under Hubie Clark's guidance, the members have worked in an unusual way to understand one another. One of the most successful chief executives of the 1970s, a decade when the sales of Baker, a supplier of oil-well and mining equipment, rose from $47 million in 1965 to $2.5 billion in 1982, Clark decided to use what he had learned about human relations in business to strengthen his family. Besides, unlike some executives, Clark had not sacrificed family to company. When they were youngsters, Clark joined each of his five sons in the YMCA's Indian Guides and Gray-Y clubs, because by club rules they could not belong unless he did.

At Baker, Clark helped develop a program in which executives ranked what was important to them — achievement, health, creativity, etc. — on a scale from one to five. They talked about these feelings with others in a group. "It had been very helpful in our business relationships to know what's important to one another and to respect it," Clark says. "And it seemed to me that the same logic would make sense in our family life." Lots of families do things together, but few are able to talk things out without hostility or resolve conflict before it hurts, he feels.

Clark called a formal family meeting to coincide with a vacation in Hawaii, when the children ranged in age from 14 to 26 and the two oldest were already married. Although he feared he might seem to be prying into their private lives, he asked everyone to write on a blackboard the five things most important to him or her. Some did so in tears or trembling. The most strongly felt desire of his wife, Patty, flabbergasted her husband. She wanted financial security. Over the years he had remarked from time to time that he had lost, say, $50,000 in the stock market on a given day, or that she would have to stop spending so

At Delphi's classic Greek theater, Hubie Clark catches a chorus line. From left: daughter-in-law Cindy, wife Patty, daughters-in-law Sue, Maggie, and Patti.

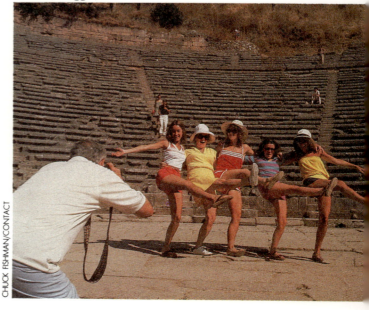

FAMILY ADVENTURES

much money because he was going into debt. He thought he was being funny, but he had failed to explain that he was borrowing money to leverage his investments, and when the market went up, he never mentioned it.

The second formal meeting of this kind, in the Bahamas five years later, included two young people engaged to marry into the family. Rebecca Clark's then fiancé, Stephen Kane, a graduate student in law and business, had a habit of ribbing her brother Ken, who was 30 and an assistant manager in a stock brokerage office. Ken told the family that he wanted to be recognized for his accomplishments, and Steve Kane came away thinking he should ease up on the kidding. Cynthia Billmeyer, a medical student engaged to Dan Clark, then a 24-year-old law student, said she wanted to feel accepted by this family she had known for two years but didn't feel a part of. "To be able to understand the needs of the human beings around you and in some ways respond is the heartbeat of a marriage and of a family relationship," Clark remarks. "Our kids began to sense that."

Clark has also encouraged his children to set their own goals. "My kids face the ever present danger of saying they all have to be as successful as Dad. We cannot try to make them carbon copies of anyone else." Between those two vacation meetings on personal sensitivity, he arranged to have a California consulting firm that Baker had used conduct a special weekend seminar for his family. The seminar focused on self-image and how to change it in formulating goals. It helped the Clark children define their goals and take steps to achieve them. Dan, then 22, had his doubts dispelled about entering law school. By their mid- to late 20s, all had settled into their careers: electrical engineer, stockbroker, video editor, lawyer, international electronics marketer, housewife and mother. With the clan expanding to include grandchildren, eight at last count, Clark is planning another family seminar conducted by professionals on child rearing and on how to enhance parent-child relationships.

Clark is convinced that money is not the tie that binds his family together. "If you plan an expensive enough trip, you can get almost every family to pull together and enjoy it," he acknowledged after the Greek trip. "To enjoy such a trip with happiness and emotional experience is the difference. And I do think that has happened in our family over the ten years we've been working to understand what's important to each member. I really think we could do the same thing around a camping trip in the mountains, and have just as much fun." Two years following their Greek experience, the Clark family visited Japan and China, where two grandchildren, 5 and 7, helped to break down barriers and open lots of doors. But when time came to plan their 1984 trip, the group numbered 20, and Clark says his children themselves decided they didn't have to travel to fancy destinations. So they rented five air-conditioned, houseboats (each at $1,750 a week) for cove hopping, water-skiing, swimming, and deer watching off the wooded shores of Shasta Lake in northern California.

FOR FURTHER INFORMATION

Greek National Tourist Organization, 645 Fifth Ave., New York, NY 10022; (212)-421-5777.

Kavos Yachting Ltd., Taxiarchon, 14 Kalamaki, Athens, Greece 17455; (30)-1-938-8411 or (30)-1-982-5701; telex 23-3876 KYGR.

Silverthorn Resort on Shasta Lake, P.O. Box 4205, Redding, CA 96099; (916)-275-1571.

PUBLICATIONS

Chartering magazine, ten issues a year, $20.75; P.O. Box 1933, Jensen Beach, FL 33457; (305)-334-2003.

Greek Island Hopping by Dana Faracos (New York: Hippocrene Books, 1982), $12.95.

A Wonderful Year in the Wilderness

■ Just after he turned 50, Alan Weeden, then president of the Manhattan-based securities firm of Weeden & Co., resolved to fulfill an old desire—to explore some of the last truly wild places on earth. As this native Californian looked back over his life, the last 20 years blurred together. To renew himself, Weeden decided to take a year off from the firm he and his two brothers had run. For an intense, indelible experience, he would camp in the wilderness over weeks at a stretch.

He found companions for his sabbatical in his children, who had all just graduated from school or college. Don, then 23, had studied anthropology at Evergreen College in Washington State. Bob, 22, had majored in psychology at

On Mount Kenya, Alan N. Weeden (second from left) tops off a year-long journey with his children, Don (left), Leslie, and Bob.

VACATIONS AND WEEKENDS

Stanford. Their sister, Leslie, 18, had finished boarding school in Connecticut. Weeden's wife, Barbara, not a camper, chose not to go.

Weeden planned an itinerary with a stunning array of Mother Earth's crown jewels: Alaska; the Patagonian fringes of Chile and Argentina; the alps of New Zealand's South Island; the beaches of southern Tasmania; the underwater splendors of the Great Barrier Reef; the bird paradises of Malaysia, Sri Lanka, and the Seychelles; the game parks of East Africa. All had plenty of wildlife in zones relatively free of disease.

Risk is always inherent in long periods in the wild, but Weeden feels the real danger lies in failing to anticipate and prepare for what might happen. Acting as his own travel agent, outfitter, and guide, Weeden leafed through old magazines, wrote dozens of inquiries, and talked to other travelers. And Bob assembled the medical kit. Even so, it would have been foolhardy to attempt such an odyssey without one member trained in the ways of the wilderness. Don, who had spent a summer at the National Outdoor Leadership School in Lander, Wyoming, climbed Mount Rainier in winter, and taught climbing and kayaking, ably filled that role. He chose the equipment, clothing, and food. Several thousand dollars worth of supplies, plus research on sites they would visit, were shipped to Alaska, Chile, New Zealand, and Australia. Half a ton of gear, including two Klepper kayaks, each capable of carrying 225 pounds of supplies, went to Anchorage. In June the four Weedens took off for Anchorage with open, round-the-world plane tickets.

The family had not seen much of one another for eight years, with the children away at school. Now they would be one another's sole companions for months, often under trying conditions. Personal relationships clearly would affect their success. Weeden had promised his wife he would personally make the final decisions where safety was involved, but otherwise agreed to the election of a leader for each leg of the trip.

On the first leg, backpacking in the volcanic wastes of Alaska's Katmai National Monument, Weeden himself was in command. Seeking a passage in the Buttress Range, he directed the hikers, with packs fully laden (60 pounds for the men and 40 for Leslie), up a precipitous 2,000-foot climb — only to find no safe way across the top and down the other side. Weeden had misread the topographical map. Back they trudged, exhausted. Next day Don located the passage, over extremely slippery shale. They had to rope together for safety. After that scary episode, Weeden agreed that Don should take over in the areas of deepest wilderness.

The youngsters soon let their father know that, crucial questions of safety apart, they wouldn't take his acting like a Wall Street executive, giving orders and creating tension. Weeden adapted gradually, noting in his diary: "I'm going through a metamorphosis. I feel like a snake who has just shed his old skin and doesn't quite know how the new one will turn out. First, I have to mellow out. I tend to organize everything and get impatient. . . . Second, the social structure has changed. The people we meet are their age, not my age." His children converted Weeden to their generation's style: third-class hotels in town, and sleeping on the fantail on a four-day ferry trip.

Away from civilization, Weeden was more than fulfilling his desire to get close to nature. On a kayaking excursion in Alaska's Prince William Sound, he saw a bald eagle in the water with a fish too heavy to pull out, a pod of humpback whales, hopping and breaching and slapping their tails. In camp he could hear the whales breathing, and watch icebergs float by. But such marvels could not ensure idyllic harmony among the humans. He wrote: "The entire trip depends on our having fun together and being supportive. I'm not sure we're working hard enough at it, as the camaraderie has begun to unravel a bit." Weeden was also disappointed at the amount of time it took to make and break camp, cook, pack and unpack the kayaks.

To adjust to one another and the rigors of the wilds took much of that Alaskan summer. Don and Bob continued to be sensitive about suggestions and criticisms from their father, and Leslie wanted more responsibility. They took a break in September, as planned, for a month in San Francisco and another living as tourists. Mrs. Weeden joined them in Guatemala, Colombia, Ecuador, and the Galapagos Islands.

The foursome next explored waterways rarely traveled by modern man. Having shipped their kayaks to Chile, they paddled down lakes and rivers, through valleys and forests with black-necked swans and Patagonian parrots, and heard from gauchos that theirs was only the third party to descend the Rio Serano in 20 years. They wanted especially to see Chile's coastal fjords, and got a permit to go as far as the Chilean navy allowed, to the Fjord of the Mountains, at the southern end of the Patagonian ice field.

To enter that fjord, a spectacular tidal inlet 30 miles long, requires negotiating rapidly changing tides, in often treacherous weather. With a UHF radio, the two kayaks set out across an open eight-mile stretch of the Golfo Almirante Montt, in calm water under a clear sky. Within an hour they were paddling in four-foot waves driven by 60-knot gusts. It took two more hours to reach an island, where they recovered from their worst scare of the year. Once into the fjord, the paddlers spent two December weeks gliding peacefully past blue glaciers among the porpoises. They camped on a beach, decorated a blossoming fuchsia with socks as their Christmas tree, and sang carols as they paddled. Together they had survived crises. On Christmas Eve, Weeden wrote in his diary: "Our spirit is excellent and I really think we have it together as a group."

In the second half of the year the Weedens abandoned kayaks to hike and climb across southern parts of the

FAMILY ADVENTURES

Eastern Hemisphere. In New Zealand's Mount Aspiring National Park they mastered mountaineering techniques — belaying and self-arrest. On a week's trek down Tasmania's southern coast they encountered drenching rains, bloodsucking leeches, and only two human beings. In Africa they climbed Mount Kenya.

The year's travels cost $53,000 (in 1976 dollars) for the four, but the experience was priceless. The children not only saw the world, but came back with enhanced self-confidence, plus convictions about what they wanted to do in life. Don went on to get a graduate degree in public health and took up field research in family planning in developing countries. Bob obtained an MBA and joined Merrill Lynch in mergers and acquisitions. Leslie finished Stanford and entered the school of journalism at Columbia. Alan Weeden returned deeply concerned about the extinction of plant and animal species and the human population explosion. Since retiring from business two years after the trip, he has devoted most of his time and management skills to the Sierra Club and other nonprofit organizations for environmental issues, resource management, and population growth.

Getting to know each other better during their family *Wanderjahr* came as a bonus. "The trip left permanent ties, really bonds," Don said afterward. "I can look my father in the eyes. We ventured something together." To his children, Weeden had changed from being not only a father but a lifelong friend as well. In 1985 Weeden, Don, Leslie, and five of their friends returned to the Chilean fjords for six and a half weeks to kayak in even more inaccessible places. "Blank spaces on the map are just magnets to us," says Alan Weeden.

FOR FURTHER INFORMATION

For those who prefer to let specialists organize their adventures or who need to learn skills for independent travel in the wilderness:

Mountain Travel, 1398 Solano Ave., Albany, CA 94706; (800)-227-2384 or (415)-527-8100.

National Outdoor Leadership School, P.O. Box AA, Lander, WY 82520; (307)-332-6973.

Outward Bound USA, 384 Field Point Rd., Greenwich, CT 06830; (800)-243-8520 or (203)-661-0797.

Sobek's International Explorers Society, P.O. Box 1089, Angels Camp, CA 95222; (209)-736-4524.

Wilderness Travel, 801 Allston Way, Berkeley, CA 94710; (800)-247-6700 or (415)-548-0420.

PUBLICATIONS

Alaska's Parklands: The Complete Guide by Nancy Simmerman (Seattle: Mountaineers, 1983), $14.95.

Darwin and the Beagle by Alan Moorehead (New York: Penguin, 1979), $10.95.

In Patagonia by Bruce Chatwin (New York: Simon & Schuster, 1978), $4.95.

Patagonia Revisited by Bruce Chatwin and Paul Theroux (Boston: Houghton Mifflin, 1986), $9.95. ■

Horsepacking in the Western Wilds

■ A horsepacking trip guided by a skilled outfitter opens up the majestic beauty of America's Western wilderness as nothing else can. A wilderness is "an area where the earth and its community of life are untrammeled by man, where man himself is a visitor who does not remain," according to the National Wilderness Preservation Act of 1964. Unlike national parks, where over 100 million visitors tour by car and bus each year, public wilderness areas are closed to all motorized transport.

Strung out along the twisting trail, a pack train of 14 horses and nine riders picks its way up the steepest part of a daylong, 18-mile climb into Montana's Beartooth Mountains. Finally on the Lake Plateau, where snowcapped granite peaks stretch on spectacularly, the horsemen make camp at 9,300 feet on the shores of Lake Pinchot. As if to impress upon them the dramatic nature of the environment, harsh to man and sensitive to his intrusion, a sudden storm churns up whitecaps on the lake and spooks the horses. Hail frosts the campers' hamburgers and ices their drinks on a July evening. But just as quickly, skies

In Montana, geologists G. A. Barber and R. N. Miller ride the trail for trout with their sons.

VACATIONS AND WEEKENDS

clear, and at seven o'clock three mule deer come placidly to the lake to drink — and punctually reappear at that same hour each morning and evening of this party's four-night stay.

Fishing and fatherhood gave extra point to this expedition into the Absaroka-Beartooth Wilderness, an expanse of National Forest lands larger than Rhode Island adjoining the northern boundary of Yellowstone National Park. R. N. "Dick" Miller, then 54, a geologist with Anaconda Copper Co. in Denver, had suggested to his colleague, G. A. "Art" Barber, then 51, the company's vice president for exploration, that they take their teenage sons on a pack trip to fish the lakes high in the Beartooth Mountains.

After Anaconda was dissolved in 1985, Miller joined Cobb Resources of Albuquerque, New Mexico, to explore and revive old gold mines. Barber went to Washington, D.C., as president of DOSECC, a government-backed corporation for deep sampling of the earth's crust. But for each, that trip in the Beartooths lives on as an indelible experience.

Neither a horseman nor an avid fisherman, Barber had warmed to the idea of a week with his 17-year-old son, Patrick, a fervent angler. Miller looked forward to comradeship with his boys, Kirk and Terry, then 15 and 17, and yearned to tryst again with the trout that had seduced him years earlier. On a prospecting trip he had paused one evening at Cimmerian Lake, and on his first cast caught a four-pound cutthroat, the biggest trout of his life.

To organize their family adventure, the two mining executives turned to the Beartooth Ranch, 90 miles southwest of Billings, bordering the wilderness near Nye, Montana. There James and Ellen Langston have been outfitting and guiding fishing and hunting parties into the Beartooth Mountains for 30 years. The Millers and Barbers brought their own tents, sleeping bags, and fishing gear. The ranch provided food and cooking utensils, as well as saddles and packhorses, and wranglers to look after them. Rates are $60 per person per day for a double room ($72 for a single), including meals and horses at the ranch.

Led by Jim Langston, 53, men and boys mounted and followed the migratory route of elk from the Forest Service trail head at Initial Creek up the west fork of the Stillwater River. On their 4,000-foot ascent, Barber, who normally would not see the forest for the rocks, discovered the plant world — from black-eyed Susans and quaking aspen in the valley to ferns and pines on lower slopes, with stately spruce at higher altitudes. After seven bumpy hours in the saddle, Barber and the other greenhorns were more than ready for their layover at Lake Pinchot and some serious fishing.

Cherishing memories of that big cutthroat, Miller was in a hurry to return to Cimmerian Lake that first morning. Others wanted to fish the chain of lakes between Pinchot and Cimmerian. So all scrambled down 1,200 feet through heavy brush and steep pitches. At the farthest end of Cimmerian, in the same hole with the same kind of fly that had produced his prize catch years earlier, a squirrel-tail streamer, Miller caught a 15-inch cutthroat.

Barber meanwhile had a rather chilling encounter. Spin-casting with his son Patrick's favorite Panther Martin lure, which had brought in more fish than any other, Barber snagged it on a rock far out in the lake. Knowing how deeply Patrick felt about that lure, Barber disrobed, waded, and swam out into the icy depths, and freed the Panther Martin.

The cherished lure proved worth retrieving. But since the anglers were releasing most of their catch, they agreed that instead of the treble hook common on this and most spinning lures, they should, on any future trip, bring single hooks without barbs, so as not to damage the fish. Twelve of the biggest trout from their daylong hike did provide a delicious breakfast next day — stuffed with bacon and onion, rolled in seasoned bread crumbs, wrapped in foil, and baked on the grill.

On the frosty morning when they broke camp, outfitter Langston, who depends on Forest Service permits to take parties into the wilderness, labored to leave as few traces as possible. The rocks ringing the fireplace were scattered and ashes dispersed. The boys dismantled their raft, made of dead trees lashed together. Back in the saddle again, dudes and wranglers climbed through Jordan Pass at 9,400 feet, detoured around a snowslide, and descended the trail along Wounded Man Creek — aptly named, it turned out.

From the start, Langston had warned the party to keep their reins firmly in hand and not to gallop. But as they headed down, the dudes grew lackadaisical, and a chain reaction rippled through the string of horses. First Langston's own mount acted skittish after he picked up a bag of pots and pans that had fallen from one of the packhorses. Just behind, Barber's horse stumbled over a log. Then Patrick's horse shot past both men and Pat's wildly sailing hat scared the Millers' horses. Terry's horse took off and his father's slalomed between the trees in a dead gallop. Slipping sideways, Miller sprawled face-down, fortunately on the only soft spot around, but the spill nonetheless left him with a painful left hip and ribs.

The 41-mile excursion ended back at the Beartooth Ranch after the riders had worked their way down the canyon of the Stillwater River with its awesome white turbulence. "I wanted to see a wilderness in action, and we did," said Barber. "Patrick and I talked in our sleeping bags the last night and I said to him, 'Do you want to do it again?' and he said, 'Sure. When?'"

FOR FURTHER INFORMATION

American Wilderness Alliance; membership, $22 a year, includes newsletter and trip announcements; Suite 114, 7600 Arapahoe Rd., Englewood, CO 80112; (303)-771-0380.

FAMILY ADVENTURES

Beartooth Ranch, Rt. 2, Box 350, Nye, MT 59061; (406)-328-6194 or 328-6205.
Dude Ranchers' Association, publishes *Dude Ranch Vacation Directory,* $1; Box 471, La Porte, CO 80535; (303)-493-7623.
Trail Riders of the Canadian Rockies, Box 6742, Station "D," Calgary, Alberta, Canada T2P 2E6; (403)-263-6963.
Travel Montana publishes *The Montana Accommodations Guide* listing ranches and outfitters; 1424 Ninth Ave., Helena, MT 59620; (800)-548-3390 or (406)-263-6963. ■

Rafting with Outward Bound

■ The name Outward Bound evokes an image of rugged, punishing wilderness trips for striplings. But the movement has by now reached out to include both sexes, all ages from 14 up, and courses ranging from the traditional mountaineering to canoeing, bicycling, skiing, sailing, and white-water expeditions. The common elements are challenge — participants are pushed beyond the limits they would normally set for themselves — and a degree of risk. But the organization reports no course-related fatalities since 1978. Applicants must sign a form acknowledging "an understanding of the rigorous nature of the course." Yet trips are sometimes undertaken by vacationers who don't fully comprehend that message.

A few of that kind took part in a summer white-water river rafting trip run by the Colorado Outward Bound School, one of five tied to Outward Bound Inc., a nonprofit organization. The occasion was a "family" course, offered a few times each year in which each participant is related to at least one other. On tour the kin are expected to break away from at-home patterns and confront problems as equals. The trip, seven days and 55 miles along the Colorado River, begins just south of Moab, Utah, winding through the sculptured red rocks of Canyonlands National Park and plunging to a finale down the 27 rapids of Cataract Canyon. The course follows part of the route explored and vividly described by geologist John Wesley Powell in 1869. The cost: $685 for adults; $400 for their children.

Among the two dozen people taking the plunge that July was Phillip Matthews, 43, who later became chairman and chief executive of Bell Sports Inc., a Norwalk, California, maker of bicycle and motorcycle accessories. Matthews had made an earlier Outward Bound raft trip and so had his son, Jay, 16. Another family group had been assembled by Robert Sonke, 50, a Merrill Lynch broker in Denver. The group included Sonke's sons, Craig, 16, and Lee, 18 (a seasoned Outward Bounder who talked his father into the trip), two brothers-in-law, and a nephew. Five couples showed up from Minnesota and North Dakota, recruited by Steve Scheel, 34, of Scheels Hardwares & Sports Shops, a chain. Scheel had kayaked Cataract Canyon as a teenager, but his wife and friends were strangers to white water. They expected a joyride.

The opening instructions from course director Sam Cox, 29, suggested otherwise. In crews of eight, including an instructor, participants were to rig, launch, and paddle three 17½-foot inflatable rafts. The crews, Cox said, would take turns preparing meals for the entire group, using supplies carried by a motorized support raft. Except for a change of clothing, a toilet kit, flashlight, and camera, they were to leave behind all trappings of civilization, including watches. As a brochure describing the course had warned, tobacco and alcohol were taboo. (Anyone breaking that ban is offered a swift ride back to civilization.)

The trip began tamely enough, in flat water, with the crews learning basic paddling and the rhythms of teamwork. As the group sweltered in 90-degree heat and got blisters from paddling, some members grew impatient. Bob Sonke later argued that crews should motor down the slow stretch of river as commercial rafting parties do. Other mutinous feelings stirred when the jug water ran out and the group turned to iodine-treated river water. Winds blew sand in the food. There was no shower, of course, and the two johns were improvised from ammunition cans. Park rules required all garbage, including human waste, to be taken out.

The hardships receded in importance as the rafts approached Cataract Canyon and the crews got schooled in white-water techniques: how to read the river for currents, eddies, and submerged rocks, and how to plot a route from shore. Paddlers practiced captaining their rafts, shouting commands to the crew.

The first major test in the rapids came on No. 5, called "Upset." Craig Sonke captained the lead raft. Next

On the Colorado River life-jacketed paddlers stoke up before braving the 27 rapids of Utah's Cataract Canyon.

35

VACATIONS AND WEEKENDS

to Craig in the stern, Cox, the director, saw the raft heading left of the intended course. Cox thought the raft could make it and, not wanting to steal Craig's sense of accomplishment, held off taking command. The raft hit a "hole," a reversal in the current, and as the raft spun sideways and tipped, both Craig and Sandra Scheel were thrown into the river. Cox and Steve Scheel hauled Craig back into the raft, then spent a harrowing moment searching for Sandra. Forced beneath the raft, she resurfaced 15 seconds later.

The rescue completed, Cox beached the raft and soberly reviewed what had gone wrong. The joyriders got the message that running the rapids in those rubber rafts was not the piece of cake they had thought, and shaped themselves into a true team. Some of the other businessmen, used to making right decisions, found their turn as captain an unsettling, humbling experience.

The onshore challenges were demanding too. Having finished off rapid No. 5 and a light supper, 14 of the group groped up a steep gulch, over slippery rock that threatened them with 100-foot falls. Finally, 1,200 feet above the river, they entered Surprise Valley, a two-mile natural amphitheater ringed by sandstone formations. Phil Matthews found that scenery, and the feat of getting there, the best part of the trip: "I never would have attempted that climb if it weren't part of something like this."

Bob Sonke and his party had elected not to go up to Surprise Valley because two of them, remembering an earlier hike, thought the overnight expedition would be too arduous. The defections disappointed the Outward Bound leaders. They, says Sonke, "found it difficult to accept that we make our own decisions."

Around the campfire on the last night, the voyagers assessed their experiences. Once inured to the hardships, the five couples from the Midwest found themselves taking to the challenge. The women especially were gratified by their ability to cope. Some complained that Outward Bound's literature should have been more explicit about the plain food, primitive facilities, and strenuous activity. Sonke later likened the course to a "military boot camp: tough, dirty, hot, and physically taxing." He says, "The biggest shocker was the muddy river. I've never been on a vacation where you couldn't get clean." He did find it satisfying to negotiate his own raft down the river, rather than be paddled by someone else. But, he cautions, "this trip is not for everyone. You ought to make sure you want to do it."

Phil Matthews enjoyed the trip as he had his first one because "it was an experience Jay and I could share as adults." Besides, said Matthews, "when I get back home, my mind's cleaner. I'm more relaxed, more physically fit, at ease with myself, and ready to deal with the world." After the rapids, and the climb, it's the world, perhaps, that looks like a piece of cake. ■

FOR FURTHER INFORMATION

Colorado Outward Bound School, 945 Pennsylvania St., Denver, CO 80203-3198; (303)-837-0880.

Outward Bound USA, 384 Field Point Rd., Greenwich, CT 06830; (800)-243-8520 or (203)-661-0797.

PUBLICATIONS

Canyonlands River Guide by Bill and Buzz Belknap (Boulder City, NV: Westwater Books), $10.95 (waterproof).

Exploration of the Colorado River & Its Canyons by John Wesley Powell (reprint, New York: Dover, 1985), $6.95.

Sierra Club Guide to the Natural Areas of Colorado & Utah by John Perry and Jane G. Perry (San Francisco: Sierra Club Books, 1985), $9.95.

Canoeing in the Arctic

■ Returning to New York via Concorde from a London business trip one Thursday in July, Robert F. Greenhill, who heads investment banking at Morgan Stanley, and John S. Wadsworth, the firm's managing director for investment banking in the Far East, collected their wives and children (three each), and set off on a totally different sort of journey. On Saturday evening three floatplanes deposited all ten of them, plus 800 pounds of gear, on an island in northern Saskatchewan's Wollaston Lake. When the planes departed, the families' last link with civilization was severed. "The moment we are left alone in the wilderness is always a high," notes Wadsworth.

On the island the New Yorkers kept a rendezvous with David Harrison, a Seattle banker, his wife, their son, and a teenage friend. The three families had spent months plotting the logistics that brought them to this remote spot.

Robert Greenhill of Morgan Stanley handled the rapids in Canada's Fond du Lac River with help from daughter Mary, then 9, and son Bobby, 11, in the bow.

FAMILY ADVENTURES

They spent the next 16 days canoeing along 200 miles of the Fond du Lac River.

Between 1965 and 1985 the Greenhills and Wadsworths made seven unique canoeing expeditions to Canada and Alaska, four of them with the Harrisons and, as soon as they were old enough, four with their children. They chose untraveled rivers and put in at points reachable only by costly chartered bush planes. And they did all their own research, outfitting, and paddling, without hiring guides. Each adventure in self-reliance brought new challenges.

The hardest journey took only the adults down Canada's Back River, which plunges into the polar sea just above the Arctic Circle. Called by some the "canoeist's Everest," the Back holds a multitude of long, difficult Class IV rapids that require precise maneuvering. Its Class V and VI rapids, the most treacherous, usually have to be portaged. The river has claimed several lives. This party's 1975 expedition was only the sixth since Captain Back ran the river in 1855, and the first with women.

Greenhill and Wadsworth had both started canoeing in Minnesota as boys, married young, and wanted their wives to share their experiments in survival in the wilderness. For the Back trip they needed a third couple so as to have at least three canoes for safety. Finding compatible companions isn't easy. Greenhill insists that on a wild river a person's mental attitude is even more important than physical strength or canoeing ability. He says, "There's a crisis, big or little, every day, and the best companions are those who are very calm." Eventually they heard of the Harrisons, who were living in New York at the time and had paddled numerous challenging courses. The three couples sounded each other out and decided to throw in their lots together.

The Back River trip had anxious moments. Two-thirds of the way through the 25-day, 500-mile journey, the Wadsworths' craft spun broadside against a rock submerged in the rapids, and was pinned there by the current. Wadsworth climbed onto the rock and, with water swirling around his legs, tried in vain to dislodge the boat. Forced to abandon ship, he and his wife, Susy, tossed their waterproof packs of food and gear into the rapids, sending them downstream to be fished out by their friends. Then Susy and Jack fought their way to shore, a ten-minute ordeal in 48-degree water.

Jack's temperature dropped to a dangerous 92 degrees, and hypothermia threatened. Judy Harrison, a paramedic, supervised his treatment — a warm sleeping bag and plenty of hot tea. Greenhill, who thrives on adversity, was invigorated by the challenge of forging ahead with only two canoes for six people.

Flying home from the Back expedition, the couples talked of taking their children on their next voyage. In 1977 they chose Alaska's Noatak River, in the Brooks Range north of the Arctic Circle. Plenty of fishing, grayling and char, and wildlife, caribou and moose, entertained the kids. The Class I and II rapids were relatively easy to deal with. The six adults and seven children, from age 7 to 16, made the 325-mile journey in two weeks. Susy Wadsworth and Gayle Greenhill shared paddling with their teenage daughters, but their husbands, who had the youngest children as mates, paddled solo almost every mile.

Two years later, on the Fond du Lac trip, the group took their six canoes through some Class III rapids. But this time Christopher Wadsworth and Mary Greenhill, both 9, could share paddling with their fathers. On its tortuous westward course from Wollaston Lake to Lake Athabasca, the Fond du Lac alternately narrows into white water and then spreads onto broad expanses of lake. Following the river proved easy, thanks to geological survey maps drawn to a scale of one mile per inch.

The big challenges, as always, were to find suitable campsites, avoid head winds, and decide whether to portage around or shoot the rapids. As a guide to the river, Wadsworth brought along a copy of the journal kept by David Thompson, who first explored the river in 1796 for the Hudson's Bay Company. It was read aloud each night around the campfire. Wadsworth also brought a summary he had made from the logs of more recent trippers, explaining how they had handled the trickiest rapids.

Finding unusually high water, the caravan made only two complete portages, carrying both their gear and the 60-pound canoes around two waterfalls. At two other points they portaged just the gear, shooting the rapids in the six unloaded canoes. About a mile upstream from breathtaking Manitou ("ghost") Falls, three pairs of the strongest paddlers shot a stretch of swirling white water, making the passage easily. Greenhill and his daughter Sarah, then 18, walked back to take another canoe through. "We got too far to the right, and met a whole new set of rapids," Greenhill later recalled. As they tried to maneuver out, tremendous waves grabbed the canoe, flipped it over, and sent both it and the Greenhills downstream. Wadsworth and Harrison, waiting in their canoes at the bottom of the rapids, came to their rescue.

Next day the group encountered the only other humans they were to see on the Fond du Lac. As Greenhill tells it, "We were roaring down Brassy Rapids, some of the longest. At the end, around a corner comes this man, with a crazed look in his eye, carrying an ax!" The families had planned to camp just at that spot, but when a second man appeared, with a second ax, the paddlers kept moving. Farther downstream they spotted a campsite, giving evidence that the ax-toting characters belonged to a crew of prospectors out cutting a survey line.

As they sat around the campfire, after a dinner of freeze-dried lasagna, or pork chops, or hamburger,

37

VACATIONS AND WEEKENDS

Greenhill entertained with endless card tricks. And Wadsworth spun a continuing ghost story that featured the "porcu-pike," a creature personifying two principal species of the river's wildlife.

The children came into their own as canoeists on that journey. The next to last day, young David Harrison and his friend carried their first canoes over a portage. "That is one of the character-building aspects of canoe tripping," his father notes. The trip ended at a fishing camp where the group found an old school bus to take them and their canoes 15 miles to an airstrip at Stony Rapids. Lifting off the dirt runway in a cloud of dust, the paddlers headed for the world of hot showers and business suits.

For end-to-end enjoyment, the three families rate highest their two and a half weeks in August 1983 on the Yukon Territories' Peel and Ogilvy rivers. Though they met long, difficult rapids and portaged six miles around Aberdeen Falls, they passed through spectacular mountain scenery in good weather, with no bugs.

In 1984 a new kind of partnership united Greenhill, 48, Harrison, 46, and Wadsworth, 44. They formed Canoe America Associates and bought *Canoe* magazine, which had printed accounts of some of their expeditions. Harrison had already shared his know-how in two books: *Sports Illustrated Canoeing*, an entry-level guide, and, with his wife, Judy, *Canoe Tripping with Kids*. So he left banking to become general manager of *Canoe*.

While Harrison was off reporting on a 1985 reenactment of fur traders boating from Lake Winnipeg to Hudson's Bay, the Greenhills and Wadsworths returned to the Northwest Territories with their children, by then ages 15 to 23. Negotiating the frigid 38-degree waters of the Burnside River that flows into the Bathhurst Inlet above the Arctic Circle, they saved some Canadian troops from disaster. After watching one of the army's rubber boats smash against rocks and another lose its gear in an eight-foot passage between 80-foot cliffs, the boys ran along the cliff tops to warn the rest of the soldiers, who were on survival training.

Shortly after returning, Greenhill, who has marshaled some of the biggest takeovers in U.S. business, quipped, "Canoes are my main interest now. Banking is a sideline."

FOR FURTHER INFORMATION

American Canoe Association; membership, $25, includes *Canoe* magazine, P.O. Box 190, Newington, VA 22122; (703)-550-7523.

Canadian Consulate General publishes lists of outfitters by province; 1251 Ave. of the Americas, New York, NY 10020; (212)-757-4917.

Ecosummer Canada Expeditions guides canoe trips in the Arctic; 1516 Duranleau St., Vancouver, B.C., Canada V6H 3S4; (604)-669-7741.

Mountain Travel conducts guided kayak trips on Alaska's Noatak and Kobuk rivers; 1398 Solano Ave., Albany, CA 94706; (800)-227-2348 or (415)-527-8100.

PUBLICATIONS

Back to Nature in Canoes: A Guide to American Waters by Rainer Esslen (Frenchtown, NJ: Columbia Publishing, 1976), $6.95.

Canoe magazine, six issues a year, $12; includes *Canoe/Kayak Buyer's Guide;* P.O. Box 3146, Kirkland, WA 98083; (800)-MY-CANOE or (206)-827-6363. Publishes *Starting Out,* annually, $3.95.

Canoe Tripping with Kids by David Harrison and Judy Harrison (New York: Viking Penguin, 1982), $9.95.

Canoeing Wild Rivers by Cliff Jacobson (Merrillville, IN: ICS Books, 1984), $14.95.

The Family Canoe Trip by Carl Shepardson and Marge Shepardson (Merrillville, IN: ICS Books, 1985), $14.95.

Narrative of a Journey to the Shores of the Polar Sea in the Years 1819-20-21-22 by John Franklin (reprint, Philadelphia: R. West, 1978), $20.

Sports Illustrated Canoeing by Dave Harrison (New York: Harper & Row, 1981), $5.95.

The World of Farley Mowat edited by Peter Davison (Boston: Little, Brown, 1980), $16.95.

Vacationing with Little Kids

■ Cruising the deep blue Pacific off Mexico, Margaret C. Whitman, 29, a management consultant with Bain & Co. in San Francisco, basked by a pool on Sitmar Cruises' luxurious *Fairsky* while her 11-month-old son, Griffith, scrambled around the playroom three decks below. Watched over by one of the ship's trained counselors, "Griff" was among 20 passengers under age 2. Later, refreshed and

On an Eleuthera beach, Club Med staffer Ann Thomas leads a towline of tots.

FAMILY ADVENTURES

relaxed, his mother took him to the children's pool, where he loved the water slide. And she loved wheeling him around the promenade deck in his stroller.

"I work five days a week, and my vacation is one time I can see my little boy. Yet I need a rest, too," says Griff's mother, who is married to Dr. Griffith Harsh, 32, a neurosurgeon. Before the cruise with his mother and grandmother, Griff had gone with his parents on a Hawaiian vacation. His mother explains, "My husband's idea of a vacation is to see his son. And most of my friends feel they don't want to take a vacation without their children, especially if both parents work."

Many young parents these days feel like Griff's. The parents of the current baby boomlet are more likely than any previous generation to be two-career couples, so their vacations do double duty: they should let Mom and Dad unwind and also provide valuable time with the children. Several travel companies offer vacations that do both.

Griff's mother chose a cruise because she found on the Hawaiian trip that moving moppets around is tough. And, she says, "kids like the routine of one place." She chose Sitmar because its ships offer separate child and teen centers staffed from 9 A.M. until midnight, and its playrooms are well stocked with books and toys. Three Sitmar ships ply the Caribbean and the Pacific. During the off-peak period from September to early December, a nine-day cruise from Los Angeles to Acapulco and back in an outside cabin costs $2,075 per adult — an inside cabin is $1,675 — plus $420 per child sharing a cabin with two adults. Prices include round-trip air fare from more than 150 cities. Other fares may be available through travel agents.

Finding trips or resorts with programs for children under 3 is not easy. Even Florida's Walt Disney World requires that children left at its KinderCare Children's Center or Mouseketeer Clubhouses be toilet-trained; it minds fewer than 50, and only on weekends and evenings. Several ski resorts welcome the extremely young, including Copper Mountain, Keystone, and Vail in Colorado, and Grindelwald and Zermatt in Switzerland.

The tiniest hedonists are also welcome at some Club Meds. The swinging singles who once peopled the resorts are growing up, so Club Med now urges parents to bring infants as young as 4 months to Baby Clubs. In Florida, Sandpiper at Port St. Lucie, 45 miles north of Palm Beach, welcomes them. Mini Clubs, six in the Western Hemisphere, take children 2 to 11. Stephanie Weisser, 34, and husband Paul, 32, part owners of Mother's Restaurant in New Hope, Pennsylvania, spent a week on Eleuthera in March with son Zachary, 2. Mornings the Weissers played tennis, snorkeled, and sailed. A G.O. (gentil organisateur, as Club Med calls members of its staff) took Zachary and a half dozen other toddlers to the beach or to the playground and gave them lunch and a nap. Afternoons the Weissers played with Zachary, then gave him supper in the children's section of the dining room. They put him back in the Mini Club from 7:30 to 9 while they ate dinner.

"We had a wonderful time," says Stephanie Weisser, "but I wouldn't do it again with a child Zachary's age." He had a hard time adjusting to a new schedule and new people. Club Med works better for gregarious older children, who on Eleuthera can learn trapeze performing, among other things. A winter week at Eleuthera's Club Med, including air fare from New York, costs $960 to $1,160 per adult, more on holiday weeks. At certain times children 2 to 7 go free to all Mini Clubs, and other ages get reduced rates.

Other choices range from bucolic to exotic. Robert Mitchell, 34, corporate controller of Scholastic Inc. in Lyndhurst, New Jersey, and his wife, Shay, 34, have taken their girls to James and Nancy Rodgers's dairy farm in West Glover, Vermont. On their first visit, Kate, 2, learned to gather eggs, and Keri, 5, watched a newborn calf with its mother. Cost: $200 a week per adult, $125 per child under 12; with shared bath, all meals, and swimming in a nearby lake.

In Nepal, families can trek near Annapurna at heights up to 10,000 feet for eight days of a 15-day trip. Small children can ride in a basket on a porter's back. One of three annual family adventures — the others are in Kenya and Peru — arranged by Mountain Travel, the Nepal Trek costs $2,490 per adult, and from $500 to $650 for children aged 2 to 14, not including air fare.

A number of European organizations cater to vacationers with youngsters. Switzerland's Happy Family Hotels, which say they are *kinderfreundlich* (child friendly), offer playrooms and free care for children 3 and up; attendants in major resort areas speak English. The Swiss National Tourist Office has details. London's Universal Aunts will take children sightseeing.

For the planning essential to a good time with kids, guidebooks pile high. *Traveling with Your Baby* by Vicki Lansky (Bantam Books, $2.95) is a primer of practical advice. *Fielding's Family Vacations USA* by Diane Torrens (William Morrow & Co., $12.95) and the newer *What to Do with the Kids This Year* by Jane Wilford and Janet Tice (East Woods Press, $8.95) describe U.S. resorts with children's programs. *Farm, Ranch & Country Vacations* by Pat Dickerman (Farm & Ranch Vacations, $9.95) is a good source for rural vacationers. *Fielding's Europe with Children* by Leila Hadley (William Morrow & Co., $12.95) includes a country-by-country guide. Special treats are highlighted in *Children's Guide to London* by Christopher Pick (London: Cadogan Books, $8.50); *Children's Guide to Paris* and *Children's Guide to Rome*, both by Irma Kurtz and Clive Unger-Hamilton (Harper & Row, $6.95 each).

For up-to-date information, the most complete news-

39

VACATIONS AND WEEKENDS

letter is *Family Travel Times* ($35 a year), a monthly published by Travel With Your Children. Subscribers receive a hot-line phone number for limited individual counseling. The company also publishes annually revised directories, *Cruising with Children* ($29 for the U.S. or European edition). Sheets on individual ski resorts are available for a few dollars each. And if doing anything with children sometimes seems trying, remember — as grandmother will certainly remind you — they're not children for long. ∎

FOR FURTHER INFORMATION

Club Med, 3 E. 54th St. New York, NY 10022; (800)-CLUB-MED or (212)-750-1670.

Mountain Travel, 1398 Solano Ave., Albany, CA 94706; (800)-227-2384 or (415)-527-8100.

Rodgers Dairy Farm, RFD #3, Box 57, West Glover, VT 05875; (802)-525-6677.

Sierra Club, Outings Department, 730 Polk St. San Francisco, CA 94109; (415)-776-2211.

Sitmar Cruises, 10100 Santa Monica Blvd., Los Angeles, CA 90067; (213)-553-1666.

Swiss National Tourist Office, 608 Fifth Ave., New York, NY 10020; (212)-757-5944.

Travel With Your Children, 80 Eighth Ave., New York, NY 10011; (212)-206-0688.

Universal Aunts, 250 King's Rd., London SW 3; (44)-1-351-5767; cable UNIAUNTS S.W.3.

PURPOSEFUL VACATIONS

Earthwatch Volunteers

■ In a rain forest in Borneo, Lynn Dyer spent two weeks trailing and observing orangutans, the orange-haired primates that are the least known and most endangered of the great apes. Professionally Dyer, 39, is Peat Marwick's regional marketing manager in Chicago for its computer software package on corporate tax compliance. By avocation she is a student of animal behavior and anthropology. The privilege of working with the world's leading expert on orangutans, Canadian anthropologist Birute Galdikas, 39, who has studied these primates in one habitat for 14 years, came to Lynn Dyer as a member of Earthwatch.

Dedicated to sponsoring field research by outstanding scholars in disciplines from animal behavior to volcanology, and to broadening public knowledge, Earthwatch recruits citizen volunteers for fieldwork. Amateurs gain the rare experience of working with top-notch professionals, who in their turn get not only additional funds for their work, but also free labor. Most projects entail observing wildlife or excavating a site. The 1987–88 schedule listed 106 expeditions in 41 countries, to be staffed by more than 325 teams with places for some 2,600 volunteers. Spring and summer are high seasons, though the calendar contains at least a few projects every month. Anyone from age 16 to 85 may join, with no expertise required—only curiosity, adaptability, and willingness to apply eyes, ears, hands, plus assorted skills, to the tasks assigned.

Besides their services, volunteers on a project contribute a share of its research costs. Since Earthwatch is a nonprofit, tax-exempt organization, volunteers can take these contributions off personal income taxes. Dyer and each of 100 Earthwatch volunteers on the orangutan project during 1985 contributed $1,395 apiece toward costs that included their bed and board for two weeks, all tax-deductible. Travel and meals to and from the field were also deductible. Dyer could deduct her round-trip air fare from Chicago to Borneo via Hong Kong and Singapore, but not expenses on vacation days she took in those cities en route.

The 1986 Tax Act looks more strictly at deductions for travel expenses. Earthwatch suggests that volunteers who take vacation days going to or from the staging areas for their fieldwork keep a log and prorate their air fare accordingly.

With ten other volunteers, Dyer left civilization behind at Borneo's small southern port of Kumai for a five-hour boat ride upriver to the Orangutan Research and Conservation Project. The 13.5-square-mile study area in a national park in the Indonesian portion of Borneo is home to over 1,000 orangutans and multitudes of monkeys. The research aims to construct a life history of the orangutans, which can be determined only by observing the same individuals over and over. Dyer was assigned to some of the 40 formerly captive "orangs" that had been illegally kept as pets until Indonesian authorities confiscated and released them to the research center. One task was following particular females, on two-hour walks morning and afternoon, with another volunteer and a local guide. Looking high in the forest canopy, they recorded the females' relationships with their offspring—how near they stayed, where, when, and how they ate, slept, and played.

Beneath the honeycombed roof of Baker Cave in southwest Texas, archaeologists and volunteer helpers sift the debris of millennia searching for the unwritten records of Stone Age man.

VACATIONS AND WEEKENDS

Following Princess, a new mother, turned into a disarming adventure. She was carrying her new baby when several of her ex-captive friends came out to tease and chase her. To protect the baby she ran away into the swamp, until apes and humans were knee-deep in mud. Exhausted, Princess turned to the Indonesian guide, put her hand on his hip, and looked at him in an appeal for help. When the pursuing orangs sensed she was under his protection, they left. Princess set about making a nest with leaves where she could nurse her baby; the guide wadded some into a pillow for her. "That communication between orang and native human was one of the most magical moments," says Dyer.

Life at the center was dormitory style, with two meals a day — one if on duty in the forest — of rice and vegetables, usually with fish. Any available fruit went to the ex-captive orangs. Plumbing was a hole in the ground. Bathing in the river was an evening event with ex-captive orangs joining in. Mimicking their human friends, they stole soap, lathered themselves, and ran off with towels and shoes.

On archaeological expeditions, volunteers dig and sift for traces of life long gone. J. F. "Jerry" Wilbur Jr., 64, a Kentucky Coca-Cola bottler and banker turned Arizona rancher, has gone on 12 Earthwatch digs. He started with paleontology, uncovering bison bones in Nebraska and working at the great mammoth graveyard in South Dakota. But in 1976 Wilbur discovered archaeology, and prefers it because the findings belonged to man.

In a remote corner of southwest Texas, Wilbur had joined an expedition led by Thomas R. Hester, 43, of the University of Texas, to explore the lifestyle of cave dwellers. There he encountered drenching rains, flash floods, swarms of gnats, and hours of grinding toil. Finally, sitting in a pit at the bottom of light and airy Baker Cave, Wilbur scraped away powdery limestone with a trowel and uncovered a smooth round stone. It was a hammer, worn from repeated blows struck by an ancestor of the Coahuiltecan Indians, as he fashioned his flint tools and spear points. When Wilbur picked up that hammerstone, his was the first hand to hold it in probably 9,000 years.

"If you don't enjoy something like Baker Cave, don't go," Wilbur warns. "It's no place to goof off." He didn't mind the digging, but found the screening detail a hot and dirty job — "bad news." Buckets of diggings were dumped on framed screens and shaken vigorously. From the material remaining on the screen, workers picked out bone, wood, charcoal, flint chips, nuts, and seeds for analysis back at the university labs. Thirty boxes of artifacts and soil samples collected on that dig would tell much about what life was really like in Texas long before the dawn of history.

Meeting new people is one feature of Earthwatch that Wilbur most enjoys. In Texas he struck up a friendship with teammate Frank Spingola, 58, office manager of American Licorice Co. in Union City, California. Every year since, when the Earthwatch catalogue of trips arrives, they consult on their choice, and go together. "You are getting into areas you couldn't as a tourist," says Spingola. Among their favorites: Swaziland in 1981 for a long-term study of early man in Africa under David Price Williams of the University of Botswana and Swaziland. One teammate was Lynn Dyer, on her first expedition. It inspired her to do graduate study in anthropology back in Chicago.

Not all foreign expeditions go to less developed countries. On Cyprus, Wilbur and Spingola helped excavate a Crusader castle and lived in a modern apartment. In Spain they worked on a Bronze Age village and stayed at a youth hostel with hot showers and the good cooking of Aragon. "With Earthwatch you are deepening your education in a field of your choice, and traveling as a non-tourist," notes Wilbur.

Involvement doesn't end with the expedition. Membership of $25 per year brings a quarterly magazine and newsletter to keep volunteers up to date on new and continuing projects. And dedicated alumni meet often to hear reports from some of the leading scientists. Now that's a real fringe benefit.

FOR FURTHER INFORMATION

Earthwatch, P.O. Box 403, Watertown, MA 02272; (617)-926-8200. ∎

Friends of French Art

∎ "Friends" who donate nominal sums to a museum or university can often join foreign study tours that promise entrée to places not open to tourists. But a few independent nonprofit organizations dedicated to preserving art and architecture offer members exceptional private visits. Friends of French Art succeeds well in its dual purpose. It conducts a tour with a mission: to select and finance the conservation of endangered works. FoFA's movable house party, open to donors of a tax-deductible, $5,000 each, visits Paris and a different region of France every year: Bordeaux, Provence, Alsace, Brittany, Burgundy, and more. The trips are popular because these Friends can view art and meet personages that tourists cannot. In appreciation for FoFA's help in preserving the patrimony of France, private collectors reveal their treasures and château owners wine and dine the Friends. They chat with prime ministers, businessmen, and old nobility whom they wouldn't have a chance to know on their own.

Formerly, as ordinary tourists, some FoFA members had filed through the grand salons and gardens of Vaux-le-Vicomte, the magnificent 17th-century château 30 miles southeast of Paris that served as a model for Versailles. As Friends of French Art, they could sit down one splendid

PURPOSEFUL VACATIONS

June evening and dine in candle-lit conviviality with the owner, Count Patrice de Vogüé, 58, and his wife, Countess Cristina. A contingent of Rothschilds turned up, and one of the banker brothers, Baron Elie, 69, had sent up several cases of his own 1966 Château Lafite for the party.

Limited to 32 member-donors, the FoFA house party usually consists of a number of business executives, spouses, and other art lovers. The group who dined at Vaux-le-Vicomte included a California developer of shopping malls and hotels, a homebuilder, a Hollywood producer, a Denver banker, a Connecticut real estate investor, a Canadian gallery owner. Beverly Hills investment adviser Daniel Renberg, 55, returned on several later tours, only to have the duties of FoFA treasurer conferred upon him. Harry Wetzel, 66, former chairman of Allied-Signal's Garrett Corp. in Los Angeles, claims he had first "been dragged along kicking and screaming" by his wife, Maggie, in 1981. That year invitations to Bordeaux's wine châteaux helped to lure Wetzel, who owns a vineyard and winery in California's Alexander Valley. Since then the Wetzels have gone on every FoFA tour.

The Friends were impressed with how deeply some Frenchmen care about preserving their country's artistic heritage. Vaux-le-Vicomte stood as the grandest château in France when it was finished in 1661. Louis XIV, supposedly affronted by the ostentation of its owner, Nicolas Fouquet, the treasurer of France, jailed him for life. The Sun King then hired the same architect, painter, and landscape gardener to fix up his own château. As the Friends dined in the very rooms where the ill-fated Fouquet had entertained the king, Patrice de Vogüé explained that his family was the fourth to own Vaux-le-Vicomte. He opened it to tourists in 1968, but he says gate receipts still do not cover expenses. "Keeping the place up and restoring it is passionate work. We do it because we have the reward of the fun," declared de Vogüé. "People write letters saying they appreciate that this is a private, not a state, effort."

Friends of French Art dedicate themselves to conserving artworks that other, more powerful benefactors might overlook. The French government has been pumping more money into art restoration in recent years, and in times past the Rockefeller family spent millions in France. But most of those funds have gone into preservation of well-known masterpieces. FoFA spreads its largess in small donations over dozens of sometimes obscure but important treasures: Marie Antoinette's harp, Joséphine Bonaparte's clothing, the only oil portrait of Montesquieu, whose ideas helped form the Constitution of the United States. And FoFA sows seed money. The mill in Pontoise, which Cézanne painted, had been slated for demolition. FoFA's $20,000 commitment to restore it moved the town council to create a park there. The Grand Théâtre of Bordeaux got one of FoFA's largest grants: $31,000 to build a scaffolding for restoration of a ceiling full of allegorical figures by 19th-century painter William Bouguereau. Not all of FoFA's dollars leave the U.S. In San Francisco they helped refurbish the Louis XV–style theater in the California Palace of the Legion of Honor, a museum devoted to French art.

"We are not regilding Versailles. We are helping restore things much closer to people," explains FoFA's founder and president, Mrs. Kelvin Cox Vanderlip, widow of a California developer. From 1979 through 1986 the organization, based in Palos Verdes, California, gave over $1 million to art restoration and to exchange fellowships for French and American students of art conservation. Most of the money came from donations related to the annual tours. "FoFA's participation encourages the French to see that if foreigners care enough to do something, so must they. It makes for a warm people-to-people *fraternité*. And by rescuing works in peril, it alerts their custodians to the need for continuing preventive conservation," notes Elin Vanderlip.

The inspiration for the organization came from Mrs. Vanderlip's daughter, Katrina, a professional art conservator, whose French husband, Charles de Carbonnel, is with Citibank in Switzerland. Through a French colleague, Katrina and her mother met Baroness Elie de Rothschild, who entertained FoFA's first tour group and has continued to open doors for the Friends.

To welcome one group, Michel David-Weill, 53, the senior partner of Lazard Frères in Paris and New York, and his wife, Hélène, entertained the Friends in their elegant old Left Bank mansion and garden. To help, they invited nearly 100 French artists, collectors, curators, ambassadors, statesmen, and financiers.

At Vaux-le-Vicomte the Friends of French Art are welcomed by their president, Elin Vanderlip (center, glasses), and by their hostess, Countess Cristina de Vogüé (foreground), who lives at the château with her husband, Patrice.

VACATIONS AND WEEKENDS

For David-Weill, support of art is as strong a family tradition as investment banking. Following his grandfather, David, and his father, Pierre, both of whom once headed Lazard, he has added to the family art collection, serves on the artistic advisory council of the national museums of France, and has been elected to the Académie des Beaux-Arts. "I was raised with the appreciation of art not only as something to own, but very much as something that contributes to the world," he says. He is fond of quoting his father, who used to say: "I love the American Declaration of Independence, but alongside the right to happiness, I would like to inscribe the right to beauty."

After a two-day whirl around Paris, this FoFA group descended on Aix-en-Provence in the south of France. There they toured the old town, visited the private home where Cézanne had lived with his parents, and inspected much of the art that their contributions would help restore. The most ambitious project would be 18th-century Chinese paintings on silk that cover entire walls in the Hôtel de Ribbe, a private house. Splitting and frayed, the paintings depict rice cultivation and scenes of daily life in minute detail. The restoration will begin with a grant from the Friends. With this as a pledge, national and departmental governments will then kick in up to 75% of the total bill because the de Ribbe house is classified as a historical monument.

At the Château d'Ansouis, a combination medieval fortress and Renaissance palace perched on a rocky summit north of Aix, FoFA contributed to the repair of delicate 18th-century carved plaster wall decorations that had cracked under the stress of a collapsing roof. The septuagenarian Duchess Roselyne de Sabran-Pontevès charmed the Friends with tales of how the château has remained in her late husband's family for over 1,000 years. For three generations the place had stood abandoned until she and her husband, newly married, began to resurrect it in 1936. After downing an alfresco lunch the duchess had prepared, several guests went for a swim in her spring-fed pool, once a Roman bath.

The 36 stops programmed by Elin Vanderlip and her French lieutenants challenged the Friends with eight 15-hour days, each ending with a dressy party. Dan Renberg, who had come on the tour because he needed a vacation, now and then longed for a pause in the action. But after restoring themselves, the Friends began counting the houses and artworks they had added to their own collections of memories. And when they thought about the people they had met, they realized that the keepers of the art were as fascinating as the art itself.

Itineraries have since been tailored to about 24 stops. Besides their $5,000 donations, FoFA tour members pay their own air fares, hotel bills, and their share of the group's travel expenses in France. Their hosts contribute the cuisine and the ambiance.

FOR FURTHER INFORMATION

Friends of French Art; membership, $100 a year, includes *Annual Report* on each tour, illustrated in color ($25 to nonmembers); Villa Narcissa, 100 Vanderlip Dr., Portuguese Bend, CA 90274; (213)-377-4444.

Two organizations that also arrange visits to private houses and châteaux in France for their benefactors:

La Demeure Historique, c/o the Versailles Foundation, 420 Lexington Ave., New York, NY 10017; (212)-867-8280.

Friends of *Vieilles Maisons Françaises,* membership $75 a year; c/o Isabel C. Stuebe, 180 Maiden Lane, 34th Fl., New York, NY 10038; (212)-734-1651.

PUBLICATIONS

Historic Houses, Castles and Gardens of France (Paris: The French Ministry of Culture with the cooperation of *La Demeure Historique,* 1987; distributed by Seven Hills Books, Cincinnati, OH, 513-381-3881), $14.95.

Knopf Traveler's Guide to Art: France by Michael Jacobs and Paul Stinton (New York: Knopf, 1984), $14.95. ∎

Fighting Fat

∎ If you are overweight and over-stressed, you have a wide choice of so-called fat farms. You can settle for a cosmetic figure-trim at a stylish spa or go to a no-nonsense health center and learn how to change your way of life. The big differences between spas and health centers are not only in diet, exercise, and pampering, but in medical supervision, educational programs, and counseling to effect a manageable change in lifestyle. The 30- and 40-year-olds of the 1980s, with much of their life ahead, are opting more and more for the lifestyle change rather than for the quick fix at a body shop. Some places combine both types of program. How safe, effective, and expensive are these assorted regimens — and how long do their effects last? Repeat visits seem to be the pattern, at least until the lifestyle changes are ingrained.

At 40, John E. Maxwell, a first vice president at Prudential-Bache, held a high-pressure Wall Street job running a department for joint marketing of securities and insurance. He weighed 320 pounds, consumed 5,000 calories a day (a habit formed as a college athlete), and felt too tired for regular exercise. But he had devised an elaborate plan for regular personal investing so he could retire at 55. Then it dawned on him: "What good is a plan for future financial security if I have a heart attack in my forties?"

To work out a regular health plan to help prevent life-threatening disease, Maxwell and his wife, Linda, went through the Life Fitness program directed by a physician at the luxurious La Costa Hotel and Spa in Carlsbad, California. As at most health centers and some spas, the visit began with medical and fitness evaluations, including blood tests for levels of cholesterol and triglycerides. Maxwell and his wife began each day with a brisk 6:30 A.M. walk on the golf course, one of three daily exercise pe-

PURPOSEFUL VACATIONS

riods, and followed an 800-calorie diet. Three breaks for massages and hot tubs eased this stringent regimen, which ended at 9:30 P.M. after a class on health and nutrition.

Those educational sessions proved the most beneficial part of the program, which the Maxwells followed for ten days. Vivid videotapes showed how fatty foods build up plaque in blood vessels. "I won't eat doughnuts and red meat now because I am afraid of what they will do to me," says Maxwell. He also discovered how to relieve stress through meditation. "I now break at eleven o'clock for 15 minutes. That's my time and nobody can have it." Twelve weeks after entering the program, Maxwell had lost 50 pounds and was playing squash three nights a week. "My wife and I hugged on the golf course one day, because after ten years of living with our weight out of control, we finally had it under control." The La Costa program costs $3,200 per person for a minimum of seven nights in a double room. Maxwell urges a longer stay to adjust to new habits.

The Pritikin Longevity Centers in California and Pennsylvania adhere strictly to the legacy of Nathan Pritikin, who believed that diet and exercise could control or prevent stress and many medical problems, from hypertension to diabetes and heart disease, without medication. (He took his own life at age 70 in 1985 when leukemia hospitalized him.) The Pritikin diet includes very little fat, moderate animal protein, no sugar or salt additives, no alcohol or caffeine, and lots of complex carbohydrates (whole grains, vegetables, and fruit). The Pritikin Centers in California and in Pennsylvania are among the least luxurious but most expensive. A 26-day stay for persons with difficult health problems costs $8,308; and 13 days, for people with mild health and weight concerns, cost $4,805. A Pritikin franchise operates a similar program in Miami Beach.

Some Pritikin clients find that stringent diet and exercise dramatically lower artery-clogging cholesterol and triglycerides. In 26 days at the Pennsylvania center in Downingtown in March of 1984, Robert Gintel, 57, chairman of Gintel Equity Management, a Greenwich, Connecticut, mutual fund firm, cut his weight from 252 to 232 pounds. His cholesterol count went from an unhealthy 253 to 193, considered good for Americans over 30. After that visit, Gintel went back for a 13-day refresher course, and eventually dropped to 207 — but later went to 230 again, despite visits to various spas.

Pritikin is not for everyone. David Stafford, 41, a sales vice president of Norwegian Caribbean Lines in Miami, completed the 26-day program at age 34 and found the diet too restrictive. By 1983 he weighed 365 pounds and was diabetic. His boss sent him to Duke Diet and Fitness Center, associated with the university's medical center, in Durham, North Carolina. There is a $600 initial medical fee; the rest of the program, including 800-calorie-a-day meals but not a room, costs $2,000 for two weeks, $2,350 for four weeks. Guests arrange for their own rooms, and

are asked to come alone, at least for the first week, so that they can concentrate on committing themselves to gradual behavioral modification without distractions. Stafford lost 30 pounds in five weeks. On his own he has twice returned to Duke for two-week stays, when he got down to 285 pounds. He has followed the regimen, continued to lose, and his diabetes is under control. "I am surprised at their high success ratio," he says. "I cannot say enough nice things about those folks."

Instead of changing home habits, some executives simply get into the spa habit. Harold Honickman, 53, chairman of Pepsi-Cola Bottling and National Brand Beverages Ltd., goes with his wife, Lynne, from New York to Palm-Aire, a luxurious 1,500-acre resort and spa at Pompano Beach, Florida, twice a year. In nine days, six-footer Honickman drops from over 200 to under 190 pounds by means of aerobic exercises and a diet of 800 or fewer calories a day. At Palm-Aire, muscles are eased by herbal wraps, whirlpool baths, and massages — amenities neither offered nor recommended by Pritikin Centers. Honickman, who claims that business entertaining precludes sticking to a diet, says: "When the jackets feel tight and the pants won't button, I know it's time to go back to Palm-Aire." The cost: $540 a day per couple.

Some executives use spas as retreats. Robert M. Topol, 60, executive vice president of Shearson Lehman Brothers in New York City, visited the small, serene Golden Door, in Escondido, California, 30 times between 1975 and 1985, and kept on going. Before he started going, he recalls, "I ate a lot, drank too much, and worried." Each day at the Golden Door, modeled on a Japanese inn, begins with a pre-breakfast hike up a small mountain. On his first visit, Topol could not make it to the top until the fifth day. When he finally got there, he says, "I had a feeling of physical and emotional well-being, pleasure with myself that I never want to lose. Now the Door does more for my head than my body." The cost: $3,500 a week for a single room. There are no doubles.

FOR FURTHER INFORMATION

Aerobics Program for Total Well-Being, 12230 Preston Rd., Dallas, TX 75230; (800)-527-0362 or (214)-239-7223.

La Costa Hotel & Spa, Costa del Mar Rd., Carlsbad, CA 92008; (800)-854-6564 or (619)-438-9111.

Duke Diet and Fitness Center, 804 West Trinity Ave., Durham, NC 27701; (919)-684-6331.

The Golden Door, P.O. Box 1567, Escondido, CA 92025; (619)-744-5777.

Hilton Head Health Institute, P.O. Box 7138, Hilton Head Island, SC 29938-1910; (803)-785-7292.

Pritikin Longevity Center, 1920 Ocean Front Walk, Santa Monica, CA 90405; (800)-421-9911 or (213)-450-5433; in Downingtown, PA: (800)-344-8243 or (215)-873-0123.

The Spa at Palm-Aire, Pompano Beach, FL 33060; (800)-327-4960; from Canada or Florida, call collect (305)-972-3300. ∎

PART TWO

SPORTS AND GAMES

FOR FITNESS AND FUN

In the Competitive Swim

■ A paragon among sports for fitness and fun, swimming can keep a body buoyant for life. Add the zest of competition, with lap after lap of training, and you've got extra incentive for vigorous workouts. United States Masters Swimming Inc., a nonprofit organization of 20,000 members, holds regional and national meets. Men and women from 25 to 90 don goggles and dash down lanes. More than half had never raced before joining one of the 350 USMS clubs. But a third are coaches or are otherwise professionally involved with swimming, and all compete in the same five-year-age groups. The YMCA offers a similar program sanctioned by USMS.

"Swimming is a lifelong fitness program that's very uplifting, and the best exercise you can get," says Stephanie A. Walsh, 36, who coached at Harvard for five years. She is a certified life underwriter with Walsh Associates, a family-owned insurance firm in Wayne, Pennsylvania, and mother of two teenage sons. At the USMS 1985 short (25-yard) course and long (50-yard) course national championships, she finished first in five of her six events and repeated the performance in an international competition. Four younger Walsh sisters have also made a big splash in USMS and other contests.

Swimming strokes right past running and bicycling in working nearly every muscle, without the overheating and weight-bearing stress on the joints that often mar those sports. "It's like returning to the womb. You don't have to worry about the traumas of contact with other surfaces," explains David L. Costill, 50, director of the human performance laboratory at Ball State University in Muncie, Indiana. An injury diverted Costill's own athletic career from longtime runner to masters swimmer. Still, competitive swimmers are not immune to sprains and strains of shoulders and knees that come from moving wrong or training too hard.

Since you exercise lying down, supported by water, swimming usually takes more time than cycling or running to burn up calories and to give heart and lungs an aerobic (oxygen-demanding) workout. That means raising the heartbeat to within 60% to 75% of capacity and holding it there for 20 minutes. Aerobic fitness requires working out at least three times a week. Once swimmers stop training, Costill's research shows, they lose most of their conditioning within six to eight weeks, sooner than runners, because they don't use their upper bodies much in daily living.

Lots of former varsity athletes get turned on by the chance to compete again. W. R. "Tim" Timken Jr., 48, chairman of Timken Co., in Canton, Ohio, had swum on Stanford's outstanding team. But after graduation, "nobody invited you over for a race in the backyard," he lamented. Timken played a little tennis and golf while rising through the ranks of the steel-bearings company founded by his great-grandfather. But "essentially I just degenerated at my desk," he admitted, until a big new pool

W. R. Timken Jr. practices the butterfly for the masters championships.

SPORTS AND GAMES

was opened in his home town. Timken, then 36, helped organize a masters team, and members followed a rigorous training program laid out by their coach: an hour of daily stretching, for flexibility, and weight lifting, to strengthen muscles, plus an hour of timed laps in the pool several days a week. Timken lost 25 pounds, and in his first USMS national championships placed among the top ten in that most demanding stroke, the butterfly. Though the pressures of business and public service have forced Timken to cut back on training, he competes when and where he can.

In San Francisco, where duties as a Stanford University trustee frequently take him, Timken swims at the Olympic Club. He led the club's six-man relay team across the English Channel in 1981. It set a record for swimmers over 40, according to the Channel Swimming Association, completing the crossing in nine hours, 20 minutes. And in 1984 in a world masters competition in New Zealand, the Olympic Club team took two firsts, and Timken's butterfly earned him a second and a third.

Experts debate whether swimming, and other regular aerobic exercise, can delay aging. Medical research has established that after the age of 25 there is an average annual decline of 1% in physical work capacity, or the heart's ability to pump and distribute oxygen-loaded blood to muscles and tissues. But a few studies show that habitual exercise may affect this decline. In research on both swimmers and runners active for over 20 years, Costill and colleagues have found the decay of aging to be very small through the years of the 50s. He believes that "if one trains fairly regularly between the ages of 20 and 50, there's a fairly small drop in capacity."

In fact, some college stars of the 1960s are outdoing themselves in the 1980s. The 1968 National Collegiate Athletic Association champion in the butterfly was Fred Schlicher, then a senior at Southern Methodist University in Dallas. In 1985 Schlicher, 37, a packager of oil and gas investment properties in Roswell, New Mexico, beat his NCAA time, swimming the 200-yard butterfly in 1:53.88. "That was a real thrill," admits Schlicher, who won six USMS events in the 1985 short- and long-course nationals. Wising up to "Fast Fred," many avoid the events he has entered.

Lucy Johnson, 38, a vice president of Los Angeles' Security Pacific National Bank, and a competitor since age 9, has also outdone herself by winning the long-course 50-meter freestyle event in 1985 with her best time ever. As a banker she gets in intensive one-hour evening workouts only three times a week. But, she says, "when I was swimming 26 hours a week as a kid, I just thought of them as a very lengthy, tiring process I simply sought to survive. Now I have such limited time that I'm much more willing to work very, very hard for that hour I'm in the water." Even on business trips, masters competitors manage to train because friends they make at the nationals let them know where to find the good pools.

FOR FURTHER INFORMATION

National YMCA Aquatics Program, Oakbrook Square, 6083-A Oakbrook Parkway, Norcross, GA 30093; (404)-662-5172.

United States Masters Swimming Inc.; annual membership fee, $15, includes the magazine *Swim*, which publishes results of national meets; 5 Piggott Lane, Avon, CT 01001; (203)-677-9464.

PUBLICATIONS

The Complete Book of Swimming by James Counsilman (New York: Atheneum, 1977), $5.95.

The Wet Workout by Jane Katz (New York: Facts on File, 1985), $8.95. ∎

Business Cyclists

∎ Cycling has broken away in the 1980s, wheeling up 75 million Americans, 12 million of them adults who hopped on bikes at least once a week in 1985. Commuting, touring, or training to race, regular riders bank fitness as they pump away. A first-rate aerobic exercise, vigorous, rhythmic pedaling forces the heart and lungs to supply oxygen to leg and thigh muscles over a sustained period, building up the body's capacity to use oxygen. And a cyclist's feet pushing pedals pass on much less stress to bones and joints than a runner's feet pounding the ground.

Thomas "Thom" Weisel, 44, the senior partner in San Francisco's Montgomery Securities, and an intense competitor in half a dozen sports, shifted from running to cycling to train for downhill ski racing. President of the U.S. Ski Team and an ex-Stanford football player, he discovered at 41 that his knees had worn out and he was constantly injuring himself. Pedaling the steep rises near his Marin County, California, home with his wife, Vicki, 27, he finds "it's beautiful being able to go 40 to 50 miles a day over different kinds of countryside instead of the five to eight miles of a run-is-a-run-is-a-run." And he pedals short, high-speed bursts for indoor-track racing with the Berkeley Bicycling Club. "I don't have a lot of time, so whenever I get on a bike I've got to make it count," says Weisel. "You can do hard workout on top of hard workout, and maybe your stamina can't take it, but your skeletal structure can, and that's a major plus, especially the older that people get."

Stamina has improved with age for Robert S. Holdsworth, 64, a vice president in W.R. Grace's Pacific Container Division in Lexington, Massachusetts. He bought his first bike at age 56 to commute seven miles each way to work during the 1979 gas shortage, and still does it when roads aren't icy. In 1983 he began road racing with Boston's Northeastern Bicycling Club, and finished the 1985 season as club champion in the Grand Masters (ages 59 to 65) division. "I can do all kinds of things physically that I could not do even as a much younger man," says Holdsworth, who has whittled his 6-foot, 4-inch frame from 200

FOR FITNESS AND FUN

down to 165 pounds. He credits cycling with putting him in shape to withstand the rigors of foreign business travel. The only problem is that he can't pack up his wheels and take them along.

Bicycling clubs, for nominal dues and entry fees, organize events and offer the convenience, discipline, and motivation of camaraderie in regular training rides. Some 750 racing clubs are affiliated with the U.S. Cycling Federation Inc., the governing body for indoor, or velodrome, racing and road racing. Though still a tiny percentage of all cyclists, racers have been gaining fast. The Boston Road Club, formed in 1981 by 30 novice racers, had spun to 300 members in 1985. The new popularity of triathlons, which combine races in swimming, running, and cycling, has geared up wheelmen. And so has the success of U.S. racers in the 1984 Olympics and other international contests. The USCF not only picks the national teams, but sanctions over 1,000 races annually from April to October for cyclists in four categories of ability. Business cyclists rarely have time to train enough to move into categories 1 and 2, but USCF offers spring and fall training camps for racers in categories 3 and 4 as well. Beginning road racers start with the "criterium," a contest on a one- to three-kilometer course with no traffic. Then they go to time trials of ten to 40 kilometers over trafficked roads. Stage races combine a criterium, time trial, and another road race.

Christopher J. Mailing, 30, a collections officer at Chase Manhattan Bank's credit-card division in Garden City, New York, wheels 6,000 miles a year with three clubs. To race, Mailing spins with the Century Road Club Association, rising before sunup for training rides in Forest Park, Queens, three times a week. He also keeps in gear with his home town of Detroit's century-old Wolverine Sports Club, which has produced 61 U.S. biking champions. Mailing is a regular at the Wolverine's cycling camp each February at a Florida YMCA near Orlando. The $175 weekly fee includes coaching, bed, and board. For touring and long-distance training, Chris Mailing pedals with the New York Cycle Club. Touring and pleasure-riding clubs, 500 strong, make up the Baltimore-based network long known as the League of American Wheelman.

Awareness of the risks in cycling can help prevent injuries. To avoid overtaxing the cardiovascular system, novices are advised to increase the length and speed of workouts gradually. Racing cyclists especially may develop knee problems by using the wrong gears, or by positioning the saddle at the wrong height. All cyclists risk crashing, even on an indoor track. Injuries are usually no more serious than abrasions, but concussions and fractures are common. In June of 1985 a red-light-running auto left Chris Mailing with a broken elbow. Collisions with motor vehicles account for only around 10% of all cycling accidents, according to the Bicycle Federation of America in Washington, D.C. But motor vehicles are involved in most of the serious cycling injuries that require medical treatment, one million in 1984, and in 95% of all biking fatalities, three-quarters of which result from head injuries.

Hence a helmet heads the list of proper apparel for the cyclist, at $35 to $75. Other typical costs: touring shoes, $30 to $50; racing leather footwear with cleats, $50 to $90. Shorts, of three-quarter length, form-fitting, and lined with chamois to prevent chafing, start at $25.

A properly fitted bicycle is essential, and varies according to the cyclist's chosen activity. For riding in flat country, a general-purpose English-style bike with three gears costs from $175 to $400. A touring bicycle for easy pedaling uphill, with loaded packs, may have 15 to 19 gears and costs from $400 to $2,000. A racing bike, with skinny saddle and thin-rimmed wheels set closer together than on others, has ten to 12 gears. Racing bikes are custom-fitted to leg length and torso, and are often assembled from French and Italian frames and selected parts. They cost from $550 to $2,500. Holdsworth, the Grand Masters club champion in Boston, owns two made-to-measure racing bikes, one costing $2,300. In his stable, Thom Weisel, the San Francisco financier, keeps ten bikes. But Chris Mailing manages with one 14-speed Raleigh he put together in 1981 for $1,000.

FOR FURTHER INFORMATION

League of American Wheelmen; membership, $22 a year, includes *Bicycle USA* magazine, nine times a year, including the annual *Bicycle USA Almanac,* with a directory of touring clubs and a "TourFinder" issue; Suite 209, 6707 Whitestone Rd., Baltimore, MD 21207; (301)-944-3399.

United States Cycling Federation; membership, $32 a year, includes *Cycling USA* magazine (racing), monthly; 1750 E. Boulder St., Colorado Springs, CO 80909; (303)-578-4581.

PUBLICATIONS

Backcountry Publications issues a series of touring guidebooks for several northeastern states and the New York City area, priced from $6.95 to $8.95; P.O. Box 175C, Woodstock, VT 05091-0175; (802)-457-1049.

Beginning Bicycle Racing by Fred Matheny (Brattleboro, VT: Velo-News, 1987), $14.95.

Bicycling, ten issues a year, $15.97; Rodale Press, 33 E. Minor St., Emmaus, PA 18098; (800)-441-7761 or (215)-967-5171.

The Complete Bicycle Fitness Book by James C. McCullagh (New York: Warner Books, 1984), $8.95.

Effective Cycling by John Forester (Cambridge, MA: MIT Press, 1984), $15.

Velo-news (racing), 18 issues a year, $18; Box 1257, Brattleboro, VT 05301; (802)-254-2305. ∎

Running: Marathons and Less

∎ With the evening sun of August glinting off Lake Michigan, 6,500 runners from 400 companies raced out of Chicago's Grant Park in the 1985 Manufacturers Hanover

SPORTS AND GAMES

Corporate Challenge. This series of 3.5-mile races sponsored by the New York City bank in cities from San Francisco to London has drawn nearly 70,000 competitors from 4,000 companies annually. Winning teams get trips to New York for a championship race in November.

Robert Barocci, chairman of McConnahghy Barocci Brown, a Chicago ad agency, began running at 40 when a company team drafted him for a race. At 43 he won the male chief executives' section of that Corporate Challenge in Chicago. In New York another 43-year-old advertising executive, racing in a July 1986 Corporate Challenge, died of a heart attack.

As legions of corporate runners pound purposefully across America, new questions arise about the benefits and risks in running and other strenuous exercise. Experts are reconsidering the amount needed for fitness — the body's ability to use oxygen in physical activity.

Scientists still debate whether vigorous exercise can prolong life. Dr. Ralph S. Paffenbarger, 63, a professor at Stanford University's medical school, and a long-distance runner, argues that it does. He has followed the histories of 16,936 men who entered Harvard from 1916 through 1950. In 1984 he reported that the death rate from cardiovascular disease was almost twice as high among sedentary men as among those who burned up 2,000 or more calories a week, equivalent to briskly walking 20 miles. His further study revealed that death rates from all causes were one-fourth lower among those who had exercised than among those who had not. However, he found the benefits of exercise peak at the burning of 3,500 calories a week, equal to 20 miles of running plus a couple hours of singles tennis.

The conundrum is that people with and without cardiovascular disease can benefit from exercise, but during vigorous exercise they are at risk. A study completed in 1981 by Dr. David Siscovick, then 30, of the University of North Carolina medical school in Chapel Hill, examined the cases of 133 apparently healthy Seattle men with no known history of cardiovascular disease. All had experienced cardiac arrest, nine while exercising. Reviewing the habits of these men, Siscovick calculated that for both sedentary and active victims the risk of cardiac arrest went up during vigorous exercise, but for regular exercisers the overall risk was only 40% that of sedentary men.

To evaluate an individual's tolerance for exercise, physicians generally recommend that persons over 35 who embark on a strenuous program should first have a medical checkup. But passing the standard stress test on a treadmill or stationary bicycle does not guarantee against accident; it is only one of several barometers. Family medical history and personal habits are also important indicators of risk.

Strong advocates of aerobic exercise have been reducing their prescriptions. Dr. Kenneth H. Cooper, 55, founder of the Aerobics Center in Dallas, helped launch the fitness boom in a 1968 book that called for running 20 miles a week, or the equivalent in other aerobic activity. But his 1985 book, *Running Without Fear*, written after the death, while jogging, of running guru James Fixx, suggests that merely walking three miles in 45 minutes five times a week suffices.

William L. Haskell, 49, director of the Center for Research and Disease Prevention at Stanford University School of Medicine, and a past president of the American College of Sports Medicine, told the 1985 ACSM convention that its standards for keeping fit may be unnecessarily high. Its widely accepted prescription called for 15 to 60 minutes of continuous large-muscle activity three to five days a week, raising the pulse rate within 60% to 90% of the heart's maximum rate, or capacity to use oxygen. Haskell concluded that if the habitually sedentary exercise at a slower pace, they can still significantly increase aerobic capacity.

An estimated seven million Americans were running in 1986, though only about 10% were racing. As a path to fitness, or a way to compete, running clearly leads in convenience and economy. It has social appeal, too. At 38, Mary Gordon, a Manhattan bank vice president, entered her first Boston Marathon. It was the fourth for a New York banker unknown to her, Donald M. Roberts, then 42. Both soon appeared in a *Fortune* article on executive marathoners. Months later, Roberts, who had admired Miss Gordon's picture, introduced himself. They entered

In Manhattan's Central Park stockbroker Mary Gordon Roberts trains regularly.

FOR FITNESS AND FUN

the next Beantown classic together and a June wedding followed. Through job changes — Gordon to Kidder Peabody and Roberts to executive vice president at United States Trust Co. — as well as parenthood, both kept running, but on separate courses.

As a working mother of their sons, 4 and 6, Mary Roberts puts in five relaxed miles a day, but does not train with her husband or race. "I feel a lot of pressure just now and I'm not looking for any more. I run to have an outlet," she says. Women, more and more of whom began running in the last decade, during their child-bearing years are less subject to cardiovascular problems than men. But scientists believe that loss of body fat and hormonal imbalances attributable to vigorous exercise cause interruption of the female reproductive cycle. Already 40 when she considered pregnancy, Mary Roberts stopped running upon her doctor's advice for several months before and after each birth. Some physicians regard running as safe for young expectant mothers.

Disruptions in women's reproductive cycles, usually reversible when exercise is reduced, were long viewed as benign. But in 1984 Barbara L. Drinkwater, 57, a research scientist at the Pacific Medical Center in Seattle, reported reduced bone density in 14 non-menstruating women, ages 18 to 35, who ran over 20 miles a week. The mineral content of their vertebrae was equivalent to that of 51-year-old women with low levels of estrogen.

Unlike his wife, Don Roberts sticks with the hard core who run for more than fitness. He enters a couple of marathons a year. For each he trains 70 miles per week, and 50 off-season, with an eight-minute mile. At 48 he achieved his best time, 2:55:09, in an autumn marathon in Massachusetts. "My ambition is to hang on as long as possible," he said, just past his 50th birthday.

The 26.2-mile marathon is a once-in-a-lifetime event for some executives. Bob Barocci, that Chicago advertising executive who had won a Corporate Challenge event, entered the 1985 New York City Marathon. At lunch and on weekends he trained 75 miles a week, with a coach's help. But caught up in the excitement of the Big Apple, he ran ahead of his intended pace, a common error. Extra tired, he fell behind, and finished over his target time of three hours, in 3:05:00. "It's a spectacular sporting event, with the skyline, and fireboats spouting," he says. "But I won't try another marathon. The training takes too much time."

Many racers apparently agree. Marathons in the U.S. slowed from 353 in 1981 to only 200 scheduled in 1986. Meanwhile shorter races have picked up the pace. Five-kilometer (3.11 miles) events more than doubled, from 12,000 in 1984 to 29,000 in 1985. Men and women over 30 can enter local and national masters races from five kilometers to marathons recognized by The Athletics Congress (TAC), the national governing body for track and field events.

A gamut of ailments threatens runners, and other athletes, who overdo or fail to train properly. Dr. James Nicholas, 65, founder and director of the Nicholas Institute of Sports Medicine and Athletic Trauma at New York City's Lenox Hill Hospital, warns that people over 35 are especially vulnerable. Muscular strength and flexibility decline with age, while blood pressure and pulse usually rise, so a person tires more easily.

Risk of acute injuries, such as sprained joints, strained muscles, torn cartilage, and ruptured tendons, can be reduced. Sports medicine experts recommend stretching for five to 15 minutes before and after running to make muscles and tendons more flexible. Warm-up and cool-down periods of slow-motion running should follow. Training with weights can strengthen muscles.

Runners with knee and low-back pain are often referred to podiatrists. When a foot hits the ground, it rolls from outside the heel to inside the toe; flat feet do this to an extreme, causing the lower leg to twist inward, damaging tendons. A pair of orthotics, soft plastic supports made from a cast of the foot and worn in shoes to prevent feet from excessive turning, can solve some knee problems.

Knees, the most frequently injured body part, may require surgery. But instead of opening a knee to remove torn cartilage, today's orthopedic surgeon can often insert via tiny incisions an arthroscope, a telescope no wider than a straw, with a tiny light. Watching what the scope sees projected on a video screen, he makes microsurgical repairs. This method shortens the patient's recovery from months to weeks. Attorney William Rainey, 40, vice president of Southwest Forest Industries in Phoenix, had arthroscopies in both knees when he lived in Seattle, and was running one week after each operation. Four years later he had had no more trouble, but had stopped racing and cut his distance.

"Overuse" accounts for most maladies, such as Achilles tendinitis, an inflammation, or stress fractures, those tiny cracks in the bone that come from wear and tear. "If you run more than three to five miles a day, faster than three miles in 30 minutes, and total more than 15 miles a week," says Dr. Kenneth Cooper, "the chances for injury increase exponentially." C. Michael Jacobi, 44, marketing and sales vice president of Timex Corp. in Middlebury, Connecticut, modified his program after marathon training gave him a knee problem. Three or four times a week he starts a four-mile route in the hills with a ¾-mile brisk walk, speeds up for a two-mile run, and ends with a walk.

Despite inevitable afflictions, some elite runners go out for ultra distances. After finishing over 70 races of marathon length and more, including three triathlons (see page 53), and winning numerous 50-mile runs, Carol La Plant, 39, an attorney with Heller Ehrman in San Francisco, succumbed to stress fractures in both legs and ruptured disks in her lower back, and suffered nerve damage. But one month after back surgery, she was running a few miles

SPORTS AND GAMES

a day. She re-entered the annual Western States 100-mile run, a mountainous course from Squaw Valley to Auburn, which she had completed in fourth place in 1985, in 22 hours and five minutes. In 1986 she again finished in under 24 hours, winning another massive sterling-silver belt buckle, engraved with her name and the figure of Hermes. "I'm intensely competitive in both the sports and the professional sides of my life," she says, "and could not be happy doing one without the other."

FOR FURTHER INFORMATION

The Aerobics Center, 12200 Preston Rd., Dallas, TX 75230; (214)-239-7223.
The Athletics Congress/USA (TAC), Suite 140, 200 S. Capitol Ave., Indianapolis, IN 46225; (317)-638-9155.
Manufacturers Hanover Corporate Challenge, Special Events, 140 E. 45th St., New York, NY 10017; (212)-808-8505.
Road Runners Club of America, Henley Gibble, President; 8208 E. Boulevard Dr., Alexandria, VA 22308; (703)-768-0545.

PUBLICATIONS

The Complete Sportsmedicine Book for Women by Mona Shangold, M.D., and Gabe Mirkin, M.D. (New York: Simon & Schuster, 1985), $9.95.
The Exercise Myth by Henry A. Solomon, M.D. (New York: Bantam, 1986), $2.95.
Fitness on the Road: Where to Stay to Stay Fit by John Winsor (Tucson: HP Books, 1986), $7.95.
National Masters News, monthly, $18.75 a year; NMN, P.O. Box 5185, Pasadena, CA 91107; (818)-577-7233.
Runner's Handbook by Bob Glover and Jack Shepherd (New York: Penguin, 1985), $7.95.
Runner's World, monthly, $19.95 a year; Rodale Press, 33 E. Minor St., Emmaus, PA 18098; (800)-441-7761 or (215)-967-5171
Running Without Fear by Kenneth H. Cooper, M.D. (New York: M. Evans & Co., 1985), $12.95.
The Self-Coached Runner by Allan Lawrence and Mark Scheid (Boston: Little, Brown, 1984), $7.70.
The Self-Coached Runner II by Allan Lawrence and Mark Scheid (Boston: Little, Brown, 1987), $9.95.
The Sportsmedicine Book by Gabe Mirkin, M.D., and Marshall Hoffman (Boston: Little, Brown, 1978), $12.45.
Stretching by Bob Anderson (New York: Random House, 1980), $8.95.
TAC Stats (statistics on racing), 7745 S.W. 138 Terrace, Miami, FL 33158; (305)-255-1405.

Triathlons for Ultimate Athletes

■ At 7:30 A.M. one August Saturday in Chicago, 2,400 athletes plunged into chilly Lake Michigan and thrashed nearly a mile, past the Adler Planetarium. Dashing ashore, they hopped on bikes to ride almost 25 miles along Lake Shore Drive. With a ten-kilometer (6.2 miles) run back to the Planetarium, they topped off the morning, and the world's biggest triathlon. Chicago's is one of 12 in the annual Bud Light U.S. Triathlon Series of regional events. "I did better than I expected," said Sarah Linsley, 28, an attorney with the Chicago law firm of Wilson & McIlvaine, after the triple challenge in 1985, her first triathlon. A runner good enough to have been asked to the U.S. Olympic marathon trials, she had never before swum so far.

Triathlons, those back-to-back tests of endurance and speed, have picked up popularity in the 1980s as fast as marathons did in the Seventies. In 1986 over 1,500 triathlons, treble the number in 1983, were on the calendar in places as far apart as Anchorage and Fort Lauderdale. Major events, listed in *Triathlon Today* and *Triathlete* magazines, draw over a half-million entrants each year. In colder climes, canoeing or cross-country skiing may replace the swim, or for variety, sailboarding. Distances stretch from a beginner's "tin man" of, say, a half-mile swim, a six-mile bike ride, and a three-mile run, to the gargantuan laps of Hawaii's Ironman Triathlon World Championship: a staggering 2.4-mile swim, 112-mile bike ride, and 26.2-mile marathon.

Why are so many business people pushing themselves into the rigorous triple training regimens that triathlons require? Advertising executive Phil Slott, 44, chairman of BBDO Ltd. in London, who has been running since high school, and entered half a dozen tin-man triathlons before leaving New York, believes "this kind of survival fitness event makes you your own hero. And opportunity for heroism is sorely lacking in modern-day life."

It all started over a few beers — *of course,* sedentary types might aver — after a relay-race awards ceremony in Waikiki, where Navy Commander John Collins challenged the assemblage to compete on a single day in a combination of Oahu's three endurance events and settle

After swimming 1.5 miles, banker G. H. "Denny" Denniston and teacher Denise Hannon get a quick rinse before pushing off on a 25-mile bike ride and ten-mile run in Long Island's Mighty Hamptons Triathlon.

FOR FITNESS AND FUN

the question of who were most fit: runners, bikers, or swimmers. In 1978, 15 men took up the challenge — including Collins (he came in ninth).

The Ironman later moved to the big island of Hawaii, in October, to allow summer for training, and at full moon, to light Kona's black lava fields for runners still on the course after dark. At 5 A.M. entrants start assembling along the Kailua-Kona pier, splash off en masse at 7, and by midnight must finish the entire 140.6 miles, through constant wind, intense heat, and an uphill bike route. In the 1986 event, Dave Scott, 32, a professional triathlete and winner of five Ironman races, set a new record of 8 hours, 28 minutes, and 37 seconds.

As the Super Bowl of triathlons, the Ironman attracts so many applicants that getting one of the 1,250 places is about as complex as getting into graduate school, complete with a $125 fee, refundable to those turned down. Placing well in certain other triathlons, or finishing a previous Ironman within a time limit, qualifies 700 entrants for the "gruelathon," as one fitness professional describes it. To keep the Ironman accessible to new competitors, places are reserved for foreigners and for 150 entrants chosen by lottery. Crazies? Not entirely. In 1985 chief executive officers or business owners accounted for 30% of the entrants. Over a quarter of the male competitors were between 30 and 39.

Finding time to train is the biggest challenge for executives. Richard W. Decker Jr., senior vice president of First Interstate Bank of California in Los Angeles, hit the luck of the Ironman draw at 37 in 1983 and in 1984. In the second year he cut his finishing time by one hour to about 14. It helps to have a leg up in one of the sports. Decker grew up on a swim team. In his 30s he ran 15 marathons, and finished a dozen endurance events on horseback.

With goal setting, time management, and the ability to tolerate stress, Decker fit in at least six months of training for each Ironman, even while working 12-hour days. Rising at 3:30 A.M. weekdays, he ran with a group up to ten miles from 4 to 5:30, getting to work by 7. At lunch he swam a mile at an athletic club twice a week. Three nights a week, one of them with a coach, he biked in Griffith Park, 30 to 40 miles in two hours, since the 114-mile ride is such a long segment of the Ironman and Decker's weakest sport. Saturday mornings he rode from Santa Monica to Ventura and back, 120 miles in six or seven hours. Saturday afternoons he swam two miles from Manhattan Beach to Hermosa. Sunday mornings he ran 23 miles around Palos Verdes. Sunday afternoons he napped.

"The Ironman is not something you do for the rest of your life," says Decker. "But it forces you to become organized. What you learn in endurance events can improve your business and personal life. A family can be part of the team, rather than mere spectators, on the outside looking in." Decker's wife, Suzanne, a psychologist, has a positive attitude toward these events.

Training for three sports instead of one tunes the body from head to toe, and relieves the monotony and stress of working the same set of muscles day after day. Moreover, a phenomenon known as cross-training sets in, whereby exercising one set of muscles strengthens others. When the opposite occurs, and fatigue hits all three sets at once, triathletes call it "cross-bonk."

Traveling on business an average of three days a week gives New Yorker Richard L. Harris Jr., a Morgan Stanley principal in public finance and a three-time Ironman competitor, an extra training challenge. He stays at hotels with pools and tethers himself to the ladder, to maintain an uninterrupted rhythm swimming in place. With clients he dines lightly so that afterward he can run. "I find I am more effective in my job when I train," he says. "I have less time overall, so I am more efficient." He keeps entering triathlons because "I can see significant improvement and the challenge of training gives me something to focus on." In 1985, at 40, he entered a London-to-Paris triathlon as a member of a four-man relay team that ran to the Channel on Thursday, swam from Dover to Calais on Friday, and biked into Paris on Saturday.

Women account for 17% of Ironman athletes. San Francisco attorney Carol La Plant (see "Running," page 51), who entered with her husband, Pierre, a biophysicist, finished among the top ten Ironwomen in 1981 at age 34, and was invited back in 1982 and 1983. She found a certain comic relief in the helter-skelter. "When you're ripping off one set of clothes in the locker room and pulling on another," she says, "there's a kind of silly madness."

After the frustration of having her job eliminated, Mary Quinn, daughter of a former governor of Hawaii and a strong swimmer, spent eight months of her 27th year training full time for the 1984 Ironman. In the 116-degree heat reflected off the lava fields, she struggled to finish the run and came in 32nd out of 250 women. She noted afterward, "In so many phases of life you don't have control. On my job it had been everybody else's control. But in my training I held complete control." Without the self-confidence she gained from the Ironman, she doubts she would have come to look for work in New York, where she became a research assistant in oil equities at Morgan Stanley.

The 1985 winner of the women's division, Joanne Ernst, 27, a 1981 Phi Beta Kappa graduate of Stanford, had turned down admission to both Harvard and Stanford business schools so she could compete in her peak years. In five years after college she estimated she earned as much in triathlon winnings, taking firsts in 15 out of 30, as she would have had she gone to business school.

FOR FURTHER INFORMATION

Triathlon Federation USA; membership, $15 a year, includes ten issues of *Triathlon Today;* P.O. Box 1963, Davis, CA 95617-1963; (916)-757-2831.

SPORTS AND GAMES

Bud Light U.S. Triathlon Series, P.O. Box 886, Solana Beach, CA 92075; (619)-436-5050.

Ironman Triathlon World Championship, Suite 815, 1100 Ward Ave., Honolulu, HI 96814; (808)-528-2050.

PUBLICATIONS

Cross-Training by Katherine Vaz (New York: Avon, 1984), $9.95.

Dave Scott's Triathlon Training (New York: Simon & Schuster, 1986), $9.95.

Triathlete magazine, monthly, $19.95 a year; 1127 Hamilton St., Allentown, PA 18102; (800)-441-1666 or (215)-821-6864.

The Triathlon Training and Racing Book by Sally Edwards (Chicago: Contemporary Books, 1985), $8.95.

Ultrasport magazine, bimonthly, $13.50 a year; P.O. Box 5262, Boulder, CO 80322. ■

Soccer: The World's Most Popular Sport

■ Soccer had passed the century mark and scored as the world's most popular sport before American converts began getting their kicks out of this international brand of football in the late 1960s. By the 1980s the game was drawing more than 30 million registered and countless unregistered players around the globe, and 1.5 million Americans had turned it into this country's fastest-growing team sport.

The "laws," or rules, of soccer prohibit the use of hands or arms for playing the ball or blocking an opponent, and so distinguish the game from its rougher offspring, rugby and American football. In 1863 the six English public schools that agreed on those laws formed an association, and "Assoc. Football" ("soccer" for short) circled the globe.

Robert Genetski, 44, chief economist and senior vice president of Chicago's Harris Bank, and his family have added their own numbers to the sport's vigorous U.S. growth. In a men's summer league he kicks and runs on Saturday afternoons; in fall and spring he coaches his youngest son's team twice a week; from October to April he plays in an indoor arena on three teams, changing position with the level of competition. On a squad composed of business and professional men over 30, he runs as a forward; with two older collegian sons, on what he calls a "cutthroat team," he moves back to defense; and on a coed team with his wife, Maureen, he plays mid-field.

Genetski discovered soccer in the late 1970s when his two older sons began playing in the park district program of suburban Wheaton, Illinois. Bored with simply running for fitness, he thought "soccer added a dimension and looked like more fun." One of the nation's leading monetary theorists, he finds soccer an ideal diversion. "You're concentrating on the game at the same time you're exerting yourself, so it is impossible to think about anything else," he says. "And once I've finished, I'm simply exhausted. I've absolutely no trouble sleeping, ever."

Competition demands neither the heft of football nor the height of basketball. A fit body, quick mind, coordination, and stamina to run turf at least the size of a football field for two 45-minute periods, substitutes excepted, are what a player needs. While the laws call for fielding 11 players on each side, it's possible to get a game together with only six per side. Except for shouldering, allowed only when the ball is within playing distance, direct body contact is against the laws.

The risk of injury is low, but no one is exempt, especially not one who plays as often and as hard as Genetski. In the coed Friday-night social league, competitive pride felled him and he tore ligaments in his knee. Major surgery for repairs laid him up for two months in 1983. A year of therapy and rehabilitation followed. And, on the advice of his sons, he adopted a muscle-strengthening regime of push-ups and weight lifting. Then, for some high-level excitement, he joined an all-star squad of coaches of youth teams in a challenge to the Chicago Sting, a pro team.

The professional teams that kicked off the game in the U.S. in 1967 have won few fans among spectators addicted to American football. But to promote the game, some pro teams helped finance neighborhood youth leagues and coaching clinics. So did the U.S. Youth Soccer Association, a division of the U.S. Soccer Federation, the amateur sport's governing body, and the American Youth Soccer Organization, an independent outfit. By 1985, 1.2 million players, ages 5 to 19, were registered. The game's low cost in manpower and gear by then had inspired colleges to field more soccer teams, 549, than football varsities, 510.

This explosion of zeal produced such a shortage of coaches that parents were pressed into service with the younger squads. Fathers of foreign birth or upbringing are more subject to the soccer-coaching draft than most, since many grew up with the game. Hendrik J. Hartong Jr., 47, chairman of Air Express International in Greenwich, Connecticut, had played 365 days a year in his native Holland before attending the University of Cincinnati and the Harvard Business School. After moving to Old Greenwich, Connecticut, in 1968, he was urged to start a boys' soccer program by a mother whose son had been cut from the community football team. "We started with 18 boys who didn't make the football team," recalls Hartong. That Old Greenwich community program grew to several hundred boys, ages 6 to 14. In 1978 Hartong started a second group, the Greenwich Soccer Club, that included his own three sons. And in 1984 he was persuaded to admit girls, a new experiment for him and some other fathers, because in Europe and Latin America girls don't play soccer. By 1986 that group included over 415 boys and 115 girls.

"The emphasis is on participation," says Hartong. "Every kid gets to play." For fees of less than $50 (which

FOR FITNESS AND FUN

provide a soccer shirt, a contribution for trophies, and insurance), plus purchase of soccer shoes, each child can play ten weekends from early September through November. The boys are distributed among 34 house-league teams, averaging 14 players per squad to compete among each other, and six travel teams, selected from the best players, to compete with other Connecticut teams.

"The strength of the club comes from the tremendous number of volunteers we have among all the parents," notes Hartong. When the youngsters register each year, they are asked to indicate on their forms whether their fathers are interested in helping out as coaches or referees, and whether their mothers will help in team administration.

A number of different groups share the organization of amateur soccer. The overall governing body of the sport, the U.S. Soccer Federation in Colorado Springs, is mainly concerned with developing national teams from the best players for international competition. Two divisions help organize recreational leagues in each state: the U.S. Senior Soccer Division for players 19 and over; and the U.S. Youth Soccer Association for youngsters from 5 to 19 years. The American Youth Soccer Organization, an independent group, organizes coaching and competition in 35 states. Many local communities organize their own unaffiliated leagues, as Hartong did in Connecticut, through their parks departments or other facilities.

Women's teams were growing faster than all others in the mid-1980s. The number registered with the U.S. Soccer Federation in 1985 totaled some 1,000, with about 20,000 players. In the states of Washington and Texas especially, women's soccer is booming. For some, soccer has opened up a new world of personal and professional development. In Dallas, Betsy Boockoff, 41, manager of product marketing at Docutel-Olivetti, a manufacturer of computerized bank cash machines, had never been interested in sports. But in 1976, when her daughters started to play soccer at ages 5 and 7, she came out to watch their 5:30 P.M. practices. Two weeks into the season, the regular coach left town on a business trip and turned the girls' team over to her. "We got a goal scored against us because I didn't know the rules," she recalls. Chagrined, she joined a women's team, and not only learned the game but loved it. "As a player I found that I could do something that is 100% for me, totally away from being a working person or a wife."

Betsy Boockoff's natural talent for taking the initiative and for organization soon got her elected team captain and she rose through the administrative hierarchy to become North Texas state commissioner for women's soccer in 1981. She credits her experience in the soccer world with enhancing her office capabilities and advancing her from a purely technical to a managerial role. "In the soccer community I have had to get involved and communicate, and have done well. That in turn has given me more confidence

to do the same thing in my job," she says. She continued to play Sunday afternoons with Cross-Fire, a team composed of women of all ages, including some mother-daughter combinations. "I'll keep on as long as it's fun," she says. "That's what counts now."

Indoor soccer, on a playing area smaller than an outdoor field, is another rapidly growing branch of the sport. It permits banking's soccer-fiend, Genetski, to play year-round in Chicago. "I happen to enjoy the indoor version of the game more than the outdoor," says Genetski of play in a Carol Stream, Illinois, arena. "It's faster, more interesting, and you get to play the ball a lot more. Quick-action plays are very similar to exciting hockey."

FOR FURTHER INFORMATION

United States Soccer Federation, 1750 E. Boulder St., Colorado Springs, CO 80909-5791; (303)-578-4678.

United States Senior Soccer Division, Suite 2107, Viscount Hotel, JFK International Airport, Jamaica, NY 11430; (718)-917-8484.

United States Youth Soccer Association, Inc., c/o Holiday Inns, Inc., P.O. Box 18406, Memphis, TN 38181-0406; (901)-363-0010.

American Youth Soccer Organization, P.O. Box 5045, 5403 W. 138th St., Hawthorne, CA 90251-5045; (213)-643-6455.

PUBLICATIONS

Soccer America, weekly, $33 a year; P.O. Box 23704, Oakland, CA 94623-0704; (415)-549-1414.

Sports Illustrated Soccer by Dan Herbst (New York: Harper & Row, 1984), $12.95. ■

Fitness for Your Kids

■ The fitness boom has bypassed America's kids. Most are fatter, many weaker and slower than they used to be, according to government surveys. While their parents work out in record numbers, half the nation's 26 million fifth- through 12th-graders probably do not get enough exercise to develop sound hearts and lungs. In 1972 Congress required U.S. schools receiving federal aid to offer girls the same athletic opportunities as boys, yet recent studies show that girls' fitness has declined even more than that of boys.

Why these troubling contradictions? Many health professionals blame the ways of modern living: riding instead of walking to school or play, sitting for hours before computer games or TV, and eating high-fat fast foods. Physical educators point to cutbacks in gym classes as many schools have instituted no-frills programs to emphasize the three R's. Half the nation's high school students get no physical education in the 11th and 12th grades, and only

55

SPORTS AND GAMES

two states, New Jersey and Illinois, require physical education in all 12 years.

Unfit kids are ultimately parents' problems — and not easy to solve. Parents who rush to get their children into competitive sports early may do more harm than good. Dr. Lyle J. Micheli, 46, an assistant clinical professor at the Harvard Medical School and chief of sports medicine at Children's Hospital in Boston, reports that youngsters are suffering an explosion of sports injuries — stress fractures in the legs, Little League elbow, swimmer's shoulder — rarely seen in children until recent years. He explains, "Overall fitness is down, so that if children do an intensive athletic activity for an hour five times a week, it's a setup for injury."

Dr. Micheli points out that in their extremities and spines, children have specialized growth cartilage more susceptible to damage than adult cartilage. And when adolescents experience growth spurts of their bones, muscles and tendons catch up more slowly and may become temporarily tight and inflexible. Without adequate conditioning exercises to stretch and strengthen ligaments and muscles, children are particularly vulnerable to injury.

Zealous but unsophisticated coaches, some of them parent volunteers, may not realize that they cannot turn every kid into a superathlete, since a lot of sports skill is inherited. To avoid hurting young bodies and feelings, nonprofessionals can consult *Coaching Young Athletes* by Rainer Martens, professor of sports psychology at the University of Illinois.

Before putting Johnny or Janey on a rugby team, concerned parents should first try to learn how their child's fitness compares with national norms and where he or she needs improvement. An estimated 18 million children (in a school population of 45 million) are tested for physical fitness annually. Testing can begin in kindergarten, but most schools start in the fifth grade. The American Alliance for Health, Physical Education, Recreation, and Dance (AAHPERD), a nonprofit organization, has designed two widely given tests.

In September and usually again in the spring, gym teachers give the Youth Fitness Test, with norms introduced in 1975. "The President's test" is what many children call it, because the best-performing students get the Presidential Physical Fitness Award. But the standards are so tough that only about 5% win. Some educators think the test discourages children, since 95% win no award. In addition, many educators and other specialists feel the Youth Fitness Test emphasizes athletic aptitude, since it measures mainly strength, endurance, and speed. For these reasons, AAHPERD developed the shorter Health Related Test in 1980. Less widely administered than the Youth Fitness Test, it replaces some of the athletic measures with gauges of flexibility and body fat, measured by a skin-fold test. Physical education teachers may make the test scores available to students and to parents on request.

To get the most benefit from the tests, parents and teachers should consider the Fitnessgram, developed by Dr. Kenneth Cooper's Institute for Aerobics Research in Dallas. It turns the results of either test into an individual fitness report card that shows each student how he or she ranks against other students nationwide, gives the student an exercise prescription for improvement, and records changes since the last test. With Campbell Soup Co. footing the bill, the computer software needed to turn out Fitnessgrams is available free to any school district from the Youth Fitness Institute for Aerobics Research, 12330 Preston Road, Dallas, Texas 75230. Forms for printing the results cost 6 cents apiece. The tests suggest good news: In a sample of 16,000 students, scores in the 1985–86 academic year improved over the previous year.

More important than any test is the exercise habit. Dr. Paul Dyment, 50, chief of pediatrics at the Maine Medical Center in Portland and chairman of the sports medicine committee of the American Academy of Pediatrics, says: "By the time a child is 5 the whole family should regularly be doing something together, say walking or biking, so that the child grows up with physical activity as part of its culture. Doing it early develops a habit, just like brushing your teeth." A good example: Mel Kornbluh, 40, a partner in Vineland Syrup Co. of Vineland, New Jersey, and wife Barbara, a professional pianist, have toured on their bikes with daughter Natalie since she was 2 and son Jed since he was even younger. At first the parents rode a tandem bike with the kids in a Bike Caboose trailer. Then they switched to two tandem bikes, each with a child in the aft seat. Tandems can be rigged with a raised seat, handlebars, and pedals behind the parent so small children can pedal according to their abilities.

The popular infant and toddler gyms, such as Gymboree and the YMCA's You & Me Baby program, where parents or baby-sitters help little ones work out, may be a lot of fun but do not speed development of a baby's sophisticated motor skills, according to David Gallahue, professor of physical education and childhood motor development at Indiana University in Bloomington. He says they don't do any harm either.

But swimming programs for children under 3, even under close supervision, find little favor with physicians. They say babies in diapers can spread infection in pools and can get convulsions from swallowing too much water. The notion of drown-proofing a child at a tender age is a myth: Having learned not to fear water, a very young child may charge into a pool and not be able to get out.

Preschoolers can benefit from simple gymnastics under professional supervision and delight their parents in the bargain. At the Harris YMCA in Charlotte, North Carolina, fathers help their 3- to 5-year-olds jump off the pommel horse and make like monkeys on uneven parallel bars. Then all join in the Mousercize routine, following Mickey's recorded directions. John C. McCombs, 39, area manager

FOR FITNESS AND FUN

for solid-state power devices at Allen Bradley Corp., and his 4-year-old daughter, Leslie, have enrolled in their third five-week session of the program, called Pops-n-Peanuts. "Saturday mornings at the Y are what Leslie and I both look forward to most for the weekend," says McCombs, who joined the Y's adult fitness classes when he started accompanying his daughter. He lost 35 pounds in three months.

Nearly 60 ski areas nationwide offer the Skiwee program of children's instruction, which teaches kids from 3 or 4 through 12. By age 8 most children can comfortably join their parents on the slopes. For further information, consult *Ski* magazine's regular Skiwee page.

For children with serious weight problems, the 12-week Shapedown program for teenagers is offered at 400 hospitals and family medical centers nationwide. In the program, developed at the medical school of the University of California at San Francisco, parents must attend at least four counseling sessions apart from those their children attend, in order to understand and help reinforce changes.

Linda Taylor, 35, a claims adjustor for United Pacific Insurance in Spokane, and her husband, Michael, a civil engineer, enrolled her reluctant son, Bill White, when he was 11 and 30 pounds overweight. Much of the program is based on taking responsibility for oneself and the psychology of self-esteem, which Bill did not grasp the first time around. He made little progress. But when he and his mother repeated the program, it took. Watching his diet,

riding his bike, and working on the family farm, Bill lost 18 pounds, and joined the junior high school football team.

Making kids more fit can be trying, since they can scarcely imagine that they might later pay gravely for a lack of conditioning today. Health educators overwhelmingly recommend a different way of motivating: Just show the kids that fit is fun.

FOR FURTHER INFORMATION

American Alliance for Health, Physical Education, Recreation, and Dance (AAHPERD), 1900 Association Dr., Reston, VA 22091; (703)-476-3400.

President's Council on Physical Fitness and Sports, Suite 7103, 450 Fifth St. N.W., Washington, D.C. 20001; (202)-272-3421.

Gymboree, Suite 400, 577 Airport Blvd., Burlingame, CA 94010-2022; (415)-579-0600.

Shapedown, Balboa Publishing, 101 Larkspur Landing, Larkspur, CA 94939; (415)-461-8884.

Ski magazine's Skiwee program, c/o Michael McMenamy, Suite 200, 3000 Pearl St., Boulder, CO 80301; (303)-449-7961.

YMCA of the USA, 101 N. Wacker Dr., Chicago, IL 60606; (312)-977-0031.

Youth Fitness Institute for Aerobics Research, 12230 Preston Rd., Dallas, TX 75230; (800)-527-0362 or (214)-239-7223.

PUBLICATION

Coaching Young Athletes by Rainer Martens and others (Champaign, IL: Human Kinetics, 1981), $12. ∎

WITH RACKET, CLUB, AND MALLET

High-Tech Golf and Tennis Schools

■ Computers have been goading big-time athletes and their coaches to peak performance for several years. Now this technology is reaching the after-hours athlete. Fancy high-tech teaching aids to make over your golf or tennis game are off to a swinging start.

The Jack Nicklaus Academy of Golf in Orlando, Florida, built near the Grand Cypress Resort golf course designed by Nicklaus, aims to develop the perfect golf swing for every comer. Nicklaus also created the academy's three practice holes, which include the hazards, traps, and tricky lies a golfer might meet anywhere. W. Whitley "Whit" Hawkins, 55, a senior vice president for marketing at Delta Air Lines, his wife, Betty, and nine other students began a session by standing before two video cameras at the welcoming cocktail party. Then Ralph Mann, 37, an Olympic hurdler and a specialist in the computer analysis of body movements, went to work.

By filming 50 touring pros, including Nicklaus and Arnold Palmer, Mann has devised a model of what he considers the perfect swing. To tailor the swing for the students, Mann takes data on their physiques from the video images and sends the information to a computer. The computer adapts Mann's model to the student's measurements to produce the ideal swing for each golfer. This appears on the screen as a stick figure overlaying the image of the student.

During three days at Grand Cypress, each student gets a daily 45-minute lesson in front of the video cameras. The stick-figure model always shadows his image on the monitors. Instructor and student can then compare how the stick figure executes a swing with the student's actual movements. Fred Griffin, 30, the academy director, or Phil Rodgers, 48, an adviser to Nicklaus and author of *Play Lower Handicap Golf* (New York: Simon & Schuster), critiques the swings and records all his comments, thus giving students a permanent audiovisual record to review at home. The price: $1,200 for the classes, two meals a day, and accommodations in luxurious villas. The fee rises to $1,600 when Rodgers teaches.

Delta's Hawkins, a 25-handicapper who learned his golf from friends, says he left Grand Cypress with "an ability to control the ball better and with a much better understanding of the subtleties of the short game — pitching, chipping, and bunker play." His wife, a beginner with a 36 handicap, used every shot she had learned as she played the practice holes; she even parred one of them.

The instructors warn students not to make bets on their games immediately. It takes at least three weeks of practice, they say, before a made-over golfer feels comfortable with his new skills. After a session with Rodgers, John A. Fennie, 54, president of Celanese Textile Fibers in New York, entered a Florida tournament. "I was a total disaster the first day, but on the third day I played my best ever," says Fennie, a 9-handicapper. "The academy put a lot of new things on me: grip, setup of the ball, position of hips, head, and shoulders. You can't turn off your old game one day and turn on your new game the next."

Some authorities question how valuable the computer-generated swing is for recreational players. Gary Wiren, 51, master teacher at the PGA National Golf Resort in Palm Beach Gardens, feels that while the computer model may help skilled golfers, it is overkill for the high handicapper. But, says Wiren, "the level of golf instruction has been raised because of Grand Cypress, and will therefore make the game more fun."

Simpler golf computers that do not produce a model can also track the actual motion of a swing, yielding detailed information on why a golfer may bogey instead of birdie. A leading golf analyzer, GolfTek, was invented by Charles H. Blankenship, 53, an electronics engineer who quit Silicon Valley for Lewiston, Idaho. His company now manufactures three models — one for individual use ($495) and two sold mainly to clubs and pro shops ($1,495 for the popular Pro III).

GolfTek measures the speed and path of a golfer's club during a swing. In addition to a computer, the device consists of a base with a tee and light sensors. Indoors it requires overhead light and, of course, a net to catch the

WITH RACKET, CLUB, AND MALLET

balls. When the golfer hits the ball and the club head passes over the sensors, they detect the angle as well as the speed of the head as it moves through the shot. Those data are processed by computer and displayed on a console. The display tells the club head's speed (for example, 106 mph) and how many yards such a stroke would send the ball (perhaps 220). The device also gives the time between the beginning of the backswing and the conclusion of the downswing. (A good swing takes from .8 to 1.4 seconds; most good amateurs take between 1 and 1.2 seconds.) Then diagrams on the console light up to show the path of the swing and what that means for the flight of the ball — hook, slice, or right down the middle.

As teaching aids, golf computers are most helpful on the full swing, to show the golfer the path and position of the club face. "The factors the golf analyzer is measuring are those that account scientifically for the ball going straight," says Tag Merritt, 50, a pro at Fairbanks Ranch Country Club in Rancho Santa Fe, California. "From a GolfTek reading, I can be sure of the direction the person is hitting, though I can't see it with the naked eye, because it happens so fast."

One criticism of the machine is that it's no help solving a golfer's problems. "You can figure out what the numbers mean," says one low handicapper, "but you need someone to look at your swing and tell you what adjustments to make." Machines are no threat to golf pros.

At the United States Open Tennis Championships and many major pro events, Chris Evert and other top-ranking players have had their matches analyzed by CompuTennis, a computer that charts matches to identify players' strengths, weaknesses, and strategies. The inventor, former Wimbledon player William Jacobson, 49, was a computer systems engineer before he founded Sports Software in California.

The Van der Meer Tennis Center on South Carolina's Hilton Head Island was among the first to use Compu-Tennis as a coaching aid for adult amateurs. Phil Frohlich, 33, a tax accountant in Tulsa, and Robert Martin, 44, partner in a family-owned Manhattan advertising agency, hovered quizzically over the small courtside computer after a seven-game match. On a $2\frac{1}{4}$-inch-wide tape a trim little machine called the CompuTennis CT120 Courtside Computer printed a breakdown of strokes and points in the match that Frohlich had just won from Martin during a week-long tennis clinic. For each player the computer listed the number and percentage of serves and returns won and lost, plus other scoring plays and errors — forehand, backhand, and net play.

The camp's summer director, Louie Cap, 41, a nuclear physicist and computer hobbyist, had keyed in each basic stroke, the court area from which it came, and how each point was won and lost. Once the match ended, the print-out began to emerge.

The printout showed that Martin, the loser of the match, won 65% of his first serves, but scored points on return of serves only twice. In his comments, Cap used the computer's calculations to reinforce his own observations. "Work on return of serves and volleys," he told Martin. "Come to the net more," he advised both players. The computer provided irrefutable evidence that his advice was sound. As a teaching aid, CompuTennis is often used as an adjunct to videotaping, which helps players perfect strokes.

The heart of the CompuTennis system is a four-pound, battery-powered computer with program, microcassette drive, and microprinter. Price: $1,970. You don't have to buy the machine. PC CompuTennis, a software program for personal computers, costs $195. Or CompuTennis score sheets can be sent to California for analysis at $25 per match.

"Sometimes people have a funny idea of why they win or lose," says Cap. "We are all very subjective as far as errors are concerned. But if you have something that says, 'Look, this is where the problem is,' players can see it. And it's right there, very relevant."

The Nick Bollettieri Tennis Academy in Bradenton, Florida, doesn't try to create new strokes for adults. Known as a stern molder of aspiring juniors, Bollettieri, 56, says, "We work within the scope of an adult's own game." It's not that Bollettieri feels old dogs can't learn new tricks. Instead he believes it is more important for his adult students to develop the right attitude than the perfect stroke. The Bollettieri Academy stresses what it calls mental toughness and uses high-tech aids to help develop it. This part of the program is under the direction of James E. Loehr, 43. A tennis pro with a doctorate in counseling psychology, Loehr has advised such world-class players as Johan Kriek, Tom Gullikson, and Kathy Rinaldi. He recently co-authored *Mentally Tough: The Principles of Winning at Sports Applied to Winning in Business* (New York: M. Evans).

Loehr defines mental toughness as the self-control that enables players to rise to a challenge without choking, getting angry, or losing concentration. "Mental toughness is an emotional skill athletes can learn," he says. One of Loehr's chief teaching aids is a heart monitor. A player's pulse rate in competition not only reveals just how hard he is working, but shows his emotional state as well. Twice during their week at the academy, students wear chest-band transmitters and computerized wristwatch receivers that display and store their pulse rates.

In one demonstration Loehr had his students play a tie breaker. To make the game extra stressful, he gave them dead balls and required them to exchange rackets. Periodically Loehr asked the players to read off their pulse rates. Afterward he remarked that one of them, Reginald Ridgely, 53, of Vitro Corp., a shipbuilding consultant to the Navy, had not shown the drop in heart rate that ideally occurs between points when a player feels he is doing well.

SPORTS AND GAMES

His opponent, Joseph H. Spencer Jr., 42, who runs his own engineering firm in Charlotte, North Carolina, consistently registered a pulse rate too low to rouse him to a high level of play. Loehr asked all students to take their pulse whenever they felt they were playing their best, and then aim to keep it there. "We find that players perform best within a narrow range of heart rate," he explains.

Joe Spencer, who plays four times a week, developed a ritual to focus his attention on the ball before serving or receiving. At Loehr's suggestion, he bounced on his feet to get his heart rate up, and he breathed out at the moment of the racket's impact on the ball. The payoff came immediately as he split sets with both a ranked junior at the academy and the director of the adult tennis program. Spencer found Loehr's insights the most valuable part of his week.

The Bollettieri Academy isn't a resort. New facilities for 32 adults, separate from those for 200 juniors, include condominium suites, a dining room, and a swimming pool. Cost: $745 per week or $275 per weekend. Don't expect all the high-tech aids to prevent aching bodies. In six hours a day of hard activity at the Nicklaus and Bollettieri academies, students discovered muscles they never knew existed.

FOR FURTHER INFORMATION

Jack Nicklaus Academy of Golf, Grand Cypress Resort, 1 N. Jacaranda St., Orlando, FL 32819; (800)-835-7377 or (305)-239-1975.

Nick Bollettieri Tennis Academy, 5500 34th St., Bradenton, FL 34210; (800)-USA-NICK or (813)-755-1000.

Van der Meer Tennis Center, P.O. Box 5902, Hilton Head Island, SC 29938; (800)-845-6138 or (803)-785-8388.

Golftek, 631 24th Ave., Lewiston, ID 83501; (208)-743-9037.

Sports Software, Suite 201, 949 Sherwood Ave., Los Altos, CA 94022; (415)-941-6363.

Low-Handicap Golfers

■ "Some play golf and some do not!" wrote the satirical poet Samuel Hoffenstein in enumerating differences among people. He might have added that some play the game a whole lot better than others. But handicaps, at least theoretically, are the great equalizers among golfers, allowing duffers and very good players to meet on reasonably even terms.

Handicap strokes are deducted from scores each player cards at the end of a round; the better the player, the lower the handicap. The average handicap of the serious U.S. amateur is 17 for men and 31 for women, according to the U.S. Golf Association, keeper of the rules on how these ratings are calculated. Some of the best golfers are rated at scratch — that is a handicap of 0 — better than all but a small portion, generally professionals, of the eight million Americans who ply the links with passion.

To determine his or her USGA handicap, a golfer must play at least five rounds on a course. But ideally, the sum of the best ten of the scores for the most recent 20 rounds is averaged and compared with the USGA rating for that course — the number of strokes a true expert would take to go around. If the course rating, par, is 72 and a player's ten rounds average 85, it might seem he had a 13 handicap. But the USGA's computation of the handicap multiplies that crude 13 handicap times the ten rounds, and then takes 96% of that figure — 12.48%. Handicaps cannot be fractionalized, so 12.48 turns into a handicap of 12.

A handicap is not constant; it moves up and down with a player's skill. But, starting in 1987, it may also move up and down with different courses. As every player knows, a 12 handicap gained on a course in Podunk does not equal a 12 earned at Pebble Beach. So the USGA has devised a system, known as the USGA Handicap Slope, to refine its method of rating courses. It takes into account the characteristics of their fairways, rough, greens, hazards, etc. A hypothetical national average course has a rating of 113. A player's handicap is converted to an index representing how he would play that average course. He checks his index against the rating of each course he plays to find his handicap on that particular course.

Advancing age does not always wither a good player's rating. E. M. de Windt, former chief executive of Eaton in Cleveland, where he plays at Pepper Pike, had a handicap of 2 in 1973; ten years later at 63 he had improved to a

Investment banker Amy B. Lane, at Navesink Country Club, in Middletown, New Jersey, ranks with the best of male executive golfers anywhere.

60

WITH RACKET, CLUB, AND MALLET

handicap of 1. John Baldwin, 44, national sales manager at the investment banking firm of First Boston in New York City, graduated from the University of North Carolina at Chapel Hill with a scratch rating, granting no handicap, turned pro for three years and improved to + 1.5, meaning close to one below par. Except for a later temporary lapse to 2, he has held his amateur game at scratch at the Meadow Brook Club in Jericho, New York.

The way to the low handicap, judging by the experiences of Baldwin and several other players from New York's financial community, is to learn the game in one's early or pre-teens (Baldwin started at 10), get professional instruction, and compete on a high school or college team. Then, in adult life, work and loved ones permitting, practice or play at least twice a week, preferably three or four times, with good golfers. Enter lots of tournaments, but keep an even, relaxed temperament. "You get to a point in the game, when you've been playing 25 years, and your swing is pretty grooved, where the real difference in how you perform competitively is 90% mental," says Baldwin.

Staying fit and limber is important, but beware of overworking the upper body. Weight lifting could tighten muscles, upsetting the smooth movement of the good golfer's grooved swing. Avoid tennis, especially during golf season. "Tennis is a very right-handed game that builds up your right arm and shoulder, and throws off your timing," Baldwin asserts. "Golf is left-handed."

Continual work on both long and short shots is a must for many. Tom T. Hamilton, 38, a vice president and security analyst at General American Investors in New York City, with a 0 handicap at the Greenwich Country Club in Connecticut, practices an hour and a half two nights a week in golfing season: 45 minutes on drives off the tee, and 45 on chip shots onto the green plus putts. He plays Saturdays and Sundays, entering tournaments monthly from May through September. In winter he hits the southern fairways once a month.

However, Baldwin doesn't touch a club from November to February. "You need an away time from the game," he feels. To gear up for the season, he joins 20 players with handicaps from 0 to 15 for a four-day weekend in March at a resort where they play 36 holes a day. During the season he spends an hour three times a week putting or chipping before playing.

Golf schools and private lessons have helped Tom Hamilton. Annoyed at always losing tournaments by only a few strokes, at age 28 he signed up for a week at one of the many schools run by *Golf Digest* magazine from time to time at various locations. An instructor found Hamilton's swing too upright and his upper body tight. So he prescribed drills to build up the left side. And for Hamilton's clubs he recommended a flatter lie, the angle where the shaft meets the club face. The next year his handicap dropped from 4 to 2. But it took two more years of practice before he won any club championships. Reverting to a losing streak in 1981, he started the 1982 season with a week at another *Golf Digest* school. Tuition at these schools varies from $1,050 to $3,900, depending on the location.

Videotaping and analysis of Hamilton's swing by the pro at the Greenwich club proved useful. "It's helpful to see your own swing, because it confirms problems someone else may have told you about, but you didn't really believe." Working with an outside pro at $60 an hour in 1985, he had a computer analysis of his swing to determine club-edge speed and angle of approach. Hamilton won the Greenwich Country Club championship in 1983 and 1985, and set his sights on the amateur championship of the Metropolitan Golf Association of Greater New York.

In business social life, where golf has taken an upswing in the 1980s, a low handicap is a mark of distinction. "On Wall Street, golf helps you to be remembered if you have talent," says John Baldwin. "Everybody in this business is out to sell the same products to the same accounts. What separates you from the rest is something personal."

Amy B. Lane, 34, a principal at the investment banking firm of Morgan Stanley, and 17-time women's champion at the Navesink Country Club in Middletown, New Jersey, couldn't agree more. "It's unique for a businesswoman to be a really good amateur golfer," notes the 5-handicapper. Lane is among a small but growing number of women who mix business and golf. Several times a year Morgan Stanley has asked her to join colleagues in entertaining clients on the fairways. A better player than most of her male counterparts, she doesn't have to keep to the women's tees, but can play off the full 6,400-yard men's tees. That's an asset any company would appreciate.

FOR FURTHER INFORMATION

United States Golf Association; membership, $25 a year, includes *Golf Journal*, eight issues a year, *Rules of Golf*, and travel discounts; Golf House, Far Hills, NJ 07931; (201)-234-2300.

Golf Digest Schools, 5520 Park Ave., Trumbull, CT 06611-0395; (800)-243-6121 or (203)-373-7130.

PUBLICATIONS

Ben Hogan's Five Lessons by Ben Hogan and Herbert Warren Wind (Trumbull, CT: Golf Digest, 1986), $16.95.

Golf Digest, monthly, $19.94 a year; 5520 Park Ave., Trumbull, CT 06611-0395; (800)-PAR-GOLF or (203)-373-7000.

Golf Magazine, monthly, $15.95 a year; P.O. Box 2786, Boulder, CO 80322-3733.

Sports Illustrated Golf by Mark Mulvoy (New York: Harper & Row, 1983), $8.95. ∎

SPORTS AND GAMES

Championship Tennis for Amateurs

■ Playing at the National Tennis Center in New York during the United States Open Tennis Championships, Keith Bailey, 31, a Peoria, Illinois, salesman for the Standard Register Co., which makes business forms, and his wife, Wendy, 25, were down love–3 in their third set. A couple of great retrieves by Wendy helped them take the match, 4–6, 6–4, 6–3, and win the husband-wife title in the Equitable Family Tennis Challenge. Returning to the women's locker room where she had left their 16-month-old son, Nathaniel, with friends, Wendy found Hana Mandlikova relaxing before her final match by tossing balls for Nat to swing at with his miniature racket. The Baileys and Nat then watched Mandlikova beat Martina Navratilova and take the women's silver trophy. Moments later, the Baileys and the other finalists from the Equitable contest stepped onto the stadium court and got their own double-handled cups — pewter, not silver.

National competitions in which adult amateurs win much more than trophies have bounced onto the tennis scene in recent years. Several corporate sponsors serve up tournaments for amateurs, rewarding regional winners with trips to play championship matches. "The opportunity to win a trip attracts players," says Richard O'Sullivan, 27, a contract analyst with Deltak Training Corp. in Naperville, Illinois, and a competitor in several of these tourneys. "Trophies gather dust. Trips give you photos and good memories."

The oldest of the sponsored amateur contests — the Equitable Family Tennis Challenge, the United States Tennis Association/Volvo Tennis League Program, and the Lipton Iced Tea Amateur Mixed Doubles Championship — offer competition to hundreds of thousands of weekend players in hundreds of clubs and tennis centers nationwide. Successful qualifiers advance through district and/or regional play-offs. In 1985 USTA/Volvo sent over 1,600 players to three-day championships in Las Vegas or Delray Beach, Florida; Lipton brought 64 players to a resort near Tampa, Florida, and Equitable Life Assurance brought 192 finalists to New York. Buick and Ford have been sponsoring similar tournaments for adult players. The Buick locals, many of them played indoors during fall and winter, lead to spring playoffs. Winners in these contests also advance to championships.

These sponsored contests are totally separate from the USTA's many amateur programs, which offer plenty of competition in special categories, such as family pairs, or seniors over 35, with a chance for a prestigious local, state, or national ranking. None of these sponsored tournaments earn ranking points.

Of all the sponsored amateur tournaments, the Equitable Family Challenge, in its 14th year in 1987, brings winners closest to the greatness and glory of tennis. Equitable Life gives six winning family pairs — father-son, father-daughter, mother-son, mother-daughter, husband-wife, and brother-sister — from 16 regional competitions all-expense-paid, four-day trips to New York for play-offs at the site of the U.S. Open pro championships in September.

After Robert Sharp, 47, president of the Peninsula Motor Club, an American Automobile Association affiliate in Tampa, and Robin Sharp, 18, had won the father-daughter finals, Robin telephoned a friend from the locker room. Overhearing the good news, Navratilova congratulated Robin, who has earned a four-year tennis scholarship at Auburn University. Says her father, "Those are the kinds of things that an 18-year-old will never, never forget."

Doubles, usually mixed, predominate in these sponsored tournaments, but in the USTA/Volvo leagues players compete on separate men's or women's teams of eight, and may choose to play singles or doubles. To enter the Volvo League competition, players must be members of the USTA. They have to be over 21 in the Volvo, Buick, and Ford contests. The Volvo and Ford contests try to equalize competition through the National Tennis Rating Program. Players are asked to rate themselves on a standard scale of 1.0 (a beginner) to 7.0 (a McEnroe). USTA observers may verify these ratings. In the USTA/Volvo, players from 3.0 (moderately adept at shot placement and rallying) to 5.0 (consistent and capable of most strokes) compete against other teams at their level. Ford pairs compete at two levels with combined ratings above or below 8.0; amateurs of any rating can enter the Buick and the Lipton.

Winners of the Ford National Mixed Doubles Championships in 1985 were Mary Prebil, 26, a claims representative for Aetna Life & Casualty in McLean, Virginia, and David Tober, 32, a Falls Church, Virginia, agent for E. F. Hutton Life Insurance. Ford paid travel and living expenses for the 72 competitors at the PGA National Resort in Palm Beach Gardens, Florida, site of the Ford Challenge Cup, in which Chris Evert defeated Hana Mandlikova. Just before the pro matches, Billie Jean King, then director of the Ford amateur tournament, introduced Mary Prebil and David Tober to the crowd at the stadium court.

Prebil and Tober also reached the 1985 USTA/Volvo national championships in Delray Beach, Florida. Volvo and USTA contributed $1,000 to each eight-member team, but players had to cover the remaining expenses. Says Prebil of the corporate-sponsored contests she has entered: "I've gotten a couple of trips and some lifetime experiences."

The Lipton Mixed Doubles amateur tourney offers the keenest competition, according to veterans of several of these sponsored tournaments. It comes closest to being an open contest, with no age limits. An amateur is defined as someone who has not accepted money for tennis in the preceding 18 months before entering a local qualifying match. These are followed by sectional and regional playoffs. At the Saddlebrook Golf and Tennis Resort near Tampa, Florida, where the players got luxurious condominium accommodations, plus three days of food and festivities, the 1985 championship contenders ranged from 16-year-old high school girls to 46-year-old matrons. They included a former pro, as well as a 38-year-old stockbroker, William A. Beckwith, from Phoenix, Arizona, who didn't take up the game till he was 30. With an exceptionally strong partner, JoAnne Murto, 22, a student at Grand Canyon College in Phoenix, Beckwith made it to the semifinals. They lost to a pair of 18-year-old college students.

In the other Lipton semifinals match, the Hartford, Connecticut, team of Cherie Baker, 24, an underwriter at Travelers Insurance Co., and David Hodges, 40, a psychotherapist, met Timothy L. Garcia, 29, a former pro and now a tax lawyer in Santa Fe, New Mexico, and Mari Forbes, 21, a student at the University of New Mexico. In a hard match, fought under a broiling October sun, the Connecticut pair won 6–3, 3–6, 7–5. On Sunday morning in the finals, the two 18-year-olds from Charleston, South Carolina — Angelo Anastopoulo and Sharon Kidney — took the first set 7–5. In the second set Hodges and Baker were ahead 5–3, with Hodges serving. At this critical point, the South Carolinians broke his serve and then, says Hodges, "they played some very strong games. We really didn't figure them out." Anastopoulo and Kidney again won 7–5 and took the championship. "Win or lose," says Cherie Baker, "that was a great tournament."

FOR FURTHER INFORMATION

United States Tennis Association; membership, $16 a year, includes *World Tennis,* monthly; 1212 Avenue of the Americas. New York, NY 10036; (212)-302-3322.

Buick, Professional Sports Marketing, Suite 108, 17430 Campbell Rd., Dallas, TX 75248; (800)-2 CAN WIN or (214)-380-5859.

Equitable Family Tennis Challenge, Capital Sports, Inc., 280 Park Ave., New York, NY 10017; (212)-087-2125.

Ford–Sports Tennis Championships, Advantage International, 1025 Thomas Jefferson N.W., Washington, D.C. 20007; (800)-635-1355 or (202)-338-3838.

Lipton Iced Tea Amateur Mixed Doubles, GD/T Sports Marketing, P.O. Box 0395, 5520 Park Ave., Trumbull, CT 06611-0395; (800)-344-4469 or (203)-373-7000.

PUBLICATION

Tennis, monthly, $17.94 a year; 5520 Park Ave., Trumbull, CT 06611-0395; (800)-247-5470 or (203)-373-7000. ■

WITH RACKET, CLUB, AND MALLET

Squashing the Competition

■ It's the brisk pace of the game that attracts half a million players, more than half of them executives, to 3,000 squash courts several times a week, year-round. In this racquet game, 45 minutes is all it takes for an exhausting match, compared with an hour and a half for tennis, and players earn a greater return in exercise. The court's size — a quarter as large as a tennis court — helps to explain the speed of the game. The ball ricochets off the walls at up to 110 miles an hour.

One executive calls squash, always played indoors, "a little cockfight of highly condensed, ferocious activity." On a four-walled court both opponents face the front wall. From his service court the server aims the ball to hit the front wall above a service line so that on the rebound it strikes the floor within the opposite service court. The receiver must return the ball to the front wall before it hits the floor twice. Meanwhile the ball may strike any of the walls, either on the rebound from the serve, or on the return. Players alternate hitting returns until one misses, and the other thereby wins the point. Fifteen points win a game and three wins make a match.

"I get a kick out of figuring it out," says Clare Muñana, 32, a management consultant with Grant Thornton International in Chicago, and a nationally ranked player. "It's something that a woman can do well. It's not just based on brute strength. It's a thinking game." You have to learn to play the angles off the walls, devise a game plan, make

In the U.S. Squash Racquets Championships at Princeton University, Leonard Bernheimer (left) beat Pablo Pick in the semifinals for the 35-and-over age group. A camera mounted at the base of the front wall took this view.

63

SPORTS AND GAMES

split-second decisions, and season all this with deception.

Instead of the smooth consistent strokes the tennis player cultivates, squash requires a choppy stroke, with a deep V at the elbow, and a snap of the wrist. The backhand gets a workout because a player doesn't have time or room to maneuver around the ball to the forehand side.

There's a bigger arsenal of shots in squash than in tennis, because the four walls and corners make for fascinating geometric complexities. In the trickiest shot, a three-wall nick, the ball is angled onto a side wall, then bounces off the front wall and hits the other side wall in the nick, or angle, where wall meets floor. It requires superior racquet handling, or "touch," but properly executed, with great force, it's almost impossible to return. "It's a shot that adds a point, and one I've worked very hard to perfect," says Leonard Bernheimer, 44, president of United Lithographers Inc. of Somerville, Massachusetts. Bernheimer has three times won the national singles championship title in the 40 to 44 age division.

Thanks to the United States Squash Racquets Association, which Bernheimer served as president from 1984 to 1986, players can compete against others of matching ability and age. The USSRA sanctions 500 tournaments a year for its 10,000 members, who pay $25 annual dues, plus entry fees. Players are rated, men and women separately, according to their level of ability: A, B, C, or D. Players over age 35 compete not only within their rating level, but within five-year age divisions, up through 70 and over. Some 7,800 players at the B, C, and D levels enter local club and regional tournaments leading to national championships, all sponsored by Insilco of Meriden, Connecticut.

A-level players and all under 35 qualify for their national championships by competitive ranking in local leagues. The principal sponsors of these top-level tournaments in 1986 were companies headed by squash players. For example, Coca-Cola USA had as president Brian Dyson, 50, who competes in Atlanta. Business players also have their own leagues, in which 150 corporations field teams in five Eastern cities, with intercity play-offs and championships, all sponsored by Insilco.

The sport remains predominantly amateur, though many a college star is tempted by the lively pro circuit, where various members of the legendary Khan family rank among the top 20 players. James W. "Jamie" Barrett, with the up-and-coming Minneapolis advertising agency of Fallon McElligott Rice, played at Princeton to become one of the top U.S. amateurs. For one year after graduating in 1983 he played the amateur circuit nationwide, "to see how far I could advance in the squash world," he says. He reached the No. 5 ranking for 1983–84, but realized it could take another four years before he might rise to the top ten on the pro circuit, and make the game pay off. His arrival in Minnesota in the fall of 1984 raised the caliber of amateur play there to an unprecedented high.

Hazards of injury lurk in ankles, knees, and heels, which take a pounding when players stop and change direction fast. At 55, Jeffrey Pettit, who runs the appraisals department at the investment banking firm of Morgan Stanley in New York, ruptured an Achilles tendon. It required surgery and a vigorous six-month rehabilitation program before he could resume play. Eyes have been hurt seriously by blows from the ball or racquet. Plastic goggles, required for top-level tourneys in 1986, became mandatory at all levels of tournament play in 1987.

Equipment for squash would seem a simple matter. A conventional wood-framed $7\frac{1}{2}$-inch racquet costs as little as $20, though a composite frame can go to $150. Jamie Barrett's Head graphite SX-2 racquet, which cost $110, should last two seasons. But it's the $3 balls that have complicated the game in the 1980s. When English schoolboys at Harrow invented the game by improvising their own version of the game of racquets, in place of the hard leather ball, they hit a "squashy" rubber ball against the schoolyard wall, whence the name "squash racquets." To this day the English squash ball, and the one used in international competition, is a lot squashier than the ball most widely used in the U.S., which has the size (44 millimeters around), firmness, and color of a lime. In 1983 the USSRA sanctioned softball championships. The softball game demands more of an athlete because the ball hangs for a split second, which gives a player time to retrieve shots that he would not even consider in the hardball game. And it is played on a wider court. The harder softball game is gaining popularity in the U.S.

FOR FURTHER INFORMATION

United States Squash Racquets Association, 211 Ford Rd., Bala Cynwyd, PA 19004; (215)-667-4006.

PUBLICATIONS

The Book of Squash: A Total Approach to the Game by Crawford W. Lindsey Jr. (Dallas: Taylor Publishing, 1987), $12.95.

The Secret of Squash: How to Win Using the 4-CRO System by John O. Truby Jr. and John O. Truby (Boston: Little, Brown, 1984), $8.95.

Squash News, monthly, $12 a year; Box 52, Arcadia Rd., Hope Valley, RI 02832; (401)-539-2381.

Winning Squash by Jahangir Khan and others (Englewood Cliffs, NJ: Prentice-Hall, 1986), $8.95.

Winning Squash Racquets by Jack Barnaby (*Squash News,* 1985), $15.95. ∎

Croquet's New Version

∎ Croquet has struck off in a new direction since the mid-1970s, from a casual summer lawn game to a competitive sport, complete with national championships. The new version manages to be more wicked than the old, with only six instead of nine wickets, at greater distance from one another on a larger court. A slower game, it entails two-way traffic, very long shots, and mental as well as manual agility for shotmaking and planning several shots ahead. "You can be the best shotmaker, but if you don't understand the strategy, you won't win," says David E. Skinner, 64, co-owner of the Seattle Seahawks pro football team, a director of Boeing, among other companies, and president of Skinner Corp., a Seattle investment firm. Skinner began playing croquet in the 1950s, but in 1980 his local club switched to the new game. "We really find it better, and much tougher," he admits.

The rules of the U.S. Croquet Association, organized in Manhattan in 1977, combine most features of the formal British contest with some from the familiar American game. In 1966 the Westhampton Mallet Club on New York's Long Island had brashly challenged London's hallowed Hurlingham Club to a contest on the Britishers' six-wicket courts. The British humiliatingly routed the Westhamptonites, but in doing so they persuaded the Long Islanders of the superiority of their layout. Soon thereafter five Eastern clubs joined to draw up a new set of rules incorporating the six-wicket layout.

The USCA has grown to 250 clubs, from Poughkeepsie to Puget Sound. Members, who pay $25 in annual dues, compete under uniform rules, in flights according to ability — from C for beginners to championship for experts. Five regional tournaments lead to the national championships. The pace of the association's growth seems limited only by the need for precisely suitable grass. Serious shotmakers demand a playing surface as smooth as a pool table — a sleekness best attained by underground watering and drainage systems plus constant care. Places with lawn tennis can easily add croquet courts; the Meadow Club of Southampton, Long Island, put in two. And some dedicated players build their own. In Phoenix, Ren Kraft, 40, president of the David R. Jones Real Estate Group, which has fielded several national champions, installed a quarter-acre court next to his home at a cost of $20,000. It requires daily watering, trimming thrice weekly, and monthly fertilizing.

The object of the six-wicket game is to send the balls, still the accustomed blue and black against red and yellow, around the big 105- by 84-foot court twice and hit the finishing center stake ahead of your opponent. Instead of the conventional double-diamond layout of nine wire wickets, in the six-wicket game one cast-iron rectangular wicket is placed in each corner of the court, the other two on either side of the center stake. Players, in singles or doubles, move their balls clockwise through the four corner wickets, next run the two center ones, and then turn back to repeat the course counterclockwise. Hence they meet each other coming and going. They can carom strokes off each other's balls and need intricate battle plans for both defense and attack. Experienced competitors try never to leave one ball alone and exposed on the court when the other side has a pair together. To escape attack, players sometimes shoot out of bounds. Unpredictable long shots can change the character of a single game several times.

On a roll in 1984 and 1985, players from the Arizona Croquet Club swept both national championships, for clubs in March in Palm Beach and for individual players in September in New York. Thus ended years of domination by the Long Island–Palm Beach circuit players, who had formulated the rules and organized the association. Ray Bell, 38, one of the expert players at the real estate group in Phoenix, had a hand in most of Arizona's triumphs. In 1984 at the club-team tourney, a doubles event, Bell took the championship with an Arizona photographer as partner. And Bell won the national doubles title in September, in partnership with James Bast, 31, a manager with Continental Airlines. That same week Arizona's Bast took the national singles title.

And in the 1985 spring club-team tournament, Bell's boss, Ren Kraft, whom Bell had introduced to the game, was rewarded for putting in that expensive home court. Kraft and an engineer at the real estate firm, Donald Stallings, 40, held on to the team title for the Arizona club. In September, Bell was back in New York's Central Park to take the national titles in both singles and doubles, the latter in partnership with Palm Beach golf pro Dana Dribben, 36. The 1985 victories were especially sweet because in both March and September the Arizona players defeated USCA co-founder and President Jack Osborn, 56,

At Palm Beach in the U.S. Croquet Association's national club team championships, David E. Skinner of Seattle aims to earn extra strokes by glancing his blue ball off that of his home-town partner, John McCallum.

SPORTS AND GAMES

and his son Johnnie. "If there's somebody to beat, you might as well beat the guy who started the tourneys," says Kraft.

These Arizona players attribute much of their success to their club's custom of playing frequently by British rules even before the USCA got started. And some of these championship players bring skills from other games. Kraft is a chess strategist. And Bell, as a 10-handicap golfer, is accustomed to the mental tension of shotmaking. Stallings, also a golfer, now prefers croquet because, unlike golf where the chief opponent is the course itself, he notes that "I'm doing things on the court that affect my opponent's game, and vice versa, so we actually have a battle."

The weapons in this battle can be personalized to suit each player's grip, stroke, and build, and players may change them as often as they like in the course of a match, except during their own turns. Mallet heads, usually of hard wood, often metal-weighted for strength, may be either cylindrical or rectangular, so long as they are symmetrical. The ash or hickory shafts are about a yard long, but may be custom-fitted, along with their handy octagonal grips. The British firm of John Jaques & Sons Ltd. has been turning out classic equipment since 1850, available in the U.S. through the USCA. Jaques mallets for tournament play cost from $35 to $160 each, and entire croquet sets run from $260 to $1,080. An American-made beginner's set, from Foster Manufacturing in Wilton, Maine, costs about $200.

Even with the elevation of croquet from a pastime to a sport, the contest preserves its languorous charm. No lung-splitting, muscle-wrenching exercise is required. Men and women, young and old, compete as equals, perspire only from the sun, and may cavalierly drink and smoke on the court. Short of the occasional chance of getting hit by a mallet furiously hurled skyward by a frustrated opponent, the risk of memorable injury is minimal.

FOR FURTHER INFORMATION

U.S. Croquet Association, 500 Avenue of Champions, Palm Beach Gardens, FL 33418; (305)-627-3999.
Instructional videotapes, a primer, and a shotmaking feature are available from the USCA at $50 each.

PUBLICATION
Winning Croquet by USCA President Jack Osborn and Jesse Kornbluth (New York: Simon & Schuster, 1983), $9.95. ∎

Polo's Perilous Pleasures

∎ If the idea of hockey on horseback intrigues you, then polo could be your game. That is, if you've got the guts to risk your neck and spend thousands of hours and possibly hundreds of thousands of dollars for the ticket. Invented by the ancient Persians and taken up by British Army officers in India, with lots of time and horses on their hands, polo has never been cheap or easy. But the once elitist game has turned popular at new polo centers where beginners can learn and top-level professionals play for corporate sponsors. In 1986 the United States Polo Association counted 27 schools and colleges with polo programs, 228 clubs, and over 2,600 individual members in the U.S. and Canada eligible to enter its sanctioned competitions. Many more play informally. Cowboys, horsey heirs of wealthy families, highly paid Argentinian pros, and highly competitive businessmen and women meet on vast fields in passionate combat.

"I've always liked complicated and dramatic sports," says Michael Levin, 36, chief executive of Titan Industrial Corp., a steel import-export company in New York City. At 32, Levin sold his 43-foot ocean-racing sloop and took up polo. He and his wife, Laurence, each compete on separate men's and women's teams.

The game demands innate hand and eye coordination. Four players, each wielding a $4\frac{1}{2}$-foot wood and bamboo mallet with one hand and reining his or her mount with the other, make a team. The object is to drive a $3\frac{1}{2}$-inch solid white ball between goal posts at each end of nine groomed acres of grass, 25 times the area of a hockey rink. Rules center on the "line of the ball," its course over the field that establishes a right-of-way which an opponent must not cross. But a player can "ride-off" an opponent, pulling alongside to force him off the line, or, in the body-checking style of ice hockey, bump an opposing horse parallel to his own. A match consists of six "chukkers," each lasting

Gould's former Chairman William T. Ylvisaker, wearing the red helmet, played a hard-driving game in Oak Brook, Illinois, in the No. 3 position—polo's equivalent of the quarterback.

WITH RACKET, CLUB, AND MALLET

seven minutes. Players take fresh mounts for each chukker, so everyone wants six horses for a match and must have at least three.

Riding should be second nature, just as skating is to a hockey player. Michael Levin had taken riding lessons as a teenager and resumed when his wife started lessons. He discovered his feel for polo at the Casa de Campo resort in the Dominican Republic. Having played a lot of squash and tennis, he found that a mallet feels much like a racket. Levin signed up for daily stick-and-ball instruction with the Dominican coach. A 45-minute lesson costs about $30 per person. Week-long polo clinic and hotel packages from January through May cost from $680 to $1,045, depending on the dates.

To try the game before making a deep-pocket commitment to owning horses, some clubs offer guest cards to novice players for clinics. Several commercial stables and polo centers teach mallet technique and the rules. The Los Angeles Equestrian Center and San Antonio's Retama are two of the nation's largest. The United States Polo Association's training foundation funds several clinics. At the University of Virginia in Charlottesville it runs one-week sessions from mid-May through June, at a fee of $900.

At the Palm Beach Polo & Country Club, a week's 25-hour clinic with Major Hugh Dawnay, an Irish master of the game, costs $1,000, horses and equipment included, from mid-December through April, February excepted. One of the world's major polo centers, this club is the creation of William T. Ylvisaker, 63, chairman of Gould, the electronics corporation in Rolling Meadows, Illinois, which owns and developed the 1,650-acre condominium sports resort. A onetime professional player for a Rothschild team in France, Ylvisaker competes in some of the top international tournaments held on the club's 11 polo fields.

For starters, a new player may want to try arena polo, indoors on an area one-third the size of an outdoor field, with only four chukkers per match. In this game a player can get by with only two horses, and even rent them at a few clubs. Levin joined Ox Ridge Hunt Club in Darien, Connecticut, popular with beginners, which requires a $2,000 bond plus dues of $1,500 a year. It offers arena polo in winter and the regular game outdoors in summer. To improve their outdoor game the second winter, Levin and his wife commuted to Florida on weekends.

Handicaps are awarded annually by the United States Polo Association to every player registered with a member club, based on performance observed in club and tournament play. Unlike golf, where lower means better, polo's best players get the highest numerical ratings. Top 10-goal status was granted to only five USPA registered players for 1986, all Argentinian. About 70% of U.S. players hold ratings of −1, the lowest, 0, or 1. Levin improved from 0 to 2 goals in just two years.

A team's rating is the sum of its players' handicaps.

Teams rated 16 or better are termed high goal, often include professional players, and compete in major national and international tournaments. Medium-goal teams, rated 16 to 8, and low goal, less than 8, flourish in regional and local club competitions. In a match the lower-rated team is usually spotted enough goals to make opponents theoretically equal.

A player is only as good as the horses under him, some say. The ponies, so called because rules once limited their height, gallop at 30 miles an hour and come snorting off the field with nostrils flaring. A pony needs a good disposition, good legs, and quick response. Training horses to stop, turn, bump, and race can start when they are 3, and takes a couple years. But then they can compete until their late teens.

You can get started in polo for as little as $10,000. You'll pay $2,500 to $3,500 each for a couple of racehorses, retired from the track, buy a used horse trailer and truck, plus tack and equipment. Maintenance can run another $4,500 a year, if you keep horses on your own property. But tournament players who travel can easily spend $75,000 a year. Top-quality, fully trained Argentinian horses, reputedly polo's best, cost up to $25,000 each, even $40,000 for a champion. To outfit yourself with helmet, boots, mallets, gloves, knee guards, and the de rigueur white britches costs about $750.

Injuries are part of the price. Bill Ylvisaker once stood before the Queen of England to accept the Coronation Cup, which his American team had won from the British, with eyes blackened and head bandaged from a ball's blow. Mallets fly, players and ponies fall, or, worst case, a pony can fall on top of a player.

Michael Levin suffered no more than a broken nose in three years of play, despite a big commitment to the sport. Starting with two horses, he and his wife eventually owned 14, mostly Argentinian, cared for by two grooms and boarded in South Carolina between the Florida and Northeastern playing seasons.

A promising player with fine horses is in demand. Levin has played with some of the world's best players at the Greenwich Polo Club in Connecticut, at the invitation of two 5-goal patrons of the game he met in Florida. In 1984 he teamed up with Peter M. Brant, 40, the president of Brant Allen Industries, a Greenwich-based newsprint manufacturer, and the developer of nearby Conyers Farm, a residential community with polo fields. They hired Argentinian pros Ernesto Trotz, then 9 goals, and Benjamin Araya, then 8 goals. And in 1985 Levin helped Peter Orthwein, 40, a New York financier and member of the Anheuser-Busch clan, assemble a team with Stewart Armstrong, 30, rated 6 goals, from the King Ranch in Texas, and Argentinian pro Alfonso Pieres, then rated 9 goals.

"Polo is an incredibly intricate game. No matter how hard you work at it, there's always that last bit you can't reach," says Levin, who aims to play more high-goal polo

67

SPORTS AND GAMES

and earn a 4- or 5-goal handicap by the time he is 40. Once mastered, though, age is no barrier; players in their late 60s still relish the combat.

FOR FURTHER INFORMATION

United States Polo Association; membership, $100 per year, includes *Polo* magazine; 120 N. Mill St., Lexington, KY 40507; (606)-255-0593.

Casa de Campo resort, P.O. Box 140, La Romana, Dominican Republic; (800)-223-6620 or (809)-682-2111.

Palm Beach Polo & Country Club, 13198 Forest Hill Blvd., West Palm Beach, FL 33414; (800)-327-4204 or (305)-793-1113.

PUBLICATIONS

Polo: The Manual for Coach & Player edited by Peter Cutino and Dennis Bledsoe (Inglewood, CA: Swimming World, 1975), $13.45.

Polo magazine, ten issues a year, $24; Fleet Street Corp., 656 Quince Orchard Rd., Gaithersburg, MD 20878; (301)-977-0200. ■

ON THE WATER
Board Sailing for Stand-Up Thrills

■ The starting gun sent a kaleidoscope of sails across Wisconsin's Lake Geneva. Each of the 138 skippers was sailing not a boat but a board of foam-filled polyethylene fitted with a mast and sail. When the wind cranked up, some skimmed across the choppy lake faster than any America's Cup contender. In July 1986 a sailboard clocked a record as the fastest sailing craft afloat, 38.86 knots, almost 45 mph, in the Canary Islands.

Board sailing was launched only in 1967, when Californians Hoyle Schweitzer, a surfer and computer engineer, and Jim Drake, an aeronautical engineer and sailor, stuck a sail on a surfboard. To attach the sail they used a rotating universal joint, for maximum maneuverability, thereby succeeding where others had failed. First called "windsurfing," after Schweitzer's Windsurfer-brand board, the sport caught on in Europe before breezing over to the U.S. The 1984 Los Angeles Olympics put an official stamp on board sailing, and by 1986 the number of U.S. skippers on boards had swelled to 1.2 million.

Sailing boards is a lot less contentious than sailing boats, in the opinion of George Callum, 42, who entered that Wisconsin regatta with his family when he was with Goodyear in Akron, Ohio. For years Callum had raced a 25-foot sloop with his wife, Janice, 39, a marketing services representative for Polaroid, and their three children. "I was the skipper and told everyone what to do. The summer ended with everyone mad. With boards, everyone is his own skipper," says Callum. Boards and boats compete under virtually the same international yacht racing rules, but "board sailing is a more lighthearted sport," says Janice Callum. And, notes George, "when you drop back on that boom and hit 20 knots, it's awfully exhilarating."

The board sailor's arms substitute for part of the rigging found on a sailboat. No wire shrouds secure the mast; no mainsheet or line control the boom and angle of sail; nor is there a rudder for steering. To steady the swiveling mast and turn the free-moving sail, the board skipper applies his muscle directly to the wishbone-shaped aluminum boom surrounding the sail. To head away from the wind, he tilts the mast forward, and backward to veer toward the wind. All this takes upper-body strength. But balance, flexibility, and coordination are even more important in shifting body weight to help maneuver the board. Skiers make good board sailors; their foot finesse controls the edges of their boards as they bounce through waves.

"You use every muscle," says Jack L. Rivkin, 46, executive vice president and director of research at Shearson Lehman Brothers in New York. After a season of sailing, he had to order his custom-made shirts a size larger — the old ones got too tight across the chest. Weekends from May to November, he sails around eastern Long Island, often with his teenage son and daughter. In a wet suit he ventures out even in December and February.

Wind at five to eight knots (6 to 9 mph) gives a nice ride. Racers need ten to 14 knots. Gusts to 20 knots start to stretch the skills of fun-loving amateurs. "You're on that very line between falling and acceleration — that's why I like board sailing," said Peter Milhaupt, 37, a vice presi-

Peter Milhaupt of First Boston takes a last gasp before ending up in Nantucket Sound.

SPORTS AND GAMES

dent at First Boston Corp., the investment banking firm, who learned to board-sail off Cape Cod.

Mastering the craft may take several lessons for an able body who has never sailed. Some board makers license their own schools and dealers give instruction. Lists of dealers by area are available from the American Boardsailing Industries Association. Distributors of Mistral, the Swiss-made board, offer 200 instructional programs in the U.S. and arrange excursions to tropical waters. International Windsurfer Sailing Schools teaches at 300 locations in the U.S. and abroad. Lathrop Sports Vacations offers week-long instructional packages in the Caribbean, with equipment included. And the United States Boardsailing Team gives weekly racing clinics from mid-January until mid-May in Melbourne, Florida.

"You don't become good unless you compete," Janice Callum believes. She organized Akron's first one-design fleet of Windsurfer sailboards on the Nimisilla Reservoir. The Callum family practiced evenings, and on weekends went to one-design regattas organized by Windsurfing International. From over 25 districts in the Western Hemisphere, these led to the annual Windersurfers championship. The Callums later switched to Mistral boards and races. Some 1,200 one-design regattas divide classes by sailors' weight; light winds favor lightweight skippers.

The United States Board Sailing Association (USBA), a division of the United States Yacht Racing Union, sanctions 50 open regattas, admitting boards of any make, and includes masters divisions for sailors over 35. A few yacht clubs have added board sailing to their racing programs. Other groups organize long-distance races, such as the 18.5-mile crossing of San Francisco Bay and return. In 1986 two Frenchmen on a tandem board with a tiny hull crossed from Dakar, on Africa's coast, to Guadeloupe in the Caribbean in 24 days, 12 hours, and five minutes. They had no competition.

Boards are easy to rig, long lasting, nearly maintenance-free, and transportable on a car top. Cruising yachtsmen sometimes carry them for entertainment in uncrowded anchorages. They cost from $400 to $2,000, in three basic types. The "all-round" board, for gentle waters and beginners, measures about 12 feet and weighs up to 45 pounds in durable plastic. "Funboards," usually under 40 pounds, may have a daggerboard for stability, foot straps, a sliding mast track, adjustable boom, and sails that perform best at 12 to 15 knots. "Short boards" for high winds and waves measure only eight or nine feet, made of fiberglass usually, with no daggerboard. Jack Rivkin uses an all-round board on Gardiners Bay, and a short F2 brand "jumper" for the ocean off Amagansett on Long Island's south shore.

With a life vest and a buddy, sailboards are relatively safe. Only four board-sailing deaths have been recorded in the U.S. in 14 years: two sailors were blown offshore in very high winds and two nonswimmers fell off and failed to cling to the board. If a skipper, overpowered by wind or waves, lets go of the boom, the sail falls on the water, and is supposed to stay attached and afloat as a sea anchor to keep the board in one place. But if equipment fails, a sailor can be in trouble. On Jack Rivkin's short board the universal joint broke twice in heavy wind far from shore. He had to roll up the sail, swim and paddle back, an exhausting and frightening experience.

"The same crowd that skis together in winter board-sails in summer. That's what is so much fun about it," says Christopher Phillips, 35, vice president at Spaulding & Slye, a Boston commercial real estate development firm. His crowd celebrated his marriage to Allyson Button with a prenuptial house party on Cape Cod that included a mile-long sail by 23 guests on boards.

For their honeymoon the couple went to the Hawaiian island of Maui, one of the world's board-sailing hot spots. A combination of waves and trade winds of 20 knots or more make Maui's eastern shore just right from mid-April through October. The newlyweds rented short boards and like most Easterners started in the somewhat tame waters of Kanaha Beach. They advanced to Sprekelsville, which demands more wave riding and jibing and finally tested themselves at Hookipa State Park, mecca for hot shots who jump their boards off cresting waves into the air.

Two years later, Allyson Phillips, by then 27 and president of A.B. Phillips & Co., her own Boston advertising agency, returned with Chris for more of Maui's thrills. Reefs off Hookipa's crescent beach turn ocean swells into long 25-mph waves. You can tack across one breaker all the way to shore. Back home in New England, Chris eagerly awaits storm fronts with high gusts to go out with friends on his F2 Bullet, a high-performance short board. "You can become a sailboard snob," he confesses, "so you want to go out only when it's blowing hard."

FOR FURTHER INFORMATION

American Boardsailing Industries Association, Dept. B, 223 Interstate Rd., Addison, IL 60101.

International Windsurfer Sailing Schools, 2006 Gladwick St., Compton, CA 90220; (213)-608-1651.

Lathrop Sports Vacations, Suite 310, 1430 Massachusetts Ave., Cambridge, MA 02138; (800)-222-LATH or (617)-497-7744.

Mistral, 7222 Parkway Dr., Dorsey, MD 21076; (301)-796-4755.

United States Boardsailing Team Racing Clinics, Box 360804, Melbourne, FL 32936; (305)-242-2424.

United States Boardsailing Association, c/o United States Yacht Racing Union, Box 209, Newport, RI 02840; (401)-849-5200.

PUBLICATIONS

Basic Boardsailing Skills by Derek Wulff (Ottawa: Canadian Yachting Association, 1984), $9.95.

ON THE WATER

Solo Sports Video, P.O. Box 357, Dana Point, CA 92629; (800)-233-6625 or (714)-240-6778.

Sports Illustrated Boardsailing by Major Hall (New York: Harper & Row, 1985), $7.95.

Windrider magazine, seven issues a year, $12.97; World Publications, Suite H, 809 S. Orlando Ave., Winter Park, FL 32790; (305)-628-4802.

Wind Surf magazine, monthly, $19 a year; P.O. Box 561, Dana Point, CA 92629; (714)-661-4888.

Rowing: For Getting an Oar In

■ At 43, John McGowan discovered rowing. At 47, he placed among the top 12 oarsmen in national singles team trials. For 20 years this vice president for program sales at the Tribune Co.'s WPIX-TV in Manhattan and its syndicated Independent Network News, had flailed away at racquet sports without the distinction he had once enjoyed as a youthful long-distance swimmer in California. Then, intrigued by the sight of oarsmen from the New York Athletic Club who trained near his Westchester County home, he started working out with them. His 1983 performance in open competition earned him an invitation to the national sculling camp in Hanover, New Hampshire, where rowers half his age were training for the Pan American Games and the Olympics.

Personal recognition comes more readily in the small pool of rowers than in the vast field of runners or tennis players. The United States Rowing Association totaled some 13,000 members in 1985, eligible to compete in regional and national championships. They stroke alone in a single shell, or in crews of two, four, or eight. And masters competition by age groups starts at an early 27. Stuyvesant Pell, 54, a senior underwriter at Chubb & Son in New York, won national singles championships three times, 1983–85, in the 52 to 59 age category.

Very popular in the 1870s when Philadelphia painter Thomas Eakins depicted the muscular bodies of oarsmen in motion on the Schuylkill, rowing is enjoying a renascence reaching beyond the old clubs and Ivy League colleges that came to dominate the sport. The USRA expanded from 285 clubs in 1980 to 365 organizations in 1985.

Rowing's biggest pull, strengthened by the incentive of training to race, comes from a total workout of arms, back, and legs. Starting with knees bent up against the chest, each stroke requires four movements. The catch puts the oars into the water. The pull-through lengthens the stroke, adding power with a forward thrust of the legs and backward move of the body on a sliding seat — a distinct improvement on the original greased pants — but "shooting the can" by moving too quickly is a no-no. The finish takes the oars out of the water; and in the recovery the rower slides forward with oars above water, careful not to "sky" them. Repeating that routine 34 times in one minute was McGowan's goal when training for the Olympic singles trials. And in a crew, an oarsman should never stop, because his idle oar will interfere with the strokes of the others.

No athlete burns up more energy than the rower. An elite crew of eight college oarsmen stroking a 2,000-meter course (just under 1.25 miles) in five to six minutes drains the energy stored in their muscles in the first 500 meters. Then the aerobic, oxygen-demanding, metabolism takes over. To get the six liters of oxygen per minute required, each of those oarsmen has to inhale more than twice what an unconditioned person inhales while exercising. Although a master rower may not pull as hard as his collegiate competitor, he is still likely to consume four to five liters of oxygen per minute. Thus rowing helps maintain a high level of cardiovascular capacity. But, as in any strenuous exercise, the athlete should first try to determine whether he is free of cardiovascular disease and able to withstand the stress.

Except for occasional back strain, rowing is practically injury-free. Instead of jolting the body, as running does, stroking simply stretches the muscles. Tipping over in cold water is one of the few hazards, especially for rowers eager to start outdoor training as soon as the ice breaks.

Competitors contend with the unique challenge of propelling themselves backward, facing aft with no view of what's ahead. That can be risky for crews without a coxswain, that extra non-rowing crewman who faces forward and calls the strokes. D'Arcy MacMahon, a planning associate at John Hancock Mutual Life in Boston, in 1976 at age 39 qualified with three friends to enter the class of four without cox in Britain's prestigious Henley Royal Regatta

Showing the strain of the National Masters Rowing Championship, Stuyvesant Pell tries to overtake John McGowan.

71

SPORTS AND GAMES

on the Thames. An Irish crew moved illegally into their lane. As the crews repositioned their shells, a crosswind blew the Americans off course, smashing their shell into a barrier and out of the race. When the Irish were declared winners, MacMahon requested and got a tradition-shattering re-row. The reprieved Americans won.

Training for high-level competition demands dogged dedication. When John McGowan, the tyro from TV, went out for an Olympic berth, he trained from 5 until 7 A.M. and from 7 P.M. until 8:30 most weekdays, plus six hours on weekends, usually with his son, James, 18, also an Olympic aspirant. And McGowan's wife, Carol, took up rowing, too. In winter a lot of rowers turn to cross-country skiing. But the McGowans worked out indoors on their home rowing machine and lifted weights to build strength. Their Olympic campaign ended when father and son, along with many more seasoned competitors, missed the team boat in the open trials for singles and doubles. Returning to age-group competition, in the 1985 USRA masters national championships, McGowan won in the singles and, with his wife, in the mixed doubles.

New designs in boats have helped make recreational rowing popular. Wooden shells, which cost up to $3,200 for a single, $4,000 for a double, have largely given way to fiberglass and other moldable materials that are easy to repair and maintain. For beginners a 24- to 30-inch-wide recreational craft is more stable than an 11-inch-wide racing shell. The Alden Ocean Shell by Martin Marine costs $1,515, with oars. Separate high-quality 9½-foot Sitka spruce oars, called sculls, may cost $260 apiece, the same price as a pair of the now preferred synthetic sculls made of carbon fiber, fiberglass, and plastic. The USRA publishes an annual guide to equipment.

Instruction for adults is available not only through clubs but increasingly through the parks departments of certain cities. In Seattle, which claims the largest per-capita boating population in the U.S., rowing is drawing many hundreds of men and especially women to programs for masters, from beginners to advanced. "It's so exciting to be sharing the sport that I love with new people," says Carol Brown, 33, a manager with Altac Corp., which bottles and distributes Pepsi and 7-Up. As a Princeton undergraduate, Brown was a member of the first U.S. women's pair to advance to the finals in international competition. And she earned spots on the national team each year save two from 1974 through the 1984 Olympics. Since switching to recreational rowing at the Lake Washington Rowing Club and at the parks services' new Mount Baker Rowing & Sailing Center, she is particularly pleased to see women, many over 45, come out at 5 A.M. to train. "There's just a tremendous response from women who've always wanted to be athletes and never had an opportunity earlier," says Brown.

The annual Head-of-the-Charles Regatta in Cambridge, Massachusetts, launched in 1965 by D'Arcy MacMahon

with two fellow oarsmen, aimed to attract student and recreational rowers. MacMahon's idea has been to change the spirit of rowing — away from the stern image of the young competitor whose tough training regimen makes the sport all work and no play. The October Sunday contest has grown into the world's largest, limited to 720 boats powered by 3,200 oarsmen competing in 18 events, according to ages and abilities. In a daylong pageant of rowing against the clock, they go off seconds apart, cheered by thousands of spectators along the three-mile up-river course. While acknowledging that you can't compete if you're out of shape, MacMahon says, "It's just fun to get out and see what you can do, especially for people over 40." This regatta has served as a model for other "head" races. And in winter the Crash B Sprints, for Charles River All-Star Has-Beens, takes place on rowing machines in the gym of the Massachusetts Institute of Technology in Cambridge. Progress over a theoretical five-mile course is displayed by computer on a huge screen. Similar events have stroked off around the country.

The social dividends of racing have become more important than the athletic rewards for one very exceptional Olympic crew. They call themselves *Alte Achter* — the "old eight." In the Munich Olympics of 1972 they flew through the water to win a silver medal for the U.S. Every year since then that crew, which includes two pairs of brothers and six who had rowed together at Harvard, has assembled from points as remote as Hawaii and the Virgin Islands to compete amongst the Championship Eights in the Head-of-the-Charles. The crewman who organizes their reunion, Franklin Hobbs, 39, a managing director for mergers and acquisitions at Dillon Read in New York, says, "Rowing is unique for building friendship. It's exhausting, and teamwork is everything. We liked each other so much — maybe the word is loved — that it was very important to stay together and to try to row as a team once a year."

FOR FURTHER INFORMATION

United States Rowing Association; Master's membership, $25 a year, includes *Rowing USA*, bimonthly; Suite 980, 251 N. Illinois St., Indianapolis, IN 46204; (317)-237-2769.

Florida Rowing Centers, Palm Beach Polo & Country Club, 13198 Forest Hill Blvd., West Palm Beach, FL 33414; (800)-327-4204 or (212)-996-1196.

PUBLICATIONS

The Amateurs by David Halberstam (New York: William Morrow, 1985), $14.95.

Rowing for the Hell of It: A Manual for Recreational Rowers by Peter Raymond (Cambridge, MA: Charles River Publishing, 1982), $11.95.

Stroke: A Guide to Recreational Rowing by Bruce Brown (Camden, ME: International Marine, 1986), $14.95. ∎

ON THE WATER

White Water's Seductive Challenge

■ When snow melts or rains swell mountain streams from Maine to California, thousands of men and women slip into canoes and kayaks to ride the rushing rivers. In their light and seemingly fragile craft, with nothing to aid them but their own skill, muscle, and sense of the river, they negotiate a twisting course between rocks and ledges, propelled by a tremendous force of foaming, white water.

"Your adrenaline is running all the time," says Paul Kendall, 44, vice president for properties management of the greater New York YMCA. Kendall and his wife, Sharon Rives, 43, a Citibank vice president for product development, first took to wild rivers in open canoes in their mid-30s, for a change of pace from hiking and biking, and for an intense commitment.

The Kendalls joined a white-water canoeing group in the Appalachian Mountain Club's New York–New Jersey region, one of 13 spread from Maine to Virginia. "You gain a confidence here you don't have elsewhere in your workaday life," Kendall notes. His wife feels that, in the supportive environment of a group, white-water canoeing especially helps women build confidence. And she points out that the mental challenges, good judgment, and quick decisions are the type most business people thrive on.

In spring and early fall the Kendalls spend a couple of weekends a month leading or helping out on canoe trips for the club. "It's a wonderful way to see natural beauty, and in some places there's no other way," says Kendall, who keeps three canoes in the courtyard of the Manhattan apartment building where he lives.

Business men and women have made a daring, low-cost sport of what was serious business for Eskimos, Indians, and fur-trading voyageurs. Those paddlers of cargo-carrying craft — dugouts and skin or birch-bark kayaks and canoes — portaged around serious rapids. But after World War II, aluminum, fiberglass, and other moldable or inflatable substances produced boats light enough to carry, yet tough enough to run the rapids, withstand pounding on the rocks, and easy to repair. In a kayak, narrower and more maneuverable than a canoe, the boater sits tightly in the hull and alternately works both port and starboard sides with a paddle bladed at each end. In a canoe he usually kneels in the classic Indian position.

No one should venture onto white water alone, or without knowing the special techniques of paddling and the hazards that lurk in a roaring river. While a command of the basic strokes used in flat-water canoeing is fundamental, it is far from adequate. "When you get rocks or trees in the way, twists and turns in the river, and currents pushing you down or crosswise in the waves, it becomes a different kind of paddling experience," Kendall observes.

As enthusiasm for white water rose in the 1970s, so did fatalities. Equipped with little more than bravado and a six-pack, some novices tried the sport after viewing it in the 1972 Olympics or the movie *Deliverance,* released that year, which had been filmed on the Chattooga River that flows between northern Georgia and South Carolina. In the three years following, the Chattooga took ten lives.

With training and precautions, the sport can be both safe and thrilling. "Those attracted to this sport usually combine an analytical mind and a physical ability to connect mind and body," says Ray McLain, 49, a chemical engineer for Procter & Gamble's paper products in Green Bay, Wisconsin. He has served on the American Canoe Association's instruction and training committee for a decade. "We're folks who are very careful about our risk management. We're going to understand what we're doing and why we're doing it and ask if we can handle it."

The American Canoe Association, the Sierra Club, and the American Red Cross all offer white-water instruction through local clubs or chapters, where old hands are eager to guide new ones. *Canoe* magazine frequently publishes directories of commercial schools as well as an annual guide to schools, outfitters, and equipment.

Paddlers divide into four categories — novice, intermediate, advanced, and expert — according to their ability to handle six standard international classifications of white water, from I to VI: easy, medium, difficult, very difficult, exceedingly difficult, and nearly impossible water that should be attempted only by teams of properly prepared experts. Novices advance from class I in a few months to class II, where they learn to maneuver the boat around rocks.

Bracing his kayak through a rapid on the Chattooga River in the Carolinas beats any white-water experience that Joseph W. Terrell III, an Anchorage contractor, has found anywhere.

SPORTS AND GAMES

Key to success is working with the force of water, not against it. A beginner tends to "horse" the canoe, trying to move it by strength. The futility of that is illustrated in *Basic River Canoeing* by Robert E. McNair, a hydraulic engineer formerly with Westinghouse and a pioneer in the sport. A canoe two feet wide and 15 feet long hurled against a rock by a current moving at 10 mph could be held there by a force of over four tons. That's such a common predicament that winching procedures for wresting loose a canoe pinned to a rock are given in the Appalachian Mountain Club's *White Water Handbook.*

"Reading" the river ahead, to tell what the contours say about its navigability, and choosing the best course can make the difference between a good and bad trip. It's impossible to memorize a river totally, because a rise or fall in the water level can transform it overnight. At flood stage, submerged trees are unseen hazards. Joel DeYoung, 39, a patent attorney with Chevron Research in California, once lost control of his kayak on the Feather River, hit a large branch, and was almost tossed into the air.

After two years of white-water paddling with the Appalachian Mountain Club, the Kendalls enrolled in an advanced five-day clinic for solo paddlers ($400) at the Nantahala Outdoor Center on the edge of the Smoky Mountains in North Carolina. "You can never stop learning about the forces of nature and how to use them to help you," says Kendall. To get beyond class III, into waters where only the most experienced paddlers should venture, and earn expert ratings took the Kendalls four years from their start in the sport.

Mastery of the "Eskimo roll" is necessary for Class IV water and above. Dunked in the drink, the river runner in a kayak or decked canoe, still snapped inside his cockpit, can right himself with the Eskimo roll. Upside down with his head in the water, and his paddle parallel to the gunwale, he leans forward, arcs the blade horizontally from the bow through the water toward the stern and thrusts his hips in the opposite direction. If he shifts his weight correctly, the boat rolls right side up.

Some white-water enthusiasts thrive on competition. The American Canoe Association, national governing body of competitive paddling on all types of water, sanctions more than 100 white-water race meets a year. Three types of boat — single kayak, single canoe, and tandem canoe — compete in separate open classes. And age-group categories for juniors (under 18), submasters (30 to 40), and masters (over 40) are added to the largest races.

Donald R. Sorensen, 49, a cafeteria and farm owner from Albert Lea, Minnesota, and Procter & Gamble's Ray McLain from Wisconsin have paired in the men's double-canoe slalom as national masters champions for three years, 1983–85. McLain holds several open titles as well. A standard slalom race covers a 600-meter course (just over one-third of a mile) over which paddlers must pass through a series of 20 to 25 gates. McLain and Sorensen also compete singly and together in "wildwater" events, running a downstream unmarked course for four to six miles of exhausting nonstop paddling in water moving at 5 to 15 mph.

For a business person to excel in competition takes tremendous effort and an extraordinary amount of time. Sorensen, who started competing in 1973 to test himself against the performance of his son and daughter, then 13 and 11, spends half his days either at his duties as chairman of the ACA's National Slalom and Wildwater Committee, which oversees all racing, or in training for the watery course.

Be it racing or running rivers, the total concentration required to cope with white water makes the sport a complete break from the cares of business life. Within driving distance of most major metropolitan areas, white water in an unspoiled environment offers a feeling of oneness with nature, and at the same time gives the boater a sense of mastering it, of exercising control over a raw elemental power that is stronger than man.

Compared with other boating, white water is not expensive. New paddlers can rent Appalachian Mountain Club equipment — a place in a canoe, a paddle, and a life vest all for $12 a day; AMC weekend trips cost about $25. For under $1,000, a white-water boater can be totally equipped. A kayak costs from $300 to $650. Canoes can run from $450 to $1,200. Paddles cost $40 to $150. Helmet, life vest, and wet suit, vital when water and weather temperature total less than 100 degrees, may cost $200. But by an act of Congress in 1796, all navigable rivers are free.

FOR FURTHER INFORMATION

American Canoe Association; membership, $25, includes *Canoe* magazine; P.O. Box 190, Newington, VA 22120-1190; (703)-550-7523.

Appalachian Mountain Club; membership, $40 a year, includes *Appalachia,* monthly; 5 Joy St., Boston, MA 02109; (617)-523-0636.

Nantahala Outdoor Center, Box 41, U.S. 19W, Bryson City, NC 28713; (704)-488-2175.

Sierra Club Outing Department, 730 Polk St., San Francisco, CA 94109; (415)-776-2211.

PUBLICATIONS

Canoe magazine, six issues a year, $12; includes *Canoe/Kayak Buyer's Guide;* P.O. Box 3146, Kirkland, WA 98083; (800)-MY-CANOE or (206)-827-6363. Publishes *Starting Out,* annually, $3.95.

Canoeing Wild Rivers by Cliff Jacobson (Merrillville, IN: ICS Books, 1984), $14.95.

Rivergods by Richard Bangs and Christian Kallen (San Francisco: Sierra Club Books, 1985), $18.95.

The White-Water River Book: A Guide to Techniques, Equipment, Camping, and Safety (Seattle: Pacific Search, 1982), $12.95.   ■

ON THE WATER

Water-Skiing, from Slalom to Jumping

■ A Minnesota teenager discovered man's power to ski, if not walk, on water in 1922 when, clasping a towrope attached to a motorboat, he wobbled across Lake Pepin on eight-foot pine boards he had curved up at their tips with steam. Ralph Samuelson's exhibitions soon made water-skiing a hit from the Midwest to the French Riviera. The stunt turned competitive in 1939, with the American Water Ski Association's first championships at Jones Beach on New York's Long Island. Now there's a move afloat to make water-skiing an Olympic sport by 1992. But fun seekers far outnumber competitors.

The tug of the towline, the sting of the spray, and the challenge to stay upright thrill some 15.5 million Americans a year. On calm water almost anyone with access to a small motorboat of 40-or-so horsepower can learn to get up on skis in an afternoon. In half an hour the impatient can master "kneeboarding," a 1980s innovation that lets you kneel on one surfboard-like ski with a belt strapped across your thighs.

"With a good boat driver, the world's worst water-skier can have a good time," says Hobart Fischer, 51, president of Bearings & Motive Specialties Co. in White Plains, New York. Life vest on and feet in rubber bindings, the skier yells, "Hit it!" His driver accelerates in a gradual takeoff, looking out for traffic and, with help from an on-board observer, keeps a backward eye on his skier at the end of a 75-foot line. Comes a fall, the skipper comes about, cuts his engine, and picks up his skier.

"It's a great sport for families," notes Fischer, whose three children and three stepchildren have skied together. After his first daughter learned how at age 10, Fischer, age 38, traded his golf clubs for water skis. Children can start as soon as they feel comfortable in water; some get the hang of it at age 2 but 6 is more usual. A ten-minute turn is time enough, with half a dozen tries over the day.

Fischer's enthusiasm led him to buy a couple of lakeside properties, with the prospect of operating commercial water-skiing facilities as his activity in retirement. "Fischer's Folly" at Uxbridge, Massachusetts, hosted the 1986 Eastern regional tournament, one of the American Water Ski Association's five annual regional contests.

Tournaments feature three main events: slalom — tight turns around buoys on a prescribed course — tricks, and jumping. Serious contenders buy boats especially designed for water-skiing that cost around $20,000 and use from five to seven gallons of gas an hour. While a good pair of recreational skis costs under $200, a slalom ski, with bindings for both feet on a single tapered ski with a fin, costs $350; a ski for tricks, $200 or more. Jump skis spring to a minimum $1,200 and jumpers need helmets. Only the

hardy attempt "barefooting," a special event without skis.

Safe skiing, recreational or competitive, means avoiding collisions with docks or submerged objects or getting run over by another boat. Under the controlled conditions of competition sponsored by AWSA, however, there has never been a fatality. Sprains and strains do occur, particularly in jumping, but serious fractures are rare.

Competitive skiing requires months of strenuous practice. AWSA headquarters in Winter Haven, Florida, will steer you to one of its 450 affiliated clubs. AWSA sanctions 350 tournaments a year in which skiers compete in men's and women's age divisions and according to skill ratings, from novice to master for amateurs. At the Bantam Lake Ski Club near his former home in Connecticut, Fischer started competing in slalom and jumping at age 45 in the veterans' division for men 45 and over.

For the slalom, Fischer throws his hefty body (6-foot-2 and 240 pounds) into a marine version of crack-the-whip. As the boat moves straight ahead along the 850-foot course, Fischer zigzags back and forth across the wake to round three buoys on each side of the course, covering about a third more distance than the boat. So with the boat going up to 34 miles per hour, standard in Fischer's division, he accelerates to as much as 60 mph crossing the wake by pressing down on the back of his ski. To slow down to 20 mph for the next turn, he shifts his weight forward, turns his ski on edge, and presses up a wall of spray. Perfect timing and rhythm are crucial; turning a fraction of a second late, the most common fault, can throw a skier off course for the next buoy. With each successful pass through the entire course, skiers in the expert and master classes are required to make their task harder, shortening the towline by specified amounts. The shorter the line, the farther out the skier must lean in his tug-of-war with the boat as he rounds each buoy.

Trick skiing seems like toe dancing, compared with the swerving glissades of slalom. But to learn tricks takes more time, and more falls, than anything else. Thomas F. O'Donnell, 52, treasurer of Resorts International, holds an expert rating in tricks, as well as in slalom and jumping. But he spent an entire winter at the Greater Miami Ski Club simply learning to turn from front to back on one ski. While the boat moves at about 15 miles per hour, the skier on one, or two, short, wide skis without a keel, executes a routine of turns, from 90 to 360 degrees. Skiers get points for the number and difficulty of tricks performed in 20 seconds. Experts can do most maneuvers on one foot, while holding the towline with the other.

Jumping is the riskiest event, demanding the most exact timing. Competitors are judged on the length of their jump from the top of a ramp to splashdown, and they must ski away upright. With a 133-foot jump, Robert Corson, engineering director of TeleSciences Inc. in Mount Laurel, New Jersey, set an Eastern regional record in 1975. Though that distance has since been beaten, Corson was

75

SPORTS AND GAMES

New Jersey jumping champion in 1985 at age 36, and again in 1986. For conditioning he runs 25 miles a week and works out in a gym year-round. In summer he skis two hours each day.

The jumper first makes a double cut across the wake, left, then right, as the boat heads for the ramp. Then the boat heads right of the ramp, and the skier veers left, aiming to hit the ramp near the lower right-hand corner. Just before reaching it, traveling at his peak speed of, say, 50 miles per hour, he flattens his skis on the water, crouches a bit, and flexes his knees. He glides diagonally up the ramp, five to six feet high, and at the top he straightens his legs with a push, and "gets his pop," as skiers call their liftoff. O'Donnell, who has a friend videotape his practice jumps for review, says, "If you have built up enough speed on that cut, then you will spring into the air and hopefully stay up there forever. It's a great thrill."

Show skiing, a specialty with a limited number of AWSA amateur tourneys, follows the style of professional acts at Florida's Cypress Gardens and some West Coast marinas. Garry Stout, 43, a financial analyst with IBM's information network division in Tampa, Florida, and his wife, Debbie, 35, each spend 40 hours a week producing and performing with the U.S. Water Ski and Show Team. This group puts on some 20 performances a year, from Las Vegas to Tennessee. Besides the awards the club has won, Stout's daredevil spinning leaps from a helicopter onto the water earn him the applause all performers treasure. "I've spent 20 years with IBM," says Stout, who transferred from California's Silicon Valley in 1980, "and I hope to spend 20 more. But at no time do I expect I'll ever get a standing ovation from 10,000 people for it." Defending his heavy commitment to show skiing, Stout says, "The fact that I enjoy my hobby keeps me in good shape physically and mentally and helps me on the job."

FOR FURTHER INFORMATION

American Water Ski Association; membership, $15, includes *The Water Skier,* seven issues a year; P.O. Box 191, Winter Haven, FL 33882; (813)-324-4341.

PUBLICATION
WaterSki magazine, eight issues a year, $15.97; World Publications, 809 S. Orlando Ave., Winter Park, FL 32789; (305)-628-4802. ∎

ON WHEELS AND WINGS

Auto Racing: Vroom at the Top

■ On his 45th birthday, Jerry Clinton drove a secondhand Datsun in the first auto race of his life — and won. "At my age a person may not be able to win footraces against younger runners, but he can buy a set of wheels," says the chairman of Grey Eagle Distributors in St. Louis, one of the top Budweiser wholesalers in the U.S. Clinton was drawn into the sport by business. When actor Paul Newman, a highly successful amateur racer, was competing at St. Louis, Budweiser, one of his sponsors, asked Clinton to lend Newman his air-conditioned motor home to use at the course. Clinton met Newman, watched the races, and got hooked.

A prodigious drive for achievement sends men and women by the tens of thousands to gritty tracks where they climb into powerful machines to see how fast they can go round and round a course. From local club events to International Grand Prix races, there is an emotional pull to this peculiar scene — the spectators camped out in rock-concert fashion, the camaraderie with mechanics and helpers amidst the pre-race din of hammering and tapping, the whiff of hot rubber, and the deafening crescendo of engines accelerating across the starting line.

The Sports Car Club of America, a 36,000-member, nonprofit organization, sanctions 250 amateur races a year at road courses from Lime Rock, Connecticut, to Riverside, California. Drivers must have completed SCCA certification. Cars compete in five categories, from showroom models that roll off production lines to "formula" cars built purely for racing. Categories are further divided by engine size and performance into 22 classes.

Amateur racing appeals to people in business because, while hardly cheap, it offers spirited competition without the big cost and time commitment of far-flung professional circuits. Drivers race, usually in 30-minute sprints, on weekends in their regional and geographic divisions.

The sport is relatively safe. In 25 million miles of SCCA club racing from 1981 through 1986, there were 45 serious smashups but fewer than ten fatalities. Because the hard tops and roll cages inside help ensure safety, Jerry Clinton opted for the GT, or Grand Touring, category. Fenders help too. If open-wheel, open-top formula cars bump tires, they can flip end over end.

He found a Datsun 510 with a 1,600-cc engine that had raced several seasons and once reached the national championships. It cost $10,000, about average for a well-tuned secondhand race car in most classes, and he plowed $3,000 into reconditioning it. By buying a proven car, though, he avoided the costly and time-consuming process of stripping down and modifying a new one. "The GT is a demanding car to drive," says Clinton, "looser in the handling than a formula car. I felt that the training would be an excellent foundation for improving my driving skills."

To get a regional license, Clinton had to attend two drivers' schools. He chose the four-day "grand prix" course in road racing at the Bob Bondurant School of High Performance Driving near Sonoma, California (cost: $1,800), and a one-day session in Oklahoma. Race-driving schools emphasize smoothness, concentration, and consistency. The technique of cornering requires a narrow

Racing in a Sports Car Club of America event, drivers whip out of a turn on a track near St. Louis.

SPORTS AND GAMES

course between spinning out and losing a lot of speed. To straighten out the curve as much as possible, each driver chooses the most direct line for his car. He gets a rhythm going and repeats each lap as mechanically as he can. Clinton's instructors told him speed would increase once he learned to shift and brake more smoothly and maintain concentration.

A regional race often combines with a qualifying event for national championships, so several classes compete at once and 20 to 50 cars career around the course simultaneously. Cars blast to over 145 miles an hour on the straightaway, brake, and downshift from fifth to third or second through ten or 12 turns, some blind, some with increasing or decreasing radii. The deafening whine lasts 12 laps in a regional race, 16 in a national qualifier.

Once he completed six regional races, Clinton was eligible for a national license and started piling up points to get to the national championships at Road Atlanta, a track near Gainesville, Georgia, that is mecca for amateur racers. Each fall, the seven divisions send their four top point winners from each class, 500 of the nation's best amateurs, to Road Atlanta. In only his second year of racing, Clinton qualified, and returned the next two years after winning the Midwest Division in his class.

To win one's class on Road Atlanta's 2.52-mile, 12-turn course is the ultimate achievement for amateur club racers. After qualifying 12 times, John O'Steen finally won the E Production class, for older modified sports cars, when he was 37 and an industrial-relations manager for Procter & Gamble. O'Steen finds it helps his concentration to run each race in his mind ahead of time. That 1981 victory in a 1957 Porsche Speedster made it probably the oldest car ever to take an SCCA national championship. An engineer by training, O'Steen had kept the Speedster competitive for nine years. Unlike formula race cars, which have only a couple of useful years because the technology keeps changing, production cars can have long careers.

Mechanical know-how helps good drivers go faster. After his Road Atlanta victory, O'Steen graduated to a 1981 Porsche 924 with a good racing record in the D Production class. Working with two friends, O'Steen lowered the rear chassis three inches. Then, to keep the wheels in proper alignment, they changed the mounting points on the suspension. In its first race the car ran 1.2 seconds per lap faster than it had in a race on the same track the year before. "Knowing exactly what a car is doing on the track and being able to relate that to what needs to be changed takes years to learn," notes O'Steen. After leading all the way in that car at the 1982 championships, he lost in his class by one second.

To get on the road to Atlanta costs anywhere from $5,000 for the purchase of a used Formula Ford ($15,000 new) to as much as $60,000 for a new turbocharged Dat-

sun, including the expense of preparing it for racing. But, like Commodore Vanderbilt's yacht, it's not the initial investment, it's the upkeep that costs. A season's expenses may run from $15,000 for a competitor who might not travel outside his division to the several hundred thousand dollars that sponsors have committed in one year to Paul Newman. Repairs are the costliest items, and engines have to be rebuilt often, sometimes after running only six hours. For most events, drivers like new tires, at about $500 a set, and use around 30 gallons of high-octane racing gasoline. O'Steen figured on $40,000 for 12 races in one year, high for an amateur. But he's good enough to pick up sponsors to pay most of the bills. One sponsor, Cincinnati Microwave, which makes radar warning systems for cars, liked O'Steen so well it asked him to join the company, and made him president in 1985.

Professional racing with its longer, faster contests, more powerful engines, and purses to help defray bigger expenses, ultimately proves irresistible to many an accomplished amateur. The SCCA sanctions eight road-racing series in which some 500 drivers compete for over $2.2 million. Its Trans-Am series of 100-mile sprint races is for highly modified touring sedans and Grand Touring sports cars. A similar series, the Camel GT, is sanctioned by the International Motor Sports Association, better known as IMSA. Endurance racing, of more than 125 turns around a course, in which drivers usually team up to spell each other, is an IMSA specialty. But both SCCA and IMSA have in recent years introduced endurance series for showroom stock cars, with very few changes from street cars allowed.

Robert G. Kirby, 61, chairman of Capital Guardian Trust Co. in Los Angeles, which manages almost $15 billion in assets, has driven around the amateur and pro auto-racing circuits for over 30 years. "You are trying to drive as slow as possible and still win," he says, "but to win you have to finish." In 1984 Kirby finally won his first SCCA national amateur championship, with a Porsche 914 in the E Production class for older modified sports cars. But he admits being really "hooked on endurance racing." In Florida he has competed in both IMSA classics: the 12 hours of Sebring, 15 times; and the 24-hour grind at Daytona, 12 times. In the 24 hours of Le Mans, organized by France's Automobile Club de l'Ouest, Kirby has driven four times. His team finished once in the top ten, and once in the top 15. Racing for Kirby is an escape from running money: "It's most refreshing to go through the looking glass, where you find people from other walks of life. They are a polyglot group of guys from everywhere."

For all race drivers, results come quickly and clearly. Returns on a business investment may not show up for five years. But after each race, competitors know whether they did the right things and start getting the car ready for the next one.

FOR FURTHER INFORMATION

Sports Car Club of America; membership, $45 a year, includes *Sports Car* magazine; 9033 E. Easter Pl., Englewood, CO 80112; (800)-255-5550 or (303)-694-7222.

International Motor Sports Association, 860 Clinton Ave., Bridgeport, CT 06604; (203)-336-2116.

L'Automobile Club de l'Ouest, circuit de la Sarthe, Cedex 19, 72040 Le Mans-Gare, France; (33)-1-43.72.50.25.

Bob Bondurant School of High Performance Driving, Highways 37 and 121, Sonoma, CA 95476; (707)-938-4741.

PUBLICATIONS

Drive It!: The Complete Book of High Speed Driving — On Road and Track by Peter Wherrent (Newbury Park, CA: Haynes), $9.95.

Driving in Competition by Alan Johnson (New York: Norton, 1975), $8.95.

National Speed Sport News, weekly, $22; P.O. Box 608, Ridgewood, NJ 07451-0608; (201)-445-5117.

On Track, weekly, $37.50; OT Publishing Inc., P.O. Box 8509, Fountain Valley, CA 92728; (714)-966-1131. ∎

Motorcycling: Free and Close to Nature

■ The old Hell's Angels image of motorcyclists disappeared in the dust thanks to the gas shortages of the Seventies and a fresh-air-and-fellowship campaign. Not only convenience and economy, but freedom of the road atop a powerful machine more challenging, and more risky, than a car appeal to many executives. When George L. Bunting Jr., 46, president and chief executive of Noxell Corp. (Noxzema, cosmetics), wants a little solitude, he vrooms off on his BMW-RT100. Even in a pack of biking buddies, he says, a cyclist is on his own. "That's a refreshing switch from the business world where I communicate all the time."

The choice of motorcycle depends on what route the rider fancies. With other motorized traffic — in town, on the highway, or on a road-racing track — road or street "bikes" prevail. Dirt bikes, usually smaller and lighter, can handle off-road trail riding or competing.

A longtime sports-car fancier, Bunting once disdained all motorcycles as "terrible." Then he noticed a lot of trail bikes zipping around the countryside near his Maryland farm. A lifelong love of machines proved stronger than his prejudice and he picked up one of his own. Later he discovered that a Noxell executive owned a BMW touring bike. Bunting took a spin on the "Beemer," and was captivated. He later bought trail bikes for his three sons, and a road bike for his wife, Anne, who really prefers horses.

For a getaway, Bunting tours with his oldest son and a group of senior executives from several companies. In over 35,000 miles on the road, he has ridden along the Blue Ridge Parkway not too far from home, as well as in New England and the U.S. and Canadian Rockies. The men say the trips give them a surpassing sense of freedom and closeness to nature. As they rhythmically balance their 500-pound machines, leaning into the curves and tasting the wind, they feel in tune with the world around them. Bunting likens the sensation to skiing; a companion who soars finds it more like flying.

These efficient machines can produce 90 horsepower or more and accelerate to 60 miles per hour in 4.6 seconds. Accidents are a constant threat on the road. While Oklahoma, Idaho, and West Virginia let motorcyclists use their auto drivers' licenses, motorcycles registered elsewhere for highway use accounted for approximately 3.1% of all motor vehicle registrations in 1985. But motorcycles tolled 10% of all motor vehicular fatalities. As in auto accidents, drunken driving is a major factor. In 1985, 4,627 motorcyclists, most on road bikes, were killed, and police reports showed 45% of them were legally drunk. Though the need for appropriately designed safety helmets is obvious, motorcyclists are an individualistic bunch who in most states have staved off legal requirements to wear them. The Motorcycle Safety Foundation of Costa Mesa, California, has designed a 6½-hour "Better Biking Course" covering all types of road hazards, available at many spots nationwide.

On his Can-Am trail bike, Jack Noga, of Hitchiner Manufacturing, makes a splashy finish to a 60-mile "enduro" at Sturbridge, Massachusetts.

SPORTS AND GAMES

Bunting and his group, who always wear helmets, have so far escaped accidents. But like most riders, they have a near-miss story. Narrowly avoiding collision with a truck in Tennessee on one of their early tours taught the men to be extra alert. They avoid most major highways, in favor of back roads, where the scenery is more spectacular anyway, and most ride with headlights on even in daylight to make their small silhouettes more visible to other motorists.

The American Motorcyclist Association and its affiliates around the country organize annually more than 1,000 road-riding meets for their members (annual dues: $20). The AMA offers independent tourers a Mac Pac with suggested routes marked for any itinerary desired. The AMA's *International Help 'N Hands Directory* lists cities and phone numbers of members willing to help travelers with mechanical problems.

Motor-psyched amateur competitors can match skills and bikes, classed by engine size, from 125 cc to 1,000 cc in AMA events. A special license is required for road racing. In addition to on-road races, competition includes sprint and endurance road racing, motocross (one to two miles of tight turns and jumps on a closed dirt track over natural terrain), and dirt-track racing. On trails in the woods, hare scrambles follow no time schedules, but competitors in "enduros" are tied to a schedule, each lasting two to four hours. The AMA can furnish details on its racing schools and championship cup series.

Trail riders, whether touring or competing, get plenty of action from rocks, sand, trees, and swamps, often on old carriage roads or fire roads, over rough terrain, through stream beds and brush. To keep peace with environmentalists, the New England Trail Rider Association, an independent group, has developed and mapped for its members over 2,000 miles of trails in six states, along clearings for power and gas lines, and abandoned roads where the knobby treads of trail bikes do minimum ecological damage.

In enduros, similar in format to auto rallies, riders are scored on how well they maintain an average speed usually set between 18 and 30 miles an hour, over a bone-jarring 60- to 120-mile route, mostly off-road. When they were some years younger, Duncan Fordyce, 44, a vice president at the Common Fund, money managers in Fairfield, Connecticut, and John S. Noga, 50, chief financial officer of Hitchiner Manufacturing in Milford, New Hampshire, entered a Massachusetts springtime enduro known as the "Cookie Buster." Fordyce bounced his 230-pound Austrian-made KTM bike over half the rutted, hilly 60-mile course. Then, because he had to stay in low gears most of the way owing to soggy ground, the bike ran out of gas. After walking the bike for two miles, he was able to borrow enough gas to make it to the 40-mile checkpoint, only to be disqualified because he was so far behind. Noga ran out of gas, too. But he managed to beg some fuel from a woman mowing her lawn. His boots full of water and his Can-Am bike caked with mud, he finished the course. Both Noga and Fordyce were delighted with the day.

San Francisco's Montgomery Street Motorcycle Club puts bikes to a more practical use. The club was founded in 1969 when Bank of America Vice President Charles Stuart Jr., then 41, and several friends began motorcycling to their jobs in the financial district. Many members — some 40 business executives and professionals — still do. But they hardly leave it at that. Nine short outings plus three or more weekend trips, usually riding "two-up" with wives or girl friends, make up their calendar.

The Montgomery Street Club's year tops off with a black-tie banquet Saturday night before Christmas. Next morning, the revelers take a ritual Sunday ride over a route favored by hundreds of motorcycle fanatics, 35 miles of tight turns and fast straightaways north of San Francisco on Highway 1, from Tamalpais Valley to Inverness. Only instead of the customary protective leather outfits, they wear tuxes to prove, in a display of lighthearted snobbery, that motorcyclists can be gentlemen. The ride ends with a champagne breakfast.

FOR FURTHER INFORMATION

AMA Championship Cup Organization, P.O. Box 447, Skyland, NC 28776; (704)-684-4297.

American Motorcyclist Association, P.O. Box 6114, 33 Collegeview Rd., Westerville, OH 43081-6114; (614)-891-2425.

New England Trail Rider Association, P.O. Box 478, Ellington, CT 06029; (203)-875-5757.

PUBLICATIONS

American Motorcyclist, monthly, $10 (free to AMA members).
Cycle, monthly, $13.98; P.O. Box 2776, Boulder, CO 80302.
Rider, monthly, $15.98; 29901 Agoura Rd., Agoura, CA 91301; (818)-991-4980. ∎

Ballooning, with the Wind

∎ Man's oldest form of flight celebrated its bicentennial in 1983 amidst an exuberant renascence. In June an international flock of balloonists dropped in on Annonay, France, a town where the brothers Joseph and Etienne Montgolfier lofted the first hot-air balloon. Theirs was a paper-lined linen bag inflated with the smoke of burning wool and straw. The 1983 visitors manned balloons of flameproof nylon or polyester, and used liquid propane burners to heat the air that fills and lifts the bag. But the idea was the same: hot air is lighter than cold, and once the air inside gets hotter than the air outside, the balloon ascends. The new technology of using liquid propane, developed by the U.S. Navy in the 1950s, replaced prohibitively expensive hydrogen and helium balloons and made sport ballooning

ON WHEELS AND WINGS

popular. From a handful of adventurers who founded the Balloon Federation of America in 1961, pilot members had grown to some 3,000 in 1986, about half of the nation's balloon pilots.

As those great, gaudy bubbles float overhead, giant toys come to life, their passage inspires awe in spectators below. The earthbound exchange shouted conversation with the aeronauts: "Where are you going?" "With the wind." And so you are, because you can't steer a balloon; it drifts at whatever speed and in whatever direction the wind is running. You can control only its ups and downs, by raising or lowering the inside air temperature. But since wind directions vary with altitude, vertical maneuvers may find a breeze going your way.

Aloft, aeronauts enjoy serenity and exposure to earth's natural beauty, coupled with enough spice of risk to set them apart, or so they feel, from their peers beneath. There is a glorious uncertainty about the destination and a superlative pleasure in just happening upon scenes and events 1,000 to 2,000 feet below. The landscape appears to unreel as if on film, and smells waft up — the sweet scent of a meadow freshly mown. Stillness is broken periodically by the roar of the propane burner, as the pilot keeps the air in the envelope hot.

If ballooning is one of the most uplifting pastimes, it's not low cost. In 1986 a new balloon averaged around $15,000, depending on size. Most come with envelopes inflatable to 56,000 or 77,000 cubic feet; a wicker or aluminum gondola with room for two to four passengers and a couple of 10- or 20-gallon propane tanks; an adjustable burner; fire extinguisher, radio, and some electronic instruments. The Federal Aviation Administration requires balloons, like other aircraft, to be registered and inspected periodically. When depreciation, plus costs of operating, maintenance, and insurance — increasingly hard to get — are computed, a balloonist who flies 75 hours a year would pay about $80 an hour for the pleasure, says Thomas F. Sheppard, 56, president of the Balloon Federation of America in 1984–86. He's also president of Sheppard-Spaeth Associates of West Bend, Wisconsin, which sells telecommunication testing instruments.

Nor is ballooning to be practiced casually. In recent years the National Transportation Safety Board has counted two to three dozen accidents and up to two fatalities annually. The deadliest hazard is collision with power lines, which can slice through the rigging like a torch or electrocute balloonists. Trees, fences, and fields with livestock or crops are to be avoided. And sudden storms can create problems. Even the most skilled balloonists are at risk. Maxie Anderson, who in 1978 crossed the Atlantic with two other pilots in the Double Eagle II, a helium balloon, was killed in 1983 during a hot-air balloon race. While he was trying to avoid crossing into East Germany, his equipment malfunctioned and he crashed in a Bavarian forest.

Stringent FAA requirements for a private pilot's license have improved the sport's safety record. The license takes at least ten hours of in-flight training, though 12 to 14 hours are the norm, at about $100 an hour. You must pass a written exam that includes meteorology, and take a flight test. And you need to be recertified every other year. Many pilots enhance their skills with a commercial license, requiring 35 hours of training. Some earn an instructor's license. John R. Hager, 57, of Lancaster, Pennsylvania, traded a 28-year career in retailing for land development to devote more time to ballooning. He has trained 30 pilots, four of whom became state champions in competition, and he has served as an FAA examiner.

You'll need clear, cool days with light, variable winds. High winds can drag the gondola of a partially filled balloon across the ground. Breezes stiffer than eight to ten knots make a launch difficult, and over 15 to 20 knots, impossible. You'll also need a little help from your friends and family, and a lot of patience. Inflating a balloon is almost as challenging as flying one. The pilot and ground crew of half a dozen spread the envelope on the ground and use a big inflator fan to fill it partially with air. When the burner is turned on, the crew strains to hold the mouth of the envelope open. Then as the inflated balloon towers 50 or 60 feet, the crew holds down the basket until the pilot is ready to ascend.

As the balloon drifts away, the crew hops into vans and gives chase to be on hand for the landing in a couple hours. By tradition, when a balloon bumps down in some remote field, champagne is broken out to be shared with the ground crew and some surprised landowner suddenly called upon to welcome these unexpected visitors as guests, not trespassers. Deflated, the huge bag folds into a compact bundle that fits inside the gondola.

With helping hands to get him aloft, builder Al Desmond (third from left) of Aurora, Illinois, steps into his gondola.

81

SPORTS AND GAMES

For all its apparently aimless drift in slow motion, sport ballooning has since the early 1970s generated local, national, and international competitions. Most are announced in *Ballooning,* the quarterly sent to members of the Balloon Federation of America, or in its monthly, *Pilot News.* In all of these events, the main test is navigational skill.

Every August some 100 contestants head for Indianola, Iowa, headquarters of the BFA, to vie in the U.S. National Hot Air Balloon Championship. The challenge consists of a series of five-mile, point-to-point flights on each of three legs, repeated over several days. Scoring is based on how close a pilot comes to each leg's target, plus time in flight. The 1986 high scorer was Sidney Cutter, president of World Balloons in Albuquerque, New Mexico.

The World Hot Air Balloon Championship drew 100 competitors and 85 fun-fliers from 22 countries, including Poland and China, to Battle Creek, Michigan, in July of 1985. Competitors in this seventh biennial event had to perform 11 tasks in one week. David Levin, 38, a lawyer and entrepreneur from Boulder, Colorado, came down as champion. This contest first got off the ground thanks to balloonist Donald N. Kersten, 61, an attorney and former Air Force officer from Fort Dodge, Iowa. Kersten persuaded the *Fédération Aeronautique Internationale* in Paris, world governing body of sport aviation, to sanction an international championship, and to let Albuquerque, New Mexico, host the first, in February 1973. The eighth world championship was scheduled for Austria in September 1987, and the ninth for Japan in November 1989.

Albuquerque, where the climate permits ballooning practically year-round, stages its own week-long International Balloon Fiesta every October. It draws close to 500 balloonists. In several "convergent navigational tasks" pilots pick their launching spot within one to three miles of a designated target and drop a marker as close to the target as they can maneuver. In one spectacular event, they try to grab a set of car keys off a 25-foot-high pole. The winner gets the car.

Competitive ballooning is a way of life for Albuquerque resident John C. Davis IV, owner of a restaurant and nightclub called the Launch Pad, and his family. Since their first ascent in 1972, when both were 27, Davis and his wife, Carol Rymer Davis, a radiologist and specialist in nuclear medicine, have entered competitions in 30 states, usually taking their two daughters with them. The younger got her first ride in a swinging balloon basket at 3 weeks, and from age 10 both children have helped the ground crew. At 16 they will be eligible for their own pilot's licenses. John Davis is New Mexico's 1986 champion and Carol Davis holds 15 world records.

Setting records is yet another challenge for high-flying balloonists. The National Aviation Association in Washington, D.C., tabulates statistics submitted on all types of exceptional flights by category of aircraft, and forwards these to the FAI in Paris for determination of world records. Dr. Davis set her records in category AX-5, a relatively small, 42,000-cubic-foot balloon. The three standouts: altitude, 31,300 feet, close to six miles, or cruising altitude for 727s; distance, 136.77 miles; and duration of flight, 6:29:1 hours.

The *Diplôme Montgolfier,* ballooning's highest honor, awarded by the FAI for outstanding contribution to the sport, was given to Dr. Davis in 1981 for her record achievements. In 1986 Malcolm S. Forbes, 68, editor-in-chief and publisher of *Forbes* magazine, and best known of all executive balloonists, was named a Montgolfier award winner for personally introducing the sport to China and sponsoring a Chinese team in the world championships. Forbes has also opened a museum of ballooning at his Château de Balleroy in Normandy.

Most balloonists find reward enough in simple ascent, which calls up childlike wonderment. Fritz Rosendahl, 52, chairman of First Federal Savings & Loan Association of Estherville, Iowa, named one of his balloons *Gulliver's Travels.* "When you leave the earth, it miniaturizes. People, cattle, fields, all shrink while you grow magically larger," he said. "It's almost like falling into a storybook."

FOR FURTHER INFORMATION

Balloon Federation of America; membership, $30 a year; P.O. Box 264, Indianola, IA 50125; (515)-961-8809.
National Aeronautic Association, 1763 R St. N.W., Washington, D.C. 20009; (202)-265-8720.
Albuquerque International Balloon Fiesta, Inc., 4804 Hawkins N.E., Albuquerque, NM 87109; (505)-344-3501.

PUBLICATIONS
The Aeronauts by Donald Jackson (Alexandria, VA: Time-Life Books, 1980), $14.95.
The Eagle Aloft; Two Centuries of the Balloon in America by Tom D. Crouch (Washington, D.C.: Smithsonian, 1983), $49.95.
Hot-Air Ballooning by Charles Coombs (New York: Morrow, 1981), $11.75. ∎

Learning to Fly

∎ Your instructor climbs out of the plane and says, "Now you take it up by yourself," slams the door, and walks off. You had steeled yourself for this moment. You had taken the two-seater around the flight pattern and landed at least 15 times. You were ready for your first solo, after, say, 15 hours of flying. Comfortable as you had begun to feel at the controls, you find the plane seems awfully empty without your instructor.

You taxi down the runway, reminding yourself to steer with your feet, not your hands. You go through the pre-takeoff checklist, pick up the mike, and say in your new, officious radio voice: "Robbinsville Traffic, Cessna 922

ON WHEELS AND WINGS

departing on runway 29." You turn, straighten out, taxi a few feet, and then push the throttle in all the way. The engine roars. The plane shakes, picks up speed, wanders a little, and then, as you pull the controls back at 55 knots, she lifts off.

Why anyone would want to take his life in his hands by learning to fly is a mystery to most people. Yet high-priced executives, entrepreneurs, and professional people in their 30s and older are learning in great numbers to take off, roll out of turns, nose over out of stalls, fly by instrument, and flare their landings.

Charles I. Robins, 55, president and owner of Met-Chem Testing Laboratories in Dearborn, Michigan, was 40 when he took to flying for the convenience it offers. His business requires visits to clients in the auto and aircraft industries from northern Michigan to southern Florida. Robins had wearied of being at the mercy of commercial airline schedules, and long hauls on the highway. The drive to a Chrysler plant he visits in Van Wert, Ohio, takes three hours. "Making that six-hour round trip in one day just wipes you out," notes Robins. In the single-engine, six-seat, pressurized Piper Malibu, equipped with telephone, that his company keeps at the Detroit City Airport, Robins can get to Van Wert's small airport in 30 minutes. "The nice thing is I can come to the office in the morning, jump in the plane, go do what I have to do, take the guys to lunch, and get back to my office for a couple more hours of work."

A weekend flight to Mackinac Island, the historic summer resort in northern Michigan, takes Robins 50 minutes, to a landing field right on the island. To drive from Detroit takes five hours plus a ferry ride — Mackinac Island allows no cars. When Robins flies the Piper for pleasure, he pays his company the going rate for renting that model.

Many executives find both personal and business reasons for learning to fly. Airline deregulation has cut point-to-point service between small and medium-size cities. Besides the time saved, keeping your own plane airborne is so mind-consuming that you leave other problems on the ground. Though 937 people were killed in private planes in 1985 compared with 638 on commercial flights, the accident rate for general aviation, which consists of private noncommercial planes, has been improving.

The main problem with flying is learning how. It requires lots of spare time, at least $3,000 for lessons and plane rentals, and a willingness to tackle the rudiments of aerodynamics, navigation, meteorology, radio communications, and a pack of FAA regulations. The FAA requires medical, written, and oral examinations, plus a minimum of 20 hours with an instructor and 20 hours of solo before you can take the flight-proficiency test. Most candidates take it after about 50 hours. A good part-time training schedule would be three flight lessons a week of one to two hours each and another three hours of ground school. On this schedule, a student ought to get a private pilot's license in three to four months.

Before you think of taking flight instruction, you should have some specific reason for piloting yourself regularly, whether it's going to a Wisconsin lake every weekend or making business trips. Whatever proficiency you gain to obtain your private pilot's license will soon fade if you don't use it. The recreational pilot flies 50 to 100 hours a year. Some instructors recommend as many as 100 hours to keep up your skills for visual flying. For those licensed to fly by instrument, at least an additional 50 hours in actual instrument flight conditions is recommended.

Many people start flying in one of the programs that Cessna, Piper, and Beechcraft franchise. These courses come with textbooks, audiovisual presentations, home-study tape kits, ground schools, and flight training by FAA-approved instructors. There are also independent schools such as American Flyers/Aviation Training Enterprises, a national chain, with schools in Illinois, California, Texas, Florida, and New York. Aviation Seminars of Princeton Junction, New Jersey, provides accelerated ground-school training in 160 places around the country.

The proximity of an airport to home tends to be the first consideration in choosing a school, but it may be worth going farther afield. Private airports near big cities are often crowded with corporate jets that get priority over student pilots for takeoffs and landings. Meanwhile you wait on the ground with your meter ticking at $35 or more an hour. It's hard enough learning to coordinate wing flaps and airspeed without having to worry about other airplanes and static-filled radio communications with cryptic air controllers.

The school should be FAA-approved. If there is no ground school and you are given only a handbook and tapes to study at home, try elsewhere. If the maintenance area looks messy with parts strewn about, walk out. Sloppy maintenance can be fatal. Seek the advice of someone who flies a lot and can recommend an instructor. Even at the best schools, instructors are underpaid and most teach only to accumulate the flying hours that will open up aviation's more lucrative jobs. The FAA requires an instructor to have a commercial license, which takes a minimum of 250 hours in the air, but ideally he or she should have flown 500 hours and have an instrument rating. Most schools offer package deals that guarantee you a pilot's license for a fixed price. The package should also include liability coverage for accidents.

Your private pilot's license once earned is really just a license to learn. True proficiency comes only after hours of practice flights. Chuck Robins went on to get a few additional certificates, including a commercial pilot's certificate, so he can carry passengers with confidence and for hire, and an instrument flight rating to get up and down in bad weather. In about 400 hours of flying a year Robins puts in five hours of instrument flying each month. When weather is really bad, you should leave your plane on the ground and either skip that important meeting, or take a

SPORTS AND GAMES

commercial flight. To get an instrument rating will probably cost at least another $5,000, for instruction and plane rental.

Many executives buy a plane. Entrepreneurs who spend more than half their time in the air on business trips may be able to claim accelerated depreciation for tax purposes. And trading up may help. Robins, whose company bought his $450,000 Piper Malibu in 1986, is depreciating it at about $60,000 a year, over five years. Production of the most popular single-engine plane ever made, the Cessna 172 Skyhawk four-seater, has ceased. But on the brisk market in used aircraft it has been selling from $11,000 to some $50,000, depending on the year it was made.

Once you're airborne, the chief thing on your mind, besides takeoffs, climbs, and turns, is landing. Your biggest problem may be judging the distance for the approach. On your first solo you do as you have been told: get in perfect position, reduce your airspeed by manipulating the flaps, hold up the nose, cut power, float right down, and pull back the controls. The wheels give a little yelp, but hold the ground. Then follows a little ritual for first solos: your instructor grabs your shirt, cuts off the tail, and hangs it on the school's wall with your name on it. So don't solo in your best Brooks Brothers shirt.

FOR FURTHER INFORMATION

Aircraft Owners and Pilots Association; membership, $35 a year, includes help with flight planning and legal services, and *AOPA Pilot* magazine ($16 to non-members); 421 Aviation Way, Frederick, MD 21701; (301)-695-2000.

SCHOOLS

FlightSafety International; maintains training centers at 16 airports; Marine Air Terminal, La Guardia Airport, Flushing, NY 11371; (718)-565-4130.

Franchised flying school headquarters:
Beechcraft's Aero Clubs, Wichita, KA: (316)-681-7111.
Cessna Aviation Education, Wichita, KA: (316)-685-9111.
Piper Aircraft Flight Centers, Vero Beach, FL: (305)-567-4361.

PUBLICATIONS

Trade-A-Plane, three times monthly, $22 a year; 410 W. 4th St., Crossville, TN 38555; (615)-484-5137.
Flying magazine, monthly, $15.97 a year; includes annual "Buyers Guide" ($3.95 to non-subscribers); P.O. Box 2772, Boulder, CO 80321; (800)-525-0643.
On Extended Wings by Diane Ackerman (New York: Atheneum, 1985), $17.95. ∎

Civil Air Patrol: Knights of the Sky

■ Early one evening in August 1983, businessman Jan Ostrat, 43, found himself flying two dogs from San Francisco to Redding, California, 200 miles to the north. For Ostrat, who runs a San Francisco company that makes building products, it was yet another mission for the Civil Air Patrol, the civilian auxiliary of the U.S. Air Force that aids in rescuing small downed aircraft and missing people. The animals were search dogs to be used by the Shasta County sheriff's department in looking for a person who had wandered away from a camp for the handicapped.

Midway in the flight, Ostrat received an emergency radio message from a CAP mission coordinator: would he in his single-engine Cessna 206 listen for radio distress signals from an aircraft in trouble? A small plane had been last heard from going down in the mountains west of Redding. Ostrat promptly delivered the dogs and their handlers, and at the Redding airport took aboard three CAP observers to conduct an airborne search.

The missing plane's last, faint message, picked up by another plane's radio, contained the word "Bally." Back and forth through the night Ostrat and his crew flew over and around Shasta Bally Mountain, 15 miles west of Redding. The observers scanned the group for flares or a fire and listened for the "wuup, wuup, wuup" of radio signals from the emergency locator transmitter, or ELT, that all noncommercial civilian aircraft must carry. The transmitter goes on automatically in a crash. Finding nothing, the team returned to Redding at midnight. Talking to the missing pilot's wife, they learned he had taken off that morning, headed for Oregon. Aloft again at daybreak, Ostrat and crew concentrated on an area 40 miles northwest of where they had searched the night before. They flew near Weaver Bally Mountain, close to the Salmon-Trinity Alps wilderness.

This time they picked up an ELT signal, and at 7 A.M. spotted the missing Cessna 152 in a brush-filled canyon.

Wisconsin Civil Air Patrol Commander James W. Heintskill (left) and pilot Raymond Fiorina check a T-34 Beechcraft in Milwaukee before a search-and-rescue training exercise.

ON WHEELS AND WINGS

They immediately called for a Forest Service helicopter and led it to the site. The plane's pilot and passenger were seriously hurt but alive. Ostrat later learned that the passenger, suffering from severe internal injuries, would probably have lived only an hour or two more if he hadn't received medical attention. "That find was a very gratifying experience, to say the least," Ostrat recalls.

Ostrat, who puts in 100 to 200 hours a year flying for CAP, joined in 1980, after he learned to fly and bought a plane. Many of his pilot friends were members, and the work sounded interesting. "CAP gives you a chance to get away from the hubbub of business," he says. "You never know where you are going to fly. Today the Bay Area, tomorrow the desert, or the High Sierra." And, he points out, "you are doing something to help a fellow pilot. Someday you might require the same assistance." In the fall of 1984 Ostrat and a CAP observer found two crash survivors in a mountain pass in the Yosemite area, at 10,000 feet in fresh snow. Ostrat's search-and-rescue work earned him an award from the governor and the job of CAP's deputy director of emergency services for the state of California.

In 1985 the U.S. fleet of 213,000 private aircraft sustained 2,742 accidents; 490 of those took 937 lives. If your plane, or your company's, disappears in flight, CAP volunteers will probably look for it. CAP puts in 80% of the search hours flown on missions directed by the Air Force Rescue Coordination Center, which coordinates all search-and-rescue efforts in the continental U.S. CAP's nearly 11,000 pilots take wing in 9,430 of their own planes, plus some 545 military hand-me-downs. The low-flying, slow-flying Cessnas, Beechcrafts, and Pipers popular among civilian pilots are better suited to conducting visual searches than most military aircraft. In 1985 CAP teams, in the air and on the ground, made 1,593 finds. But the missions can be dangerous. In June of 1985 a CAP crew of three on a search in the Oregon mountains and another of four on a practice mission in Washington State lost their lives in crashes.

CAP teams log a lot of time on disappointments — most of their finds turn up no survivors. And many missions do not end with a find. In September of 1984, for example, CAP pilots from California, Arizona, and New Mexico logged 540 hours of flying looking for a plane that disappeared on a flight from Carlsbad, California. They never found it. Over 95% of the ELT signals investigated turn out to be false alarms.

Disaster relief and the transport of blood and organs for transplant make up the rest of CAP's emergency services. Less time-consuming and more certain of success than searches, medical missions help CAP build its count of lives saved. Total 1985 saves: 116.

You don't have to be a pilot to belong to CAP. Radio buffs operate a network of more than 29,000 stations over special frequencies, providing an independent communication network. They report emergencies, including natural disasters such as hurricanes and floods, and marshal help. Intelligence officers develop a description of a missing plane and leads on where it might have gone, often by talking to airport personnel or the pilot's friends and family. About half the planes in distress that the Air Force and CAP search for have not filed flight plans. Aerial observers look for telltale marks — a swath of sheared trees — and ground-to-air signals: an X of stone, wood, or cloth means survivors need medical assistance.

Wilderness trackers and emergency medical technicians form ground teams to rescue victims at accessible sites. Michael Curry, 29, a software engineering manager with Ingersoll Milling in Milwaukee, trains CAP cadets in land rescue. His wife, Elizabeth, 29, an engineer with General Electric's medical systems, works in mission control to help coordinate all of these specialists. You can learn many of these skills from CAP courses that are offered evenings or on weekends.

Much of the work is not of the drop-everything-and-take-off immediately variety. CAP pilot Raymond Fiorina, 58, vice president for manufacturing at A. O. Smith Automotive Products Co. in Milwaukee, spends a lot of Saturdays repairing and maintaining the patrol's planes. General Dynamics lets Betty Decker, 57, a project representative in Pomona, California, operate as mission controller out of her office.

Unlike the military reserves or National Guard, none of CAP's 41,570 senior members or 24,000 cadets (boys and girls age 13 to 21) get paid. Volunteers on an authorized mission, including pilots flying their own planes, are covered by government insurance. Crews draw reimbursement only for fuel, oil, maintenance, and communications costs. Those payments totaled $1.47 million in 1985 for 13,234 hours of flying done by CAP.

If you're intrigued by the prospect of adventure and ready to take an oath "to save life and to aid the injured . . . placing these duties before personal desires and comforts . . . that others may live," you can join CAP anywhere in the U.S. Check the phone book or ask your local airport for the address of the nearest unit.

FOR FURTHER INFORMATION
Civil Air Patrol, Maxwell AFB, AL 36112; (205)-293-5463. ■

IN WINTER

Ski Racing Alpine Style

■ Zigzagging down flag-marked slalom courses has picked up speed among the 9.5 million U.S. downhill, or alpine, skiers. At major ski areas, hundreds of thousands of racers bear down on their poles and burst through electronic starting gates. On a quarter-mile giant slalom course, they carve long open turns through a couple of dozen gates in less than a minute. It's "like driving a high-powered sports car, with no blinking red cop lights following you," said Jack Gaar, 36, proprietor of an accounting firm in Costa Mesa, California, and a club racer.

Ski clubs open those racing gates, even for novices, offering trips and instruction at group rates. To get started in alpine racing, you don't need special racing boots or skis. At over $300 a pair, those can wait until you're a serious competitor.

And a smorgasbord of national programs offers racing to weekenders and vacationers at nominal fees. Regional winners get free trips to finals at top resorts. Rules of eligibility keep out professionals, national team members, and recent winners.

Nastar, or National Standard Race, is the most widely available program, found at 135 ski areas. The "standard" is based on a complex national handicap system, involving a pacesetter at each course who runs it every day to establish the equivalent of par at a golf course. A Nastar competitor can run on any Nastar course, as often as he likes. His daily result is registered at a computer center, and his three best handicaps of the season are averaged to determine his final handicap and standing. The 100 best Nastar adult racers — two men and two women in five age groups from each of five regions — receive all-expense-paid trips to Nastar national championships.

"The reward is not just the paid expenses; it's the whole experience," says Richard Abromeit, a security analyst with Breau Capital Management in Waltham, Massachusetts. He won a trip to the 1985 Nastar championships in Sun Valley, Idaho. He paid for his wife's trip, and for an extra week at Sun Valley, where they found the steeps more demanding than the flatter hills they are used to at Waterville Valley, New Hampshire. They've put their 3-year-old daughter on skis, in hopes of entering the Family Ski Challenge in a few years.

Sponsored formerly by Equitable Life Assurance, this series is for family pairs: a parent and child under 19, siblings, or spouses. The two run the course separately, but in each category the pair with the best combined times wins. Local races are scheduled almost every weekend from late December through February at 50 ski areas. In 1984 Robert E. Comstock Jr., 40, a New York-based controller for SITA, a worldwide airline telecommunications

Opening the ski-club racing season in California, Jack Gaar, CPA, surges forward at the start of a giant slalom race down Fascination Run at Mammoth Mountain.

IN WINTER

consortium, and his wife, Frances, 39, each teamed up with their daughter, Jennifer, 13, for races at Killington, Vermont. Both pairs won and moved on to the Northeast regional competition, one of five nationwide. Again they triumphed, and were among 35 family teams to win three-day trips to Vail, Colorado, for the national championships.

Enjoying the luxury of deep powder, which as lifelong skiers on Vermont's tough and icy terrain they had never met before, Comstock and Jennifer's combined time was 70.72 seconds. At the awards banquet the family took double honors: second in the father-daughter category, and first in mother-daughter. In 1986, again at Vail, the national husband-wife winners were Hugh "Mac" and Susie Jacob, 30 and 29, of Cheboygan, Michigan, where he is the distribution manager for Procter & Gamble's paper products. Their combined time: a breathtaking 62.08.

Many clubs enter their fastest members in *Skiing* magazine's Ski Club Challenge at a fee of $75 per team. Each club must include a man and a woman in each of three age brackets: 21 to 27, 28 to 35, 36 and over. From six regional contests, the six clubs with the best team times are awarded expense-paid trips to the national championships in the Rockies or the Sierra Nevadas. National winners get invited back the next year to a race of champions.

Company teams have gone head to head with business peers in a couple of competitions. The Corporate Grand Prix of Skiing was started in 1986 by Worldwide Ski Corp. as an invitational series for executive-level teams of three skiers each in A and B levels. A $150 entry fee per team put those managers into one of seven regional two-day qualifying races on Nastar giant slalom courses. Winning teams got trips to Park City, Utah, for finals.

For fast-track schussers, the Corporate Ski Challenge at Alpine Meadows, California, has been open to all employees on company teams. It holds both individual and team competition in all three alpine disciplines: downhill, long and steep; slalom, 35 quick turns in a short run; and the familiar giant slalom. With no preliminary competitions, the Corporate Challenge offers no free trips. An entry fee of $450 for a team of four to six includes all course fees, use of practice courses, an alpine training program, and parties each evening of the four-day event, but it does not cover lodging. Out of 130 teams in 1987, the winner was from California: the Lockheed Missiles & Space Corp.

The United States Ski Association, governing body of the sport, offers competition at several levels, with lots of encouragement and a few freebies for recreational amateurs. In 1985 the USSA introduced alpine "citizen racing." An entrant in the USSA American Ski Challenge must be at least 21 and may not have skied on a college varsity, or even live within 15 miles of a ski area. Five regions sent 117 qualifiers to the national citizens' cham-

pionship in Crested Butte, Colorado, in April of 1986. They raced head to head on regulation parallel giant slalom and slalom courses, the latter with 58 gates to negotiate in less than 500 feet. A commercial lender for First Bank System of Minneapolis, a systems analyst for the 3M Co. of St. Paul, and an electrical engineer for AT&T in Denver were among the top six women who, along with the top six men, were designated the national citizens team. These championships aim to develop teams for competition in citizen races in Europe.

Kings of the mountains are the competitors in the masters series sanctioned by the USSA. Many are former national team members. In state, divisional, and national races, amateurs 25 years old and up compete by age classes in slalom, giant slalom, and downhill events. The courses meet official standards, with more gates and longer, steeper terrain than those used for most non-USSA races. At the national masters championships, H. Benjamin Duke Jr., 65, vice chairman of the Gates Corp. in Denver, a rubber manufacturer, was third among some 20 competitors in his class in slalom plus a combined event of all three disciplines in 1983 and 1984, and in downhill plus combined in 1985.

Some skiing champions operate camps for recreational skiers, complete with videotaping and off-slope analysis. Billy Kidd teaches at Steamboat Springs, Colorado. Lathrop Ski & Race Camps offer instruction by touring world-class competitors at major U.S. and European resorts. The Mahre Training Centers at Keystone, Colorado; Stowe, Vermont; and Heavenly Valley, California, feature instructors groomed by the Olympic gold and silver medal twins, Phil and Steve Mahre, and their coach Harald Schoenhaar, as well as visits with the Mahres.

Coin Operated Racing Systems lets racers practice on marked courses at 65 areas in North America. A token opens the starting gate. Each run is timed electronically with an instant readout at the end. The hard part, some skiers report, is getting that token in the slot with ski gloves on. Happy landings.

FOR FURTHER INFORMATION

COMPETITIONS

Corporate Ski Challenge, Alpine Meadows Ski Area, P.O. Box 5279, Tahoe City, CA 95730; (916)-583-4232.

Family Ski Challenge, Capital Sports Inc., 805 Third Ave., New York, NY 10022; (212)-319-7770.

Skiing magazine's Ski Club Challenge, Action Sports Marketing, Suite 37, 100 N. Village Ave., Rockville Centre, NY 11570; (516)-536-2130.

United States Ski Association, 1750 E. Boulder St., Colorado Springs, CO 80909; (303)-578-4600.

World Wide Ski Corp. for Nastar and The Corporate Grand Prix, P.O. Box 4580, Aspen, CO 81612; (303)-925-7864.

SPORTS AND GAMES

TRAINING CAMPS

Billy Kidd Ski and Racing Camps, 2305 Mt. Werner Circle, Steamboat Springs, CO 80487; (303)-879-6111.

Lathrop Ski and Race Camps, Suite 310, 1430 Massachusetts Ave., Cambridge, MA 02138; (617)-497-7744.

Mahre Training Centers, Keystone Resort, c/o Gordon Briner, P.O. Box 38, Keystone, CO 80435; (303)-468-4172.

PUBLICATIONS

The Alpine Training Manual by U.S. Ski Coaches Association (Box 100, Park City, UT 84060; revised 1985), $15.

No Hill Too Fast by Phil and Steve Mahre (New York: Simon & Schuster, 1985), $17.95.

Ski magazine, eight issues a year, $9.94; P.O. Box 2795, Boulder, CO 80302; (800)-525-0643 or (303)-447-9330.

Ski Racing newspaper, 20 issues a year, including *Ski Racing Redbook*, $20; Rt. 100, Waitsfield, VT 05673; (802)-496-7700.

Skiing magazine, seven issues a year, $9.98; CBS Magazines, 1515 Broadway, New York, NY 10036; (800)-525-0643 or (303)-447-9330.

Skiing Techniques and Training by Ludwig Schaller (New York: Heinemann, 1984), $20. ■

Ski Racing: Cross-Country

■ Skiing the nordic way, cross-country, has glided faster than the downhill, or alpine, variety in the 1980s, putting close to 5.5 million outdoorsmen on skinny skis. Cross-country used to be the only way of skiing before transport turned into sport. Norwegian settlers traveled about Wisconsin and Illinois on skis in the 1840s. And one "Snow-Shoe" Thompson skied the mail from California over the Sierras to Nevada. But as 20th-century recreation, alpine left nordic in the drifts until the 1960s when nature lovers began organizing cross-country tours to the wintry wilderness. Fresh inspiration for nordic competition blew in with Bill Koch's silver medal in the 1976 Olympics, the U.S.'s first Olympic award in the sport.

Easy access, relatively low cost, and a safe, simple technique popularized cross-country skiing. Independent of lift tickets and lines, you need only gently rolling ground — a golf course, river bank, or wilderness trail. A beginner may prefer a groomed, man-made track at a ski area. Skilled skiers and experienced winter mountaineers can explore virgin powder.

Some executives find in cross-country a return to a way of skiing life that seems sadly to have disappeared from downhill slopes. William M. Chester Jr., vice president and treasurer of Heil Co., a Milwaukee manufacturer of truck bodies, used to ski regularly in the Rockies but grew disenchanted with the behavior of the crowds. "You had to lock up your skis so no one would steal them. There were bad feelings when people pushed ahead of you in lift lines," he recalls. In 1979, at age 54, he took to cross-country, entering some races. "This group was friendly. People encouraged each other on the trail. The feeling was the same as when I started downhill skiing in the 1940s."

To get a sense of the sport, renting equipment is easy in most cross-country ski centers and avoids the beginner's confusion of what to buy. Nordic gear is much lighter than alpine. Boots that lace look more like shoes than the downhiller's heavy footwear. They clamp onto slender, extra-long skis only at the toe, leaving the skier free to lift his heel in a running motion.

With a kick of one foot and a glide on the other, you set off swinging your arms to help push along on your poles in what has been described as the Groucho Marx lope. Correctly called the "diagonal stride," this basic technique moves the opposite arm and leg forward together, as in a brisk walk.

Cross-country uses nearly every muscle. Sending huge amounts of oxygen to those muscles for a sustained period develops the cardiovascular system and builds endurance. Physiologists have found that among well-trained, top-flight athletes, nordic skiers, along with oarsmen, burn up more energy than competitors in any other sport, alpine skiing included, from 500 to 1,200 calories an hour, depending on pace and body weight.

Still, nordic skiing is easier on the body than most other aerobic exercise. It avoids the shock that running exerts on the back and knees. Gliding along at six to ten miles per hour means fewer injuries, next to a downhiller's average 20 mph. In alpine, if your mind drifts for a second, you risk catastrophe. In cross-country you can talk, enjoy the countryside, daydream. Oldsters, who don't want to risk brittle bones, find cross-country adds years to their skiing lives. The legendary Herman "Jack Rabbit" Smith-Johannsens of Piedmont, Quebec, was still competing at 100. And Bill

William M. Chester Jr. (left), of Heil Co., puts 17 miles behind him in a cross-country marathon.

IN WINTER

Chester, whose wife had skied as a teenager with Jack Rabbit, saw him watching a 1986 Canadian race, at 111.

Local clubs and ski centers organize races from late December to mid-March, usually in classes that conform to those of the United States Ski Association's Nordic Division. USSA license holders can accumulate points toward a ranking in certain races ranging from ten kilometers (6.2 miles) to 50 (31.2 miles). The Northeast offers the most races, including some five-kilometer races and relays, at cross-country centers such as Craftsbury Common, Vermont, and Waterville Valley, New Hampshire. A 24-hour hot line (802-254-5513) to the USSA's eastern nordic office in Brattleboro, Vermont, gives race schedules, updated daily.

Men and women compete separately, as seniors from 21 to 30 years, and masters from 30 on, in five-year age groups. There's a masters series and training camp. Chester, who in 1983 and 1986 entered the masters world championships, had looked forward to reaching the age 60-and-over division, until he saw that its competitive times were faster than those of the 50s divisions. "Apparently skiers who stayed on were the good ones," he noted.

Citizen racing of marathon proportions, long a feature of Scandinavia's winters, has swept over North America and much of the world in the last dozen years. The American Birkebeiner, the Boston Marathon of cross-country skiing, is held the last Saturday of February in northern Wisconsin. Patterned after a historic race in Norway (*Birkebeiner* means "birch-bark leggings" in Norwegian), the event draws at least 5,500 starters from all over the world. Bill Koch entered in 1985 and 1986.

With the elite leading through the town of Hayward, these legions go off in waves at five-minute intervals. The fastest travelers complete the full 55-kilometer (34-mile) distance to Telemark Lodge in Cable, Wisconsin, in under four hours. A 29-kilometer (18-mile) Kortelopet ("short race") takes them about two hours. All finishers are rewarded with a cup of steaming blueberry soup, and immense satisfaction.

A new "skating" technique has kicked up worldwide controversy between the speedsters, who want to finish first, and many citizen racers, whose challenge is simply to finish. Introduced by Bill Koch in 1982 when he won the World Cup, this method uses the inside edge of one ski as a skate, gripping the snow at an angle to the direction of travel, while the other ski glides forward. This footwork chops the snow into a series of V's, spoiling the grooved tracks that traditional striders follow. The Birkebeiner now allots half its wide trail to skaters and half to striders. But Chester, who has piloted his plane full of friends to the Birkebeiner since 1980, is learning skating.

Waxing skis, which traditionally takes much of the night before a race, may be simplified by skating. Some cross-country tourers now use waxless skis with patterned bottoms for traction, but most competitors prefer wax. They want a surface beneath the boot soft enough to grip the snow under their weight in the kick, yet hard enough elsewhere to glide forward easily. Some skaters, who can grip the snow with the ski's edge, use only the glide wax.

Big prizes have come with a couple of marathons in the Great American Ski Chase, an eight-race series sponsored by Leaf, a candy company. The California Gold Rush at the Royal Gorge resort in Soda Springs, north of Lake Tahoe, awarded an ounce of gold to the male and female winners of the 50-kilometer race in 1986. And the male winner, along with the female winner of the 1987 Silver Rush, or half-marathon, each got a free trip to Japan's 25-kilometer Uribandi ski marathon in Sapporo in 1987. In Traverse City, Michigan, the first American man and woman to finish the 50-kilometer North American Vasa in February get a trip in March to ski in Sweden's 89-kilometer (55-mile) Vasaloppet. Bjorn Kvammen Jr., 45, chief executive of CTL Engineering in Columbus, Ohio, won in 1985. Being Norwegian-born helped, and so did 625 hours of training per year. That includes summertime poling on short roller skis, with wheels at each end.

A Worldloppet series consists of the longest cross-country marathon in each of 11 countries. Starting with Austria in 1977, at age 44, Philip Erard, a senior vice president in corporate finance at Wertheim & Co. in New York (see page 23), had finished all 11 countries by March of 1987, one of more than 300 Worldloppet skiers to do so.

Erard holds the distinction of opening three Iron Curtain countries to Americans on skinny skis. After negotiating for a year, he was invited in March 1982 to attend the Festival of the North at Murmansk, the Soviets' ice-free port above the Arctic Circle. Royally received, he skied the 54-kilometer race with some 4,000 Russian comrades, most on wooden skis. They awarded their guest a silver samovar, on pretext of being the oldest competitor to complete the route. Each year since then, Worldwide Nordic USA, a Chicago travel agency that takes groups to Worldloppet races, has taken skiers to the Murmansk marathon. On his own, Erard entered citizen marathons in Czechoslovakia in 1984 and Poland in 1985, the first American in each, he was told. "Those were great person-to-person experiences," says the cross-country capitalist.

FOR FURTHER INFORMATION

United States Ski Association: Nordic Division, 1750 E. Boulder St., Colorado Springs, CO 80909; (303)-578-4600.

American Birkebeiner Ski Foundation, P.O. Box 911, Hayward, WI 54843; (715)-634-5025.

Worldwide Nordic USA Travel Service, P.O. Box 185, Hartland, WI 53029; (414)-367-7227.

PUBLICATIONS

Backpacker magazine, bimonthly, $18; CBS Magazines, 1515 Broadway, New York, NY 10036; (800)-525-0643 or (303)-447-9330. Publishes *Ski X-C*, annually, $3.95.

SPORTS AND GAMES

Birke Fever: A Ten Year History of the American Birkebeiner by Tom Kelly (Scandia, MN: Specialty Press, 1982), $12.95.

Citizen Racing by John Caldwell and Michael Brady (Seattle: Mountaineers, 1982), $9.95.

Cross-Country Ski Book by John Caldwell (Brattleboro, VT: Greene, 7th ed., 1984), $8.95.

Cross Country Skier magazine; five issues a year, $9.97; Rodale Press, 33 E. Minor St., Emmaus, PA 18090; (800)-441-7761 or (215)-967-5171.

Cross Country Skiing Right by William Hall (New York: Harper & Row, 1985), $12.45.

Ski Faster Easier by Lee Borowski (Champaign, IL: Human Kinetics Press, 1986), $15.95.

Sports Illustrated Cross-Country Skiing by Richard C. Sheahan (New York: Harper & Row, 1984), $9.95. ∎

Ski Patrol: Samaritans of the Slopes

■ Conditions at Vermont's Stratton Mountain on New Year's Day were snowy, cold, and crowded, with 6,000 skiers on the slopes. On her first run of the day, Jeri Weibel, a manager in the antitrust division of AT&T's legal department in Manhattan, was weaving down an "expert" trail called Slalom Glade. She got going too fast, caught her skis under heavy snow, and fell. Her safety bindings, fastening boots to skis, failed to release as they should have. As her right leg twisted she felt sharp pain in her knee and calf. She tried to stand, with her husband's help, but fell again as her knee buckled and seemed to swivel.

To the rescue: the Ski Patrol, nationally a force of 24,000; at Stratton a band of 70 volunteers, plus a core of 30 paid patrollers. In patrol headquarters atop Stratton Mountain, a pair of unpaid volunteers got a call for help from a lift operator and quickly fastened on their skis. John Doble, 56, president of Emergency Medical Services Co., a consulting firm in Darien, Connecticut, reached the scene of the accident two minutes later. J. King Wright, 47, a senior vice president at Shearson/Lehman Brothers in Manhattan, followed with a toboggan.

Removing his skis, Doble crossed and upended them in the snow above Mrs. Weibel, to warn off oncoming skiers, and began to ask her questions. "You keep your hands off a victim until you know what's wrong," Doble explains. In this case, the suspicion was a dislocated knee and the treatment on site was immobilization by means of a box splint. With Mrs. Weibel strapped onto the toboggan, Doble and Wright then eased their load slowly down the mountain, managing, despite 20-degree weather, to arrive at the bottom sweating. Their final task on this tour was to carry toboggan and victim into the first-aid room.

Elapsed time from the moment Doble and Wright got their call: 55 minutes. Cost of the rescue to Jeri Weibel: zero. Diagnosis: a sprained knee, the most common of skiing injuries. Since the accident, Mrs. Weibel has skied with a brace. "But without the Ski Patrol, it might have been much worse," she says.

Nationwide statistics suggest three injuries per 1,000 "skier visits." Total injuries at Stratton that day: 19, including 12 victims brought in on toboggans by ski patrollers. The parent organization behind this action, the National Ski Patrol System (NSPS), was founded in 1938 with the notion that skiers willing to risk the perils of the mountain for sport should be willing also to look after one another. Charles Minot Dole, a New York insurance broker, conceived the idea after he broke his ankle while skiing at Stowe, Vermont, and had to be carried down by his wife and friends on a sheet of old roofing metal. After the start of World War II, Dole talked General George Marshall into adding ski troops to the U.S. Army.

Today 90% of all NSPS patrollers, identifiable by the gold cross on pack or parka, are unpaid volunteers. Most serve on weekends and holidays. But some resorts, such as Aspen and Vail, that do a big vacation business use only paid help.

To become an NSPS patroller, on downhill or cross-country trails, a person applies to a local ski area. He must be a competent skier and equipped with a certificate in advanced first aid from the Red Cross or credentials as a state-certified Emergency Medical Technician. He also needs current certification in CPR, or cardiopulmonary resuscitation. Once accepted as a candidate, a skier trains for a year, then takes exams to get his badge. Each year thereafter, he takes refresher courses, catching up on the latest in rescue and first-aid techniques.

Besides limb injuries, the patroller's medical training focuses on treatment of exposure, frostbite, and hypother-

Volunteer ski patrollers John Doble (left) and King Wright splint Jeri Weibel's hurt knee before carting her down Stratton Mountain on a toboggan.

mia. Legends about St. Bernard dogs to the contrary, brandy won't do as a remedy. The best treatment for hypothermia is to put the victim in a sleeping bag next to a warm body, ski-patrol variety or otherwise. The trainee must also learn to handle the rescue toboggan, a job that increases in difficulty with the weight of the patient. Wright and a partner once rescued a man weighing nearly 300 pounds, bringing him down a trail sheeted with ice.

It's also essential to learn less common kinds of rescue. When a ski lift breaks down, usually because of mechanical failure or high winds, it must be evacuated. Typically, the Ski Patrol hurls or shoots a weighted rope over the lift cable, then from the ground attaches the rope to a seat called a T-bar, and hoists it up. The lift passenger, securing himself to the T-bar, rides it down as patrollers feed out the rope. Jo Ann Duthler, 36, an assistant vice president of Bank of America and a branch manager in Santa Rosa, California, has worked on several such rescues, once dealing with passengers stranded 40 feet up.

As a Western patroller, skiing on steep mountains that get heavy snows, Duthler has also trained for avalanche rescues — and unfortunately has had to use that training. After an avalanche at Heavenly Valley, the vast ski area straddling the California–Nevada line, she joined an unsuccessful search. The victim's body was recovered only after the spring thaw.

Patrol work is not for slackers. Members must ski in all conditions, blizzards included, and on all kinds of surfaces, from powder to blue ice. All patrollers in the NSPS must work at least ten days each season, and most ski areas want even more devotion. Work may begin at 8 A.M. Operating in pairs, patrollers are assigned to stand by for accident calls, or to patrol a succession of trails for casualties or reckless skiers who need reprimanding. About 4 P.M., when the lifts close, all patrollers gather at the summit for a final sweep of the mountain to make sure no laggards are left. On that last run it may be dark.

A big set of satisfactions balances the hardships. On-duty patrollers do not have to wait in lift lines and they get to ski free — no small perk in these days of steep prices ($27 per day at Stratton). Camaraderie in a patrol tends to be great. Patrollers have even been known to have a few beers together at day's end (drinking on the job is forbidden).

The deeper satisfactions have to do with rescues, some dramatic. John Doble holds a Purple Merit Star, the patrol's highest award, given for saving a life — in his case, that of a young woman who missed a turn, crashed through a fence, and plunged into a ravine. When Doble and two other patrollers got to her, she was alive, but bleeding badly, with broken ribs coming out her back and chest. Six more patrollers were summoned to help move her down the mountain. Doble and a partner then sustained her on the ambulance ride to a hospital. Recovered, she returned to skiing at Stratton, and waved every time she saw Doble.

Doble's patrol training in emergency treatment actually led to a change in career. Once an advertising executive, he got to thinking there should be a system for quickly delivering medical services in the workplace. His Emergency Medical Services Co. develops programs for corporate clients who wish to train their employees in emergency first-aid procedures. Owing to other commitments, he has reluctantly given up ski patrolling.

For many seasoned skiers, patrolling provides an incentive to stay with the sport. One executive who put in over 30 years said, "People are very fortunate when they can combine their interests in a manner that does something for themselves, the way skiing does, and lets them help others, the way the Ski Patrol does."

FOR FURTHER INFORMATION
National Ski Patrol System, Inc., 2901 Sheridan Blvd., Denver, CO 80214; (303)-237-2737.

PUBLICATION
The National Ski Patrol by Gretchen R. Besser (Woodstock, VT: The Countryman Press, 1983), $10.95. ∎

Senior Hockey: More Brains, Less Brawn

■ The high point of the ice-hockey year comes in July in the heart of California wine country for some 800 amateurs lucky enough to play in the Snoopy Senior World Hockey Tourney. This contest is the loving production of *Peanuts* cartoonist Charles Schulz, 63, whose addiction to

In Connecticut the Greenwich Skating Club takes the puck up-ice after a save by their goalie in a contest with New Jersey's Essex Foxes.

SPORTS AND GAMES

hockey started in Minnesota school days. At the Redwood Empire Ice Arena he built in Santa Rosa, he has hosted his tourney since 1975 and skated with his Diamond Icers, lately in the AAAAA division for players 60 to 64 years old.

You have to be at least 40 to smack a puck in this event, except goalies, who must be between 30 and 40. Up to 40 teams of 20 players each can field several six-member squads in different five-year age divisions. Applications are accepted first come, first served before a May deadline. Each team entering pays a $250 fee plus its own expenses. From Tokyo and Helsinki, but mostly from the U.S. and Canada, they arrive, gear and wives in tow. With three evenings of square-dancing and barbecue, formal dancing and socializing as guests of "Sparky" Schulz and his wife, Jeannie, the tourney is a grand reunion for repeaters and players who may have faced off years ago in other arenas.

Key to the athletic success of the Snoopy Tourney, and other senior amateur contests, are the modified National Hockey League rules that make the sport safe for players who can't afford time out for injuries. Risks of getting hit by an errant stick, a screaming puck, or a bone-crunching body check into the boards have been all but eliminated. At Santa Rosa the modified rules forbid body checking and slap shots, where the stick's blade rises above the knee on the backswing, so skaters don't have to dodge pucks flying at 135 mph.

"When checking is removed from senior hockey, you don't have to retire from play. It's a more durable game, with fluidity and grace," says Michael Hanson, 42, the owner of two radio stations in Norwalk, Connecticut, who captained varsity hockey at Yale in the 1960s. Hanson first entered the Snoopy Tourney as goalie for the Commuters All Stars. In the 1985 finals he played in the A division (40 to 44) of New York's St. Nick's Oldtimers. They beat the Vancouver Flames, 4–3, and won a gold trophy topped with a triumphant Snoopy.

Winning under modified rules, which prohibit taking an opponent out of play by brute force, is still a strenuous game that demands tireless legs, good wind, split-second reactions, and upper-body strength for stick work. But players have to rely more on technique and strategies and less on brawn. Denver real estate broker Val Senter, 55, who took up hockey only at 32, and plays left wing with the Denver Centennial Stars, feels that the no-checking rule brings out the best-finessed hockey. The Santa Rosa tourney, which they've entered every year, is what keeps the Centennial Stars playing back home. Senter's squad won the AAA (50 to 54) division's gold trophy in 1985.

Some die-hard old-timers have argued that the modified rules emasculate a sport with manly traditions that go back to 1879, when two Canadian university students put English field hockey on ice. Others complain that the no-body-checking rule can ruin a game if referees call it too closely. It's hard to play defense without bodily contact.

The Amateur Hockey Association of the United States, governing body of the sport and developer of national

teams for international competition, has modified its rules in the 1980s to allow degrees of roughness in different classes of member teams. AHAUS teams in the "Over 30" class prohibit body checking and slap shots. The "Senior Nonchecking" class, which accounts for half of AHAUS adult teams, has a minimum age of 18 and bans only checking, not slap shots. "Senior Open" teams, which have 20 as the minimum age and include a number of former professional players, follow regular AHAUS rules that allow both checking and slap shots. But Tom Uber, 30, a stockbroker with Manley Bennett McDonald in Detroit, who played semi-pro hockey after college, prefers to skate his twice-weekly recreational games in a nonchecking league with a couple of teammates pushing 60.

Before joining a team, players should read its rules. The 750 adult teams registered with AHAUS in 1985 represent a mere quarter of all U.S. adult amateur hockey organizations. And 40% of AHAUS adult teams are in Michigan, where Detroit businessmen pressed for the modified rules so they could keep on playing with less hazard. Non-affiliated teams set their own rules. The Commuters League in the New York metropolitan area consists of a northern division in suburban New York and Connecticut, where players over 35 play a no-checking, no-slap-shot game, and a southern division in New Jersey, where half of the over-35 squads permit full body checking. When the two divisions meet for the championships, nonchecking applies.

Helmets with chin straps are compulsory for all AHAUS member teams, and face masks for players under 18. The Snoopy Tourney does not require helmets, but many older players voluntarily don both bonnets and bird-cages to keep their toothy grins intact.

Coaching youngsters means added ice time for hockey enthusiasts. Fred Filoon, 44, a senior vice president and director of Wood Struthers & Winthrop Management Corp. in New York City, plays forward left wing two evenings a week from November through February with the Greenwich, Connecticut, Skating Club in the Commuters League. And as head coach for the traveling team of Greenwich Squirts, 120 boys and girls ages 10 and 11, he lines up other volunteer coaches and spends weekend mornings and afternoons drilling with them and their charges on Greenwich's outdoor rink. As AHAUS registered coaches and teams, they have access to a detailed instructors' program and receive inexpensive liability and accident insurance coverage.

Beginners' hockey isn't for kids only anymore. Frustrated parents and fans who yearn to score, but can't even skate, can apply to the National Novice Hockey Association, a for-profit outfit founded in 1980 to cater to the fantasies of men and women over 21. In 16 locales, with more promised, in the Northeast, Middle West, and Southwest, new NNHA members start in October an eight-week course in skating, stick handling, shotmaking, and game strategies. Cost: $250. For another $400 the

IN WINTER

tyros will be assigned to 18-member coed teams with a coach and issued colorful professional-style uniforms and protective gear. Under no-checking, no-slap-shot rules, they play eight weekly games against other NNHA teams. An April tourney determines local champions. For a second season, these new players can re-enroll for games as "advanced beginners."

The Nelson family of Middletown, Connecticut, converted their tennis court to a winter arena when dentist Peter Nelson, 38, and his wife, Joan, 37, were in their first NNHA season. "It's a little more of a physical game than tennis," notes Dr. Nelson, who plays first-line defense on the advanced Yellowjackets team in the Hartford League, where he has spent more time in the penalty box than any other player. "It brings out the kid in all of us." The Nelson parents grew so fond of the game that they signed up for a three-week hockey day camp at the Drummond Hockey School in Westhaven, Connecticut, with their son, Lester, 8, and daughter, Svea, 6. It's never too late to learn.

FOR FURTHER INFORMATION

Amateur Hockey Association of the United States, 2997 Broadmoor Valley Rd., Colorado Springs, CO 80906; (303)-576-4990.

National Novice Hockey Association, Box 437, 8375 Leesburg Pike, Vienna, VA 22180; (703)-448-8284.

The Snoopy Senior World Hockey Tourney, Cecilia Shortt, coordinator, (707)-539-9023; Redwood Empire Ice Arena, 1067 W. Steele Lane, Santa Rosa, CA 95401; (707)-546-7147. ∎

Curling, with Broomsticks and Stones

∎ Imagine you're watching a curling match. Seven grownups look on as an eighth slides a polished granite spheroid down a long sheet of ice. The stone rumbles ponderously forward. Two players are now mincing along ahead of it, scrubbing and thwacking the ice vigorously with *brooms!*

Suddenly the sweeping stops as the stone slides into a large target area composed of concentric circles. Stones lie jumbled inside the target, and more are scattered off to the sides, out of play. When the score is posted — "red two, white nothing" — it bears no obvious relationship to the random-looking scatter on the ice.

What's going on is not nearly as lunatic as it seems. More than other sports, perhaps, curling has to be known to be loved. And it promises to get better known at the 1988 Winter Olympics in Calgary, Alberta, where it will be a demonstration sport, with hopes of becoming a medalist sport in future years. This venerable pastime originated in the 16th century, possibly in Holland, but more likely in Scotland. Yet anyone who knows the Italian game of bocce would feel at home in a curling match. More familiarly, the techniques are something of an amalgam of bowling and

shuffleboard, with the mental aspects of billiards or chess.

Curling has attracted a following of quite rational executives. Los Angeles-born Kaytaro G. Sugahara, 50, chief executive of Fairfield-Maxwell Ltd., a Manhattan-based $100-million holding company, plays three times a week. "It is a game in which one can become relatively proficient rapidly. It's a team sport and you contribute right away to the progress of a contest," says Sugahara, who was introduced to curling at age 35. At the Ardsley Country Club in Ardsley-on-Hudson, New York, he got help at a clinic with Ray Turnbull, a Canadian from Winnipeg who tours to teach.

The logistics of curling are really quite simple. Two four-person teams — they're called "rinks" — compete; each player has two stones to shoot. The object of the game is to cause a stone weighing no more than 44 pounds to slide down a 140-foot "sheet" of ice and come to a pinpoint halt inside the target area, 12 feet in diameter, called the "house." The task requires a certain finesse, especially if the desired destination is blocked by one or two stones in front of it. The curler's basic approach, in fact, is not a straight shot but a gentle arc, from which some say the game derives its name: the stone "curls" into its resting place as it reaches the house.

Getting a stone to curl is not especially difficult, but it takes skill, and the help of teammates. For delivery the curler grasps the stone by a handle on top. As he slides his stone forward on the ice, his opposite foot slides too, advancing his position. And the broom in his opposite hand helps balance or brace his body. When he releases the stone, he twists the handle slightly, which sets the stone to spinning lazily as it rumbles down the ice. Depending on whether the wrist is twisted toward the body, an "in-turn," or away from it, an "out-turn," the stone will rotate either clockwise or counterclockwise. As the stone starts to slow down toward the end of its run, the rotational forces overcome the forward momentum, and the stone begins to curve in the desired direction — to the right if it's spinning clockwise, or vice versa.

And now the mystique of the sweeping emerges. Originally done to clear snow from outdoor ice, the idea is still to improve the sliding surface. The ice on a curling sheet is not glassy, but pebbled with drops of frozen water. Vigorous sweeping causes the ice to melt slightly, and the stone, in turn, to travel faster and farther. Besides lengthening a stone's travel by 10 to 15 feet, sweeping flattens the arc of the curve because the stone does not slow down as soon as it otherwise would.

What type of broom gives the best results is a matter of preference: the Scottish scrub-type brush or the Canadian straw broom. The Canadian brooms require more vigorous strokes. Whatever broom is used, sweeping requires fine judgment. If the moving stone is what curlers call "light" — meaning it's moving so slowly that it may stop short of the desired point — the sweepers sweep mightily. Should it be "heavy," or fast moving, they step aside.

93

SPORTS AND GAMES

The ideal shot always requires a little sweeping. If you put your shot in the house and don't need any sweeping, you're lucky to have it stop where you want it. Curlers operate under a rigorous code of honor. If a sweeper happens to "burn" a stone — that is, graze it with even a single straw — he is honor-bound to declare the mishap and remove the stone from play.

The ultimate authority of any curling rink rests in each team's "skip," who is team captain. Most of the time the skip stands in the house and, signaling with the broom, tells his teammates where to place the next stone — whether it's to be a draw, meaning that it simply comes to rest at a certain point, possibly blocking an opponent's stone, or a takeout, intended to knock an opponent's stone out of the house. The skip also indicates whether to use an in-turn or an out-turn. He must be a good tactician and anticipate what the other skip can do to counter. "Curling is like a gigantic, ongoing game of chess played on ice," says Steve Brown, 40, skip of the 1986 U.S. men's championship team, and a manager of health-claims underwriting for American Family Insurance Co. of Madison, Wisconsin.

The game is broken down into eight or sometimes ten innings, called "ends," during which each player shoots two stones. Scoring is an all-or-nothing proposition: the winner of the end is the rink with any or all of its stones closer to the tee, or button — the center of the target — than any of the other rink's stones. If red has three, four, or even eight stones in the house and white has only one, but that one is closest to the tee, white wins the end, 1–0.

Toward the finish of a contest, each rink may have three or four stones within the house, and the last shots are the most crucial. These are always taken by the skips. In countless games, skips have turned the tables dramatically with their last stones, transforming, say, a potential one-point loss to a two-point victory by edging an opponent's stone out of its position.

During a two-hour match a player slides a stone 16 times, walks several miles from one end of the sheet to the other, and sweeps very hard. And practicing shots during the October-to-May season can be even more exhausting. "Because of wear and tear on knees and back, the most obsessive curler can work out only an hour daily," says Steve Brown, who not only captained Madison's 1986 men's national champions, but coached the 1985 championship team from Wilmette, Illinois.

In Canada close to a million regular curlers slide the rocks. Some "bonspiels," or tournaments, draw hundreds of players and offer such prizes as new automobiles. But even in Canada, curling is resolutely nonprofessional.

In the U.S., curling has kept to a relatively small band of around 20,000 devotees. To make the sport better known, Kay Sugahara, the New York financier, has been a recent patron of curling. Twice he helped sponsor the world championships, as well as telecasts of the event and demonstrations in New York's Rockefeller Center skating rink. "I'm anxious to make curling a more 'in' sport, and get more people to play what I consider a terrific game," he says.

Few public ice rinks offer curling, and the game is mostly played under the aegis of 133 clubs governed by the U.S. Curling Association. The fine old traditions of curling may have flourished because of the game's tightly knit and fraternal atmosphere. In the East, from Virginia to Maine, many curling circles are affiliated with country clubs, and to play it's often necessary to belong to the parent club.

In the northern Midwest, curling's heartland, independent clubs make it easier to get into the action. The St. Paul club, the largest, with 600 members, can hold eight games at once on its eight sheets. Seattle's 300-member Granite Curling Club has won 13 national championships since 1957.

In California, curling is definitely an oddity. That hasn't deterred Christopher Goldsmith, 30, in the Los Angeles office of Wyatt Co., a consulting firm for employee compensation and benefits. As a teenager, he learned curling at the Ardsley club in New York and later joined the Los Angeles Granite Curling Club. To practice, those players can rent ice only after 9 P.M. on Sundays. With little local competition, the club has represented the California–Oregon region at the men's national championships three times in the 1980s.

Curling is not expensive. Special shoes with soles of Teflon cost $50 to $120; or one may wear a $12 slip-on Teflon slider when shooting. Sturdy stretch-twill trousers are best, and pliable deerskin gloves let hands move easily. Brooms cost $30. The stones, of Welsh or Scottish granite, are $700 for a set of two. Dues at an independent club may range from $70 in small towns to $300 in big cities.

Sociability is a big part of the sport. In a tradition surviving from curling's early days, when a stiff measure of whiskey punch was served to ward off the chill of playing on a windswept frozen pond or river, no match is really finished until both rinks share refreshments.

FOR FURTHER INFORMATION

United States Curling Association, Box 971, 1100 CenterPoint Dr., Stevens Point, WI 54481; (715)-344-1199.

United States Women's Curling Association, Winnifred Bloomquist, President; Rt. 1, Box 100, Drayton, ND 58225; (218)-455-3863.

PUBLICATIONS

Curling to Win by Ed Lukowich, A. L. Hackler, and Rick Lang (New York: McGraw-Hill, 1987), $11.95.

North American Curling News, official publication of the United States Curling Association and the United States Women's Curling Association; six winter issues, $7; Summit Publishing Inc., 214 Summit St., Portage WI 53901; (608)-742-3853.   ∎

TO CHALLENGE THE MIND

Bridge in the Big Leagues

■ "If you like to read poetry and you hate math, I would say that you shouldn't play bridge," remarks Alan "Ace" Greenberg, 58, chairman of Bear Stearns & Co., the Wall Street investment firm. He is one of many expert players who feel that a mathematical bent, a logical turn of mind, and a good memory are essential qualities for a good player. Typically, many computer specialists figure among the 300,000 members of the American Contract Bridge League and those who play regularly in league-affiliated clubs. But plenty of poetry lovers and math haters can also be found among the estimated 12 million Americans who enjoy bridge simply as a social activity. What draws all players is a game of mental agility that is not as protracted as chess, does not depend on a throw of the dice, as does backgammon, and is, for them, the most challenging card game in the deck.

Bridge today means contract bridge, the game that Harold Vanderbilt adapted from auction bridge in 1925. With two partners facing each other at a table of four, each holding 13 cards, competitive bidding determines what suit shall be trump and the number of tricks over the "book" of six that the high-bidding pair must take. This is their contract. If they make the number of tricks they have contracted for, they score. If they don't, their opponents score.

Where "shuffle and deal" social bridge requires four people, a minimum of eight (two tables) is needed for duplicate bridge, the form of the game played in competitive tournaments. Bidding follows the same process, but in duplicate the pairs take turns playing hands with identical cards, and the pair that scores best wins. These hands are coldly dealt by computer, from more than 635 billion possible combinations.

Bidding is the critical element in duplicate, and the skilled player is one who can convey most accurately to his partner what cards he holds. This is done through assorted conventions and systems. In the Blackwood convention, a bid of "four no trump" asks the partner how many aces he has; a reply of "five diamonds" means he has one ace. In a system like Precision Bidding, invented by the late shipping magnate C. C. Wei, the player can bid, say, "one club" when he really means that he has a good holding in spades. Of course, a pair's bidding can also reveal their holdings to their opponents. As bridge authority Alfred Sheinwold has noted, "Bridge is the only game in which you tell your opponents exactly what cards you have and what you're going to do with them, and then dare your opponents to stop you."

Except for world championships, which require qualifying, tournament bridge is open to anyone. It helps to belong to the American Contract Bridge League ($15 per year). Members regularly receive lists of tournaments nationwide. The league sponsors about 820 sectional tournaments, more than 85 regional ones, and three annual North American championships. Players compete in

In trials for a world championship, Alan Greenberg of Bear Stearns opened bidding with a club. Then with only a singleton ace, he supported the hearts bid by his partner, pro Jim Jacoby, who held king, jack, and five small hearts. They made a small slam, but so did their competitors, playing the same hand at another table.

SPORTS AND GAMES

pairs, or in teams of six — four play while two rest. Other tournaments are held by the American Bridge Association, made up principally of black players, and the World Bridge Federation.

All one needs to enter a tournament is time (they usually last three days), the entry fee (from $12 to $20 per day), and travel money. If you lack a regular partner, professionals are available, from around $40 for a three-hour session to thousands of dollars, depending on the status of the pro and the tournament, and whether the pro gets a bonus for performance. No cash prizes are offered, as they are in other countries. All that awaits the winner are match points for one's team, master points for oneself, and the ineffable satisfaction of winning at a game that puts one's powers of thinking and concentration to the utmost test.

Part of Alan Greenberg's success dates from the day in 1968 when Jimmy Cayne, a young municipal bond salesman, entered his office looking for a job. Greenberg, an amateur magician of note, asked about hobbies. "Bridge," said Cayne. When Greenberg, who had taken up bridge in college, asked how well he played, Cayne, who had won a few national and regional titles, replied: "Frankly, Mr. Greenberg, you will never know as much about the game as I do, even if you spend the rest of your life learning." Despite this assessment, Cayne got the job. He played only an occasional social game of bridge with his boss until 1975, when Greenberg popped the question: "Do I have the makings of a tournament player?" Deciding that he did, Cayne trained Greenberg by hiring a pair of professionals and the four entered local and regional competitions. They won every major team tournament in New York, then moved on to national victories. The pressure of work and other interests have caused Greenberg and Cayne, 51, chairman of Bear Stearns's executive committee, to give up tournaments, though they still play at the Regency and Cavendish bridge clubs in New York City.

Other executives continue to pursue challenge in the big leagues of tournament bridge. Douglas Drew, 55, of Toronto, vice president for manufacturing at Noma Canada, a producer of electrical products, and the current chairman of the ACBL, says he manages because "bridge is my only hobby." Starting young and sticking with it helps keep skills sharp. Charles Burger, 49, an attorney in West Bloomfield, Michigan, began as a sophomore at the University of Michigan and was competing in tournaments before graduation. Of the move from classes to cards, he says: "Both are competitive outlets. It's civilized warfare wherever you play." Burger has won many major national events and played on the winning team in a 1985 national tournament in Las Vegas. Malcolm K. Brachman, 59, president of the privately held Northwest Oil Co. in Dallas, was trained as a physicist at Harvard, and did not consider himself a natural player. But he trained his memory and

fielded a team that won the World Bridge Federation Championship in 1979. In 1985 and early 1986 he entered four major tournaments: the Summer North American Championship in Las Vegas; the Fall North American Championship in Winnipeg, Canada; the Mid-Winter Holidays tournament in Reno; and the Bols tournament in Rotterdam.

Women make up about 60% of ACBL's members, but the most serious women players are not in business. One exception is Dorothy Moore, 57, of Dallas, a financial planner with the Phoenix Mutual Insurance Co. She introduced her former boss, the late Ira G. Corn, founder of Michigan General, a diversified manufacturing company, to bridge and they became active tournament competitors and promoters. Mrs. Moore, who recently resumed tournament play, feels that young women who might make good tournament players are too busy carving out their careers.

Combining business and bridge, Katherine Wei, 55, one of the world's top competitors, is a professional player as well as a senior vice president of Falcon Shipping Group, founded by her husband, C. C. Wei. A gold medalist in the 1978 World Bridge Olympics, played every four years, Mrs. Wei led a group of American players to her native China in 1980 to play in the Shanghai International Friendship Tournament. One of her partners was China's leader, Deng Xiaoping, an ardent player. The next year she was back in China to welcome the Falcon Shipping Group's *Pride of Texas,* the first American flag carrier to deliver grain to China under the China–U.S. Maritime Treaty.

Playing with some of the 4,200 bridge clubs affiliated with the ACBL is a good way to start prepping for tournament play. Most welcome new members. Fees for joining range from $5 to hundreds of dollars. Excellent instruction is often available. New York City's Beverly Bridge Club, for instance, offers more than a dozen courses designed for every level, at $110 for ten lessons. Supervised evening practice sessions cost $6. Hundreds of books on the game range from classics such as Alfred Sheinwold's *First Book of Bridge* to esoterica. A spate of programs, with names such as "Cybron," "Parlor," and "Baron," have been written for the home computer and one to four players.

"One of the charms of this game," notes Charles Burger, the onetime collegiate competitor, "is that you can play it forever, as long as you have a mind. You're not limited by, 'No, you can't return his serve anymore.'"

FOR FURTHER INFORMATION

American Contract Bridge League; membership, $15 a year, includes *Contract Bridge Bulletin,* monthly; P.O. Box 161192, 2200 Democrat Rd., Memphis, TN 38186; (901)-332-5586.

PUBLICATIONS
Commonsense Bidding by William E. Root (New York: Crown, 1986), $19.95.
Duplicate Bridge by Alfred Sheinwold (New York: Dover), $3.
The Precision Bidding System in Bridge by C. C. Wei (New York: Dover, 1973), $3.

Chess vs. the Computer

■ Computerized chess sets caught the eye of Chicago investment banker Burton J. Vincent, 61, a decade ago, soon after they came on the market. The executive vice president of Cleveland-based Prescott Ball & Turben has since matched wits with a succession of four electronic opponents, including a couple that talk. As he caught on to their often predictable games and as better models appeared, he upgraded his sets. Now eligible for rating by the U.S. Chess Federation on the same scale as humans, from 1000 for novices to 2000 and over for expert players, these microprocessors have improved dramatically in the 1980s. So has Vincent's game. As a tournament player against live opponents, his rating has risen from 1386 to over 1500. He gives much of the credit to practice, battling his electronic partners.

Chess players have argued passionately about how skillfully the computer can play chess and whether humans should let cybernetic competitors into their game. Long described as "the art of human reason," chess probably started in India, reaching Europe by the 13th century. Since the 1950s, computer scientists have used chess as a model for developing artificial intelligence — the computer's capacity to perform operations analogous to human learning and decision-making. Giant research computers started beating a few chess experts in 1977. A decade later no machine had yet reached the very top echelons of U.S. or world championship players. The best, a research unit at Pittsburgh's Carnegie Mellon University, was rated over 2300.

But by August 1986, microprocessors had advanced to a point where, in the U.S. Chess Open tournament, an experimental model from Fidelity International of Miami beat an international master rated 2533, David J. Strauss of the University of California's statistics department in Riverside. Top-of-the-line models already on the market in 1986 were rated at 2100, better than 90% of the U.S. Chess Federation's 55,000 members.

These machines still fail to entice some very high caliber players. James T. Sherwin, 53, vice chairman of GAF in Wayne, New Jersey, is one of 50 American international masters. Having outplayed such greats as Samuel Reshevsky and a teenage Bobby Fischer, and served as commentator for a PBS TV presentation of some Kasparov-Karpov matches in the World Chess Championship, Sherwin doubts that a machine could provide the competitive stimulus on which he and many other players thrive.

TO CHALLENGE THE MIND

"The element of human combat is lacking," he avers. "A really good chess player has got to have a killer instinct like any athlete. You are always thinking about whether you are getting your opponent down. But how do you psych out a computer? You can't exhaust the possibilities in chess through scientific analysis. You have to rely on intuition and talent, and ultimately those elements conspire to achieve beauty. Chess is an art form that can be created only with someone on the other side of the board building tension. The distillation of all your experience and some creativity, some unknown factor, are at work, and that would be terribly difficult to program."

Sherwin concedes that in the 1990s computer chess may become capable of the strategic thinking of world-class players. He even admits to owning a chess program that he has toyed with on his Apple home computer. Software programs playable on general-purpose personal computers and devices used only for chess all play according to the same basic principles.

To choose a move, the computer goes through a two-part process. First it laboriously scans all available moves and considers the opponent's possible responses. The number of moves a computer can examine depends on the size of its memory and the speed of play. If, for example, the computer has a choice of 30 moves and it looks only three turns ahead, it must examine $30 \times 30 \times 30$, or 27,000, possibilities.

Next the computer evaluates each potential move according to pieces defended or captured and the position attained on the board. The program assigns different values to each piece — a pawn may be worth only one, while a rook may count as much as five or six. To assess the more complex factor of position, the program assigns a

Favoring human over computerized chess opponents, GAF Vice Chairman James T. Sherwin (right) beats Vladimir Gostkhorhevich in a timed 14-minute game at a Manhattan club.

SPORTS AND GAMES

positive value to the squares that are important to control, and it accentuates the positive. Most programs can compete at several levels or speeds. The longer a computer takes on each play, the further ahead it can look. Burton Vincent's Fidelity Elite Avant Garde has 15 selectable levels, including eight pre-set levels, from blitz (two to five seconds) to tournament speed (two to three minutes). The longer it takes, the better it plays.

Both hardware and software have overcome annoying shortcomings of early consumer models, to give computer chess more human ways of thinking. Playing at a high level, a small machine used to take 48 hours on the millions of calculations required for one move. That didn't bother players of postal chess who correspond on each move, and whose tourneys last for years. But to make the game more appealing to less patient competitors, certain features have been included in the programs. Instead of idling while waiting for the human player to complete a move, virtually all chess computers think about position on their human opponents' time. Early programs favored capturing material above all else, lacking the ability to sacrifice a piece to improve position, but new models have overcome that tendency.

Most computers used to play conservative and predictable opening and middle games and a weak end game. The best of today's computer chess sets give the human opponent the option of choosing the computer's opening and playing both sides until the game reaches the point that the person wants to work on. Chess computers are now capable of recognizing draws, and some models are able to accept or reject the offer of a draw.

The U.S. Chess Federation publishes an annual buying guide in its magazine, *Chess Life.* Its 1986 recommendations for stand-alone sets included the Fidelity Elite Avant Garde 2100, listed at $550, and Fidelity's Par Excellence model with the same 2100 rating, but with six instead of eight pre-set levels of play, at $200. Among the foreign makes available in the U.S. are models from Novag, a Hong Kong-based producer, known for aggressive extra fast chess, priced from $250 to $700. From Hegener & Glaser of West Germany, the Mephisto models have extra powerful hardware for speed and cost from $395 to $2,000. SciSys models from Switzerland, also sold under the Radio Shack label, range from a hand-held portable Express 16K to the Turbostar 432 at $250. The latter, instead of looking at all possible moves by brute force, selects some likely ones, then searches their consequences in depth.

Software programs usable on most home computers include "Paul Whitehead Teaches Chess," an introduction for beginners to middle-level players, published by Enlightenment Inc. More advanced players can look for challenge in "Sargon III" from Spinnaker Software of Cambridge, Massachusetts; "Chess Master 2000" from Software Toolworks of Sherman Oaks, California, distributed by Electronic Arts of San Mateo, California; and an English import from Psion Ltd. of Oxford called simply "Chess." Most are priced between $40 and $50.

FOR FURTHER INFORMATION

United States Chess Federation; membership, $25 a year, includes *Chess Life,* monthly; 186 Rt. 9W, New Windsor, NY 12550; (914)-562-8350.

PUBLICATIONS

Let's Play Chess by Bruce Pandolfini (New York: Simon & Schuster, 1986), $6.95.

The New Computer Chess Book by Tim Harding (Elmsford, NY: Pergamon Press, 1985), $14.

Principles of the New Chess by Bruce Pandolfini (New York: Simon & Schuster, 1986), $6.95. ■

PART THREE
HOBBIES

PERFORMING
Jamming in a Jazz Band

■ Nostalgia for the popular music of their younger years has sent scores of business executives back to the bandstand to play the kind of jazz their generation knew and loved best. Blowing brasses and slapping the bass in hundreds of six- or seven-piece combos, and big bands, too, these players find in jazz a natural expression, an uninhibited part of the personality that bubbles up like a friendly conversation.

Up in the Boston suburbs, the New Black Eagle Jazz Band holds forth each Thursday night at the Sticky Wicket Pub in Hopkinton. Anthony Pringle, 50, principal engineer for Prime Computer of Framingham, has been raising an 80-year-old silver cornet to his lips, squinting, and taking the Eagles on a tear through some of the hottest rags east of Seventh Avenue.

Away from business, executives are free to be artists, and making music gives a joyful release of tension. The Eagles — an architect, pediatrician, sales promotion director, two engineers, and a clinical psychologist — stop just short of a full-scale commercial operation. All are union musicians. To leave time for their careers and families, they limit themselves to 120 performances a year, in the U.S. and occasionally in Europe. More than a dozen of their records and cassettes have won critical acclaim. By keeping music an avocation, they enjoy the best of two worlds.

Most people know jazz when they hear it, but many would have trouble putting a finger on what makes it jazz, what ties the traditional New Orleans style to the later Dixieland, swing, bebop, post-bebop, and more recent forms. Jazz evolved in America during nearly 300 years to emerge at the turn of the century in the distinctive improvisations of black musicians blending African and European melody, harmony, and rhythm. Traditional jazz melodies carried by the front line — trumpet, trombone, and clarinet — developed from the calls, cries, hollers, and wails of church and work singing. But the pliable human voice that the wind instruments imitate can produce more variations in tone than the keys of a piano, the basis for the standard diatonic scale.

To come closer to the voice, jazz uses it own special "blues scale," which "flats" the third, seventh, and frequently the fifth note of the octave — turning them into "blue notes." The harmony underneath the melody generally holds to the standard scale. This combination produces the blues harmonies intrinsic to jazz. Hitting adjacent black and white piano keys simultaneously approaches this sound.

Rhythm comes from the drums, piano, banjo, or guitar, and tuba or string bass. The tempo usually carries the 2/4 beat of ragtime, or the 4/4 beat of march time. Syncopation in the melody accents unexpected beats and skips the accent on beats where it would normally fall.

The age of traditional jazz had virtually ended by the time Prohibition was repealed in 1933. But a revival began in San Francisco in 1940 when Lu Watters and his eight-piece Yerba Buena Jazz Band started to reconstruct the 1920s recordings of trumpeters Joe "King" Oliver and Louis Armstrong. In 1945 trumpeter Bunk Johnson, then 66, was brought out of obscurity and up to New York,

The New Black Eagle Jazz Band rocks the jazz boat in Boston Harbor as adman Stanford Vincent belts out a request for "Basin Street Blues."

99

HOBBIES

where his New Orleans Band split apart the steamy old Stuyvesant Casino down on Second Avenue. Youngsters jammed the place, danced all evening for a dollar, and bought pitchers of beer for 50 cents.

By the 1950s virtually every white campus in the country had its jazz band, and the future Eagles were beginning to soar. At Dartmouth, Peter Bullis, an associate with the Boston architectural firm of Notter Finegold & Alexander, was picking banjo with the Indian Chiefs. At Brown, Stanford Vincent, president of Vincent-Curtis advertising consultants in Boston, was sliding his trombone with the Brunotes. As the infatuation spread abroad, Tony Pringle taught himself cornet in his home town of Liverpool, England, and later got thrown out of the RAF Marching Band for swinging up "Sussex by the Sea."

The Eagles go back to the traditional style of ensemble playing perfected in the Teens and Twenties in New Orleans by such black musicians as Jelly Roll Morton and his Red Hot Peppers. They refuse to rely on hackneyed war-horses—the "Saints" or "Muskrat Ramble"—but have built a repertory of more than 500 old tunes. Since little of this music was written down at the time it was created, Pringle and Bullis have spent hours listening to re-issues of rare recordings, many of them from Europe, and to tapes of old 78-rpm records sent in by fans. Some of their happier finds: "King" Oliver's "Working Man Blues," originally recorded in 1923, and Oliver's first recording of an up-tempo rouser aptly named "Shake It and Break It."

Together since 1971, the Eagles long ago tuned in to one another well enough to improvise collectively. Their listeners hear many voices, each speaking in its own tongue, but exquisitely blended into a common conversation. That close-knit quality takes cultivating. On the bandstand each player gets a chance to choose the tunes for one set. At regular monthly meetings chaired by piano player Robert Pilsbury, the clinical psychologist, everybody gets an opportunity to air his gripes—about tempos, interference with another player's solo, which engagements to accept, what to wear. The meetings are sometimes stormy, but, says Pilsbury, "everyone leaves with a great sense of exhilaration—and the focus is always on the band."

Playing Dixieland, which was developed from black music by whites and flourished in Chicago, usually does not require such an intimate relationship. The members of the front line trade off solos, backed up mainly by the basic chords, so the intricate coordination of tight ensemble playing is less important.

Sitting in with local jazz groups gives a lift to Jerry T. Silverman, 57, president of Retail Ventures in Warrendale, Pennsylvania, on visits to some 200 of his company's stores in 35 states. Silverman, who played professionally in his teens and 20s, and holds a card from the American Federation of Musicians, seeks out jazz clubs or locally advertised open jam sessions. Often he's asked to join in with his flügelhorn. Similar to a cornet, this instrument's wider, shorter bore produces a mellower sound. "The repertoire is practically international. Everybody knows the same pieces," notes the itinerant sideman.

Hosts can quickly hear whether a guest can lip the notes. "If you play well, they're happy to have you make their lives more interesting for an evening," observes Silverman, who has jammed from Rio to Paris. At the very least, he practices in his hotel room. Brass and woodwind players need almost daily workouts to maintain the embouchure, or lip, required to play for hours at a time and hit the high notes.

The swing era's big-band style of the late 1930s and early 1940s made a comeback in the 1970s and 1980s. Unlike the small improvisational jazz and Dixieland ensembles, the big-band sound takes 16 or so musicians who play from "charts," or written arrangements, so that all the saxophones, for example, come across as one disciplined section.

The Jack Lantz Big Band, founded in 1981, plays mostly arrangements of 1930s music in the Count Basie tradition. "We're disciplined," says Lantz, "but we may open up space in the middle of, say, 'Satin Doll,' to stretch out an improvised solo." Lantz, 39, vice president of operations of Q-Tech Corp., a Los Angeles supplier of microelectronic products to the military, majored in musical composition at Yale, then secured his financial future with an MBA from Harvard. "It's hard to make it in music, but a band makes a super avocation," he notes.

His 16-piece outfit includes four trumpets, four trombones, five saxophones, a bass, drums, Lantz himself on an electronic keyboard, and a vocalist. "It's easy to find players, but it's hard to find good players," the leader remarks. A third of the members are professional musicians. To audition, players sit in Tuesday nights when the band meets at a club to work up new tunes. After a particularly tough rehearsal, one of the amateurs asked to quit, but Lantz reassured him. With help from agents, they play about one local engagement per week, for weddings and parties. The band charges union-scale rates, and from those engagements members walk away with $100 to $200 a gig.

Not content to rely on the historical repertory, James M. Benham, 51, founder and chairman of the Benham Capital Management Group in Palo Alto, California, makes sure that his groups perform and record works by new young composers. Treasury notes by day and trumpet notes by night fill his calendar. A pioneer in money-market funds based on U.S. government securities, Benham and his company manage $3.3 billion for 160,000 investors. As a teenage trumpeter, Benham, who comes from a long line of classical musicians, dreamed of winning first chair with the National Symphony. But on a band scholarship at Michigan State, where he majored in finance, his room-

PERFORMING

mate turned him on to jazz. In 1975 Benham joined a casual rehearsal band led by a colleague. They converted it to Full Faith and Credit, a 17-piece operation that includes professional musicians. In 1981 Benham formed Palo Alto Records. It finally broke even in 1986.

"I think of playing as a form of meditation," Benham says of his practicing in the master bedroom every night before dinner. "The breathing processes it takes to get hot air to move through a trumpet, to make it 'speak,' get rid of all those business thoughts that are on your mind. That's when you can escape into the experience, be really into it, and all the other problems of the day, the week, the year, they're out of your mind."

FOR FURTHER INFORMATION

Elmhurst College Summer Jazz Camp, c/o Doug Beach, Music Department, 190 Prospect, Elmhurst, IL 60126; (312)-279-4100, ext. 357.

Jazz West Summer Camp, University of Southern California, MUS, 102-A, University Park, CA 90089-1851; (213)-743-2627.

PUBLICATIONS

Early Jazz: Its Roots and Musical Development by Gunther Schuller (New York: Oxford University Press, 1986), $8.95.

Jazz by G. Collier (New York: Cambridge University Press, 1975; Resources of Music Series), $16.95 with tape.

The Mississippi Rag, monthly tabloid, $15 a year; P.O. Box 19068, Minneapolis, MN 55419; (612)-920-0312. ∎

In Tune with the Classical Beat

■ In business life, Ralph Lane, 51, has protected Raid, Pledge, and other products from trademark pirates, as associate counsel for S. C. Johnson & Son in Racine, Wisconsin. In his after-hours life, Lane acts out a fantasy that has surely penetrated the mind of many an executive. He conducts a symphony orchestra—the 70-member West Suburban Symphony, based outside Chicago. In elegant command during performance, Lane turns and bows at the end of Beethoven's *Emperor* Concerto, to thunderous applause. He bids the orchestra rise with the aplomb of a Bernstein.

The scene does not entirely befit a maestro of world renown. The West Suburban Symphony regularly performs in a Hinsdale, Illinois, high school auditorium. Its members are accountants, doctors, engineers, salesmen, scientists, students, teachers, and homemakers. But all are trained musicians and many have auditioned for their chairs. Lane auditioned for the podium, competing against other guest conductors and winning the job by vote of the orchestra's members and its board.

The West Suburban Symphony may be exceptional in having a businessman as conductor, but it is typical of close to 1,000 low-budget "community" and "urban" orchestras, so identified by the American Symphony Orchestra League, that draw musical talent from other professions. More flexible than major orchestras, these groups bring classical music to new audiences, offer it free or at low cost, perform new compositions, and provide a showcase for rising young artists. And they give talented amateurs a chance to perform.

Players who step up to this chance let themselves in for a fairly structured existence of practice and rehearsals. Some say they need to be at their instruments at least once a day to keep up their skills. And, unlike many improvisational jazz players, classical musicians must play what the composer wrote. At home Ralph Lane studies scores, and every Monday evening from September through April he drives 150 miles round-trip to rehearse the West Suburban. He also conducts the Wheaton, Illinois, summer symphony orchestra.

Commitments such as these enable Lane, and others with a dual calling, to resolve career conflicts. Lane studied the French horn and conducting in his youth. Inducted into military service after he finished Harvard Law School, he got the job of leading the Seventh Army Symphony Orchestra in West Germany. As a civilian he returned to law, practicing in Chicago. But music drew him away to

In Hinsdale, Illinois, corporate lawyer Ralph Lane conducts the West Surburban Symphony Orchestra in Beethoven's *Emperor* Concerto.

HOBBIES

earn a graduate degree from the Eastman School and a position as dean and professor of music at a small Midwestern university. Those duties left little time for conducting and weren't too remunerative either. So in 1971 Lane joined S. C. Johnson's legal department, where he spent 15 years as a contented businessman-lawyer pursuing music on the side. He gets paid for symphony conducting, but the money amounts to only a small fraction of his income. The psychic income counts more. "Musicians," Lane says, "need to make music."

At least one business executive with no musical training yielded to an obsession to conduct by creating his own podium. Gilbert E. Kaplan, 45, publisher of *Institutional Investor*, got a notion to conduct Mahler's overwhelming Second Symphony, complete with chorus. He studied with a coach, hired the American Symphony Orchestra, and led it through the work before an invited audience at New York's Avery Fisher Hall in 1982. Kaplan has since conducted the Second many times in the U.S. and abroad.

"Your confidence goes up when you play with people better than you are," says Haskell Edelstein, 53, senior vice president and general tax counsel at Citicorp in Manhattan. He gets invitations to do so frequently because he is a bassoonist. And bassoonists, says Edelstein, "are not exactly a dime a dozen." The instrument is exceedingly difficult: pitch is harder to maintain than on most other reeds and the fingering is arcane. "Can I play this piece perfectly?" Edelstein says he always asks himself before a performance. The answer was a rare yes when he undertook Mozart's Quintet for Four Woodwinds and Piano at a concert of Manhattan's Riverside Orchestra.

Founded and managed by Ephraim Rubin, a clarinetist and president of Optimal Analysis, a consulting firm, this 60-piece organization presents five concerts per season. These often feature premières and members of the New York Philharmonic as soloists. Edelstein, a founding member, eventually gave up playing with the orchestra in favor of three or four chamber music groups. "I've played most of the orchestra music for bassoon that I am capable of," he explains. "There's more stuff to play in chamber music, and it's more fun." But bassoonist Bryn Douds, 31, an actuarial director for Prudential Insurance in New Jersey, kept right on coming into Manhattan for Riverside's Monday rehearsals.

In place of the dynamic excitement of the orchestra, many string and woodwind players prefer the intimate teamwork of chamber music, in conductor-less groups with one instrument to a part. Small and usually informal, they can sight-read and the audience, if any, may be just family members and friends. The Amateur Chamber Music Players Inc. publishes directories of instrumentalists in America and around the world who are available for impromptu musicales. On a business trip, Peter A. Benoliel, 54, chairman of Quaker Chemical Corp. in Conshohocken, Pennsylvania, bowed his violin in Detroit, Los Angeles, and—relying on music as the universal language—Tokyo and Osaka.

Summer workshops for chamber players, listed in a directory from Chamber Music America, have attracted Edelstein for a number of years. His wife, Joan, a senior research scientist at New York University Medical Center, went too. But "I felt ostracized as I sat musing in the sun," she recalls. As a defensive maneuver, she took up the flute. Since then both Edelsteins have had a good time at the Chamber Music Conference in Bennington, Vermont, and other New England workshops, as a musical pair.

FOR FURTHER INFORMATION

Amateur Chamber Music Players Inc.; minimum annual contribution, $10, includes *North and Central American Directory* of players; additional copies, $10; *Overseas Directory*, $5; 545 Eighth Ave., New York, NY 10018; (212)-244-2778.

American Symphony Orchestra League; associate membership, $25, includes bimonthly *Symphony* magazine; 633 E St. N.W., Washington, D.C. 20004; (202)-628-0099.

Chamber Music America; associate membership, $25, includes *Chamber Music* magazine, quarterly; biennial *Directory of Summer Chamber Music Workshops, School and Festivals*, $8; 545 Eighth Ave., New York, NY 10018; (212)-244-2772.

■

A Place in the Chorus

■ The voices that fill America's concert halls with soaring choral music pour mostly from the throats of enthusiastic amateurs. From Carnegie Hall to Silicon Valley, former college or choir singers, and even bathtub vocalists, concertize in thousands of community choruses. Many major symphony orchestras depend on amateurs to perform the great choral works. Under professional direction these singers get some musical education, socialize with fellow choristers, and lift their spirits. In some cities even those too busy to join a chorus can drop in for sing-alongs. The truly dedicated can take singing summer vacations.

Business voices have a place in the 150-member Fairfield County Chorale in Westport, Connecticut, where men and women from Exxon, ITT Rayonier, GE, Pfizer, and Stauffer Chemical join in song. The 110-member Bach Society of St. Louis numbers McDonnell Douglas engineers in its ranks, and the 150-member Houston Symphony Chorale includes oil and engineering company managers. Many corporations sponsor their own choruses, which help the cares of work to evaporate.

"The music we rehearse and perform becomes part of my body and soul, running through my head as I prepare a financial contract," says bass Peter J. Pettibone, 46, a partner in the law firm of Lord Day & Lord. He has served as president of Manhattan's 125-member Canterbury

PERFORMING

Choral Society, which gives four concerts a year at the Church of the Heavenly Rest.

"In choruses there are no heroes," notes John Hoyt Stookey, 56, chairman of National Distillers & Chemical. He and his wife, Katherine, have sung with the Canterbury Choral Society for 29 years. "For an hour or two each week, you are simply one of the tenors or sopranos," he says. Teamwork is the keynote of choral music, with singers grouped according to vocal range — soprano and alto, tenor and bass. The singing of each part by many voices in unison distinguishes a chorus from an ensemble, where only one or a few people sing each vocal line.

To join almost any chorus, a singer has to audition, usually in late summer or early fall, before the start of a concert season. Typically the prospective member must perform a solo of his or her choosing, then sight-sing from a score the director picks, and run through scales to show the voice's range. When Henry Mader, 41, a building products marketing manager at Koppers Co., tried out for Pittsburgh's Mendelssohn Choir, which regularly appears with the Pittsburgh Symphony, he was intimidated by the musical standing of the director, Robert Page, 52, who also leads the Cleveland Orchestra chorus. "I was scared to death when I sang my solo, 'The Lord's Prayer,' recalls the bass-baritone. "I felt as if I were taking a Hollywood screen test." Mader finds the intensive rehearsals for up to ten programs a year equal to individual instruction.

Most community choruses present three or four programs per season and rehearse one evening a week from September until May, with extra rehearsals before each concert. Singers who miss more than two or three rehearsals usually must drop out of the next performance. Many choruses tour occasionally. California's Santa Clara Chorale has gone to Europe every other summer.

Besides voices, executives often contribute business skills and funds to their choruses. The New York Choral Society, composed of 190 avocational singers, has an annual budget of $250,000 and no paid administrator. A 16-person board of singing members runs the society. Second soprano Mary Lee Duff, 38, a vice president and portfolio manager at J. & W. Seligman & Co., investment advisers, serves as president and devotes most of her free time to the organization. The Choral Society presents three concerts of classics and new works in Carnegie Hall each season, with a paid professional orchestra and soloists, and has made several recordings sold commercially.

The University Glee Club of New York, established 92 years ago, preserves a tradition of male choral singing and conviviality. The 135 members are mostly businessmen. They shun long works in favor of folk songs, spirituals ("Shadrack"), an occasional Bach fragment ("Sheep May Safely Graze"), and drinking songs.

"We are really a singing fraternity," says Danilo J. Mena, 47, president of Williams Equity Group, an investment banking and leasing company, and president of the University Glee Club. Weekly rehearsals start with drinks and a buffet dinner. To join, singers must be nominated by members, pass an audition, and then survive a probationary six-week period to determine how well they blend socially as well as musically.

For sing-alongs you don't have to audition or attend scheduled rehearsals. At Christmas time an audience of 3,000 becomes the chorus for the *Messiah* Sing-In at New York's Lincoln Center organized by the National Choral Council, a professional group that provides the direction. Many cities celebrate the season with similar do-it-yourself *Messiahs.*

And summer offers unique opportunities to sample choral singing without joining an organization. The New York Choral Society schedules Summer Sings each Tuesday and Thursday evening from June to September. Professional conductors from the New York metropolitan area take turns leading all comers through sight-readings of 35 choral masterworks, from Bach to Bernstein, with sheet music and refreshments provided. The cost: $5 an evening.

For a singing summer vacation, adults with previous choral experience have an unparalleled opportunity in the Berkshire Choral Institute held at the Berkshire School in Sheffield, Massachusetts. Founded in 1982 by John and Katherine Stookey, the institute offers singers a chance to rehearse a different choral masterpiece each week in July under America's outstanding choral conductors. On Saturday evenings they present the work in concert for an audience of 800 at the Berkshire Choral Festival. Students get classes in sight-singing and vocal techniques, with afternoons free to enjoy tennis, swimming, canoeing, or golf on the 500-acre grounds. The cost: $420 per week ($275 for a second week), in a double room ($50 extra for a single), meals, campus facilities, and passes to the Tanglewood music festival included. The 1986 schedule featured a week of opera choruses, when you could belt it out under the Metropolitan Opera's chorus master, David Stivender. Admission is limited to 150 singers per week, first come, first served.

FOR FURTHER INFORMATION

Berkshire Choral Institute, Sheffield, MA 01257 (413)-229-8526.

The National Choral Council, 1650 Broadway, New York, NY 10019; (212)-333-5333.

The New York Choral Society, 165 W. 57th St., New York, NY 10019; (212)-724-6633.

Musical America, 825 Seventh Ave., New York, NY 10019, publishes an annual *International Directory of the Performing Arts* ($55), which lists more than 100 choral groups, professional and amateur, that tour in the U.S.

For information on thousands of unlisted choruses, consult local church choir or orchestra directors. ∎

HOBBIES

Barbershop Harmony

■ Many who yearn to lift their voices beyond the confines of the shower find their perfect medium, plus a lot of fun and fellowship, in barbershop quartets. If travel schedules make it impossible to attend a quartet's every rehearsal, executives can join barbershop choruses where an occasional absence won't be missed. A good ear attuned to following the melody counts for more than formal training. Rhythms and meters are uncomplicated, and lyrics are easy to voice in a traditional repertoire of such old favorites as "Shine On, Harvest Moon" and "Good-Bye, My Lady Love." Men who harmonize tend to treat each other as fraternity brothers and it's hard to go home grouchy after an evening of song.

"Singing is a terrific release," says John D. Miller, 36, NBC-TV's vice president for advertising and promotion. Encouraged by his parents, professional singers, Miller formed his own quartet in a Chicago suburb in fifth grade. Except for the early 1980s, when he was making his way in network TV, he has sung bass with one foursome or another ever since. "Barbershop singing, something I'm pretty good at, takes care of those urges to perform that as a television executive I don't always get the chance to satisfy," notes the media manager.

In Los Angeles, Miller joined three other experienced harmonizers in 1983 to form the New Tradition. Lead singer and quartet manager is Dan Jordan, a computer software distributor; John Sherburn, an X-ray technician, sings tenor; and Bob Gray Jr., a defense contract product manager, is a baritone. They perform 20 weekends a year, embellishing song with comic routine. For their rendition of "Come, Josephine, in My Flying Machine," they appear in uniform as World War I aviators.

Musically, barbershop singing is a particular style of harmony and, like jazz, a genuine American folk art. The four unaccompanied voices form a chord on every note of melody. Unlike conventional men's glee clubs and choirs, where the high tenor carries the melody, in most barbershop groups a second tenor sings the lead while the first tenor harmonizes above, the baritone and bass below.

Another earmark of the genre is the dominant seventh chord, used in barbershop more than in most other music. The dominant seventh puts one part seven full notes above the bass, rather than the more frequently heard eight notes, or octave. In most arrangements of "Sweet Adeline," the "sweet" and the "del" are sung in dominant sevenths.

The tradition of making music in barbershops dates back to Elizabethan England, when barbers kept guitars in their parlors to amuse waiting customers. But the singular barbershop sound is usually traced to black singers improvising in the South in the early 1800s. What finally welded the sound to the shop was the publication in 1908 of a hit called "Jefferson Lord, Play That Barbershop Chord." Those last four syllables were all rendered in the unmistakable dominant seventh.

The Society for the Preservation and Encouragement of Barbershop Quartet Singing in America was founded by a tax attorney and an investment banker in Tulsa in 1938, a time when radio threatened to drown out local performing. In 1986 membership totaled 38,000 individual singers in 2,000 registered quartets and 800 choruses, all male. Women dedicated to the barbershop style sing with one of 700 chapters of the Sweet Adelines, or with Harmony Inc.

The SPEBQSA, now headquartered in Kenosha, Wisconsin, sponsors sing-offs in 16 districts to qualify 16 choruses and up to 50 quartets to compete for titles as international champions. In a glorious songfest during Fourth of July week in a different city each year, these qualifiers are judged on sound, interpretation, stage presence, and arrangement.

The Vocal Majority of Dallas, a men's chorus of over 150, many of them executive voices, won the SPEBQSA's choral championship four times from 1975 to 1985. (Win-

The Schizo-Phonics started in the Wheeling, Illinois, barbershop of Craig Huotari (standing, left). Co-founder Donald Reid (standing, center), head of Ashwell & Co. in Chicago, had to drop out, but entrepreneur Charles Nicoloff (right) and realtor John Gatto sing on.

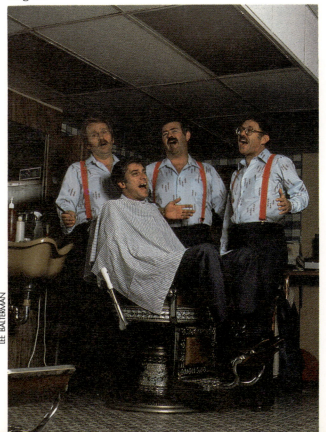

PERFORMING

ning choruses have to skip two years before competing again.) Douglas Maddox, 36, has sung with eight quartets or choruses from Pasadena to Atlanta in his 13-year career with Burroughs. When he came to Dallas in 1983, where he is regional product center manager, one of the great attractions was the chance to join the Vocal Majority. "Singing as intensely as we do in a good rehearsal or performance is almost athletic. I look forward to it every week," says the tenor. As 1985 champion, the Vocal Majority was invited to perform at the 1986 contest in Salt Lake City, and was thrilled to combine voices with the famed Mormon Tabernacle Choir. "We get such a reward from performing when the people go crazy and stand up," Maddox admits.

The quartet championship trophy went to those entertaining Californians, the New Tradition, in 1985. "Good singing combined with a little off-the-wall wackiness" helped, in the opinion of bass John Miller of NBC. For their final appearance, the foursome offered "Lydia, the Tattooed Lady" in their Marx Brothers' guise, with Miller as Groucho. He then claimed the second gold medal of his barbershop career, having sung with the winning Grandma's Boys in 1979.

Interpretation, the combination of tempo, diction, and phrasing that gives artistry to a song, sent the winning Boston Common soaring so far above other finalists in 1980 that five years later a judge wrote of it in *The Harmonizer,* the society's magazine, as "a rare experience." Their resonant presentation of "That Old Quartet of Mine," written for barbershop by Arthur Godfrey's brother Bob, brought the audience of 15,000 out of their seats. Terence Clarke, 49, president of Clarke Goward Fitts, a Boston advertising agency, and contact man for the quartet, said afterward: "There are moments when you become the song. On those rare occasions, a song is like a conveyor belt — you climb on it and it carries you off. This is an almost spiritual experience."

Success threatened to run away with the lives of the Boston Common, who performed everywhere from Carnegie Hall to the QE-2, where they warbled their way around the Caribbean. In the year of their championship they averaged a concert a week, before cutting back to spend more time with their families. Finally in 1983 they had to disband after two members dropped out.

But the urge to harmonize is irrepressible. In 1985 Clarke, who sings bass, and baritone Larry Tully, 37, president of Appleton Corp., a real estate management firm in Holyoke, Massachusetts, recruited two new voices to form the Boston Consort. By rules of the society, if two singers drop out, the quartet's name must change. The group practices twice monthly and tape-records those sessions so that each member can rehearse on his own.

Americans have carried their art form abroad. In the summer of 1986 the Boston Consort traveled to England and Wales to appear before chapters of the British Association of Barbershoppers, with their interpretations of "Roses of Picardy" and "Pack Up Your Troubles in Your Old Kit Bag."

FOR FURTHER INFORMATION

Society for the Preservation and Encouragement of Barbershop Quartet Singing in America Inc., 6315 Third Ave., Kenosha, WI 53140-5199; (414)-654-9111.
Sweet Adelines, P.O. Box 470168, Tulsa, OK 74147; (918)-622-1444. ∎

The Rewarding Applause of Theater

∎ Sweeping on stage with an arrogance befitting their station, the Earls Tolloller and Mount Ararat vied in song, and in vain, for the hand of the lovely but lowly born Phyllis in Gilbert and Sullivan's *Iolanthe.* "An enjoyable team," said the New York *Times* of the earls in a review that found the entire performance "flawless . . . with polish on all levels."

That would be welcome praise for any performers, but it was especially sweet for the earls, who spend most of their time behind desks. Johnson deF. Whitman, 51, a vice president of Morgan Guaranty Trust, and Clifford Lefebvre, 57, a corporate lawyer with the New York firm of Morris & McVeigh, have been treading the boards after hours for 25 years with Manhattan's Blue Hill Troupe.

They are among thousands of executives and professionals across the country who have joined amateur theater groups. In the 1980s stagestruck adults numbered more than 12 million, according to a survey by Louis Harris & Associates. Some 3,500 privately supported, volunteer community theaters put on shows. Their repertory has extended from *Ghosts,* at Minneapolis's Theatre in the Round, to *Jesus Christ Superstar* in Midland, Texas.

For executives onstage, applause is the reward. They also prize the theater's power to liberate them from the stress and routine of their business lives. Whitman says getting out of himself and into another character is "a total catharsis." For most performers, he thinks, acting does what it did for Henry Fonda, who said in his autobiography: "One of the beautiful things about the theater for me is that it's therapy. I don't have to be me. I've got the mask on."

Manhattan's Blue Hill Troupe has refined its act mightily since its debut 58 years ago, when some New York families summering in Blue Hill, Maine, produced *H.M.S. Pinafore* on the deck of a yacht. Still unwaveringly dedicated to Gilbert and Sullivan, today's Troupers command Broadway prices. From the annual spring production,

105

HOBBIES

which runs for seven performances at Manhattan's Hunter College Playhouse, as much as $60,000 goes to charity.

As do many amateur groups, the Blue Hill Troupe hires professional stage and musical directors for the 13 Gilbert and Sullivan operettas in its repertory. But the performers on stage are all amateurs. Winthrop Rutherfurd Jr., 44, a partner in the Wall Street law firm of White & Case and a veteran of 11 roles, says the troupe's professional directors help overcome self-consciousness. "You have to give yourself over to the director and permit yourself to do whatever he recommends." he states, "even though that may be out of character with your personality." For *Iolanthe* Rutherfurd transformed himself into young Strephon, the romantic lead who is half man and half fairy, in a performance that the New York *Times* found "outstanding."

In recruiting new members, the troupe seeks first-rate talent. It also wants to be sure both performers and backstage volunteers can get along together through months of rehearsals. Candidates must be sponsored by members and pass muster at a series of fall parties. Singers then audition.

When Whitman joined Blue Hill at age 24, his tenor voice got him the role of Nanki-Poo, the young hero in the *Mikado,* even though he had done no acting. "That scared the devil out of me. I was stiff as a rail at rehearsals," he recalls. "But as soon as the footlights came on for the performance, a total transformation came over me. The role just worked itself out. The makeup, the costume, the lights separate you from all those people out there, and keep them from getting inside your head."

Experience in the theater can develop skills that apply at work. Susan M. Getzendanner, 42, a vice president of Fiduciary Trust, has served as president of the Blue Hill Troupe, which has a board of directors and ten committees. "Getting 200 people to work together toward one production was the most thrilling and scary thing I have ever done," she says. She transfers some of her organizational techniques to the bank, where, among other duties, she heads training. Theater can train managers in communicating. Acting skills help to dispel the uncomfortable feeling many senior executives experience when called upon to speak at dinners and conventions. And the theater also teaches quick reaction to unexpected events. As an old vaudevillian used to say, "Whatever you do wrong, make it look like it's supposed to happen."

Some groups enlist corporate talent to create original shows. In Franklin Lakes, New Jersey, a New York City suburb, Warner-Lambert's vice president for public affairs, Ron Zier, 56, has scripted two productions for music and direction by Kathleen Kelley, a pianist and wife of a retired AT & T senior vice president. The congregation of the Church of the Most Blessed Sacrament produced both. Zier's idea for *The Gifts, A Christmas Fable,* presented in

November 1986, turned on a mandate given the Three Kings. They were to sell their gifts and, in return for immortality, use the proceeds to create a foundation to support good works, such as converting missile factories to consumer product plants. Frequently rising at 5 A.M. on Saturdays, Zier spent a year writing the work, which included 20 musical numbers performed by a troupe of 40, half from the business world.

Rehearsing almost nightly for eight weeks was more time than some executives had bargained for, but it brought the group together socially as well as musically. Robert Rittereiser, 49, president of E. F. Hutton, played Secretary of State. Tenor Paul O'Brien, 47, vice president of New York Telephone customer services before transferring to Boston as chief operating officer of New England Telephone, taped his part as King Balthazar and practiced while driving to work. Originally pushed into performing by his daughters, O'Brien says, "Being in a musical allows you to interact with people you wouldn't normally. People surprise you with how much fun they are." The entire community turned out to see the show during its three-night run. O'Brien notes, "This event gives one a sense of contributing not only to the well-being of the parish, but of the town."

New York's amateurs compete with a rich theatrical scene. But on the bare high plains of West Texas, the Midland Community Theatre is the main cultural resource in the city of 100,000. The center of the richest oil field in the U.S. outside Alaska, Midland started attracting aggressive young wildcatters, engineers, geologists, and MBAs generations ago. The theater began in a Quonset hut in 1946, and one young participant in the early days was George Bush, who wound up in a lengthy Washington run.

Today Midland has a $2.2-million performing-arts complex, built largely with contributions from oilmen and their foundations. The theater organization puts on at least 12 adult productions a year and welcomes all comers to try out for parts, or to work backstage, under the direction of a permanent professional staff. The theater is a good place for newcomers to get acquainted — there aren't many other things to do with your evenings. Auditions for the 1970s rock opera, *Jesus Christ Superstar,* brought out over 200 would-be thespians, most in their 20s and 30s. One father and son duo sang in the chorus. At first some local conservatives thought the show might be a bit far-out for Midland. But it proved so popular, the run was extended an extra weekend. The oil business may have faltered in Texas in the 1980s, but culture is holding up just fine.

Such an efflorescence of community theaters has sprouted in Texas that "play-offs" are held in four quadrants of the state prior to a statewide competition. Nationwide, the American Association of Community Theatre, which accepts individual as well as group memberships,

PERFORMING

oversees contests for its theater groups. Some 300 troupes enter the preliminaries. The winners hit the boards every other year in a national community theater festival.

FOR FURTHER INFORMATION

American Association of Community Theatre; individual membership, $40 a year, includes a bimonthly newsletter, *Spotlight;* c/o James Carver, President, Kalamazoo Community Players, 329 S. Park, Kalamazoo, MI 49007; (616)-343-1313.

Ballroom Dancing

■ He takes 35 business trips a year, but James Tillotson doesn't let a hectic schedule cut in on his favorite exercise: ballroom dancing. Vice president for research and development at Ocean Spray Cranberries, Tillotson, 57, has waltzed, rumbaed, and tangoed from Shanghai to Zurich. "I could sit in the hotel and get fat or drink a lot," he says, "but I prefer to skip dinner and go dancing." Executives at Ocean Spray kid him about his passion, but he doesn't mind. Since he began dancing seven years ago, the 6-foot 2-inch Tillotson says he has lost 40 pounds, improved his posture, and become more confident in social and business situations. One other attraction he cites: "There's no other sport where you can walk into a room and within 20 minutes have all of the women in your arms."

Ballroom dancing is on an upswing across the U.S. The surge started with the discomania of the mid-Seventies, which ignited widespread interest in dance, even among men notoriously bashful, if not terrified, around dance floors. Dance teachers say the Public Broadcasting Service has chipped in by carrying major ballroom dance competitions since 1981. Then, in the fall of 1985, the all-dance revue *Tango Argentino* became one of the hottest tickets on Broadway and propelled interest to the loftiest heights in years. Pinning down the number of U.S. dance students is impossible because most teaching studios are small and independent, but the figure is surely rising. At the two major nationwide teaching chains, Fred Astaire International Dance Association and Arthur Murray International, combined new enrollments rose from about 85,000 in 1982 to about 96,000 in 1985.

Some foxtrotophobes don't call the dance school until they have to — daughter's wedding is three weeks away — but many others take up dancing for exercise or to relieve tension. Many men, such as Jody Simons, 58, manager of the Drexel Burnham Lambert investment firm's Boston office, just got fed up with being klutzes. Despite his wife's urgings at business and social affairs, he refused to dance. "My feet just wouldn't move." he explained. In 1984, on a whim, he signed up for lessons with a local instructor, and his wife joined him three weeks later. Two years later, he said, "I go dancing at every opportunity. We hardly ever go to the movies anymore."

For some ardent hoofers, especially those who have excelled in sports or are overachievers at work, dancing for the simple fun of it is not enough. They need to compete. They have plenty of opportunity. Dance studios set up a lot of competitions so students can mingle and because students take more lessons when gearing up for a championship. Scores of other regional and national contests give chances to dancers of almost any ability. The National Dance Council of America sets the judging standards, and two newsletters report the competitive calendar in detail: *Dance Week* and *The Amateur Dancers.*

Some competitors become obsessed with their hobby. John Gay, 35, a senior vice president at Southeast Bank in Miami, rarely dances socially anymore. He and wife Lori, a professional dance instructor, have for several years been U.S. theatrical dance champions in the pro-am division. Gay practices about 20 hours a week. Ronald Ford, 36, a senior business analyst at Amoco Chemicals Co. in Chicago, won the U.S. Amateur Ballroom Championship in 1981 and turned pro two years ago. Practicing, teaching, and competing take him about 40 hours a week. He spends $10,000 to $12,000 a year on dancing, which is more than his teaching income.

Other aspiring Freds and Gingers remain more footloose. Rod Reader, 42, after competing for about a year,

James Tillotson, Ocean Spray vice president, had plenty to smile about once the dancing was over. He won four gold medals at a New England Imperial Competition in Boston.

HOBBIES

insisted that he "will never turn my hobby into a monster." Says Reader, a partner in Downes & Reader Lumber Co. of Stoughton, Massachusetts: "I never lose because I go for fun." Richard Cyphers, 36, manager of E. F. Hutton's Hartford office, takes a similar attitude: "I look at a competition as being in a land-of-make-believe for a weekend. We get dressed up and show off our skills."

Finding dance instruction is easy practically everywhere in the U.S. The two major chains, Arthur Murray and Fred Astaire, together have about 400 franchises. To find the nearest, call national headquarters or check the yellow pages. You will also probably find listed several independent studios, which outnumber the franchises by about 6 to 1. Many colleges and universities offer day and night classes in ballroom dancing. Learning need not cost much. An Astaire studio in New York City, for example, offers an introductory package of four lessons for $12; after that, group lessons cost $15 an hour. Private lessons are expensive: generally $30 to $50 an hour, often much more for the time of teachers who turn out champions.

Most major cities have public dance halls for ballroom enthusiasts, usually offering live music and often charging admission. Go alone without qualms. Everyone is there to dance and expects to ask or be asked. And the dance halls and their denizens have largely left behind the slightly less-than-wholesome aura some once had. Among the standout spots:

• NEW YORK CITY. Roseland (239 West 52nd Street; 212-247-0200) is mecca for serious dancers. A surprising blast from the past: taxi dancers, who will spin around the floor with the customers for a dollar a dance.

The Red Parrot (617 West 57th Street; 247-1843) was once a roller disco, but is now a nightclub with dancing until 4 A.M.

• BOSTON. Moseley's On The Charles (Dedham, Massachusetts; 617-326-3075) is a giant ballroom (10,000 square feet) for serious dancers on Wednesdays and Saturdays; 11 miles from downtown.

Parker House Hotel (60 School Street; 227-8600) caters to a young crowd; good food is available.

The Bay Tower Room (60 State Street; 723-1666) draws a well-to-do crowd and offers a spectacular view of Boston harbor; the dance floor is small and the food is good.

• CHICAGO. Willowbrook Ballroom and Restaurant (Willow Springs, Illinois; 312-839-1000) has dancing Thursdays, Saturdays, and Sundays; 18 miles from downtown.

• DALLAS. Four Seasons Ballroom (4930 Military Parkway; 214-349-0390) has dancing Wednesday and Friday nights.

• SAN FRANCISCO. Hyatt Regency hotel (5 Embarcadero Center; 415-788-1234) holds tea dances in the Atrium lobby every Friday afternoon from 5:30 to 8:30.

Cesar's Latin Palace (3140 Mission Street; 648-6611) is a converted bowling alley that holds 1,000 people. Thursday, Friday, and Saturday are Latin nights, from 9 P.M. to 5 A.M. A rose for clenching in the teeth is optional.

FOR FURTHER INFORMATION

Arthur Murray International, 1077 Ponce de Leon Blvd., Coral Gables, FL 33134; (305)-445-9645.

Fred Astaire International Dance Association, 11945 S. W. 140th Terrace, Miami, FL 33186; (305)-238-7911.

United States Amateur Ballroom Dancers Association; membership, $8 a year ($12 for competitors), includes *The Amateur Dancers,* bimonthly; 125 Hillside Ave., West Caldwell, NJ 07006; (201)-226-9140.

PUBLICATION

Dance Week, $22 a year; Telemark Dance Records, Richard S. Mason, P. O. Box 55, McLean, VA 22101; (703)-356-9113.

∎

CREATING

Working Your Way with Wood

■ In the well-appointed shop of his spacious Georgian-style home on Long Island, Enrique Senior, 42, an investment banker with Allen & Co. in New York City, lovingly planes a piece of black walnut. "There's a great sensual pleasure in planing — the odors, the colors that come up as you shear," notes the Cuban-born financier. "I think planing is the most satisfying part of woodworking." That piece of walnut will form the base of a display case Senior has designed, with hidden hinges and heavy bevel-edged glass, for his collection of late 19th-century firearms, selected for the beauty of their craftsmanship and wooden mountings.

Senior finds woodworking absorbs his mind as well as his hands, relieving him from the high-pressured business of advising corporations. He personally conceives the design of everything he makes, from a six-foot carved oak mantel for his family room, to a mahogany-veneered bookcase for a particular spot in a partner's office.

The challenge in making fine furniture of any design turns upon mastery of the skills of woodworking — cutting, shaping, and joining. The ancient art of joinery, the shaping of parts to fit and hold together without fasteners, in dovetails or other mortise-and-tenon joints, starts with understanding the properties of wood, its strengths and weaknesses. "Wood is alive. It expands and contracts with the seasons, as the humidity changes," explains Senior, who got to know a lot about wood as a teenager with a home workshop in Havana. As a student of architecture at Yale, he grew to appreciate fine fittings and joinings, especially those of Japanese craftsmen.

The not-so-handy, who may have come late to the woodworker's craft, need some formal instruction in the basics. University extensions, museums, and dealers in woodworking tools frequently offer courses and workshops. So do YWCAs and YMCAs. Richard Ravitch, 52, a New York City builder and developer, who served as chairman of the Metropolitan Transportation Authority before taking on the chairmanship of the Bowery Savings Bank, has confessed: "I was a real klutz with my hands and there was a family joke that I could never do anything." But when he was in his mid-30s, the gifts of a power drill and electric handsaw, thrust upon him by his mother, challenged him to try to make a table.

Summoning all the help he could get, Ravitch bought a particular radial-arm power saw because five free lessons came with it. He cultivated the acquaintance of an expert professional cabinetmaker. He took a two-day course in wood-turning on a lathe from a craftsman in England, and a refresher course from another in Vermont. He pored over Andrew W. Marlow's *Fine Furniture,* and glossy issues of the magazine *Fine Woodworking.* Ten years of work and study paid off in more than 30 items, most of them re-creations of American museum pieces.

Today's woodworkers have a great advantage over craftsmen of their great-grandfathers' day who produced those original museum pieces: the array of sophisticated power tools that enable them to perform many tedious tasks quickly and precisely. As their skills and ambitions sharpen, woodworkers avidly equip their shops with more and better power tools. Senior's workshop contains 20 machine tools, worth $39,000, from a $10,000 table saw to a $50 sander. For their major stationary tools, Senior and Ravitch each purchased machines of industrial quality, which do more precise work than the ones designed for home use.

Delta International of Pittsburgh is a major manufacturer of industrial models, while Sears' Craftsman brand has equipped many a home workshop. Jimmy Carter's White House staff presented him with $8,000 worth of Sears tools when he left office. Some home craftsmen prefer to buy all-in-one equipment. The Shopsmith Co. in Dayton, Ohio, makes a multipurpose contraption with a single motor plus attachments that perform as table saw, disk sander, drill press, lathe, and horizontal boring machine, at a cost upwards of $3,000.

Hand-driven tools for, say, shaping and finishing — saws, planes, chisels, awls, gimlets, files, rasps — turn many woodworkers into collectors. They cherish the craftsmanship in the making of the tools themselves. Senior has acquired 345 hand tools, from dovetail saws to

HOBBIES

Japanese water stones, used for sharpening fine tools. Some covet old tools. Ravitch is very proud of his 1983 purchase, in an auction bid by mail, of an old English Norris plane. "That's as fine a plane as there is," he explains. "I'm not interested in older tools for their antique value, but because they function better and are more precise."

Working drawings guide the artisan from start to finish. Those who design their own pieces, as Senior does, make their own drawings. Others, who copy museum pieces, have a rich selection in the plans drawn and published by Lester Margon, a designer and scholar who produced hundreds of scale drawings of museum pieces. Grandfather-clock fanciers can get plans and clockworks for reproductions of Colonial masterpieces from Mason & Sullivan in West Yarmouth, Massachusetts.

Authenticity of materials and construction preoccupies many makers of reproductions. When Richard Ravitch made a large Pennsylvania Dutch hutch, one of his favorites, he joined the front frame to the sides with wooden nails he had chiseled out himself. Some purists stop short of hand-finishing, a time-consuming, and potentially boring, process. Instead they apply varnish with an electric air compressor. But Ravitch has taught himself to do "French polishing," a process of hand-smoothing and many, many rubbings that gives an appealing antique patina to newly made furniture.

FOR FURTHER INFORMATION

Garrett Wade Co., dealers in woodworking tools; publish a catalogue, $4, with quarterly supplements; 161 Ave. of the Americas, New York, NY 10013; (212)-807-1155.

PUBLICATIONS

Complete Book of Woodworking Tools and Hardware by Charles R. Self (Blue Ridge Summit, PA: TAB Books, 1983), $14.95.

Construction of American Furniture Treasures by Lester Margon (New York: Dover, 1975), $6.

The Encyclopedia of Furniture Making by Ernest Joyce (New York: Sterling Press, 1979), $19.95.

Fine Furniture by Andrew W. Marlow (Briarcliff Manor, NY: Stein & Day, 1977), $12.95.

Fine Woodworking magazine, bimonthly, $18; The Taunton Press, Box 355, 63 S. Main St., Newtown, CT 06470; (203)-426-8171.

The New England Handcraft Catalog by Kenneth A. Simon (Chester, CT: The Globe Pequot Press, 1983), $14.95; lists schools and leading artisans.

Tage Frid Teaches Woodworking (Newtown, CT: The Taunton Press)
  Book 1: *Joinery, Tools & Techniques* (1979), $17.95;
  Book 2: *Shaping, Veneering & Finishing* (1981), $17.95;
  Book 3: *Furniture* (1985), $18.95.

Woodsmith, bimonthly, $10 per year; Woodsmith Publishing, 2200 Grand Ave., Des Moines, IA 50312 (515)-282-7000. ■

Painting and Sculpting

■ Winston Churchill called his hobby "a joy ride in a paintbox." He considered his art a first essential in keeping mentally fit. "A man can wear out a particular part of his mind by continually using it and tiring it," he wrote, "just in the same way as he can wear out the elbows of his coat. . . . The tired parts of the mind can be rested and strengthened . . . by using other parts."

For Allen Krowe, 53, a senior vice president of IBM in Armonk, New York, "Painting is a comfortable jacket and chair and book you can slip into again and again. Only you might grow tired of a book. Painting you never do." Dr. David Rogers, 60, president of the $1.5-billion Robert Wood Johnson Foundation in Princeton, New Jersey, the nation's largest health philanthropy, likens his affinity for sculpting to Linus's affection for his blanket: "When I'm upset, I'll go to my shop and whack away at something and then come back to my problem later."

Recreation through creation lets the artist compose alone, independent of partners, time, and even place, for the graphic artist, at least. Painting and sculpting engage mind and eye in directing the hand. And at the end there's something to show for the effort. After a first attempt at sculpture, one executive decided "it didn't really matter if my piece didn't look exactly as I wanted it to. It's not Michelangelo, it's not Rodin, but it's *me*, my work." Many executives find their artistic creativity has turned into more than a diversion. It heightens their awareness and becomes part of their personalities.

For IBM's Krowe, painting replaced flying at age 31,

With a sculptor's mallet, Dr. David Rogers drives a chisel into a cherry log in his Princeton, New Jersey, workshop.

CREATING

after eight years as an Air Force fighter pilot and then a stint in the Air National Guard. "Your attention and thought processes are somewhat similar, taking in everything," says Krowe, who paints landscapes and seascapes. He claims the same exhilaration from art that he once found at 38,000 feet. "Painting gives you a chance to leave your world," he explains. "Time flies, almost as if you were in a time machine. No matter how much you enjoy your job, the price of self-renewal means leaving that world."

Totally self-taught, Krowe simply plunged in, heeding the protean Churchill's advice to busy people: "There is really no time for the deliberate approach." In school, Krowe cheerfully admits, "I was always a dead zero in art class." From studying the work of painters he enjoys, he tries to learn both technique, such as the effects achieved with a palette knife, and composition. He has copied several works of the American realist Edward Hopper, those with rectilinear buildings, light, and shadows. One reminded him of his great-grandmother's house in Virginia. Sometimes he simply paints "memories or idealizations of things that were lovely," he says. He may photograph or sketch scenes he likes, such as Chesapeake Bay lighthouses and vessels, as inspirations for later canvasses.

Serendipity now and then has marked Krowe's more than 100 paintings. "If you really try, the result will be something surprising," he remarks. "You work on a painting and then you look at it the next day. You might observe that the treatment of a shadow is exceptionally good, and you know that you didn't do it purposefully — it just happened."

Sculpture, man's oldest art, entered the life of Dr. David Rogers as compensation for two unfulfilled desires, to be a painter and a surgeon. His father, Carl Rogers, a noted psychologist, developed the idea that every person needs to grow in self-esteem throughout life. Most of the family were gifted amateur painters. "But I couldn't paint worth a damn," David Rogers recalls. So in self-defense he started whittling and at 15 produced a figure of a young woman in cedar. Then at Cornell University Medical College he found that research suited his personality better than the surgery he had intended. A leading specialist in infectious diseases, Rogers has headed Vanderbilt University's department of medicine and the Johns Hopkins medical school. Meanwhile he never stopped sculpting in wood, realizing at age 30 that "it was an important part of me."

Formal instruction figured briefly but importantly in Rogers's artistic development. At Ohio State, where he started college, he took a summer course in clay modeling from the sculptor-in-residence. "I learned a lot in just one intense three-month period," he recalls, even though he went back to sculpting wood, a different technique. In clay, sculptors start from the inside and work out, making corrections as they model. In stone and wood they work from the outside in; with these less forgiving materials, carvers have to be more disciplined than modelers.

Carvers pride themselves on creating an entire sculpture from a single block of stone or wood. At the family's summer place in New York's Finger Lakes region, Rogers found twisted old cedar stumps and roots that gave shape to a 30-inch ballet dancer on point and a glowering eagle. Fallen trees from neighbors fill the Rogers garage in New Jersey. Black walnut yielded a skunk and a badger, sycamore a woman's golden torso. Mahogany that Rogers picked up beachcombing in the Caribbean turned into a mother sea lion and pup.

Looking at a log, Rogers searches for the figure that may be trapped within, and visualizes its final form — graceful, powerful, humorous. A physician's knowledge of anatomy helps give form to his subjects. The only tools he needs are a saw; a sculptor's mallet to drive the gouges that chisel away outer wood, along the grain if possible; a jackknife and rasp to carve and shape; and sandpaper for finishing. He finds it best to keep his subjects strong and simple, so that the finished piece hangs together as a work of art. In 45 years Rogers has produced 250 pieces, he reckons, though he isn't sure where they all are. He's never sold any, but gives lots away.

Though he vows to remain militantly amateur, Rogers has shyly agreed to two noncommercial public exhibitions. At a Vanderbilt exhibition of his works, which he visited alone at night, he felt what Thomas Mann called "the proud embarrassment of the artist, tasting the enjoyment of his own works with the eyes of strangers." Rogers recalls that "seeing 25 years of my work, 45 pieces around the room, was a profound experience. I thought, I really like this." Years later, a show at the Educational Testing Service headquarters near Princeton exposed Rogers to professional criticism. New Jersey artists were invited to a special viewing. With his wife, Bobbie, Rogers went to eavesdrop. "I felt real good about how pleased people were with my stuff," he says. "So I reasoned, okay, don't be embarrassed by the fact that you enjoy it."

FOR FURTHER INFORMATION

The American Art Directory (New York: R.R. Bowker, 51st ed., 1986), $94.50, lists U.S. and Canadian institutions that offer instruction. Many give courses on evenings and weekends to beginners and experienced students. A few:

The Art Students League of New York, 215 W. 57th St., New York, NY 10019; (212)-247-4510.

The National Academy of Design School of Fine Arts, 5 E. 89th St., New York, NY 10128; (212)-996-1908.

The School of the Art Institute of Chicago, 280 Columbus Dr., Chicago, IL 60603; (312)-443-3717.

UCLA Extension, Department of Visual Arts, 10995 Le Conte Ave., Los Angeles, CA 90024; (213)-206-8503. ■

HOBBIES

Through the Camera's Eye

■ Rising at four on a February morning, Arthur Dickey, 56, an architect in Edina, Minnesota, cheerfully stood in 12-below-zero weather to take pictures of St. Paul's 12-story ice palace, iridescent in dawn's early light. On the way to work in Providence, Rhode Island, banker Dean Holt, 45, spotted a pair of red shoes on gray steps, and made one of his favorite photographs. At home in St. Louis, Martha Frentrop, 46, a training executive with Southwestern Bell, focuses on the textures of food. Stephen McGrogan, 38, a computer consultant with Elxsi, in San Jose, California, and his wife, Jean, spend hours in their darkroom making prints to enter in photo contests.

Most of America's 4.5 million photo hobbyists snap shots of families and vacations for their memory banks. But more and more executives, like Holt, Frentrop, and McGrogan, have made cameras their companions and turned to photography in adult life as their medium of creative expression. Whatever the purpose, the biggest reward comes from producing an image with impact.

"The sheer ease with which we can produce a superficial image often leads to creative disaster," noted the late Ansel Adams, one of America's most admired photographers and teachers. Most American amateurs use pocket-sized "point-and-shoot" electronic cameras with automatic focus and built-in light meters that make quick work of candid shots. To broaden their choices of exposure and focus, and get a better grasp of their craft, many serious amateurs prefer reflex cameras with separate lenses and manual controls. But Edward Weston, whose sharply focused classics helped to secure photography's place as art, held that "the photographer's most important and likewise most difficult task is not learning to manage his camera, or to develop, or to print. It is learning to see photographically."

"The camera can only do part of the job," acknowledges Dean Holt, president of the business credit division of Fleet Credit Corp. in Providence, who takes his camera on business trips. "Your eye, your mind really, has to see the picture before the camera can take it. The camera is just making your mind work. That's the fun part of it."

To make a picture memorable, the photographer, like the painter, heightens reality with his own vision, and brings to it fresh perceptions that another viewer might not have grasped. "Some people can just walk up to a trash heap and produce a telling drama out of it," notes McGrogan, who is trying to develop that ability. Unlike the painter, who starts with a blank canvas, the photographer is limited in his capacity to synthesize a work of art. Outside the studio at least, he must do his best with the world as he finds it. He composes his picture by selecting forms, textures, colors that best express his idea. Then he arranges the way those elements will appear on film, usually by choosing a particular vantage point and moment. "A painting, you can work with over a period of time to create the image you want," notes Holt, who gave up drawing and painting for photography. "You can't just make a canvas of the negative. Maybe you set up a picture, but your time is limited. Light changes and light is everything in photography. Afterward you can manipulate just so much in the darkroom. Imagination has to be there when the essential picture is created."

Perceptual skills from their own particular backgrounds help many successful amateurs. Robert McCabe, 51, cofounder and president of Pilot Capital Corp. in New York City, sharpened his eye while riding radio cars and hanging around the darkroom of the New York *Mirror* when his father was its publisher. Martha Frentrop studied fashion design and advertising art in college. McGrogan, trained as an electrical engineer, approaches photography as a technician, and is surprised to see how differently he and his wife, a onetime professional photographer, look at the world. "She sees things that elude me, mostly in shadows, while I see mostly in shapes and colors."

Once the photographer's critical eye has conceived a

Photographing young children presents special challenges, as Robert McCabe knows from firsthand experience. As his son, George, demonstrated at 2, they have their own ideas about posing.

112

CREATING

picture, success in capturing it on film depends on an awareness of what his equipment can do. When humans look at a scene, the brain blocks out unimportant objects that the camera will register as clutter. And the brain tends to "see" things the camera cannot, telling us that a person in the distance is six feet tall, though he may appear only three inches high. An alert photographer with a long lens or a zoom lens can enlarge a figure. And he can etch in clouds or deepen shadows with a red filter.

Color film was the choice of 95% of America's amateurs by the mid-1980s, though many purists consider black-and-white more challenging and expressive. Robert McCabe, whose black-and-white photographs of Greece were published in a book, *Metamorphosis,* in 1979, said, "You have to be much more attentive to the idea in a black-and-white picture." However, when he no longer had time to do his own darkroom work, he switched to color, which imposes different challenges. "Color gives you another dimension in composition instead of just light, shapes, and form. But you have less latitude in exposure and you need greater sensitivity, because you can't make corrections on a slide as you can when you print a black-and-white picture." Many photographers compensate by "bracketing," or repeating the same color shot at several exposures.

A darkroom offers all sorts of creative possibilities, but can cost from $3,000 to upwards of $10,000 to install and equip. In printing black-and-white you can darken a sky by overexposing that part of a negative, or lighten skin tones by underexposing them. Or you can dip a print in sepia toner to add warmth. Engineer Steve McGrogan and his wife, Jean, the former professional photographer, have a darkroom well equipped for both black-and-white and color. New instant kits from Kodak have led other amateurs to try their own color printing and processing. In selecting a commercial processor, the novice hobbyist may get better results from a place that professionals use rather than from retail chains that offer fast, cheap service for what often turns out to be low-quality work.

Instruction is only one of many services available through the Photographic Society of America, an organization of 14,000 individual enthusiasts plus camera clubs. A one-time $5 registration fee plus $30 annual dues includes subscription to the monthly *PSA Journal,* access to workshops, correspondence courses, and critiques in eight special-interest divisions, including the pictorial print, the color slide, video and motion pictures, and photo travel. Competition through salons stimulates photographers to compare their work. Architect Dickey has enjoyed taking pictures ever since he won a Brownie camera for selling the *Saturday Evening Post* door-to-door at age 11. But the PSA, which he joined at age 40, he says, "has really taught me a great deal about photography through association with other amateur photographers."

Never underestimate the social rewards of photography. If you ask McGrogan, he may tell you how grateful he is to his mother for giving him a camera just to get him out of the house at age 21. He met his wife through a camera club.

FOR FURTHER INFORMATION

Photographic Society of America; membership, $5 initial registration fee plus $30 a year, includes *PSA Journal,* monthly; 2005 Walnut St., Philadelphia, PA 19103; (215)-563-1663.

PUBLICATIONS

Complete Kodak Book of Photography: In Association with Time-Life Books (New York: Crown, 1986), $29.95.

Edward Weston by Ben Maddow (Boston: Little, Brown/New York Graphic Society, 1978), $15.95.

The New Ansel Adams Photography Series: The Camera (1980); *The Negative* (1981); *The Print* (1983); by Ansel Adams with Robert Baker (Boston: Little, Brown/New York Graphic Society), $24.50 each.

The Photographer's Eye by John Szarkowski (Boston: Little, Brown/New York Graphic Society, revised ed., 1980), $12.95.

Popular Photography magazine, monthly, $11.97; CBS Magazines, 1515 Broadway, New York, NY 10036 (800)-525-0643 or (303)-447-9330. ∎

Photographers' Workshops

■ From the Maine coast to the Monterey Peninsula, photography workshops are drawing thousands of shutterbugs each summer and fall. These intensive sessions celebrate one of the most enduringly popular hobbies while offering picture know-how to enthusiasts of all abilities. For participants, workshops usually mean total immersion from the treasured light of dawn until well after dark; in return they give new technical skills and open eyes to new ways of seeing.

"Pretty exciting" is how Mary Nation, 38, a vice president and portfolio manager at Bankers Trust in New York, describes the first workshop she attended. Entitled "Travel Images — Bon Voyage!," it lasted four days and cost $295 at Manhattan's International Center of Photography. The seven students and their instructor, who shot color film, traveled no farther than Staten Island by ferry. But from their first assignment the class got the message that the most important voyage is in the imagination. Mary Nation went on to a workshop in basic black-and-white. "It's fun," she says. "I'm having a ball." Besides year-round instruction in Manhattan, the center offers summer workshops at scenic destinations in the United States and Europe.

With scores of operators nationwide offering hundreds

113

HOBBIES

of workshops annually, how can anyone make the right choice? Several magazines — *Modern Photography, Petersen's Photographic, Popular Photography* — publish directories of workshops. But these are usually drawn from press releases and published with no evaluation, so you will have to do some investigating. Questions to ask: Must you submit sample photographs for critique by the instructor? What are the instructors' qualifications? How many students will there be, and what is the ratio of instructors or assistants to students? How much time will you spend in the field getting hands-on experience? Will film be processed for evaluation during the workshop? Will lab facilities be available for students? Will the workshop give names of former students as references? For the most direct answers, try to talk to the instructors.

You need not even be an active photographer to attend workshops at the Friends of Photography in Carmel, California. Ansel Adams was among the founders. Its six summer workshops focus on aesthetic rather than technical concerns, using a show-and-tell format. They feature some of the finest practitioners of the art, from portraitist Yousuf Karsh, 77, to documentary photographer Mary Ellen Mark, 46. Students, divided into small groups, have a chance for discussion with several masters. No film-processing facilities are available to students, but optional shooting in the field is scheduled with workshop assistants. The cost: about $500 per workshop, including room and board.

William Guion, 36, manager of advertising and sales promotion for Pan-American Life Insurance in New Orleans, attended a Friends workshop on the black-and-white print, his first. "I just wanted to learn from the masters how to see," says Guion, who has been seriously interested in photography for a couple of years. "But I learned a lot technically too, about composition and how to communicate information by looking through someone's ground glass." On his drive back to New Orleans he looked at the country with different eyes.

Another haven for beginners as well as advanced practitioners is the Maine Photographic Workshops in Rockport, a summer colony of photographers. This school offers a 5½-day "crash course" for beginning amateurs on alternate weeks (tuition and lab fee: $360, not including room and board). Higher-level workshops here and elsewhere generally require that you know the fundamentals of photography and are able to use a manual camera, not just an automatic point-and-shoot model. In these workshops, beginners may not be welcomed by other students if they cannot keep up or demand extra time from the instructor. James McCann, 57, an Atlanta-area sales representative for H. B. Fuller Co. who has attended a half dozen workshops, complains, "Every workshop I've been in has had out-of-pace beginners."

Many workshops offer specialized instruction. One on photographing people attracted George Schneider, co-

owner of a Pittsburgh accounting firm, and his wife, Viola. "Our people were always stiff and standing in a row," says Schneider. "There had to be a better way." They drove down to Asheville, North Carolina, for a weekend with Tim Barnwell (tuition $95), director of Appalachian Photographic Workshops. "We learned that you have to develop a rapport with your subjects, and that takes time," Schneider says. "I'd been hurrying." Appalachian offers instruction all year except in December.

Nature photography workshops thrive in the West, land of dramatic vistas and primeval wilderness. The University of California extensions at Santa Cruz and Santa Barbara offer outdoor and travel workshops conducted by outstanding photographers. Wilderness Photography/Trinity Alps Workshops, a partnership of three naturalist photographers, offers sessions in a dozen North American locales, such as Wyoming in July and Ontario for fall foliage. At the Trinity Mountain Meadow Resort in northern California, Tom Cory, 41, a clinical psychologist from Chattanooga, Tennessee, and his wife, Patricia, spent a week photographing wildflowers, insects, streams, and landscapes ($750 per person, room and board included). "I've had 20 years of experience as a photographer and been to at least 15 workshops," says Cory, "but I still learned something, and I'll go back to more."

And if your companion is not the photography fan you are? Some outposts of the arts offer a solution. The Anderson Ranch Arts Center in Snowmass Village, Colorado, holds workshops in woodworking, ceramics, and painting as well as sessions with famous photographers at its new photography center (tuition and lab fees for one- and two-week sessions: $300 to $400). The Penland School for crafts, 50 miles northeast of Asheville, North Carolina, also offers several programs (tuition for two-week programs: $300; room and board: $235 to $575). Alex Radin, 65, a Washington, D.C., consultant and formerly executive director of the American Public Power Association, accompanied his wife, Carol, an artist, to the school. He took a black-and-white photography workshop, she attended one in fabric and other designs, and domestic tranquility was ensured.

FOR FURTHER INFORMATION

Anderson Ranch Arts Center, P.O. Box 5598, Snowmass Village, CO 81615; (303)-923-3181.

Appalachian Photographic Workshops, 242 Charlotte St., Asheville, NC 28801; (704)-258-9498.

Friends of Photography, membership, $36 a year, includes two periodicals. P.O. Box 500, Carmel, CA 93921; (408)-624-6330.

International Center of Photography, 1130 Fifth Ave., New York, NY 10128; (212)-860-1753.

Maine Photographic Workshops, Rockport, ME 04856; (207)-236-8581.

CREATING

Penland School of Crafts, Penland, NC 28765-0037; (704)-765-2359.

University of California Extension, Santa Barbara, CA, 93106; (805)-961-4200.

University of California Extension, Santa Cruz, CA 95064; (408)-429-2971.

Wilderness Photography/Trinity Alps Workshops, Mary Ellen Schultz, 27834 25th Dr. S., Federal Way, WA 98003; (206)-941-8884.

PUBLICATIONS

Modern Photography magazine, monthly, $13.95; ABC Consumer Magazines, 825 Seventh Ave., New York, NY 10019; (800)-666-3977.

Petersen's Photographic, monthly, $15.94; Peterson Publishing, 8490 Sunset Blvd., Los Angeles, CA 90069; (213)-854-2222.

Popular Photography magazine, monthly, $11.97; CBS Magazines, 1515 Broadway, New York, NY 10036; (800)-525-0643 or (303)-447-9330. ∎

FOR COLLECTORS AND CONNOISSEURS

Art: How Not to Get Stung

■ Saturdays bring gallery-goers to Boston's Newbury Street, to Chicago's West Superior Street, and especially to New York's 500 art showcases, uptown and down. A. Alfred Taubman, 63, chairman of Sotheby's Holdings Inc., which owns London and New York auction houses, has estimated the world market in art and other collectible items at about $25 billion a year. Legions of collectors chasing a limited supply of fine art run risks of getting stung. Homework, caution, and some professional services can limit those risks.

Experts often advise new collectors to buy not for investment, but for pleasure. Since art doesn't turn over with the speed of a blue-chip stock, it may take years to liquidate at a profit, with luck. Besides, speculators have made the market highly volatile in recent years, especially in contemporary art. Still, to avoid loss in value, buyers of art for art's sake need to pay as much attention to these acquisitions as to other assets.

Aesthetic quality, authenticity, and condition — whether a piece needs restoring or has already been restored — underlie the value of a work. Once they know what they like, canny collectors specialize. They learn all they can about their period, genre, or artists, from courses, reading, museums, dealers, auctions, and other collectors. Above all, an art lover looks and compares, developing an eye for style and quality.

Two gallery-goers who have enthusiastically adopted this practice are Herbert Glantz, 56, president of an electrical supply company, N. Glantz & Son, in Brooklyn, New York, and his wife, Kitty, 49. Saturday morning regulars at the Soho and Madison Avenue galleries that feature contemporary American artists, the Glantzes do their research and keep on top of the current, dynamic art scene. Says Glantz: "We don't want to get ripped off." His wife polished her expertise as a volunteer at Manhattan's Whitney Museum of American Art, and later moved to the Museum of Modern Art as a paid lecturer.

To avoid buying inferior works, deal only with reputable dealers and auction houses. Buying directly from another collector may fetch a better price but can be risky without expert advice. Both dealers and auction houses sift a multitude of wares, and offer warranties — sometimes limited — that what they sell is as described in catalogues or bills of sale. Christie's, another leading auction house, and Sotheby's keep large staffs of specialists, available to serious collectors. Dealers can also provide vital information. The Art Dealers Association of America publishes a list of its more than 100 members, with the specialty of each.

Dave H. Williams, 53, chairman of Alliance Capital Management, part of the Equitable Life Assurance Society, spends time each weekend enhancing his knowledge of prints through catalogues, visiting dealers, or previewing auction lots with experts. He looks for what he likes. "I react to my stomach," he says. Since his first purchase in 1969, he has assembled and catalogued a collection of 240 mostly black-and-white prints by early 20th-century

At New York's 128-year-old Graham Gallery, Herbert Glantz (center), who heads a family company, and his wife, Kitty, discuss neo-expressionist Carmen Cicero's *Puttin' on the Ritz* with Robert C. Graham Jr. The Glantzes bought the work for $8,000.

FOR COLLECTORS AND CONNOISSEURS

American artists. His collection hangs at his firm's head-quarters in lower Manhattan, and he adds to it at every good opportunity. At a 1985 spring auction at Christie's in New York, he bought a signed Winslow Homer seascape for $27,500.

Fakes, while infrequent, crop up in a sellers' market. And attribution of works to a particular artist may change with new scholarship. For a minimum $500, a New York nonprofit organization, the International Foundation for Art Research (IFAR), will get top scholars to authenticate paintings, prints, and small sculptures. In 1981 George Elvin, 43, a New York lawyer, bought some antiquities while on vacation in Jerusalem. One piece aroused suspicion: a Faiyum portrait, named for an area in Egypt rich in archaeological relics. These images of the dead, painted on wood, were customarily placed in tombs. IFAR consulted New York's Metropolitan Museum of Art and sent a photograph to the world's leading Faiyum expert in East Germany. The Met and the German expert pronounced the piece a fake. The Jerusalem dealer refunded the $2,000 purchase price, minus shipping costs.

On the condition of important works up for sale, major auction houses will, if requested, supply a report with far more information than catalogues give. Dave Williams always asks to have a print taken out of its frame, to see from the back how much restoration has been done and whether there are tears, or burns from exposure to light. The buyer of a painting, or the restorer he may consult, can examine it under ultraviolet light in a darkroom to determine the extent of restoration. Ray Hender, 42, a mutual fund portfolio manager in Boston who buys American impressionist paintings from dealers, says he would never purchase a painting without a black-light examination.

Once satisfied with quality, authenticity, and condition, the collector looks at price, which can be the ultimate sting. The standard measure of worth is the auction-price history of similar works. The presale estimates published in auction catalogues are based largely on past sales. At the low end, they are close to unpublished reserve prices, below which consignors will not sell. The major auction houses add a 10% buyer's premium to the bid price. Dealers' prices, rarely published, may be negotiable.

Prices paid at auctions are easy to determine. *International Auction Records,* published annually by Editions Publisol in New York, records auction prices worldwide. In West Newton, Massachusetts, *Leonard's Index of Art Auctions,* published quarterly, records prices from American houses. A year's subscription costs $125.

A service called Telepraisal in Garden City, New York, offers art buyers a computerized shortcut. By phoning and giving a credit-card number, a collector can get a five-year history, adjusted for inflation, of prices paid for the artist's comparably sized works. The charge: $30 a report. One satisfied customer is Nathan Smooke, 76, president of Wellman Properties, an industrial real estate firm in Los Angeles and a trustee of the Los Angeles County Art Museum. When he has to make a quick decision about purchasing one of the early 20th-century paintings he collects, Telepraisal provides a useful check.

As an experienced collector, Dave Williams feels commitment may be as important as homework. "There's nothing like getting some money involved to get your attention," he says. "If you get some money on the line, that will certainly heighten your consciousness and interest. Plunge, is my advice."

If financing presents a problem, you may even use a bit of artful leverage. Banks aren't usually enthusiastic about loans on art, but Citibank accepts major artworks as security, generally with other collateral, for loans that can reach tens of millions. "The purpose of the loan could be to buy more art, to buy a boat, a company, or real estate," says Stewart B. Clifford, 57, Citibank's senior vice president in charge of private banking and investment. "We consider lending against art very good business."

FOR FURTHER INFORMATION

Art Dealers Association of America, 575 Madison Ave., New York, NY 10022; (212)-940-8590.

International Foundation for Art Research, 46 E. 70th St., New York, NY 10021; (212)-879-1780.

Telepraisal, P.O. Box 20686, New York, NY 10009; (800)-645-6002 or (212)-614-9090.

PUBLICATIONS

Art & Auction magazine, monthly, $42 a year; 250 W. 57th St., New York, NY 10107-0004; (212)-582-5633.

Art News, monthly, $29.95 a year; 48 W. 38th St., New York, NY 10018; (212)-398-1690.

The Complete Guide to Collecting by Lee Rosenbaum (New York: Knopf, 1982), $17.50.

International Auction Records, annual, $184; Editions Publisol, P.O. Box 339, New York, NY 10028; (212)-949-2397.

Sotheby's Guide to Buying and Selling at Auction by C. Hugh Hildesley (New York: Norton, 1984), $17.95. ∎

Classic Cars

∎ Handsome lines, the growl of an elegant engine perfectly tuned, and nostalgia rule the hearts and heads of collectors of vintage automobiles. "A feeling for kinetic art" inspired Gordon Apker, he says, when he acquired a 1929 Duesenberg J white roadster. "That vehicle is an incredible piece of art from probably the finest hour of American automotive engineering," declares the 42-year-old chief of Monarch Foods in Seattle.

"The greatest boon of a vintage car is that you can have fun with it," notes Sidney Farnsworth, 59, who spent five years painstakingly restoring a 1928 Bentley he bought in 1963 and has driven it 1,000 miles a year ever since. "You

HOBBIES

don't have to hang it on the wall and simply look at it," says the vice president of John E. Cain Co., which makes condiments in Ayer, Massachusetts.

Old cars need exercise to keep them from deteriorating. Most states offer special license plates for collector cars, with limited driving privileges, since such cars do not always meet current regulations. "I drive all my cars at least once a month, on the Los Angeles Freeway and up to Malibu," says Otis Chandler, 58, chairman of the executive committee of the Times Mirror Co. in Los Angeles. His collection of ten very rare and exotic classic cars and four racing Porsches was valued at close to $5 million in 1986. That includes his one-of-a-kind blue 1932 Packard Super 8 sport phaeton and the 1969 Porsche that clocked 242 mph at Le Mans.

Investment takes a back seat with Chandler and most car collectors. But in 1985 a Midwestern pizza king shelled out $1 million each for two Duesenbergs. And in 1986 a rare 1931 French-made Bugatti Royale with a 14-foot chassis and a 300-horsepower engine was bid up to $6.5 million by a Houston shopping-center developer at an auction of 237 cars from the collection of the late Nevada hotelier and casino king, William F. Harrah. Longtime car buffs are not always thrilled by such fancy prices, which make buying harder and may only temporarily enhance the value of their own collections. In the early 1980s, prices skidded downhill when high interest rates drew funds away from tangible assets.

Gordon Apker, whose automotive ardor goes back to age 9, when he resuscitated a 1922 Dodge truck a neighbor had given him, paid $90,000 for his Duesenberg in 1979. "That was a lot of money for me," says the onetime dirt-poor farm boy who grew up to be the largest holder of Shakey's Pizza franchises in the U.S. Sidney Farnsworth paid $1,500 for his unrestored Bentley in 1963 and in 1984 discovered that it was one of only nine of a model produced with a shorter than usual chassis, making it worth an estimated $150,000 in 1986. "That's not smarts; that's luck," says the matter-of-fact New Englander. More often the price of a collectible car plus the cost of restoration add up to more than the market value of the finished product.

The world of car collecting encompasses the huge trove that had been assembled by Bill Harrah, once numbering over 1,400 historic automobiles, as well as the big, obsolete gas-guzzling "muscle cars" of the 1960s and early 1970s. Some devotees collect only vehicles from the pre-1916 "brass era," when cars were equipped with brass lanterns and fittings. Others collect certain makes, or *marques,* such as Packards; many focus on particular years, say, 1955–57 Chevys, or models, notably Fords A and T.

True fanatics own and show "classics," dating from 1925 to 1948. As defined by the Classic Car Club of America, these are limited to certain models of some 75 makes. At the club's stately national and local competitions, judges scrutinize exquisitely restored cars to verify that all equipment is authentic and in working order. Replicas have occasionally been passed off as originals to unwary collectors. Longtime car buffs Otis Chandler and Gordon Apker have both served as judges at the annual *concours d'élégance,* at Pebble Beach, California, the Kentucky Derby of car collecting. Minuscule defects can take fractional points off a score: Phillips-head screws won't do on a Duesenberg, because they weren't used in 1930s coach work. In the entire U.S., fewer than ten cars a year score a perfect 100. Apker's own 1934 boat-tailed Auburn V12 got 100 at Pebble Beach in 1982.

Younger collectors are shifting to cars of the 1950s and 1960s, reminiscent of those they grew up with and that are more affordable. Apker, who assembled his collection of 11 classic cars, among the finest in the West, before prices zoomed up, also owns half a dozen 1950s models, including one of the first Cadillac El Dorado convertibles. "I am not willing to go out and spend a million dollars. Now that I have a basic classic car collection, it's more fun to buy some of the more frivolous stuff and enhance the collection with American memorabilia." Convertibles from the 1950s decorate one of his Seattle pizza parlors.

Racing and sports car collectors, hot to compete in their Porsches, or open-cockpit Bugattis and Ferraris, have a choice of almost 100 events a year, from Lime Rock, Connecticut, to Riverside, California. They are organized by some 30 clubs dedicated to the growing sport of vintage

Sidney Farnsworth bought this 1928 Bentley in 1963, when his son, Tom, was a baby. As Tom grew up, Farnsworth worked on the car for five years before he could drive it near his Massachusetts home, and took five years more to finish details.

ARTHUR SCHATZ

118

FOR COLLECTORS AND CONNOISSEURS

racing. A list of these clubs is available from the Sports Car Club of America.

Most collectors get their enjoyment from sleuthing out great cars, tracking down authentic parts, and laboriously installing them. Every collector dreams of finding a marvelous car in a barn, relatively intact, modestly priced, but in need of a satisfying amount of work. While Farnsworth realized that dream in the 1960s with his Bentley and in the 1970s with a 1959 red Aston Martin coupe, the dream will probably remain just that in the 1980s. Barns, garages, and junkyards have long since been sifted and are not so likely to yield more treasures.

So collectors turn to the organized market of want ads, auctions, salvage yards, and swap meets. *Hemmings Motor News,* a monthly, carries nationwide classified ads for vintage cars and parts, and notices of auctions. Leake's Antique Car Auction, held in Tulsa each June, is among the major annual sales. In August, Farnsworth never misses the antique, classic, and special-interest auto auction at the Owls Head Transportation Museum near Rockport, Maine.

The vintage-car market produces its share of partially restored lemons, as a buyer may discover once he gets under the hood or on the road. Farnsworth's "car of my dreams," a Jaguar XK-120, he says, "turned out to be a slug, with an incontinent gas tank and an engine the wrong size for the model." So he sold it for $3,000 and for that exact sum bought the Aston Martin coupe to restore. Even with space for only three vintage cars in his stable, Farnsworth's zest for nosing out new acquisitions remains undiminished. In 1986, to make room for a French blue T-37 Bugatti, he had to part with a 1947 yellow MG with green leather upholstery.

Restoration takes time, know-how, and skinned knuckles. Farnsworth tries to buy cars in fairly good shape. "I really don't like to buy basket cases. They constitute too big a job of restoration," he says. When Farnsworth, who holds a Yale engineering degree, restored his Bentley, he worked from a manual, totally dismantled the car, cleaned and repaired hundreds of parts. Bentleys of that period had cylinder heads integrally cast with the cylinder block so they cannot be removed and the pistons must be inserted from below. Farnsworth pushed one of the pistons up too far and it locked in place. He spent hours cutting off the top of the piston and waited six months for another from England.

Car buffs can polish their expertise at some 80 museums listed in *Hemmings' Vintage Auto Almanac.* Some standouts: California's Merle Norman Classic Beauty Collection in Sylmar and Briggs Cunningham Automotive Museum in Costa Mesa; the William F. Harrah Automobile Museum near Reno; in Indiana, the Indianapolis Motor Speedway Hall of Fame and the Auburn-Cord-Duesenberg Museum in Auburn; in Dearborn, Michigan,

the Henry Ford Museum; in Rhode Island, the Newport Automobile Museum.

Half a dozen national clubs welcome anyone interested in a variety of cars. *Hemmings' Almanac* lists clubs of all types, from those limited to owners of particular *marques* to some that admit enthusiasts who don't even own cars. For modest annual dues, members get club publications with notices of events. Most have local groups and many organize driving tours. Oldest and largest of the national organizations is the Antique Automobile Club of America. The Veteran Motor Car Club of America unites owners of all antique cars, defined as at least 25 years old. The Horseless Carriage Club of America requires ownership of at least one pre-1916 automobile. The Milestone Car Society consists of collectors of limited production cars with certain engineering standards, made from 1945 through 1970.

FOR FURTHER INFORMATION

Antique Automobile Club of America, P.O. Box 417, Hershey, PA 17033.

Classic Car Club of America, Suite 126, 2300 E. Devon, Des Plaines, IL 60018.

Horseless Carriage Club of America, P.O. Box D76, 7210 Jordan Ave., Canoga Park, CA 91303.

Milestone Car Society, P.O. Box 50850, Indianapolis, IN 46250.

Sports Car Club of America, P.O. Box 3278, Englewood, CO 80155.

Veteran Motor Car Club of America, P.O. Box 36788, Strongsville, OH 44136.

PUBLICATIONS

Car Collector, monthly, $26; P.O. Box 171, Mount Morris, IL 61054.

Cars & Parts, monthly, $18; P.O. Box 482, 911 Vandermark Rd., Sidney, OH 45365-9978; (513)-498-0803.

The Complete Handbook of Automobile Hobbies by Beverly Kimes (Princeton, NJ: Automobile Quarterly, 1981) $9.95.

Hemmings Motor News, monthly, $17.95; P.O. Box 945, Bennington, VT 05201; (802)-442-3101.

Old Cars Weekly, $24.95 a year; 700 E. State St., Iola, WI 54990; (715)-445-2214.

Standard Catalog of American Cars, 1805–1942 edited by Beverly R. Kimes (Iola, WI: Krause, 1982), $29.95.

Standard Catalog of American Cars, 1946–1975 edited by John Gunnel (Iola, WI: Krause, 1982), $19.95. ∎

Appreciating Wine

∎ The leisurely appreciation of different wines with good food and good friends turns dining at home into an occasion. And the ability to negotiate a restaurant wine list with confidence has become a basic business skill. The variables can befuddle even the most sober executive: country of origin, region, type, variety, vintage, foreign exchange rates. Learning how to find bottles that suit

HOBBIES

palate, menu, and pocketbook takes time and an inclination to experiment.

Sniffing and sipping at organized classes can dispel the oenological fog. An easy way to find out how to distinguish between wines of, say, Bordeaux and the Rhône Valley is to enroll in a course, complete with tastings, at a wine store, restaurant, cooking school, university extension, even a YMCA. However, anyone can fill a glass and expound on the contents. So it's best to check the teacher's background. The Society of Wine Educators can direct a wine lover to reliable sources of oenological knowledge.

"Most people spend too much money on wine. A $10 bottle is usually not twice as good as a $5 bottle," noted an instructor at the International Wine Center's school in New York. A former Dun & Bradstreet executive, Albert L. Hotchkin Jr., 43, started the center in an old Manhattan carriage house. It combines a wine bar and restaurant called Tastings that serves dozens of wines by the glass, a club for weekly tastings, and a school. In the entry-level "Discovering the Pleasures of Wine," offered weekday evenings year-round, students taste and discuss some 20 wines from major regions of the world in three sessions for $125. The approach is analytical and scientific.

Even though preferences in wine are subjective, experts have agreed on a method of assessing wine, via eye, nose, and mouth, with a measure of objectivity. This enables consumer, supplier, and critic to talk approximately the same language about such things as sweetness, acidity, body, and balance.

At New York's International Wine Center, instructor Rory Callahan (standing) had students compare California and French wines. Seated (from left): Roy K. Campbell, of Dun & Bradstreet; Gary Reiswig, of the Maidstone Arms Inn; and stockbroker Keith Stern.

A good judge of wine first examines it in the glass for color — the richer the hue, the older the wine — and for clarity — murkiness indicates something has happened to change the taste. Swirling the wine to aerate it, the taster sniffs to identify the grape — each variety has its characteristic aroma — as well as the smell, or "bouquet," that comes with aging.

In describing aroma and flavor, the lingo can get terribly flowery: words such as raspberries, truffles, and violets imply that the wines carry traces of the same natural chemicals found in those plants. For example, raspberry denotes a flavor common to certain French red wines. Lest you think this is entirely scientific, experts disagree on whether Bordeaux, Beaujolais, or Rhône wines are the more raspberryish.

From start to finish, a proper tasting should take about 12 seconds. A small sip enables the expert to measure the main components in the taste: sugar, acid, and puckering tannins from skins, stems, and the oak barrels in which wine is aged. Participants in a wine-judging session record their perceptions of sweetness, acidity, astringency, and so forth on score cards.

To make the various components in the taste of wine unmistakably clear, the head of the Chicago Wine School, Patrick W. Fegan, 39, serves students in his introductory class red wine doctored with sugar, vinegar, tannin, and citric acid. "Those were awful, terrible," says Margaret Haas, 42, a vice president and portfolio manager at Stifel Nicolaus, who entertains a lot at home. "The bottom line of this course is to help us identify those wines that we like and to know how to buy them." The Chicago Wine School's beginning course costs $115 for five 90-minute sessions.

New York City offers a wide choice. Gerald M. Chaney, 39, vice president and controller of Crystal Brands, an apparel company, took the Introduction to Wine at the New School for Social Research (four sessions for $162). Its culinary-arts program offers a half dozen wine courses per semester.

Besides tasting at least six wines at each weekly session, Chaney learned some basics: how to read a wine label (French wines are usually classified by region, California's chiefly by variety of grape or generic type, such as chablis); how to store wine (never cool an unopened bottle for over a month because a refrigerator's vibrations interfere with the wine's aging); and what corkscrew to use. "I enjoy wine much more now and find it part of the entertainment to look at wine lists in restaurants and use my knowledge in picking and appreciating a wine," says the new connoisseur. While you can be assured of quality with high-priced vintages, he adds, "it's a lot of fun to experiment with less expensive wines."

The Wall Street crowd favors a glamorous setting — eight sessions at Windows on the World ($350) atop the

World Trade Center. With Kevin Zraly, 35, the wine director of Windows, students sample 100 white and red wines from Europe and California, and close with a celebration featuring champagne, sherry, and port. At New York's Connaissance & Cie., which also has branches in Boston, Washington, and Florida, specialists can find nine-session courses on the wines of Bordeaux or Burgundy ($375), as well as shorter courses on wines of Italy ($240) and California ($175).

To keep cultivating their wine sense, graduates can hold comparative tastings at home. One connoisseur suggests buying half a dozen wines of the same type, but at various prices, and inviting friends over for a blind sampling. If grape expectations fall flat, try a different wine merchant and repeat the experiment. When a good value reveals itself, you can stock up. *Mastering Wine* by Thomas Maresca offers a guide to comparing just two or three wines at once, often a California vs. a French.

For socializing over wine and food, some 250 U.S. chapters of Les Amis du Vin International Wine Society hold monthly wine tastings and dinners. The society also arranges tours to foreign vineyards. While the directors of these chapters are usually wine merchants and restaurateurs chiefly interested in selling wine, their gatherings often feature outside experts.

To keep consumers on top of news from vineyards, wineries, and the marketplace, *The Wine Spectator* appears twice a month at an annual subscription of $35. Its classified ads carry notices of publications, schools, tours, and all sorts of wine accessories.

Touring vineyards and wineries enhances a wine lover's pleasure and knowledge. The Wine Institute, a trade association for California wines, publishes a tour guide listing wineries open to the public. Many California vintners open their doors to visitors year-round. "I'm not interested in stomping grapes," says Margaret Haas, who after taking her Chicago course drove out to the Napa Valley for the Chardonnay grape harvest. "But I learned a lot about grapes and how they have improved, and the differences in the way wine is processed."

The Napa Chamber of Commerce and the Sonoma County Wineries Association in Santa Rosa gladly offer suggestions for self-guided itineraries or can arrange a private tour accompanied by a knowledgeable guide. Wine Adventures Inc. of Yountville, California, offers private one-day tours of the Napa or Sonoma valleys at $100 apiece for two people, or three days and two nights at $650. This agency also tailors group tours.

In France, visiting châteaux, vineyards, and wineries under the tutelage of an inside expert is advisable to get more than a tourist's-eye view of how great wines are produced there. From March through September the French Wine Institute in Paris accepts 15 persons for one- and two-week seminars in English in Paris with visits to

FOR COLLECTORS AND CONNOISSEURS

Bordeaux, Burgundy, and Champagne. Participants dine at some of the best restaurants in those regions. Cost, excluding transatlantic air fare: $5,860 for two weeks, or if you provide your own hotel in Paris, $4,200. *A votre santé!*

FOR FURTHER INFORMATION

Les Amis du Vin; membership, $30 a year, includes *Friends of Wine*, bimonthly; 2302 Perkins Pl., Silver Spring, MD 20910; (301)-588-0980.
Society of Wine Educators; James Holsing, Executive Director, Suite 14, 132 Shaker Rd., East Longmeadow, MA 01028; (413)-567-8272.
Wine Institute, 165 Post St., San Francisco, CA 94108; (415)-986-0878.

SCHOOLS
Chicago Wine School, 1633 N. Halsted, Chicago, IL 60614; (312)-266-WINE.
Connaissance & Cie., 23 W. 39th St., New York, NY 10018; (212)-921-1326.
French Wine Institute, 76 Champs-Elysées, 75008 Paris; (33)-1-4242-5927; telex 643-438; or c/o De Vogüé Travel Services, 3425 W. Monte Vista Ave., Visalia, CA 93277; (209)-733-7119.
International Wine Center, 144 W. 55th St., New York, NY 10019; (212)-757-0518.
New School for Social Research Wine School at The Culinary Center, 100 Greenwich Ave., New York, NY 10011; (212)-255-4141 or 741-5690.
West Side YMCA, 5 W. 63rd St., New York, NY 10023; (212)-787-6557.
The Wine School at Windows on the World, 107th Fl., One World Trade Center, New York, NY 10048; (212)-912-0344.

VISITS TO VINEYARDS
Napa Chamber of Commerce, 1900 Jefferson St., Napa, CA 94559; (707)-226-7455.
Sonoma County Wineries Assoc., 50 Mark West Springs Rd., Santa Rosa, CA 94559; (707)-527-7701.
Wine Adventures Inc., P.O. Box 3273, Yountville, CA 94599; (707)-944-8468.

PUBLICATIONS
The Académie du Vin Wine Cellar Book by Steven Spurrier (Topsfield, MA: Salem House, 1986), $19.95.
Alexis Lichine's Guide to the Wines and Vineyards of France (New York: Alfred A. Knopf, 1982), $19.95.
Alexis Lichine's New Encyclopedia of Wines and Spirits (New York: Alfred A. Knopf, 3rd ed., 1981), $40.
The Complete Guide to Wine Tasting and Wine Cellars by Michael Broadbent (New York: Simon & Schuster, 1984), $12.95.
Hugh Johnson's Modern Encyclopedia of Wine (New York: Simon & Schuster, 1986), $29.95.
International Wine Review, bimonthly, $30; Beverage Testing Institute, P.O. Box 285-F, Ithaca, NY 14851.

HOBBIES

Mastering Wine: A Taste at a Time by Thomas Maresca (New York: Bantam Books, 1985), $9.95.

Windows on the World Complete Wine Course by Kevin Zraly (New York: Sterling Publishing, 1985), $18.95.

The Wine Spectator, biweekly, $35 a year; 400 E. 51st St., New York, NY 10022: (800)-227-1617, ext. 560, or (212)-751-6500.

The World Atlas of Wine by Hugh Johnson (New York: Simon & Schuster, 1986), $39.95.　　　■

THE NATURAL WORLD

Astronomy: In Touch with the Universe

■ "For over 30 years I have had a love affair with astronomy," confesses Curtis Vaughan Jr., 58, chairman of Vaughan & Sons, a building supply company in San Antonio. "It started when I received as a Christmas gift my first telescope, a two-inch refractor made in Japan." The gift was from his mother.

In Vaughan's lifetime, astronomy, our oldest science, has revised man's concept of the universe as radically as in the previous 5,000 years. Only in the 1920s did we learn that our solar system isn't the center of the universe. Beyond our Milky Way, with its few hundred billion stars, perhaps another hundred billion galaxies swirl. And we discovered in the 1930s that not only starlight but invisible emanations come from galaxies, as faint radio signals, the poet's "music of the spheres."

A different sort of radio signals, of uniform wavelength, coming from every part of the sky, was discerned in the mid-1960s. These signals clinched the evidence for the Big Bang theory of the origin of the universe: that a very small concentration of matter and energy exploded ten billion to 20 billion years ago into a primordial, ever-expanding fireball.

"One of the fascinating aspects of astronomy is that physicists, concerned with the very smallest particles that have a lifetime of minute fractions of a second, have used ideas from astronomy's Big Bang theory of the universe," notes Vaughan, who was a Harvard physics major. Cosmic questions confront today's astrophysicists. Where is the universe going? Will it expand indefinitely? Or will it eventually devour itself, as collapsing stars get sucked into black holes?

The skyward focus of the Space Age makes ours an extremely stimulating time to be an astronomer, professional or amateur. Gigantic mountaintop telescopes, deep-dish radio antennae, satellites, and interplanetary spacecraft keep collecting new information about pulsars, quasars, black holes.

The telescope's most important function, of course, is gathering light from the heavens, and the amount it picks up depends on the surface area of the optical element that focuses the image within the tube. This may be either a lens that refracts light, a mirror that reflects it, or a combination of the two. Amateurs can select the telescope that best fits their interests and budget, or build their own.

For the serious beginner, a 2.4-inch refractor telescope, such as Vaughan's first instrument, costs from $300 to $700. Those who want a close-up tour of the solar system can do well with an element and aperture three to five inches in diameter, costing from $500 to over $1,000. For such "deep sky" objects as galaxies, star clusters, and nebulae, six to eight inches or more may be needed, and prices often start above $1,000. Celestron of Torrance, California, makes a popular eight-inch model for $2,400.

Vaughan advanced first to a 3.5-inch Questar, a handy miniaturized tabletop telescope, from New Hope, Penn-

In his home observatory, Texas lumberman Curtis Vaughan can meander among the stars.

HOBBIES

sylvania. It is built with a mixed lens-and-mirror, or "catadioptric," system. The standard model, with two eyepieces for different magnifications, weighs 14 pounds with a carrying case that fits under an airplane seat and costs $2,677.

Good visibility depends a lot on location. Throughout the Northeast, light pollution, the bane of astronomers, blanks out natural objects in the sky and warm currents make the air unstable, causing stars to twinkle. The southwestern U.S., where Vaughan lives, has some of the country's best viewing. He built his country retreat west of San Antonio, away from urban lights, and placed his observatory on concrete stilts to see above the treetops. For stability of focus he mounted his powerful 16-inch reflecting telescope, made by Ealing of South Natick, Massachusetts, on a central pier anchored in bedrock. In his splendidly laid-out home observatory, Vaughan can give his star-party guests an intimate look at the moon and planets or a trip through the Milky Way.

To locate a particular object, Vaughan consults the *American Ephemeris and Nautical Almanac,* published annually by the U.S. Naval Observatory. This gives the coordinates, known as right ascension and declination, of any identifiable sky object for the time that it will be on the Greenwich meridian. Astronomers adjust accordingly their sidereal clocks, which tell time by the rotation of the earth with reference to the stars, rather than ordinary time, which has to add a day every leap year to catch up. Vaughan then points the big telescope at the right patch of sky, and slides open the domed observatory roof. He handles the painstaking process of precisely adjusting the instrument's position by simply typing the celestial coordinates on a computer keyboard and pressing a button. A motor than moves the scope quickly into position. Behold, there is M 80, a globular cluster of 100,000 tightly packed stars far out in the Milky Way. Vaughan's computer control was custom-made, but similar devices are commercially available. Celestron's Sky Sensor, compatible with several of its telescopes, costs $950.

Photographing deep-sky objects through the telescope shows the astronomer more than he can observe. While stars almost always look white to the eye, a time exposure on color film can distinguish white-hot stars, glowing at 10,000 degrees centigrade, from the cooler yellow and red ones, at 3,000 degrees. Vaughan's eight-inch Celestron-Schmidt camera ($3,000), which operates at a relatively fast f 1.5, enables him to capture short-lived phenomena, such as the flaring whiteness of a nova, or new star, surrounded by green and orange stars.

Vaughan's solar telescope to study the sun by day has an occulting disk to block out all but the sun's edge, and a filter to eliminate all but the light emitted by glowing hydrogen. He can see hydrogen flares, which may last only a few hours, and sun spots, which may last for days or even months.

As Vaughan's interest in astronomy deepened, he developed ties with the astronomy department of the University of Texas at Austin and has served many years on the board of visitors for its McDonald Observatory in West Texas. McDonald has a 107-inch telescope, and hopes to build a 300-incher if it can ever raise the money. In 1984 Vaughan completed a series of donations to the university totaling $500,000 for an endowed chair in astronomy. It will be filled once the new telescope is a certainty.

Amateurs can add to astronomical knowledge by discovering an occasional comet, counting meteor showers, and recording data on the brightness of variable stars, which change their intensity either periodically or irregularly. So numerous are these that the major observatories cannot allot enough time to them on their big telescopes. So the American Association of Variable Star Observers, composed of professionals and amateurs, acts as a clearinghouse for sending data to major observatories. Several other organizations bridge the gap between amateurs and professionals. And the Astronomical League coordinates the work of amateur astronomy clubs nationwide.

FOR FURTHER INFORMATION

American Association of Variable Star Observers, 25 Birch St., Cambridge, MA 02138; (617)-354-0484.

NASA's Jet Propulsion Laboratory, I.H.W. California Institute of Technology, 4800 Oak Grove Dr., Pasadena, CA 91109; publishes a list of astronomical information sources.

The Association of Lunar & Planetary Observers, c/o John Westfall, P.O. Box 16131, San Francisco, CA 94116.

The Astronomical League, c/o Donald Archer, P.O. Box 12821, Tucson, AZ 85732.

The Astronomical Society of the Pacific; membership, $24, includes *Mercury,* a bimonthly; publishes list of computer programs on astronomy; 1290 24th Ave., San Francisco, CA 94122; (415)-661-8660.

PUBLICATIONS

Astronomy, monthly, $21; 1027 N. Seventh St., Milwaukee, WI 53223; (414)-272-2060.

Burnham's Celestial Handbook: An Observer's Guide to the Universe beyond the Solar System by Robert Burham Jr. (New York: Dover, 1978–79), 3 vols.: Vol. I, $9.95; Vol. II, $10.95; Vol. III, $12.95.

A Complete Manual of Amateur Astronomy by P. C. Sherrod with T. L. Koed (Englewood Cliffs, NJ: Prentice-Hall, 1981), $10.95.

Cosmos by Carl Sagan (New York: Ballantine Books, 1986), $3.

The First Three Minutes: A Modern View of the Origin of the Universe by Steven Weinberg (New York: Basic Books, 1977), $14.95.

Norton's Star Atlas by Arthur P. Norton (Cambridge, MA: Sky Publishing), $24.95.

Sky and Telescope, monthly, $20; 49 Bay State Rd., Cambridge, MA 02238; (617)-864-7360. ∎

THE NATURAL WORLD

At Home with Orchids

■ Robert P. Bauman, 55, chairman of The Beecham Group in London, England, has faced a problem common to many executive horticulturists: how to keep a big collection of plants healthy without constantly having to nurse them. "My desire is not to be controlled by my plants," says Bauman. By trial and error he has found, surprisingly, that orchids can elegantly satisfy this desire. "If you want blooms, nothing surpasses the orchid. Individual blooms last weeks to months, and plants can produce 25 to 50 blooms each. Their reputation for fragility is unfounded," he says after long experience in his former Connecticut home.

Getting to know orchids and growing them for pleasure is an affair of the heart that has enthralled more and more indoor gardeners. Though fond of gardening since his boyhood days in Ohio, Bauman bought his first orchid in his early 30s, on a Florida vacation. He couldn't resist the *Phalaenopsis,* or moth orchid, he saw in a florist's shop. More than 20 years later that plant was still rewarding him six months of the year with as many as 40 white flowers.

Orchids are nature's largest family of flowering plants, numbering some 35,000 species, and they are the youngest of all plants in the evolutionary chain. A single blossom may range from one-tenth of an inch to 15 inches across, and can yield as many as two million seeds, among the tiniest in the floral world. Some orchids, such as the lady's slipper, live as far north as the Arctic Circle, where they grow with their roots in the ground. But most thrive in high, cloud-brushed tropical forests, depending on other plants for support. These tree-dwellers take most of their nourishment from air and water.

On a business trip to Brazil, when he was with General Foods, Bauman went into the dense jungle south of São Paulo with some local associates. He looked up — and on aerial perches high in the trees sat dozens of tiny orchids. Reaching up, he carefully scraped some plants off the bark, and back in his hotel scrubbed them clean of debris so that they could pass U.S. government inspection at home.

And, like many backyard gardeners who love to start plants, Bauman once tried germinating seeds from some of his favorite blooms. He put them in the oven in a flask of agar gel, but all he got was mold. Germinating orchids in a man-made environment requires an absolutely sterile laboratory.

No longer do orchid fanciers need to resort to such practices. Plants have become widely available, thanks to new methods of reproduction that started in the late 1960s. Since each cell contains a plant's entire genetic formula, tissue culture can provide thousands of replicas exactly like the parent. Working in sterile air, with a microscope, a laboratory technician slices one-tenth of a millimeter off a tip, or meristem, of budding growth and places it in a test tube on a bed of agar containing nutrients and hormones. Once the tissue has established an independent life, it is cultivated in a succession of flasks containing various solutions that help it multiply. While specialists propagate rare specimens this way, commercial growers reproduce the more popular varieties. These sell from $3 for a small pot that will take several years to bloom to $30 for a plant five or more years old that is ready to flower. Bauman likes to buy very young plants of new hybrids to see how they will turn out.

Many orchid hobbyists relish competing with their blooms. The American Orchid Society, a nonprofit horticultural corporation, encourages advances in cultivation and hybridization through its judging system. It sanctions more than 200 shows a year and conducts some 400 monthly regional judgings. Results are published in the Society's *Awards Quarterly.*

Though he did enter a nice plant in a local show now and then, Bob Bauman is more interested in developing practical methods for the home grower, starting with himself. In 25 years of growing orchids in their Wilton, Connecticut, home, Bauman and his wife, Patricia, have learned much about these and other compatible house plants. They have received help from the American Orchid Society's *Bulletin,* which carries articles on cultivation, and from the vast educational resources of the New York

Robert P. Bauman in the greenhouse of his former Connecticut home.

HOBBIES

Botanical Garden, which holds an annual orchid show. Bauman has in recent years served on the board of the Botanical Garden, and around home was considered something of an expert. (On CB frequencies in Connecticut, his handle was "Orchid Power.") A garden club in Greenwich invited him to speak on his favorite subject: "Training Orchids and Other Plants to Adjust."

Refusing to let his hobby run his life, Bauman has given much thought to minimizing the maintenance of his 1,000-or-so plants. In 1982 he put his views and methods into a book, *Plants as Pets,* illustrated by his wife. Here he argues that you can train plants to adjust to your situation if you create an appropriate routine and permanent place for them, just as you would for your dog.

There is no great mystique about caring for orchid plants, Bauman insists. Contrary to popular belief, they include many varieties that are tough, disease-resistant, and long-lived. For the beginner he suggests two: his favorite *Phalaenopsis,* which produces a spray of two- to five-inch blooms in white, pink, yellow, or stripes; and the *Paphiopedilum,* "Paph" for short, or lady's slipper orchid, which bears a single flower per stem in a variety of hues and markings. This species periodically adds flower spikes that on repotting can be divided to make a new plant.

The trick to growing orchids lies in approximating their natural environment—sunlight, temperature, moisture, breezes, and nutrients. Bauman contrived a system that allowed him to maintain with ease a good environment for his varied collection of orchids and compatible plants — bromeliads, gardenias, hibiscus, to name a few. He accommodated most of them in a greenhouse and adjoining basement equipped with automatically timed fluorescent lights and electric fans for circulating air.

In winter the basement temperatures ranged from 60 to 70 degrees and in summer 70 to 80. The humidity was kept around 50%. To ensure against the effects of a power failure or the furnace going out, Bauman had put in a propane-driven generator and auxiliary heater. The easiest way to kill an orchid is by overwatering. Bauman varied the pots and potting materials so that plants with different moisture requirements, all standing on slatted benches for drainage, could be watered together just once a week. And to automate that chore he had installed in the ceiling of the basement, upside down, a lawn sprinkler system with timer. That meant he could leave them for up to a month at a time in summer, while he and his wife were up in Maine, playing golf.

FOR FURTHER INFORMATION

American Orchid Society; membership, $28, includes the monthly *American Orchid Society Bulletin;* 6000 S. Olive Ave., West Palm Beach, FL 33405; (305)-585-8666.

New York Botanical Garden; membership, $30, includes *Garden*, bimonthly; 200th St. and Southern Blvd., Bronx, NY 10458; (212)-9-GARDEN).

PUBLICATIONS

All About Orchids by Charles Marden Fitch (New York: Doubleday, 1981), $15.95.

Orchids as House Plants by Rebecca Tyson Northen (New York: Dover, revised ed., 1976), $2.95.

Orchids: For the Home and Greenhouse (New York: Brooklyn Botanic Garden, 1986), $2.25.

You Can Grow Orchids by Mary Noble (West Palm Beach: American Orchid Society, 4th ed., 1980), $7.95. ■

Gardening for Gourmets

■ The fitness boom and America's long-ripening affair with gourmet food are combining to give new zest to gardening, the most popular outdoor leisure activity in the U.S. Vegetable gardening occupies members of 33 million households, many of them adventurous epicures who raise flavorful imported types of greens, zippy herbs, and other goodies rarely found in supermarkets.

The demands of gourmet gardeners have brought forth new sources of seeds and plants and new fonts of how-to information. The best starting place for novices is the National Gardening Association, a nonprofit organization for backyard food gardeners. Members receive the monthly *National Gardening* magazine and replies to written queries. A directory of catalogues for vegetable seeds, fruit trees, herb plants, and garden tools costs $2.50 ($3 for non-members).

A host of new seed companies offer imports and some

Daniel Will of Lazard Frères turned over his New Jersey vegetable patch to French varieties.

THE NATURAL WORLD

old-fashioned American "heirloom" varieties usually not available from the major seed houses. These smaller companies claim their seeds yield juicier and tastier vegetables than the big sellers. However, two of the major seed companies, W. Atlee Burpee and Park Seed, in recent years have added a number of gourmet greens, herbs, and foreign vegetables to their catalogues.

At Le Marché Seeds International of Dixon, California, epicures find some 280 varieties of European, Asian, Mexican, and American vegetables in a $2 catalogue replete with growing instructions and recipes. Jill Cole, 30, a partner in Riley Cole Agency, a small Oakland, California, headhunting firm, thinks southern European and Asian varieties perform well in her Mediterranean-type climate. She planted Le Marché purple Sicilian artichokes, lavender and white Italian and Asian eggplants, an old type of convoluted Italian tomato, and American tomatillos that bear green, walnut-sized, tomatolike fruits in protective husks. She is also raising a type of watermelon once nearly extinct, the large, sweet Moon and Stars, named for its yellow spots on dark green skin. For shock value and tang in salads, Jill and husband Donald Cole, 36, use edible flowers — nasturtiums, calendulas, violets.

A cherished source of heirloom seeds for serious gardeners is the Seed Savers Exchange, a nonprofit outfit founded in 1976 by former printer Kent Whealy. Through its publications, enthusiasts trade or buy seeds of old-fashioned vegetable varieties. Information on membership ($12 a year) is available by sending a stamped, self-addressed envelope to the exchange at P.O. Box 239, Route B, Decorah, Iowa 52101.

In northern New Jersey, Daniel Will, 43, a bond trader at the investment banking firm of Lazard Frères in New York City, and his wife, Jeanne, have started a French vegetable garden. Many of their 20 or so seed varieties come from the handsome and instructive catalogue ($1) of Shepherd's Garden Seeds in Felton, California. Experienced horticulturalists who have long grown American vegetables and English herbs and flowers, the Wills are digging into the Continental adventure as an experiment, trying such exotica as the luscious Charentais melon.

Fascination with herbs has grown like a weed in recent years, with Warren and Beverly Sweeney in the thick of it. Sweeney, 60, a sales executive for White Stag Sportswear in Chicago, started growing herbs with his wife some 25 years ago, after he discovered French cuisine on buying trips to Europe. On their five acres in Barrington Hills, Illinois, they cultivate 50 varieties, including such unusual ones as wormwood and sweet woodruff. For years they have been teaching at the Chicago Botanic Garden. Both have been elected to membership in the Herb Society of America, whose purpose is furthering knowledge about the cultivation and uses of herbs. Sweeney plans to make herbs his business in retirement and is already supplying a few French restaurants.

Many gardeners are rediscovering old methods of intensive cultivation in slightly raised beds, which can reduce chores and increase yields once initial spadework is done. In Winter Park, Florida, Harry Bull, 64, owner of the Travel Consultants travel agency, grows three crops of vegetables a year. His wife, Nita, stir-fries a lot of them, and what they do not eat they love to give away. Bull's seeds are not imported, but his methods come from the ancient Chinese. With extra soil he has raised his beds eight inches above the rest of the ground to improve drainage. Before each planting he prepares the 20 four-foot-wide beds, which are eight or 16 feet long, by digging down 12 to 15 inches and mixing in a compost of lawn clippings and leaves. He sprouts seedlings indoors, then sets some out as closely as 3 inches apart. The plants' density helps crowd out weeds, so that after planting, Bull works only a couple of hours a week in his garden.

Chicago attorney John Forbes Swenson, 57, knows his onions — and garlic. He raises more than 300 varieties of them, including rare and endangered species, in half of his 5,000-square-foot vegetable and herb garden at his Glencoe, Illinois, home. He has received 75 varieties from the East German government. Swenson uses an intensive French method of "double digging" to prepare raised beds. With his English spade, from Smith & Hawken in Mill Valley, California, where he gets most of what he calls his heavy artillery, he removes the topsoil to a depth of 12 inches. Then, with a spading fork, he loosens the underlying soil 12 inches deeper before filling in the beds with a mixture of compost and topsoil. Swenson plans eventually to give his collection of plants to the Chicago Botanic Garden and other institutions. But his interest is decidedly more than academic: Swenson's eye-opening recipe for three pints of marinara sauce calls for a half pound of garlic.

A garden of delights does not grow without know-how and toil. A good deal of know-how, at least, can be free. The U.S. Department of Agriculture's Extension Service agent in each county offers information and advice; botanic gardens open to the public offer frequent workshops and occasionally plant model vegetable and herb gardens. The toil is part of the hobby's appeal. Devoted gardeners renew their spirits in the soil — and eat about as well as anybody can.

FOR FURTHER INFORMATION

National Gardening Association; membership, $18 a year, includes *National Gardening* magazine, monthly; 180 Flynn Ave., Burlington, VT 05401; (802)-863-1308.

Herb Society of America, 2 Independence Court, Concord, MA 01742; (617)-371-1486.

Seed Savers Exchange, P.O. Box 239, Rte. B, Decorah, IA 52101; (319)-382-3949.

Chicago Botanic Garden, P.O. Box 400, Lake Cook Rd., Glencoe, IL 60022-0400; (312)-835-5440.

New York Botanical Garden; membership $30, includes *Garden,*

HOBBIES

bimonthly; 200th St. and Southern Blvd., Bronx, N.Y. 10458; (212)-9-GARDEN.

W. Atlee Burpee, Warminster, PA 18974; (800)-523-6642 or (212)-674-4900.

Le Marché Seeds International, P.O. Box 190, 200 N. First St., Dixon, CA 95620; (916)-678-9244.

Park Seed, P.O. Box 31, Greenwood, SC 29647-0031; (803)-223-7333.

Shepherd's Garden Seeds, 7389 W. Zayante Rd., Felton, CA 95018; (408)-335-5400.

Smith & Hawken, 25 Corte Madera, Mill Valley, CA 94941; (415)-383-4050.

PUBLICATIONS

The Complete Book of Edible Landscaping by Rosalind Creasy (San Francisco: Sierra Club Books, 1982), $14.95.

Country Journal Book of Vegetable Gardening by Nancy Bubel (Harrisburg, PA: Historical Times, 1983), $10.

The Garden Seed Inventory edited by Kent Whealy (Decorah, IA: Seed Savers Exchange, 1985), $12.50.

Gardening: The Complete Guide to Growing America's Favorite Fruits and Vegetables by the National Gardening Association (Reading, MA: Addison-Wesley, 1986), $19.95.

The Gourmet Garden by Theodore James Jr. (New York: E. P. Dutton, 1983), $9.95.

Herb Gardening at Its Best by Sal Gilbertie (New York: Atheneum, 1980), $8.95.

Herbs: Gardens, Decorations, and Recipes by Emelie Tolley and Chris Mean (New York: Crown Publishers, 1985), $30.

Square-Foot Gardening by Mel Bartholomew (Emmaus, PA: Rodale Press, 1981), $11.95.

"The Victory Garden Vegetable Video" by Bob Thomson and Jim Wilson (New York: Crown Video, 1986), $24.95. ∎

Watching the Mystery of the Birds

∎ Spotting birds has taken flight from a casual pastime for backyard naturalists, or a hobby for eccentrics, to a competitive sport. The National Audubon Society counted 30 million American bird watchers in 1985. Many "birders" are window watchers, content to recognize what wings their way. A few are zealous amateur ornithologists who pursue their quarry on every continent, vying to sight the greatest number of the world's known species, some 9,100.

What attracts these avian fanciers? Birds symbolize freedom, says Roger Tory Peterson, 77, the artist whose first *Field Guide to the Birds* was published in 1934. "They have wings and go where they want to when they want to, even though birds are no freer than we." Watching birds soon reveals that they are bound by invisible cords to the calendar, particular habitats, even their own private territories and rituals. Trying to understand these mysteries transports the bird watcher out of man's artificial world.

Allan Keith, 48, a senior portfolio manager at Brown Brothers Harriman & Co., a private bank in New York, has seen nearly half the world's species, on visits to 48 countries. "After being desk-bound, getting into the out-of-doors on a birding vacation allows me to put completely out of my mind what I do for a living," he says. Keith got serious about birds in his teens. On his way home from school one day in May, he saw a black, white, and pink bird in the woods near his Brockton, Massachusetts, home. Checking his father's copy of Audubon's *Birds of America,* he identified it as a male rose-breasted grosbeak. Eventually, Keith says, "instead of just being an observer of what came my way, I began to actively look for birds. And the more I looked the more I enjoyed the process."

Identifying birds in the field takes an eye for detail, an ear attuned to bird song, and a good memory. A birder also needs a handy illustrated field guide and at home a more comprehensive reference work. Binoculars should be chosen chiefly for magnification, brightness, and clarity. Keith uses a Zeiss 10 × 40; it enlarges an image ten times and has a 40-millimeter lens that lets in lots of light. Its list price is about $840, often discounted to $500 or $600. Clothing should blend with nature's hues. Bright colors may scare birds away.

At some distance, the size, silhouette, and flight pattern quickly tell the observer whether a bird is, say, a duck, dove, or warbler. At closer range, the color and markings further narrow the possibilities: it's not a yellow-throated warbler, but a hooded warbler. The keen watcher never takes his eye off the bird, hoping all the pieces will fall into place like the working of a kaleidoscope.

Birders get a chance to perform a public service in the National Audubon Society's Christmas Bird Counts. When the U.S. Air Force was seeking sites for new fields, it asked the Audubon Society to map populous bird areas as ones to avoid. The Christmas Counts provided the data. In this annual census, begun in 1900, observers note all birds and species sighted on a single calendar day, selected locally between mid-December and early January, within a circular area 15 miles in diameter. In 1985 an estimated 42,000 observers participated at 1,600 locations. Findings are published in Audubon's periodical, *American Birds.* Year-to-year figures show changes in distribution and concentration.

Amateur ornithologists interested in competitive bird listing got a vehicle for their hobby with the founding of the American Birding Association in Austin, Texas, in 1969. One major game is to see how many different species ABA members can identify in a given region during a calendar year, and cumulatively over a lifetime. Using checklists of species as classified by the American Ornithologists' Union, the supreme authority on taxonomy, birders tally their sightings and report their totals to the ABA for tabulation and comparison. (They are on their honor not to

THE NATURAL WORLD

cheat.) Rankings of birders by number of species sighted are published in a supplement to *Birding,* the ABA's bimonthly magazine, in annual and cumulative lists.

Allan Keith, the investment portfolio manager, has added steadily to his avian portfolio. In the 1985 worldwide life lists, published by the ABA, his ranked 15th with 4,405 species, garnered at occasional peril. In Idi Amin's Uganda, his binoculars and telescopes prompted interrogation at roadblocks. And in Colombia part of his group, garbed in camouflaged field wear, were mistaken for guerrillas by an army guard, who escorted them at gunpoint to his sergeant.

On "Big Days," another ABA game, birders scramble in teams of six at most, staying within shouting distance of each other, to see how many species they can sight within a state, province, or country in one calendar day when birds are likely to be plentiful. All team members must see or hear 95% of the birds counted. James M. Vardaman, 64, of Jackson, Mississippi, who heads a major timber consulting company, organized his own Big Day expeditions in 1984, with teams of experts in nine countries: Colombia, Panama, Mexico, Surinam, Thailand, India, Nepal, Senegal, and, in the U.S., Texas. He traveled in Texas by car, 500 miles by airplane, five by marsh-buggy, and three on foot. With these forays, which set six Big Day records, plus longer visits to six more countries, Vardaman topped the 1984 annual world list with 2,800 species. A dozen South Pacific birds of paradise, males with dazzling head feathers sighted in Papua New Guinea, gave the birdman from Mississippi his biggest thrill. "When one of those flies down and lights on a dadgum fence in the clear sunlight about 150 feet from you, you just say, 'My God! Look at that!'"

To spot rare birds it is frequently necessary to hire local people or professional ornithologists who can distinguish among the profusion of species, because good field guides do not always exist. Keith often travels with one of a dozen outfitters that specialize in tours for small groups of birders. Victor Emanuel of Austin, Texas, is one of them.

Without leaving their offices, some lucky window watchers in Los Angeles have observed a rare species more closely than bird trippers are likely to. Early in 1984, Arco Treasurer Camron Cooper, 47, spotted peregrine falcons, an endangered species, alighting repeatedly on the rooftop of the 40-story Union Bank Building across the street. She alerted bank Chairman John F. Harrigan, 60. A lifelong naturalist who disdains "life lists" but carries binoculars in his golf bag, Harrigan called the University of California's Santa Cruz Predatory Bird Research program. These falcons had apparently been released from a captive breeding project. A nesting box was slipped onto a ledge just below the roof, and Arco loaned the researchers space with a direct view. Harrigan had a video camera aimed at the nest and a TV monitor placed in his office so he could watch the nesting. Two of the female's eggs were retrieved, placed in an incubator, and hatched. In late 1985 the male returned with a new mate.

FOR FURTHER INFORMATION

American Birding Association; membership, $24 a year, includes *Birding,* a bimonthly; P.O. Box 313, Sonoita, AZ 85637.
American Ornithologists' Union, The Smithsonian Institution, Washington, D.C. 20560; (202)-357-2051.
National Audubon Society; membership, $30 a year, includes *Audubon* magazine bimonthly; 950 Third Ave, New York, NY 10022; (212)-546-9100.
Victor Emanuel Nature Tours, P.O. Box 33008, Austin, TX 78764; (512)-328-5221.

PUBLICATIONS

American Birds, quarterly, plus "The Christmas Bird Count" issue, $25 a year; National Audubon Society.
Audubon Society Master Guide to Birding (New York: Knopf, 1983), 3 vols. with photographs, $41.85.
Birds of North America by Chandler S. Robbins and others (New York: Golden Press, 1983), $7.95.
Call Collect, Ask for Birdman by James Vardaman (New York: McGraw-Hill, 1984), $8.
Field Guide to the Birds of North America (Washington, D.C.: National Geographic Society, 1983), $15.95.
The Peterson Field Guide Series by Roger Tory Peterson (Boston: Houghton Mifflin) includes:
A Field Guide to the Birds East of the Rockies (1984), $11.95; *A Field Guide to the Birds of Britain and Europe* (1983), $17.95.
A World of Watchers by Joseph Kastner (New York: Knopf, 1986), $25.
"Audible Audubon," an audiotape with player for field use, $39.95, and "The VideoGuide to the Birds of North America," $75.95, are available from the National Audubon Society. ■

Campaigning for Top Show Dog

■ The sport of exhibiting dogs crossed over from England in the 1870s, and within the next decade two of dogdom's leading American fixtures had established themselves. New York City's Westminster Kennel Club, whose top-ranking annual show still draws the nation's finest canines, sponsored its first in 1877. Crowds crammed the Hippodrome, on the future site of the first Madison Square Garden, to view 1,201 dogs—from a huge Siberian bloodhound to two pugs with lace collars. The American Kennel Club set itself up as arbiter of breed standards and registrar of pedigrees in 1884. And August Belmont Jr.,

HOBBIES

banker and backer of railways, became its president in 1888.

Women have now practically taken over dog shows, but both men and women risk addiction to these absorbing canine beauty contests. Arden Hansen, 37, vice president of SPR News Source, a Minneapolis company that markets public affairs television shows, was asked by her friend to take an Old English sheepdog into a local show ring. The shaggy dog took the reserve winner's purple-and-white ribbon — next best after the winner's blue. Elated, Ardie Hansen bought a Chesapeake Bay retriever female puppy of show quality, named Tai. Her husband, Jack Hansen, 46, founder and president of SPR, made clear that showing dogs should be her hobby; he had no time and would not intrude. But on a chilly March weekend he drove his wife and Tai to a show in Iowa. On a lark, Hansen had also entered his occasional hunting dog, Lady, a seven-year-old purebred Chessie. Neither dog won an award, but showing dogs won over Hansen, who came away admitting he had fun. Subsequently he and his wife established the Nesnah Kennels (that's Hansen spelled backward).

To take part in showing, dog lovers join local clubs, at annual membership fees of $10 to $50. The American Kennel Club offers services to these local clubs. In 1985 more than 1,000 shows open to all 128 breeds recognized by the AKC attracted 1,367,123 entries. And clubs dedicated to a single breed put on close to 1,500 AKC-sanctioned specialty shows. To enter any of these shows, dogs must be registered, at least 6 months old, and have no disqualifying faults, such as a dyed coat or a physical disability. Dogs are judged on conformation, or how close each comes in appearance, movement, and temperament to the ideal standards for the breed as spelled out by the AKC.

Showmanship by a dog's handler plays a big part in competing. So at his wife's urging, Hansen joined her in a class on how to "stack," or pose, their dogs to show off their good features in the ring and play down their weaknesses. At a show in St. Paul, the Hansens entered Tai in the Puppy class, and Lady in American-Bred, two of five basic classes; the other three: Novice (for dogs with limited prior winnings), Bred-by-Exhibitor, and Open. Males and females compete separately. Lady won her class handily, as its only entry. Winners of those five classes then compete against each other in a "winners" class; and the winner of that class is eligible to compete for best-of-breed, against all of its kind that have previously earned a championship. Unaware of this procedure, tyro Hansen was surprised to be called to the ring twice more. Until laughing spectators told him, he had no idea that Lady had won "winners bitch," against all other females, including his wife's, and "best-of-breed." Next day, in another show, Tai won in her class, and in shows that followed quickly became a champion.

The first object of the dog-show game is to "finish" a dog as a champion by accumulating 15 points, under at least three different judges in AKC-licensed shows. A dog builds up points by being judged winners dog, or bitch, in the winners class, an honor worth from one to five points, depending on the number of competitors. But to become a champion, the wins must include two "majors" — victories worth three to five points — under different judges. Thereafter the title Ch. (for champion) precedes the dog's official name. Once a dog has earned best-of-breed at a show open to all breeds, it is eligible to compete for best in the group to which its breed belongs. The seven group winners — sporting, hound, terrier, working, toy, non-sporting, and herding — compete for best-in-show. "We treat the breed ring as a crapshoot," says Hansen. "A different judge picks a dog he or she thinks is the best dog that day. You have to keep that in mind when your own wonder-dog loses."

The Hansens added two male Chesapeake puppies to their Nesnah Kennels, and Tai's litter presented them with a few more. Keeping dogs at home means morning and evening care and feeding chores, plus an hour or so of training each evening after work. Determined not to let the dogs interfere with the rest of their lives, the Hansens limit themselves to about 20 shows a year, and compete for certificates in working-dog and obedience classes as well. But they never schedule events during hunting season, which Hansen and a couple of the dogs enjoy. Competition expenses at their level, including travel and entry fees, total about $3,000. Operating Nesnah Kennels comes to another $7,000 annually. Hansen let himself get involved, he figures, because, outside of business, "my life had been devoid of competition of a fun kind." And, rather than intruding on his wife's space, he finds "it's delightful to be sharing something we can do together until we're 80."

Executives who seek the acclaim of winning awards at important shows, especially the Westminster, held each February in New York's Madison Square Garden, are likely to spend far more than the Hansens and hire a professional handler. A mature dog with a distinguished pedigree can cost from $1,000 to $10,000, depending on the breed and whether the dog is imported. In a year of heavy campaigning, say in 100 shows, expenses can run as high as $20,000 per dog, according to William Trainer, president of the Professional Handlers Association of America. Boarding and training come to $200 or $300 a month, plus veterinarian fees. Show entry fees run about $15 each. A professional handler might charge $50 for each show, plus travel expenses, and expect bonuses for winning a group-first or best-in-show.

The payoff comes largely in prestige and trophies. Show-dog owners have little chance for the rewards that accrue to owners of racehorses, who can collect purses and steep stud fees and take advantage of tax breaks.

THE NATURAL WORLD

While a top male show dog might command a stud fee of $200 to $1,000, depending on the breed, he usually doesn't procreate enough to pay for himself. Unless the owner breeds and sells dogs as a business, it's hard to convince the Internal Revenue Service that his expenses deserve to be treated as business losses.

Harold Nedell, 57, of Houston, former president of Meineke Discount Muffler Shops, sold his yacht in 1979 to go into the business of breeding, exhibiting, and selling fox terriers. "Most years I don't make money," he says of his 13-acre Foxmoor Kennels. But Foxmoor has finished 20 champions of its own, one of which, Ch. Foxmoor Macho Macho Man, has sired 20 more champions. Nedell says his reward is chiefly aesthetic. "I can't paint worth a damn; I can't play an instrument," he says. "So creating a lovely animal gives me tremendous satisfaction."

FOR FURTHER INFORMATION

The American Kennel Club, 51 Madison Ave., New York, NY 10010; (212)-696-8200. Films (16-mm) and videocassettes are for sale at $60 and $35, respectively.

PUBLICATIONS

The Complete Book of Dog Health by William J. Kay, D.V.M., and Elizabeth Randolph (New York: Macmillan, 1985), $19.95.

The Complete Dog Book: Official Publication of the American Kennel Club (includes official breed standards) (New York: Howell Book House, 17th ed., 1985), $17.95.

How to Show Your Own Dog by Virginia Nichols (Neptune, NJ: TFH Publications, 1970), $12.95.

Pure-Bred Dogs/American Kennel Club Gazette and *The American Kennel Club Show, Obedience and Field Trial Awards,* monthlies, $18 a year each, $28 for both, published by the American Kennel Club; (212)-696-8226. ∎

Putting Hunting Dogs on Trial

■ Since the shooting season for wild game lasts only several weeks, field trials, which go on much of the year somewhere in the country, have grown as important as hunting, or even more so, to many hunting-dog owners. The American Kennel Club's licensed field trials test performance in each of 22 breeds, from bassets to Weimaraners. The original idea of the trials was to develop better dogs for hunting through breeding and training. The AKC licenses over 1,100 trials a year, which also test the skills of the dogs' handlers.

Edward K. "Edd" Roggenkamp III, 41, Chevrolet's marketing manager for national field operations based in Warren, Michigan, bought an English springer spaniel in 1980 for bird shooting, his passion. The dog performed so well under the gun that friends urged Roggenkamp to enter a trial. He did, won a ribbon, and was hooked. Roggenkamp enters a dozen trials a year, handling three or four dogs. By winning two trials, a springer is designated a field champion — FC if handled by a professional handler, AFC if handled by an amateur. In 1985 two of Roggenkamp's were amateur field champions. Since business travel does not allow him to train his dogs consistently, he has a professional handler living on his Indiana farm. He hunts extensively with his field-trial springers, but his golf has gone to the dogs.

Field trials simulate hunting, with action controlled by rules that vary for the four categories of dogs: hounds, pointing breeds (where handlers and judges ride horseback), retrievers, and spaniels (Brittany spaniels excepted). During a springer-spaniel trial, two handlers and their dogs compete at once, tramping over parallel courses, much as a pair of hunters might. Judges, one for each dog, follow. Gunners move along the edges of the course, ready to down the pen-raised pheasants placed in the grass for the dogs to flush. Though half a dozen pheasants may be killed for every dog completing a springer trial, field trialists argue that their dogs save wild birds because they can retrieve game which less trained dogs might not find, causing hunters to kill more birds to bag their limit.

On a nod from his judge in a 1985 trial in Las Vegas, Nevada, Edd Roggenkamp gave a palms-up gesture to "cast off" his dog, FC Reward's Satin Sassy, a 3-year-old female. Zigzagging through the brush, Sassy grew excited as she caught the scent of a bird. Ears flapping, she leaped toward the bird. When the pheasant took wing, Roggenkamp blew his whistle, commanding Sassy to stop. A shotgun burst brought the bird down while Sassy held her ground, marking, or watching, where the bird fell. The judge then signaled Roggenkamp to send his dog "on re-

In a New York field trial, Philadelphia developer Edwin H. Whitaker (right) commands his springer for judge Edward Faraci.

131

HOBBIES

trieve." Meanwhile, the other handler had commanded his dog to stop, to keep him from poaching on Sassy's retrieve. When Sassy brought the bird back, the judge examined it for damaging toothmarks.

Teams are judged on how well the handler controls the dog, and how quickly and carefully the dog brings back the bird. They go through three series of two retrieves, over fresh ground each time. A good handler contributes 30% to 50% of the results in spaniel trials. But luck as well as skill figures in the sport. Wind direction and temperature can affect the dog's ability to pick up a scent.

Roggenkamp and Sassy won that Las Vegas trial, and went on to the national springer-spaniel field championships at Rend Lake in Illinois over Thanksgiving weekend. To qualify for the nationals, a springer has to place among the top four in at least one licensed trial. One hundred springers qualified in 1985, and 52 entered, 29 of them handled by professionals, including Sassy this time. She placed second in the national open all-age stakes.

A new participant in the sport can buy an 8-week-old puppy (about $300 for a springer; $500 or more for a Labrador retriever) and train it at home. A 2-year-old fully trained dog with a good record in competition can cost $2,000 to $5,000 for a springer; $10,000 to $15,000 or more for a Lab. Professional training costs around $200 a month for a springer, plus the tab for birds used in training: $1.50 per bird for pigeons; $7 to $10 for pheasants. It takes ten to 15 pigeons a week to train a pup. A year's field-trial budget ranges from $1,500 to $4,000, depending on the number of trials and distances traveled.

Retrievers, the waterfowl specialists, need more training than springers. Their trials, on land and water, tax the dog's memory more, require absolute precision, and have grown harder as judges try to create new challenges on land and in water. Dudley Millikin, 54, manager of planning for small commercial aircraft engines at General Electric in Lynn, Massachusetts, and his wife, Elizabeth, train their own Labradors. After 17 years of competing from Nova Scotia to Maryland, they came up with their first field champion in 1982, seven-year-old Wingover Clean Sweep.

The retriever's capacity to learn rises and falls in a bell curve, Millikin observes. "When you start out, you just make them good citizens. Then they reach a point where the absorption level is high and the amount of training time required is tremendous. By 5 or 6 years they are peaking, and only need maintenance. Around 9 they are ready for retirement."

In retriever trials, unlike springer trials, the retriever's handler has to stay behind as his dog runs toward the fallen bird. "There can be a lot of frustration in getting your commands complied with at 100 yards in a howling gale," says Millikin. He turned to a professional trainer for help with Sweep at age 4, especially for so-called blind retrieves, in which the dog is not allowed to see the bird fall

but is sent off on a line indicated by a thrust of the handler's arm. Handlers wear white coats so their dogs can see them from a distance. This attire and the difficulty of the tests prompt the criticism that these trials set up artificial situations, far removed from real hunting.

In the silvery marshes and golden stubble fields of the Bombay Hook National Wildlife Refuge in Delaware, the Del Bay Retriever Club's all-age stakes for amateur handlers called for three marked retrieves, in which the dog watches the birds fall, and one blind retrieve, all on land. For the water series, Sweep had to make a blind retrieve through what trialists call chocolate pudding — mud and shallow water, stumps, and dead trees. He was one of 22 dogs to be called back for the final test: a "quadruple," or four marked retrieves that required swimming and running across the marshes. Sweep not only finished, an achievement in itself, but bagged a judge's award of merit. After two more years of trialing, including the national amateur championships in Idaho in 1983, Sweep ended up a field champion and amateur field champion in both the U.S. and Canada and had earned his comfortable fireside retirement.

In 1985 the AKC introduced new hunting tests for retrievers and pointers whose owners are not interested in competing for ribbons on a field-trial circuit, but want to find out what their dogs can do. Dogs are tested and scored from one to ten on marking, scenting, perseverance, style, and trainability. To qualify, the dog must repeat each test several times and the scores in each must average seven. Three levels of titles are awarded according to the number of times a dog qualifies: junior, senior, and master. And these go on the pedigree, regardless of whether a dog has any field-trial championships to its credit.

FOR FURTHER INFORMATION

The American Kennel Club, 51 Madison Ave., New York, NY, 10010; (212)-696-8200.

PUBLICATIONS

The American Kennel Club Show, Obedience and Field Trial Awards, monthly, $18; published by the American Kennel Club; (212)-696-8226.

The Labrador Retriever by Richard A. Wolters (Los Angeles: Petersen Publishing, 1983), $37.50.

Retriever Field Trial News, monthly, $30; 4213 S. Howell Ave., Milwaukee, WI 53207.

The Working Retriever by Tom Quinn (New York: E. P. Dutton, 1983), $29.95. ∎

Improving Wildlife Habitats

∎ Avid angler Robert E. Meier, 55, a vice president at Kimberly-Clark, maker of Kleenex, fishes for trout in Wisconsin streams upwards of 40 times a year. But on a fall

THE NATURAL WORLD

Saturday he was wading through a chilly stream north of Green Bay carrying a woodsman's ax instead of his rod. With two dozen other volunteers from chapters of Trout Unlimited, an environmental group dedicated to fishing, Meier was transforming a sluggish, backed-up stretch of river into a swift-running stream inviting to the wily *Salvelinus.*

Improving wildlife habitats, once the exclusive concern of state game departments or the groundskeepers of privately owned fishing and hunting preserves, is attracting thousands of conservation-minded executives. Some just give money. Ducks Unlimited raised $45 million in 1984 for large-scale water control projects to improve waterfowl nesting grounds in Canada, where 70% of North American ducks breed. While contractors handle those projects, increasing numbers of hunters and fishermen are joining organizations that take a do-it-yourself approach.

Volunteers across the country are doctoring stream beds, planting forage, and revitalizing woodlands under the supervision of such organizations as Trout Unlimited, the Wild Turkey Federation, and the Ruffed Grouse Society. Says Harold A. Levin, 55, a vice president of Abbott Laboratories, a North Chicago-based health care products company: "It's a chance to give something back to a sport that gives you so much."

Levin was one of the Trout Unlimited volunteers sprucing up the Wisconsin stream with Meier. Sweating profusely despite the cool weather, the work party hacked apart five beaver dams after trapping and killing the beavers. "We're restoring a spawning stream," Meier explains as he watches water surge past a dam's remains. "Trout like cold, clean, fast-flowing water, but beaver dams cause the water to silt up and get warm." Killing one species of wildlife to protect another may seem an odd form of conservation, but the Trout Unlimited operation had the blessing of the Wisconsin Department of Natural Resources. Beavers are proliferating in the northern part of the state. Their pelts have become less fashionable, and they have had virtually no natural enemies since wolves all but vanished a generation ago. Besides wrecking trout streams, beaver dams block drainage ditches, sometimes flooding highways.

Other members of the group pulled on waterproof wading boots to stock the nearby Wolf River — one of the state's premier trout streams — with 16,000 brown trout fingerlings supplied by a state hatchery. The men poured buckets of water brimming with fish into a fleet of inflatable rubber rafts donated for the day by a local outfitter. Then, sitting in the partly swamped boats and drifting along with the current, they dumped the tiny fish into a five-mile stretch of river.

With 414 chapters and 77,000 members in the U.S., Canada, Japan, and New Zealand, Trout Unlimited is one of the fastest-growing game preservation groups. Says President E. Harold Davis, 46, a vice president at Cum-

mins Engine in Columbus, Indiana: "We're doing something that's fundamentally right." Local chapters are improving 136 rivers and streams in 30 states. The work varies from building fences and cattle crossings, which keep livestock from muddying Virginia's Mossy Creek, to dumping hundreds of huge boulders into Oregon's Metolius River to create the eddies and riffles trout love.

In addition to fieldwork, Trout Unlimited members do wildlife research, run educational programs, and act as volunteer lobbyists in state legislatures. Says Davis, "We focus on watershed management and issues like acid rain and pollution runoff." Much of the pollution, of course, comes from companies. But executives who are also conservationists say they rarely find themselves in conflict with their employers. "There is far less of a confrontational atmosphere than in the past," says Keith C. Russell, 66, a vice president of McDonald & Co. Securities, a Cleveland brokerage firm. "Enlightened companies today understand that habitat is important not only for wild animals but also for people. Companies work with you."

Local chapters also hold fly-tying and rod-building classes and sponsor weekend fishing trips. In Wisconsin members take handicapped children to stocked trout ponds for a day of fishing. "It's really wonderful to watch them get excited," says Thomas Flesch, 40, a production planner for Oscar Mayer, a subsidiary of General Foods.

Ruffed Grouse Society members help state and private landowners cut trees in woodland areas to increase grassy meadows in which grouse thrive. Local chapters sponsor symposiums and training seminars on forest rejuvenation. "I spend as many hours in conservation meetings as I do hunting in the woods," says Douglas Wadsworth, 50, general counsel for National Guardian Life Insurance Co. in Madison, Wisconsin, and head of the chapter there.

Wild Turkey Federation members create nesting grounds by planting trees and shrubs. They also trap birds and relocate them to new breeding grounds. As a result, says Executive Vice President Robert Keck, wild turkeys now flourish in areas where they have been absent for nearly 100 years. "From 1980 to 1985 the number of states with turkey-hunting seasons had gone from about ten to 46," he says.

Though preservation groups are mainly out to create better hunting and fishing for themselves, other conservationists applaud their work. "What these folks are doing is crucial." says Jay D. Hair, executive vice president of the National Wildlife Federation in Washington, D.C. "I've never fished for trout in a place that wasn't absolutely beautiful. If you can save a stream for trout, you preserve lots of other natural values."

Levin estimates he spends a week a year on Trout Unlimited projects. "It's easy to get active in something you really care about," he says. Levin savors the thrill of the catch, not the fish itself; he releases every one he

133

HOBBIES

lands. "I have a few that I ought to make into pets," he says. "I think I've caught them a couple of times."

FOR FURTHER INFORMATION

Ducks Unlimited; membership, $20 a year, includes *Ducks Unlimited,* bimonthly; One Waterfowl Way, Long Grove, IL 60047; (312)-438-4300. "Ducks Unlimited's VideoGuide to Waterfowl and Gamebirds" is available for $79.95, via check, or via credit card from (800)-342-3825.

National Wild Turkey Federation; membership, $15 a year, includes *Turkey Call,* bimonthly; P.O. Box 530, Wild Turkey Bldg., Edgefield, SC 29824; (803)-637-3106.

National Wildlife Federation; membership, $12 a year, includes *National Wildlife* or *International Wildlife,* bimonthlies ($19 for both); 1412 16th St. N.W., Washington, D.C. 20036; (202)-797-6800.

Ruffed Grouse Society; membership, $15 a year, includes *The Drummer,* bimonthly; 1400 Lee Dr., Coraopolis, PA 15108; (412)-262-4044.

Trout Unlimited; membership, $20 a year, includes *Trout,* quarterly; 501 Church St. N.E., Vienna, VA 22180; (703)-281-1100. ∎

COMMUNITY SERVICE

Volunteer Firemen

■ One New Year's Eve, residents of the tiny (pop. 1,650), prosperous Manhattan suburb of Plandome, Long Island, were gathering for a convivial celebration in their village hall when, at 9:15, the fire alarm sounded. It took only minutes for an imposing bunch of businessmen to hotfoot it to the firehouse below the hall, exchange tuxedo jackets for firefighter's coats, and tuck striped trousers into their high rubber boots. Hanging onto their trucks, Plandome's volunteer fire department rolled a few blocks to a two-story, stone-faced house, where smoke pulsed from the eaves.

An old-fashioned Christmas tree with lighted candles had kindled the blaze. No one was left in the house. An advertising man helped lay the hose, a lawyer hooked it to a hydrant. To open the front door wide would have risked a "blow-out," or explosion, as fresh air combined with hot gases. So the door was opened just enough to let in a little water, then closed, on the theory that the water would convert to steam and put out the fire. It worked.

Then Peter Del Duca, 47, a senior vice president in the real estate firm of Cushman & Wakefield, and later Plandome's chief, donned a breathing apparatus to enter. Louis Trapp, 54, a partner in a Wall Street law firm, climbed a ladder and broke open a second-story window to let out the gases. In all, 39 firemen had turned out and, with their evening clothes a bit the worse for wear, most rejoined the party in time to ring in the New Year.

Volunteer fire associations date back at least to 1736, when Benjamin Franklin founded the Union Fire Co. in Philadelphia. As the country turned urban and suburbs consolidated, many towns turned to career firefighters. But 885,000 volunteers still serve, mainly in towns of under 10,000 and unincorporated areas. Outnumbering the full-timers four to one, these volunteers take on what is, for their career brethren, one of the most hazardous occupations in the U.S. Fatalities in the line of duty in 1985 numbered 57 career personnel and 62 volunteers.

Besides the challenge of saving lives and property, saving tax dollars keeps most volunteer forces in business. Local pride and neighborly trust also inspire householders to join. Most of the 6,000 to 7,000 annual deaths by fire occur in the home. Members of Plandome's 70-man force feel they can provide better protection to their square mile's some 420 houses, church, country club, beach club, and railroad station than outsiders. "They don't know the people and that's not the same as walking into a person's house when you've been there for a party Saturday night, or were there when the kids were christened," says Carl Meyer, a former chief of the Plandome department, and a market consultant. While commuters are away at work, Plandome's road-maintenance crew helps cover daytime calls. The village also has mutual-assistance agreements with nearby departments in Long Island's virtually all-volunteer system.

Besides fighting fires, many departments check for gas leaks and provide emergency rescue and ambulance service. Courage, commitment, teamwork, willingness to learn, physical fitness, and time are basic requirements.

For hands-on experience, the volunteer fire department in Lake Bluff, Illinois, set fire to a house slated for demolition. Insurance agency heat Robert Graham (left), then a captain, emerges from the smoky interior as his lieutenant talks to the engineer on the pumper.

HOBBIES

Commuters and business travelers take their turns answering calls on evenings and weekends. Meetings or drills usually take an evening a week. Keeping personnel and equipment at the ready uses much more time than handling emergencies, and business skills are big assets.

The chief of a volunteer department holds down a second job, without pay. In Fairfax, Virginia, 15 miles from Washington, James J. Featherstone III, 30, is a coordinator of supply shipments for Mobil's corporate purchasing in its international division. He also puts in 30 to 40 hours a week as fire chief of nearby Burke, Virginia, an unincorporated area with 40,000 people in single-family houses and offices. That department, composed of 45 volunteers and 30 career members, ties into a Fairfax County system combining volunteer and full-time forces. "My phone at work rings almost daily with fire department business," says Featherstone. "Despite my best efforts, I can never totally divorce myself from it, but my superiors appreciate what I do and are willing to tolerate it." Every chief must see that a deputy is trained to fill his boots. When Mobil sent Featherstone to Nigeria for a month and Saudi Arabia for three months in 1986, his eminently qualified deputy, a fire specialist for the Federal Emergency Management Agency, took over.

Firefighting has been good for Featherstone's business career. "When you are on the scene under the gun in an emergency, you have to decide what to do and do it. That experience in leadership at a young age, along with a management role in budgets and finance, I believe helped me," he says. "Besides, being a firefighter is not your standard leisure activity. Its novelty draws attention to you." Featherstone's generation is rejuvenating many a department. He joined as a cadet at 16, became a full-fledged firefighter at 18, the usual eligible age, stayed active through college nearby, and advanced via service and special training courses to deputy chief. When he was 26, the department's volunteers elected him chief and reelected him each year since.

To maintain standards that impress insurance underwriters is a major objective of all departments. In most states the Insurance Services Office Inc., funded by the property and casualty industry, grades municipalities on their fire protection by reviewing their records of previous years. Examiners consider such factors as qualifications of personnel, response distance, communications facilities, equipment, and water supply. Grades are awarded on a scale of one, the best, to ten, and charges for property insurance are generally scaled accordingly. A property owner in a district with a classification of nine may not be able to buy as much insurance as he wants. Plandome, Long Island, has long been rated five. Fairfax County, Virginia, including Featherstone's department and two others, has a rating of three, with an average response time of 30 seconds.

Adopting a fire code helps to upgrade a rating. Codes are often based on standards developed by the National Fire Protection Association, a private voluntary organization, as models for various types of localities. Lake Bluff, Illinois, 30 miles north of Chicago's Loop with a population of about 4,500 and an industrial park, had to change its outmoded ways in the mid-Seventies when only a few volunteers showed up, late, at a fire in a garage. A public furor erupted and several young men were concerned enough to join the department. They had to recruit new talent, upgrade their training, and modernize equipment. Robert Bruce Graham, president of Graham Insurance Agency in Skokie, persuaded the Lake Bluff village board to adopt a code. He set up a fire prevention bureau and with his men inspected industrial plants. On invitation, they also inspect homes, advise on the placement of smoke detectors, and put on family fire drills. Lake Bluff's response time went down to three minutes and its insurance rating improved from eight to six. In 1980 when Graham, then 35, was appointed chief of the department by the village president, he put in a five-year program to improve the rating to four, and succeeded.

The enviable assignment of procuring new engines, the pride and joy of every department, fell to David Graf, director of materials for Bally Manufacturing's Midway division, which makes coin-operated games. By 1976 Lake Bluff's engines, aged 19 and 23 years, were obsolete. Graf projected the department's needs, and laid out a plan with a future budget. Impressed by his unprecedentedly thorough presentation, the seven-member village board approved the program and put it out for bids. By 1985 Graf, 39, was deputy fire chief and Lake Bluff had four engines purchased over a six-year period, at a cost as high as $125,000 each. Three of them pump 1,000 gallons or more per minute. Protective gear for firefighters is constantly updated to state of the art. And to provide insurance coverage, volunteers become municipal employees during each call, drawing $4 in pay. To supplement the village budget, the annual Fourth of July dance of the firemen's association, the social event of the year in Lake Bluff, raises funds.

Concern about hazardous chemicals and other materials transported by rail and truck for increasing use in manufacturing prompted Lake Bluff to enlist 25 other Lake County departments in jointly acquiring special equipment. The unit rotates monthly to four quadrants for training. At Lake Bluff that falls to chief Bob Graham, an appointee to the Governor's Task Force on Hazardous Materials.

Training levels have risen at Lake Bluff under Graham and Graf. At the College of Lake County, Graham teaches tactics and strategies of firefighting, one of three courses required to become a certified officer in Illinois. Drills are frequent and occasionally the force joins other depart-

COMMUNITY SERVICE

ments. Once they put their skills to the test when World War II buildings slated for demolition at the Great Lakes Naval Training Station were set afire.

Satisfactions come straightaway. "It's knowing you are part of true community service, with hands-on," says Bob Graham. "If you just raise funds, you don't have direct control or impact."

FOR FURTHER INFORMATION

National Fire Protection Association; membership, $60, includes *Fire Command,* monthly ($16.50 to non-members), *Fire Journal,* and *Fire Newsletter,* bimonthlies; Batterymarch Park, Quincy, MA 02269; (617)-770-3000.

PUBLICATIONS

Firehouse magazine, monthly, $17.97 a year; Box 2481, 82 Firehouse Lane, Boulder, CO 80321; (212)-475-5400.

The Volunteer Fire Company by Ernest Earnest (Briarcliff Manor, NY: Stein & Day, 1980), $8.95.

Volunteers, a Portrait of Small-Town Firefighters by Raymond Pompilio (Trumansburg, NY: Crossing Press, 1979), $10.95.

■

Running for Office in Suburbia

■ WANTED: *Successful business or professional persons, with stamina for weekly meetings, before and after business hours, plus high tolerance for group decisions, to serve as candidates for local elective office. Applicants must undergo intense public scrutiny, and respond to public needs. Job requires up to 300 hours per year without pay.*

That imaginary, but not far-fetched, want ad describes what many municipalities ask of their public servants. The suburban villages and towns where business and professional people enjoy the good life, where more and more of them work and pay taxes, are governed by unstinting and mostly unpaid residents. Rewards come not from the power and honor that accrue to big-city politicians, but from the satisfaction of paying one's dues to the community, and of experiencing democracy in action.

Though business executives have complained more about politicians and government than any other irritation, only a tiny fraction of them ever answer that ad. A commitment of precious time could slow the climb up a corporate ladder. And in an age when respect for elected officials has turned to mistrust, it takes an indestructible ego to withstand the flak from ever more demanding citizens. But professional business skills and experience gained in other community volunteer work provide great resources for local governments to tap.

In Lake Bluff, Illinois, 30 miles north of Chicago, David Graf, director of materials at a Bally Manufacturing division in a nearby town, was one of the Young Turks who

rejuvenated the local fire department (see p. 136). He then got a call asking if he was interested in running for village trustee. Six trustees and a president govern this community of 4,500, with a paid administrator to handle the day-to-day paperwork. Graf said he would consider it.

A nonpartisan caucus recruits the candidates by distributing fliers door to door to solicit nominations. Caucus members then interview each nominee who agrees to run. Since the village elects three trustees to four-year terms every two years, the caucus puts up three nominees at a town meeting. The meeting also takes nominations from the floor, and in open vote approves candidates for the ballot. Graf, a caucus nominee, ran and won.

When his four-year term was up, Graf ran unopposed for village president, becoming, at 39, the youngest chief executive in Lake Bluff's history. "The duties seem endless," says Graf, who gives at least one night a week to the village government, plus another to the fire department as deputy chief.

The most controversial issues, as in many suburbs, concern land use and development. The average assessed valuation of a residential property in Lake Bluff was around $160,000, totaling almost $78 million in 1985, whereas the total value of commercial and industrial property came to only $14 million. One hot potato has been whether or not to annex an unincorporated area to the west, which would widen the tax base but would mean providing the area with municipal services.

No controversy surrounded the trustees' decision early in Graf's presidency to take on Lake Bluff's first debt. In 1986, 75% of the voters passed a million-dollar bond issue to raise part of the funds to build a much-needed fire and police station.

Balancing commitments to family and community tugs at the heart. "There are times when I would rather skip a meeting and play with my boys, 12 and 7, and my little girl, 4," Graf admits. And the children don't always understand why, if Dad is village president, they can't do this or that.

While exposure to governmental issues has been broadening, Graf doesn't think his public commitments have helped or hindered his business career. "The real rewards come from a deep sense of service and an ability to contribute," Graf states. "I really believe in the American system and feel I ought to participate."

The office sought the man in Graf's case. Others seek office and getting one of these unpaid posts can be an intricate and frustrating process. It was for Donald J. Kirk, who in his professional life served for many years as chairman of the Financial Accounting Standards Board. This organization sets criteria that corporations are required to follow in reporting to shareholders. Kirk decided to take on some community activity at age 38, when he settled in the affluent suburb of Greenwich, Connecticut. Home to 60,000 residents, the average assessed value of a house in

HOBBIES

Greenwich is $400,000. A number of very large companies occupy seven million square feet of commercial space there.

Kirk discovered he had a lot to learn. Shortly after moving to Greenwich, he noticed that a vacancy existed in the Representative Town Meeting, the 232-member nonpartisan legislative body, derived from the traditional New England town meeting. Kirk applied to the Town Meeting's district leader, who reminded him of a fundamental requirement: only registered voters are eligible to run for public office and newcomer Kirk had not yet registered in Greenwich. Making sure he got on the voter rolls before the next election, Kirk then gathered the needed signatures on a petition to get on the ballot. He was elected to a two-year term, and was twice reelected.

A more enticing challenge came along when a vacancy occurred on the 12-member Board of Estimate and Taxation. This body controls the purse strings of Greenwich, and Kirk's professional accounting skills would fit nicely. As a Democrat, Kirk figured his chances were good. The board is a partisan body equally divided between Republicans and Democrats, and the vacancy was on the Democratic side. Kirk put his name before the Democratic Town Committee, but it passed over him in favor of another candidate.

Persisting, Kirk again announced his candidacy before the next general election, and this time won the Democratic Committee's endorsement. But two incumbents on the Board of Estimate had been dropped by the committee and Kirk was forced to compete for the spot in a primary election. He won, and the ensuing general election simply confirmed the results. Kirk has since won reelection to four two-year terms.

In each of his terms the Board of Estimate appointed Kirk to the all-important four-man budget committee. This core group bears the brunt of the board's work by preparing Greenwich's annual budget of over $100 million for presentation to the Representative Town Meeting for a vote of approval in May. Putting the budget together involves hours and hours of public hearings and meetings with department heads to determine their needs. Three or four controversies a year that involve the budget or require new money capture local headlines: What happens to the remaining students when schools close for insufficient enrollment? Should Greenwich have a local bus system? More sidewalks? And the Board of Estimate is sometimes made the scapegoat for personnel changes within the town government. When departments want to dismiss someone, budget contraints are often given as the reason.

How did Kirk manage to put in some 300 hours a year minding the business of Greenwich while heading the Financial Accounting Standards Board? His office was nearby in Stamford, Connecticut. "I'm not dependent on train schedules," he said. "So I can do very early morning meetings or get to them shortly after work."

And he found that his work with the town benefited his professional life. "There really is a feedback about how to do certain things or staff certain functions," he notes. "And it's added to my warehouse of patience and tolerance, which is a good thing. It works both ways."

Personally speaking, Kirk says his work with the Board of Estimate has been the "most satisfying extracurricular activity that I've ever had, because I'm involved in some significant decisions about the town I live in. You get a little bit of psychic payback in that you have an immediate sense of doing something that is important to the people you like and live with."

FOR FURTHER INFORMATION

Government Finance Officers Association of the U.S. and Canada, Suite 800, 180 N. Michigan Ave., Chicago, IL 60601; (312)-977-9700. Members include officials of city, county, state, provincial, and federal governments, as well as school and special districts.

PUBLICATIONS

How to Run a School Board Campaign and Win by Cipora O. Schwartz (Columbia, MD: The National Committee for Citizens in Education, 1982), $5.95.

How to Support Your Cause & Win; Citizens' Handbooks Series (Columbia, SC: University of South Carolina Press, 1984), $14.95.

Local and State Elections: The Guide to Organizing Your Campaign by Ann Beaudry and Bob Schaeffer (New York: The Free Press, 1986), $15.95. ∎

The Joys of Hands-On Philanthropy

∎ Futures trader Paul Tudor Jones II looks out for the futures of 85 seventh graders in Brooklyn's rough Bedford-Stuyvesant neighborhood. He tells the kids that if they get into college, he'll pay for it. That ought to be a strong incentive to finish high school in a city where about a third of the students don't. "In my business, luck and being in the right place at the right time can be important to success," says Jones, 31, who manages $8 million of his own money and $65 million for customers of Tudor Investments. Breezing uptown in his red BMW, he adds: "I'd just like these kids to know that there is a rainbow, and if they work hard there is a pot of gold at the end."

With creativity, talent, and time, many executives are doing more for charity than writing checks. They are launching their own projects or signing on with others who have done so, getting a close look at the problems they're attacking, and squeezing maximum effect from their contributions. Some, like Jones, use lots of money, while others use little more than initiative and energy. All are finding satisfaction in giving to a world with too much need.

COMMUNITY SERVICE

The inspiration for Jones and 15 other New York executives who have offered to finance educations for many inner-city elementary school graduates comes from industrialist Eugene M. Lang, 67. Founder of Refac Technology Development Corp., Lang promised in 1981 to pay college tuition for 59 sixth graders from his old school, P.S. 121 in East Harlem. Nine moved away, one went to jail, and the rest were to receive high school diplomas in 1987. Lang's idea inspired similar programs in 15 cities. "Interest is spreading much faster than I have time to deal with it," says Lang. "I just can't think of anything more significant."

Salesmanship and thrift are the keys to V. R. "Swede" Roskam's scholarship plan. He and five other businessmen started Educational Assistance Ltd., to which companies donate surplus inventory or equipment — furniture, office machines, laboratory apparatus — usually taking a tax deduction. Educational Assistance sends the goods to small liberal arts colleges, which credit the value of the gifts toward tuition for needy students and award scholarships in the corporations' names. As sales vice president of Chicago-based Oil-Dri Corp. of America, which makes clay-based chemical absorbents, Roskam, 56, travels widely and gets plenty of chances to make pitches for Educational Assistance. He devotes 15 hours a week to the outfit, which in three years has arranged $1.5 million in scholarships for 350 youngsters.

To help the severely handicapped — the blind, the mentally retarded, and those with limited muscular ability — Honeywell research scientist Lee Hallgren, 51, gave the gift of time, for which there is no tax deduction. Working with the Minneapolis Cerebral Palsy Center for more than a thousand hours over $5\frac{1}{2}$ years, he has developed safe, simple electronic aids. One of them, an outsize, highly sensitive disk-shaped switch, lets an ill-coordinated person operate an electric toy or appliance. "This project was the most difficult and most exciting I have ever worked on," says Hallgren. "The exciting part is to see the look on a child's face when he does something, and to see that joy reflected in the parents." Based on Hallgren's automated learning devices, the Cerebral Palsy Center has started Ablenet, which provides education for the handicapped, counseling for parents, and seminars for teachers and therapists. The center produces and sells the devices, with handicapped persons doing some of the assembly work.

The whole wide world is the urgent concern of Robert C. Macauley, 62, the energetic founder and chairman of Virginia Fibre Corp., a manufacturer of paper products headquartered in New Canaan, Connecticut. Five years ago, after meeting with Pope John Paul II, Macauley started up the Americares Foundation, a nonsectarian relief agency that collects and dispatches supplies with the speed and derring-do of a benevolent commando operation. After the accident at Chernobyl spread a pall of radiation over Eastern Europe, a church official in Poland telexed Americares asking for milk, baby food, and vitamins. Americares volunteers and staff members sent overnight requests to pharmaceutical companies, which responded with $970,000 of dried milk, liquid milk requiring no refrigeration, vitamins, and potassium iodide to protect thyroid functions. The supplies went off in three airlifts in May, weeks before Congress appropriated far less money for the same purpose.

Managers who cannot contribute time regularly can still target their monetary giving and get a close look at its effects. Two Bear Stearns executive vice presidents were so moved by famine scenes from Africa last year that they wanted to increase their contributions to World Vision, a Christian relief and development agency — but they also wanted to see where their money was going. Thomas R. Anderson, 41, head of investment banking at the firm, and Denis P. Coleman Jr., 40 in charge of government bonds and mortgage securities, traveled to Mali, one of West Africa's poorest countries, with an official of World Vision. At the village of Menaka they saw residents and nomads line up at 5 A.M. for a daily scoop of rice. They observed how drought, deforestation, and erosion had brought agriculture to a standstill. Moving on to Burkina Faso (formerly Upper Volta), they were surprised to find crops growing and people well fed, thanks to irrigation from the Tita Dam project. Anderson and Coleman agreed to pay for a feasibility study on water and reclamation projects for Menaka, and they have pledged to raise $1.5 million over five years for long-range development projects. "I have a name and a face for Menaka now," says Anderson. "I will help Menaka, whether it's a deep-water well or a dam."

Contributors who can't make on-the-spot inspections can get acquainted with deserving projects through several organizations. InterAction comprises more than 100 reputable organizations offering overseas aid. Two services publish lists of charities that meet their standards, plus reports on 300 to 400 philanthropic organizations: the Philanthropic Advisory Service of the Council of Better Business Bureaus, and the National Charities Information Bureau. The facts these outfits furnish can also help a contributor follow Thomas Anderson's sound rules for intelligent giving: Get firsthand knowledge, target a specific project, and banish the cynical thought that an individual contribution is too small to make a difference.

FOR FURTHER INFORMATION

Council of Better Business Bureaus, Philanthropic Advisory Service, 1515 Wilson Blvd., Arlington, VA 22209; (703)-276-0100.

InterAction, Suite 1114, 200 Park Ave. S., New York, NY 10003; (212)-777-8210.

National Charities Information Bureau, 6th Fl., 19 Union Square W., New York, NY 10003; (212)-929-6300.

World Vision, 919 W. Huntington Dr., Monrovia, CA 91016; (818)-357-7979. ∎

INDEX

Abercrombie & Kent International, 26
Aberdare National Park, 27
Ablenet, 139
Abromeit, Richard, 86
Adam, Jennifer, 1
Adams, Ansel, 112, 114
aerobic exercise, 47, 48, 50, 71, 88
Africa, camera safaris in, 26–27
Aix-en-Provence, France, 44
Alaska, 32, 37
alpine skiing. *See* downhill skiing
Alpine Trails Ltd., 20
Alps, Swiss, 20, 23–24, 25
Amateur Chamber Music Players Inc., 102
Amateur Hockey Association of the United States, 92
Amboseli National Park, 27
American Alliance for Health, Physical Education, Recreation, and Dance, 56
American Alpine Club, 23
American Alpine Institute, 25
American Association of Community Theatre, 106
American Association of Variable Star Observers, 124
American Birding Association, 128–129
American Birkebeiner cross-country ski race, 89
American Boardsailing Industries Association, 70
American Canoe Association, 73, 74
American Contract Bridge League, 95
American Federation of Musicians, 100
American Flyers/Aviation Training Enterprises, 83
American Kennel Club, 129, 130, 131, 132
American Motorcyclist Association, 80
American Orchid Society, 125–126
American Ornithologists' Union, 128
American Red Cross, 73
American Sailing Association, 1
American Symphony Orchestra League, 101
American Water Ski Association, 75, 76
American Youth Soccer Organization, 54, 55
Americares Foundation, 139
Amis du Vin, Les, International Wine Society, 121
Anastopoulo, Angelo, 63
Anderson, Maxie, 81
Anderson, Thomas R., 139
Anderson Ranch Arts Center, 114

Annapolis Sailing School, 1, 2
Annapurna, 22
Antique Automobile Club of America, 119
Apker, Gordon, 117, 118
Appalachian Mountain Club, 10, 73, 74
Appalachian Photographic Workshops, 114
Araya, Benjamin, 67
Arctic, 13, 36–38, 89
Armstrong, Louis, 99
Armstrong, Stewart, 67
art collecting, 116–117
Art Dealers Association of America, 116
art study tours, 42–44
Arthur Murray International, 107, 108
Association for Adventure Sports, 20
Astronomical League, 124
astronomy, 123–124
Athletics Congress, The, 51
Atkinson, W. Gary, 19
Australia, 4, 11, 12
Austria, 10
auto racing, 77–79. *See also* cars, classic
Aviation Seminars, 83

Back River, 37
Bailey, Keith, 62
Bailey, Nathaniel, 62
Bailey, Wendy, 62
Baker, Cherie, 63
Baker Cave, Texas, 41, 42
Baldwin, John, 61
Balloon Federation of America, 81, 82
ballooning, 80–82
ballroom dancing, 107–108
Banks, Mike, 20
Banks, Patricia, 20
Barber, G. A., 33, 34
Barber, Patrick, 34
barbershop singing, 104–105
Barnwell, Tim, 114
Barocci, Robert, 50, 51
Barrett, James W., 64
Barron, Thomas A., 10
Bass, Richard, 24–25
Bast, James, 65
Bauman, Patricia, 125–126
Bauman, Robert P., 125–126
Bean, L. L., symposium, 28
Beckwith, William A., 63
Bell, Ray, 65–66

Belmont, August, Jr., 129–130
Benham, James M., 100–101
Benoliel, Peter A., 102
Berkeley Bicycling Club, 48
Bernheimer, Leonard, 63, 64
Berkshire Choral Institute, 103
Bernstein, Judith, 19
Besteman, John, 27–28
Besteman, Kay, 28
Beverly Bridge Club, 96
Bicycle Federation of America, 49
bicycling, 48–49, 53, 56; European tours, 18–19
Biggs, Barton M., 18
Biggs, Judy, 18
Billmeyer, Cynthia, 30, 31
Bimini Big Game Fishing Club, 12
bird watching, 128–129
Blankenship, Charles H., 58
Blue Hill Troupe, 105–106
board sailing, 69–71
Bob Bondurant School of High Performance Driving, 77
Bobbie Burns Lodge, 8, 9
Boinske, Charles, 16–17
Bollettieri, Nick, 59
Bonaire Island, 3
Boockoff, Betsy, 55
Borneo, 41–42
Boston Road Club, 49
Brachman, Malcolm K., 96
Braden, Forrest, 15
Brant, Peter M., 67
Briant, Andy, 5
bridge, 95–97
British Columbia, 7–9
British Open (golf), 6, 7
Brown, Carol, 72
Brown, Steve, 94
Bud Light U.S. Triathlon Series, 52
Bugaboos Lodge, 8
Bull, Harry, 127
Bull, Nita, 127
Bullis, Peter, 100
Bunting, Anne, 79
Bunting, George L., Jr., 79, 80
Burger, Charles, 96
Burns, Gerard, 5
Burns, Helen, 5
Bush, George, 106
Butterfield & Robinson, 10, 18, 20

141

INDEX

Cabo San Lucas, Mexico, 11–12
California Gold Rush (skiing marathon), 89
California Sailing Academy, 2
Callahan, Rory, 120
Callum, George, 69–70
Callum, Janice, 69–70
Campbell, Roy K., 120
Canada, 7–9, 13, 37–38
Canadian Mountain Holidays, 7–9
canoeing, 36–38, 73–74
Cap, Louie, 59
Captiva Island, Florida, 2
Carbonnel, Charles de, 43
Carbonnel, Katrina Vanderlip de, 43
Caribbean, 3, 11, 12, 39, 70, 111
Cariboos Lodge, 8
Carnoustie golf course, 6–7
cars, classic, 117–119. *See also* auto racing
Carter, Jimmy, 109
Catamount Trail, 10
Cayne, Jimmy, 96
Century Road Club Association, 49
Chamber Music America, 102
Chandler, Otis, 118
Chaney, Gerald M., 120
chess, 97–98
Chester, William M., Jr., 88–89
Chicago Wine School, 120
children: fitness for, 55–57; vacationing with, 38–40
Chile, 12, 32, 33
chorus singing, 102–103
Christie's auction house, 116
Christmas Bird Counts, 128
Church, Jim, 3–4
Church, Cathy, 3–4
Churchill, Winston, 110, 111
Citibank, 117
Civil Air Patrol, 84–86
Clark, Cindy, 30
Clark, Dan, 31
Clark, E. H., Jr., 30–31
Clark, Ken, 31
Clark, Maggie, 30
Clark, Patti, 30
Clark, Patty, 30
Clark, Rebecca, 30, 31
Clark, Sue, 30
Clark, Todd, 22
Clarke, Terence, 105
Classic Car Club of America, 118
classical music playing, 101–102
Clifford, Stewart B., 117
Clinton, Jerry, 77–78
Club Med, 38, 39
Coin Operated Racing Systems, 87
Cole, Donald, 127
Cole, Jill, 127
Coleman, Denis P., Jr., 139
Collins, John, 52–53
Colorado, 10
Colorado River, 35–36
Commuters League, 92
CompuTennis, 59
Comstock, Frances, 86–87
Comstock, Jennifer, 87

Comstock, Robert E., Jr., 87
Connaissance & Cie., 121
Connor, Kathy, 8
Connor, Nicholas, 8
Cook, John, 27
Cooper, Camron, 129
Cooper, Kenneth H., 50, 51, 56
Corn, Ira G., 96
Corporate Grand Prix of Skiing, 87
Corporate Ski Challenge, 87
Corson, Robert, 75–76
Cory, Patricia, 114
Cory, Tom, 114
Costill, David L., 47, 48
Cousteau, Jacques-Yves, 3
Cox, Sam, 35–36
croquet, 64–66
cross-country skiing, 9–10, 88–90
curling, 93–94
Curry, Elizabeth, 85
Curry, Michael, 85
Cutter, Sidney, 82
Cyphers, Richard, 108
Cyprus, 42

dancing, ballroom, 107–108
Darenberg, Carl, Jr., 12
Darenberg, Carl, Sr., 12
Darrell, Charles, 16
David-Weill, Hélène, 43
David-Weill, Michel, 43–44
David-Weill, Pierre, 44
Davis, Bob L., 17
Davis, Carol Rymer, 82
Davis, E. Harold, 133
Davis, John C., IV, 82
Dawnay, Hugh, 67
De Windt, E. M., 60–61
Dearborn, Susan, 28
Decker, Betty, 85
Decker, Richard W., Jr., 53
Decker, Suzanne, 53
deep-sea game fishing, 11–13
Del Duca, Peter, 135
Deng Xiaoping, 96
Denmark, 14–15
Denniston, G. H., 52
Desmond, Al, 81
Devlin, Sheila, 28
Devlin, Shaun, 28
DeYoung, Joel, 74
Dickey, Arthur, 112, 113
dieting programs, 44–45; for children, 57
Dixieland music, 100
Doble, John, 90, 91
Doerfling, Ralph G., 3
dogs: hunting, 131–132; show, 129–131
Dole, Charles Minot, 90
Dolomites, Italy, 23–24
Doner, Robert, 5
Doner, William, 11–12
Donley, James, 20
Donley, Mary Todd, 20
Douds, Bryn, 102
downhill skiing, 86–88
Drake, Jim, 69

Drew, Douglas, 96
Dribben, Dan, 65
Drinkwater, Barbara L., 51
Ducks Unlimited, 133
Duff, Mary Lee, 103
Duke, H. Benjamin, Jr., 87
Duke Diet and Fitness Center, 45
Dusenbury, Douglas, 7
Duthler, Jo Ann, 91
Dyer, Lynn, 41–42
Dyment, Paul, 56
Dyson, Brian, 64

Eakins, Thomas, 71
Earthwatch, 41–42
Eberly, Dale, 6, 7
Ecosummer Canada Expeditions, 28
Edelstein, Haskell, 102
Edelstein, Joan, 102
Educational Assistance Ltd., 139
Edwards, George, Jr., 5
Elvin, George, 117
Emerson, Roy, 5
England, 4–5, 15, 17, 19, 20
Equitable Family Tennis Challenge, 62
Erard, Philip, 23, 89
Ernst, Joanne, 53
Evert, Chris, 59, 62
Exum School of Mountaineering, 23

Fairfax, Virginia, 136
Fairfield Shooting School, 16
Faraci, Edward, 131
Farnsworth, Sidney, 117–118, 119
Farnsworth, Tom, 118
Featherstone, James J., III, 136
Federal Aviation Administration, 81, 83
Fédération Aeronautique Internationale, 82
Fegan, Patrick W., 120
Fennie, John A., 58
Festival of the North, 89
Field, Mitchell, 8–9
Filoon, Fred, 92
Fiorina, Raymond, 84, 85
firemen, volunteer, 135–137
Fischer, Bobby, 97
Fischer, Hobart, 75
fishing: deep-sea, 11–13; salmon, 13–14; trout, 34, 133
Fishing International, 12
Fitzgerald, Michael, 15
Fixx, James, 50
Flakne, Dawn, 9–10
Flesch, Thomas, 133
flying (airplane), 82–84; Civil Air Patrol, 84–86
Fond du Lac River, Canada, 36–38
Fonda, Henry, 105
Forbes, Malcolm S., 82
Forbes, Mari, 63
Ford, Ronald, 107
Ford National Mixed Doubles Championships, 62
Fordyce, Duncan, 80
Fouquet, Nicolas, 43
France: art tours, 42–44; wine-tasting tours, 121

142

INDEX

Franklin, Benjamin, 135
Fred Astaire International Dance Association, 107, 108
French Wine Institute, 121
Frentrop, Martha, 112
Friends of French Art, 42–44
Friends of Photography, 114
Frishman, Janet, 2, 3
Frishman, John, 2, 3
Frohlich, Phil, 59
Frontiers International Travel, 13, 14, 15
Futch, Leo, 6, 7

Gaar, Jack, 86
Galdikas, Birute, 41
Gallahue, David, 56
Garcia, Timothy L., 63
gardening, 126–128. *See also* orchid growing
Gardiner, John, 5
Garvin, Clifton C., Jr., 16
Gatto, John, 104
Gay, John, 107
Gay, Lori, 107
Genetski, Maureen, 54
Genetski, Robert, 54
Gerhard's Bicycle Odysseys, 19
Getzendanner, Susan M., 106
Gintel, Robert, 45
Glantz, Herbert, 116
Glantz, Kitty, 116
Gleneagles golf course, 6, 7
Gmoser, Hans, 8, 9
Godfrey, Bob, 105
Golden Door Spa, 45
Goldsmith, Christopher, 94
golf: low-handicap, 60–61; schools, 58–59, 61; in Scotland, 6–7
GolfTek, 58–59
Gordon, C. Athol, 13
Gostkhorhevich, Vladimir, 97
Graf, David, 136, 137
Graham, Robert Bruce, 135–137
Graham, Robert C., Jr., 116
Grand Cayman, 4
Gray, Bob, Jr., 104
Great American Ski Chase, 89
Great Lakes Kayak Touring Symposium, 29
Greater Houston Gun Club, 16
Greece, 30, 31
Greenberg, Alan, 95, 96
Greenhill, Bobby, 36
Greenhill, Gayle, 37
Greenhill, Mary, 36, 37
Greenhill, Robert F., 36–38
Greenhill, Sarah, 37
Greenwich, Connecticut, 137–138
Greenwich Skating Club, 91, 92
Greenwich Soccer Club, 54–55
Gregg, A. John, 16–17
Grey, Zane, 11
Griffin, Fred, 58
Griffin & Howe, 16
Gstaad, Switzerland, 4, 5
Guion, William, 114
Gullane, golf course, 6
Gullikson, Tom, 59

Gunflint Trail Lodge to Lodge Ski Association, 9
gymnastics, 56–57

Haas, Margaret, 120, 121
Hager, John R., 81
Hair, Jay D., 133
Hallgren, Lee, 139
Hamilton, Tom T., 61
Hannon, Denise, 52
Hansen, Arden, 130
Hansen, Jack, 130
Hanson, Michael, 92
Happy Family Hotels, 39
Harmony Inc., 104
Harrah, William F., 118, 119
Harrigan, John F., 129
Harris, Richard L., Jr., 53
Harrison, David, 36, 38
Harrison, Judy, 37
Harsh, Griffith, 39
Hartong, Hendrick J., Jr., 54–55
Haskell, William L., 50
Havens, John P., 15, 16, 17
Havens, Timothy M., 15, 17
Hawaii, 2, 11, 12, 30, 39, 52, 70
Hawkins, Betty, 58
Hawkins, W. Whitley, 58
Hawley, Elizabeth, 24
Head-of-the-Charles Regatta, 72
Heintskill, James W., 84
heli-skiing, 7–9
Hemingway, Ernest, 11, 26
Hender, Ray, 117
Henley Royal Regatta, 71–72
Herb Society of America, 127
Hester, Thomas R., 42
Highland Bend Shooting School, 16, 17
hiking in Nepal, 21–22
Hillary, Edmund, 21, 22, 24
Hobbs, Franklin, 72
hockey, senior, 91–93
Hodges, David, 63
Hoey, Marty, 25
Holdsworth, Robert S., 48–49
Holland & Holland Ltd., 15–16
Holt, Dean, 112
Honickman, Harold, 45
Honickman, Lynne, 45
Horseless Carriage Club, 119
horsepacking, 33–35
Hotchkin, Albert L., Jr., 120
Huotari, Craig, 104
Hurricane Island Outward Bound School, 28

ice hockey, senior, 91–93
Iceland, 13–14
illness: bends, 3; hypothermia, 37; mountain sickness, 21
injuries: auto racing, 77; ballooning, 81; bicycling, 49; of children, 56; hockey, 92; motorcycling, 79; polo, 67; squash, 64; skiing, 90–91; water-skiing, 75
Institute for Aerobics Research, 56
InterAction, 139
International Balloon Fiesta, 82

International Center of Photography, 113
International Foundation for Art Research, 117
International Motor Sports Association, 78
International Wine Center school, 120
International Windsurfer Sailing Schools, 70
Ireland, 7, 19–20
Ironman Triathlon World Championship, 52, 53
Italy, 18, 19, 23, 24

J World, 2
Jack Nicklaus Academy of Golf, 58, 60
Jackson Ski Touring Foundation, 10
Jacob, Hugh, 87
Jacob, Susie, 87
Jacobi, C. Michael, 51
Jacobson, Fred, 20
Jacobson, William, 59
Jacoby, Jim, 95
Jacoby, Michael, 28
jazz playing, 99–101
Johnson, Bunk, 99–100
Johnson, Lucy, 48
Jones, Paul Tudor, II, 138–139
Jordan, Dan, 104

Kane, Stephen, 30, 31
Kaplan, Gilbert E., 102
Karsh, Yousuf, 114
kayaking, 27–29, 32–33, 73, 74
Keck, Robert, 133
Keith, Allan, 128, 129
Kelley, Kathleen, 106
Kendall, Paul, 73, 74
Kendall, Sharon Rives, 73, 74
Kent, Geoffrey, 26
Kenya, 26–27, 31, 33, 39
Kerkorian, Kirk, 26
Kersten, Donald N., 82
Kidney, Sharon, 63
Kidd, Billy, 87
King, Billie Jean, 62
Kirby, Robert G., 78
Kirk, Donald J., 137–138
Kittredge, Conway, 12
Koch, Bill, 88, 89
Koch, Ehrengard, 2
Koch, Rüdiger, 2
Kornbluh, Barbara, 56
Kornbluh, Jed, 56
Kornbluh, Mel, 56
Kornbluh, Natalie, 56
Kraft, Ren, 65–66
Kriek, Johan, 59
Krowe, Allen, 110–111
Kvammen, Bjorn, Jr., 89

La Costa Hotel and Spa, 44
La Mer, 4
La Plant, Carol, 51, 53
La Plant, Pierre, 53
Labatt, Arthur S., 18, 19
Labatt, Sonia, 18, 19
Lake Bluff, Illinois, 135, 136, 137
Lane, Amy B., 60, 61
Lane, Ralph, 101–102
Lang, Eugene M., 139
Langston, Ellen, 34

143

INDEX

Langston, James, 34
Lantz, Jack, 100
Lathrop Ski & Race Camps, 87
Lathrop Sports Vacations, 70
League of American Wheelmen, 18, 49
Leahey, Alice, 2
Lefebvre, Clifford, 105
Lenser, Gerhard, 25
Levin, David, 82
Levin, Harold A., 133–134
Levin, Laurence, 66
Levin, Michael, 66–68
Lewis, Drew, 2
Lewis, Marilyn, 2
Linsley, Sarah, 52
Lipton Iced Tea Amateur Mixed Doubles
    Championship, 62–63
Loehr, James E., 59–60
Lorenz, Katherine, 20
Louis XIV, King of France, 43

Macauley, Robert C., 139
McCabe, George, 112
McCabe, Robert, 112, 113
McCallum, John, 65
McCann, James, 114
McCombs, John C., 56–57
McCombs, Leslie, 57
McCoy, Bowen H., 21–22
McGowan, Carol, 72
McGowan, James, 72
McGowan, John, 71, 72
McGrogan, Jean, 112, 113
McGrogan, Stephen, 112, 113
McLain, Ray, 73, 74
MacMahon, D'Arcy, 71–72
McNair, Robert E., 74
Maddox, Douglas, 105
Mader, Henry, 103
Mahre, Phil, 87
Mahre, Steve, 87
Mahre Training Centers, 87
Mailing, Christopher J., 49
Maine Photographic Workshops, 114
Mandlikova, Hana, 62
Manion, Holly, 8, 9
Mann, Ralph, 58
Manufacturers Hanover Corporate Challenge
    races, 49–50
marathon running, 50–52
Margon, Lester, 110
Mark, Mary Ellen, 114
Marks, Randolph A., 13–14
Marshall, George, 90
Martens, Rainer, 56
Martin, Robert, 59
Masai Mara Game Preserve, 27
Matterhorn, 23
Matthews, Edward E., 23
Matthews, Jay, 35
Matthews, Phillip, 35, 36
Maxwell, John E., 44–45
Maxwell, Linda, 44–45
Meier, Robert E., 132–133
Mena, Danilo J., 103
Merritt, Tag, 59

Meyer, Carl, 135
Mexico, 11, 38
Micheli, Lyle J., 56
Mikes, Patricia, 1
Miles, Robert, 28
Milestone Car Society, 119
Milhaupt, Peter, 69–70
Miller, John D., 104, 105
Miller, Kirk, 34
Miller, R. N., 33, 34
Miller, Terry, 34
Millikin, Dudley, 132
Millikin, Elizabeth, 132
Missildine, Fred, 16
Mitchell, Kate, 39
Mitchell, Keri, 39
Mitchell, Robert, 39
Mitchell, Shay, 39
Mont Blanc, 25
Montana, 33–35
Montauk Marine Basin, 12
Monterey Peninsula Country Club, 6–7
Montgolfier, Joseph and Etienne, 80
Montgomery Street Motorcycle Club, 80
Moore, Dorothy, 96
Morton, "Jelly Roll," 100
Motorcycle Safety Foundation, 79
motorcycling, 79–80
Mount Aconcagua, 25
Mount Elbrus, 25
Mount Everest, 21–22, 24, 25
Mount Kala Pattar, 21, 22
Mount Kenya, 31, 33
Mount Kilimanjaro, 21, 25
Mount Kosciusko, 25
Mount McKinley, 25
Mount Rainier, 23, 32
Mountain Travel, 10, 19, 20, 22, 26, 39
mountaineering, 23–26
Muirfield golf course, 6
Muñana, Clare, 63–64
Murto, JoAnne, 62
music performance: barbershop singing, 104–
    105; chorus, 102–103; classical, 101–102;
    jazz, 99–101

Nairobi, 26, 27
Nantahala Outdoor Center, 74
Nastar ski-racing program, 86, 87
Nation, Mary, 113
National Association of Underwater Instruc-
    tors, 2–3
National Audubon Society, 128
National Aviation Administration, 82
National Charities Information Bureau, 139
National Collegiate Athletic Association, 48
National Dance Council of America, 107
National Fire Protection Association, 136
National Gardening Association, 126
National Novice Hockey Association, 92–93
National Outdoor Leadership School, 25
National Shooting Sports Foundation, 16
National Ski Patrol System, 90
National Tennis Rating Program, 62
National Wildlife Federation, 133
Navratilova, Martina, 62

Nedell, Harold, 131
Nelson, Joan, 93
Nelson, Lester, 93
Nelson, Peter, 93
Nelson, Svea, 93
Nepal, 21–22, 24, 39, 129
New Black Eagle Jazz Band, 99–100
New England Aquarium, 4
New England Trail Rider Association, 80
New Hampshire, 10
New School for Social Research, Introduction
    to Wine, 120
New York Choral Society, 103
New York Cycle Club, 49
New York Sailing School, 2
New Zealand, 12, 32, 33
Newman, Paul, 77, 78
Nicholas, James, 51
Nick Bollettieri Tennis Academy, 59–60
Nicklaus, Jack, 6, 58
Nicoloff, Charles, 104
Noatak River, Alaska, 37
Noga, John S., 79, 80
nordic skiing. *See* cross-country skiing
Norgay, Tenzing, 24
North American Vasa, 89
North Berwick golf course, 6
Northeastern Bicycling Club, 48
Northwest Outdoor Center, 28
Norway, 10, 13, 89
Nottenkamper, Andy, 6

O'Brien, Paul, 106
O'Donnell, Thomas F., 75, 76
Olafsson, Jafet, 14
O'Leary, Paddy, 20
Oliver, Joe "King," 99, 100
orchid growing, 125–126. *See also* gardening
Orthwein, Peter, 67
Orvis Shooting Schools, 16
Osborn, Jack, 65–66
Osborn, Johnnie, 66
O'Steen, John, 78
Ostrat, Jan, 84–85
O'Sullivan, Richard, 62
Outward Bound Inc., 28, 35–36

Pachmayr Shotgun Hunting School, 16
Paffenbarger, Ralph S., 50
Page, Robert, 103
painting, 110–111
Palace Hotel (Gstaad, Switzerland), 4, 5
Palm-Aire, 45
Palmer, Arnold, 58
Panama, 11, 12
Parr, W. Matt, 12
Pebble Beach golf course, 6, 7
Pell, Stuyvesant, 71
Penland School of Crafts, 114
Peru, 12, 39
Peterson, Roger Tory, 128
Pettibone, Peter J., 102–103
Pettit, Jeffrey, 64
pheasant shooting, 14–15
Philanthropic Advisory Service, 139
philanthropy, 138–139

INDEX

Phillips, Allyson Button, 70
Phillips, Christopher, 70
Phillips, William, 23
Photo Bonaire, 3
Photographic Society of America, 113
photography, 112–115; astronomical, 124; safaris, 26–27; underwater, 3–4
Pick, Pablo, 63
Pieres, Alfonso, 67
Pilić, Nikki, 5
Pilsbury, Robert, 100
Pines, Irwin, 11
Pius, Charles, 6
Plandome, NY, 135, 136
Plank, Lollie, 14
Plank, Raymond, 14, 15
polo, 66–68
Portmarnock golf course, 7
Prebil, Mary, 62
Preefer, David, 1
Prestwick golf course, 6
Pringle, Anthony, 99, 100
Pritikin, Nathan, 45
Pritikin Longevity Centers, 45
Professional Association of Diving Instructors, 2, 3
Pryor, Daniel, 22
Pryor, Joseph, 22
Pryor, Samuel F., III, 21–22
public office, 137–138

Quinn, Mary, 53

racing: auto, 77–79; balloon, 82; bicycle, 48–49; motorcycle, 80; ski, 86–90
Radin, Alex, 114
Radin, Carol, 114
rafting, 35–36
Rainey, William, 51
Rainier Mountaineering, 23
Ramblers' Association, 20
Ravitch, Richard, 109, 110
Read, Al, 22
Reader, Rod, 107–108
Reid, Donald, 104
Reiswig, Gary, 120
Renberg, Daniel, 43, 44
Reshevsky, Samuel, 97
Ridgely, Reginald, 59–60
Rinaldi, Kathy, 59
Rittereiser, Robert, 106
Rivkin, Jack L., 69, 70
Road Atlanta, 78
Roberts, Donald M., 50–51
Roberts, Mary Gordon, 50–51
Robins, Charles I., 3, 83, 84
Robinson, Harrison, 7
Rodgers, James, 39
Rogers, Nancy, 39
Rodgers, Phil, 58
Rogers, Bobbie, 111
Rogers, Carl, 111
Rogers, David, 110, 111
Roggenkamp, Edward K., III, 131–132
Rosendahl, Fritz, 82
Rosenlaui mountaineering school, 23

Roseto, Michael, 6, 7
Roskam, V. R., 139
Rothschild, Baron Elie de, 43
Rothschild, Baroness Elie de, 43
rowing, 71–72
Royal and Ancient Golf Club, 7
Royal Burgess golf course, 6
Royal St. George golf course, 7
Rubin, Ephraim, 102
Ruffed Grouse Society, 133
running, 49–52; in marathons, 49–51; in triathlons, 52–54
Russell, Elizabeth Markus, 19
Russell, Keith C., 133
Russell, William F., 10
Rutherfurd, Winthrop, Jr., 106

Sabran-Pontevès, Roselyne de, 44
safaris, camera, 26–27
sailing, 1–2; board, 69–71
St. Andrews golf course, 6, 7
St. Croix, Virgin Islands, 1–2
Samburu Game Reserve, 27
Samuelson, Ralph, 75
San Juan Islands, 27, 28
Sarazen, Gene, 7
Sayers, Alan, 19
Scheel, Sandra, 36
Scheel, Steve, 35, 36
Schlicher, Fred, 48
Schneider, George, 114
Schneider, Viola, 114
Schoenhaar, Harald, 87
Schulz, Charles, 91–92
Schulz, Jeannie, 92
Schweitzer, Hoyle, 69
Scotland, 6–7, 13, 20
Scott, Dave, 53
Scott, Douglas, 6
scuba diving, 2–4
sculpting, 110–111
Sea Touring Kayak Center, 28
See & Sea, 4
Seed Savers Exchange, 127
Senior, Enrique, 109–110
Senter, Val, 92
Shapedown, 57
Sharp, Robert, 62
Sharp, Robin, 62
Shedd Aquarium, 4
Sheinwold, Alfred, 95, 96
Sheppard, Thomas F., 81
Sherburn, John, 104
Sherwin, James T., 97
shooting: pheasant, 14–15; wing, 15–17
Sierra Club, 73
Silbert, Stephen, 26–27
Silbert, Tracy, 26–27
Silverman, Jerry T., 100
Simons, Jody, 107
Siscovick, David, 50
Ski Club Challenge, 87
Ski Patrol, 90–91
Ski Touring, 9–10
skiing: for children, 39, 57, 86–87; cross-

country, 9–10, 88–90; downhill, 86–88; heli-, 7–9; water, 75–76
Skinner, David E., 65
Sloan, Stephen, 11
Slott, Phil, 52
Smith-Johannsens, Herman, 88–89
Smooke, Nathan, 117
Snoopy Senior World Hockey Tourney, 91–92
soccer, 54–55
Society for the Preservation and Encouragement of Barbershop Quartet Singing in America, 104
Society of Wine Educators, 120
Sonke, Craig, 35–36
Sonke, Lee, 35
Sonke, Robert, 35, 36
Sorensen, Donald R., 74
Sotheby's auction house, 116
Soviet Union, 25, 29
Spain, 42
Spencer, Joseph H., Jr., 60
Spingola, Frank, 42
Sporting Clays Association, 17
Sports Car Club of America, 77, 78, 119
squash, 63–64
Stafford, David, 45
Stallings, Donald, 65–66
Stern, Keith, 120
Steve Colgate's Offshore Sailing School, 1, 2
Stivender, David, 103
Stookey, John Hoyt, 103
Stookey, Katherine, 103
Stout, Debbie, 76
Stout, Gary, 76
Strauss, David J., 97
Street, Bob Allen, 23
Stuart, Charles, Jr., 80
Sugahara, Kaytaro G., 93, 94
Superior National Forest, 9–10
Sweeney, Beverly, 127
Sweeney, Warren, 127
Sweet Adelines, 104
Swenson, John Forbes, 127
swimming: for children, 56; competitive, 47–48
Switzerland, 10, 20, 23–24, 39

Tanzania, 26
Tasmania, 33
Taubman, A. Alfred, 116
Taylor, Linda, 57
Taylor, Michael, 57
Telepraisal, 117
Temba, Per, 22
tennis: camps, 4–6; championship, for amateurs, 62–63; schools, 59–60
Tennis Ranch (Carmel Valley, California), 5
Tenth Mountain Trail Association, 10
Terrell, Joseph W., III, 73
theater performing, 105–107
Thomas, Ann, 38
Thompson, Robert, 3, 4
Tillotson, James, 107
Timken, W. R., Jr., 47, 48
Timnick, Henry O., 19
Tober, David, 62

145

INDEX

Topol, Robert M., 45
Trainer, William, 130
Transpacific Race, 2
Trapp, Louis, 135
Tremblay, Gene, 7, 9
triathlons, 52–54
Trinity Mountain Meadow Resort, 114
Troon golf course, 6–7
Tropic Star Lodge (Panama), 12
Trotz, Ernesto, 67
Trout Unlimited, 133
Tully, Larry, 105
Turnberry golf course, 6
Turnbull, Ray, 93

Uber, Tom, 92
United States Amateur Ballroom Championship, 107
United States Boardsailing Association, 70
United States Chess Federation, 97, 98
United States Chess Open Tournament, 97
United States Croquet Association, 65–66
United States Curling Association, 94
United States Cycling Federation Inc., 49
United States Department of Agriculture Extension Service, 127
United States Golf Association, 7, 60; Slope Handicap, 60
United States Masters Swimming Inc., 47–48
United States National Hot Air Balloon Championship, 82
United States Polo Association, 66, 67
United States Rowing Association, 71, 72
United States Ski Association, 87, 89
United States Soccer Federation, 54, 55
United States Squash Racquets Association, 63, 64
United States Tennis Association, 5; /Volvo Tennis League Program, 62
United States Water Ski and Show Team, 76
United States Youth Soccer Association, 54, 55
Universal Aunts, 39
Utah, 35

Vanderbilt, Harold, 95
Vanderlip, Elin (Mrs. Kelvin Cox), 43, 44

Van der Meer Tennis Center, 59
Vardaman, James M., 129
Vaughan, Curtis, Jr., 123–124
Vermont, 10, 39, 89, 90, 102
Veteran Motor Car Club of America, 119
Victor Emanuel nature tours, 129
Vincent, Burton J., 97, 98
Vincent, Stanford, 99, 100
Vinson Massif (Antarctica), 25, 26
Virgin Island, 1–2, 3
Vogüé, Cristina de, 43
Vogüé, Patrice de, 43
volunteers, 41, 84, 90, 132–139

Wadsworth, Christopher, 37
Wadsworth, Douglas, 133
Wadsworth, John S., 36–37, 38
Wadsworth, Susy, 37
Waikiki Aquarium, 4
Wales, 20
walking tours, European, 19–21
Walsh, Stephanie A., 47
water-skiing, 75–76
Watson, Tom, 6
Watters, Lu, 99
Wayfarers, The, 20
Weeden, Alan, 31–33
Weeden, Barbara, 32
Weeden, Bob, 31, 32, 33
Weeden, Don, 31, 32, 33
Weeden, Leslie, 31, 32, 33
Wei, C. C., 95, 96
Wei, Katherine, 96
Weibel, Jeri, 90–91
Weisel, Thomas, 48, 49
Weisel, Vicki, 48
Weisser, Paul, 39
Weisser, Stephanie, 39
Weisser, Zachary, 39
Wells, Frank, 24–25
Wells, Luanne, 25
West Coast Sea Kayaking Symposium, 29
Westminster Kennel Club, 129
Weston, Edward, 112
Wetzel, Harry, 43
Wetzel, Maggie, 43
Whealy, Kent, 127

Whitaker, Edwin H., 131
White, Bill, 57
white-water boating, 73–74
Whitman, Johnson deF., 105
Whitman, Margaret C., 38–39
Whittaker, Louis, 25
Wilbur, J. F., Jr., 42
Wild Turkey Federation, 133
Wide World of Golf, 6, 7
Wilderness Photography/Trinity Alps Workshop, 114
wildlife habitat, improving, 132–134
Will, Daniel, 126, 127
Will, Jeanne, 127
Williams, Dave H., 116–117
Williams, David Price, 42
Wimbledon, 5
Windmill Hill Place, 4–5
windsurfing. *See* sailing: board
Wine Adventures Inc., 121
wine appreciation, 119–122
Wine Institute, 121
wing shooting, 15–17
Wiren, Gary, 58
Wolverine Sports Club, 49
Woodstock Ski Touring Center, 10
woodworking, 109–110
World Bridge Federation, 96
World Bridge Olympics, 96
World Chess Championship, 97
World Hot Art Balloon Championship, 82
World Vision, 139
Worldloppet ski marathons, 89
Worldwide Nordic USA, 10, 89
Wright, J. King, 90, 91

Yeats, William Butler, 20
Ylvisaker, William T., 66, 67
YMCA, 3, 30, 47, 49, 56–57, 109
YWCA, 109
Yosemite Mountaineering School, 23
Young, Barbara, 9
Young, Ted, 9
Youth Fitness Test, 56

Zier, Ron, 106
Zimmerman, Karen, 1
Zraly, Kevin, 121